THE TYRANNY OF COMMON SENSE

The Tyranny of Common Sense

Mexico's Post-Neoliberal Conversion

IRMGARD EMMELHAINZ

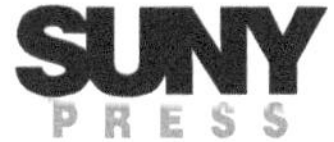

Published by State University of New York Press, Albany

Printed in the United States of America

For information, contact State University of New York Press, Albany, NY
www.sunypress.edu

Library of Congress Cataloging-in-Publication Data

Names: Emmelhainz, Irmgard. author.
Title: The tyranny of common sense : Mexico's post-neoliberal conversion / Irmgard Emmelhainz.
Description: Albany, NY : State University of New York Press, [2021] | Includesbibliographical references and index.
Identifiers: LCCN 2021001873 | ISBN 9781438485935 (Hardcover) | ISBN 9781438485959 (eBook)
Subjects: LCSH: Neoliberalism—Mexico. | Common sense.
Classification: LCC JC574.2.M6 E46 2021 | DDC 320.510972—dc23
LC record available at https://lccn.loc.gov/2021001873

10 9 8 7 6 5 4 3 2 1

To Lizzy, Layla, and Roberta.

To Nacho Sánchez Prado, Oswaldo Zavala, Dawn Paley, and Sayak Valencia, my fellow Horsemen and Horsewomen.

To David Emmelhainz.

To the women from the Grupo de las comidas de los viernes.

CONTENTS

ACKNOWLEDGMENTS

Lizzy Cancino, Roberta Sonamour, Ignacio Sánchez Prado, José García, Arturo Barranco, Eshrat and Javan Erfanian, Bruce Parsons, Silvia Gruner, Miguel Ventura, Rebecca Colesworthy; each knows why. And my teachers Amparo Fernández, Karen Cordero, David Raskin, Rebecca Comay, Sonia Nimr, John-Paul Ricco, Franco Berardi, Coni Comaleras, Fabián Sejanes, Belu Oteda.

INTRODUCTION TO THE ENGLISH EDITION

The official estimated number of the March 8, 2020, women's march in Mexico City was eighty thousand, but it definitely felt like we were many more. Knowledgeable veterans calculated up to ten times more women at the demonstration, although many had been dissuaded by physical and police barriers to make it to the Zócalo, Mexico City's main square and the symbolic center of the country. The jacarandas were with us, all in full purple bloom. A few days before that, Harvey Weinstein had been sentenced to twenty-three years in jail for various accusations of rape, abuse, and harassment. The day after the march came the strike. The strike became so important that small, medium, and big corporations either joined in or condoned the strike supporting their female workers. Giant retail companies like Comercial Mexicana and Banco Santander displayed public support for the women's general strike in banners inside their branches, while some brands' logos were disseminated on social media to symbolically strike in solidarity.

For the march, the water in the fountain on Reforma Avenue, adorned with the sculpture of Roman goddess Diana, and the water in the fountain of the wisdom goddess Minerva in Guadalajara had been dyed red as if they had begun to bleed. In Mexico City's Zócalo, the names of women murdered by femicide violence found in public records were inscribed in white-mold letters. Mothers of murdered and disappeared daughters led the multitude. The feminist march and strike were reproduced in cities across the country and in Latin America, creating waves of green (the emblematic color of the pro-abortion struggle) and purple, which in Mexico City matched beautifully with the blooming jacaranda flowers that had arrived a month earlier than usual. During the march, there was no direct repression, but as I mentioned, access to the Zócalo was dissuaded. The images of a half-empty Zócalo contrasted with

Reforma Avenue packed with demonstrators in purple and green, matching the jacarandas. A total of six people were detained for attacking protesters at the doors of Palacio Nacional (National Palace, the siege of the federal government), which had been heavily protected with metal doors. Bellas Artes Palace, hotels, restaurants, and shops along Reforma and Alameda Streets displayed similar kinds of armored protection. And yet, the hundreds of riot squad female police with faces reddened by the sun, who were stationed on the edges of the procession, passively observed the marchers through their protective masks and watched as the *morras*[1] either spray-painted or broke through the armoring and began to destroy windows, doors, and security cameras. A few meters from me, a group of *morras* had begun to smash the window of a Starbucks next to the Hilton Hotel with a long hammer and a thick wooden beam. Further along, I saw a similar group throwing rockets that exploded into loud banging noises and dissolved into pretty-colored gases. *Morras* were also releasing rocks the size of soccer balls, had burned the wooden barricades protecting the Cathedral in the Zócalo, and had begun to circle around the bonfire, chanting. To me, these expressions of rage were beautiful, and I silently thanked them for risking their skins, freedom, lives, integrity, and sanity for all of us. While these not at all sporadic episodes of vandalism occurred, many of the other women present chanted, "No violence, no violence," without knowing or understanding that those violent gestures indeed spoke on behalf of the women's struggle. "The origin of women's oppression is private property," I said to a fellow woman marching in my contingent, wishing to have a moment to discuss Engels and Federici with her, and to remind her of the Chilean hymn by LasTesis "El violador eres tú" (You are the rapist), which directly accuses the State of being founded on and maintaining heteropatriarchy and thus gender violence. Beyond the political need for an intersectional feminism, a feminist popular pedagogy needs to be more widely adopted to enable a general understanding of the links between heteropatriarchy and State indifference to gender violences. After all, it is the State that grants aggressors impunity. Mexican President Andrés Manuel López Obrador—the first ever from the left to be in power in Mexico—took the long-expired stance of universal struggle for rights and emancipation. "I am not a feminist, I am a humanist," he declared, in sync with the leftist prejudice that feminism is a petit bourgeois struggle that takes away focus from

---

1 In Mexico, *morra* means young woman. In other parts of Latin America, it can have sexist connotations.

the struggle against the main enemy. Days before, the First Lady had shared a flyer supporting the women's strike on her Instagram account, only to post a different flyer a few hours later in which she expressed support for the president and his regime. According to the president, only some of the striking and marching women were fighting against femicide, "but there is another current that is against us and they want the government to fail and prevent the consolidation of the Fourth Transformation [the self-ascribed historical name of López Obrador's regime]."[2] Paranoid, the president accused women of being conservative and wanting his government to fail, when in truth, one of the main demands of the march had been that the State cease giving impunity to gender-violence criminals. By expressing paranoia and indifference toward the women's march and strike, just as authorities behave blandly when action against women's aggressors needs to be taken, the president himself is demanding silence from the victims. This is why vandalism against official monuments (Patrimony) is a direct expression against State impunity granted to male aggressors of women. A symbolic gesture toward the Catholic Church's historical and present complicity with women's oppression during the March 8th protest took place as women "liberated" the Cathedral erected across from the Palacio Nacional by pulling away the shielding fences and leaving their bras hanging around the entrance gates. "¡Fuimos todas!"[3]

At the beginning of November 2019, the collective Mujeres Organizadas had called for an indefinite strike at UNAM to protest against gender violence. Female students took eleven out of the thirty-nine UNAM campuses, including the Filosofía y Letras and Ciencias Políticas y Sociales faculties. Despite the establishment of an institutional protocol in 2016 to deal with harassment from professors to students and male students against women, the *morras* paralyzed classes and barricaded entire sections of the university, demanding that the protocol be amended and real action be taken. This occurred against the backdrop of the long and very visible struggle in the mass and social media to bring justice to Lesvy Berlín, a UNAM student murdered on campus by her boyfriend in 2017. A judge had concluded that it had been a suicide, despite the existence of surveillance images of them having a fight and

---

2 Declaration by the president in his daily morning address on March 9, 2020, as reported in *El Financiero*, https://www.elfinanciero.com.mx/nacional/hay-una-vertiente-que-quiere-que-fracasemos-es-el-conservadurismo-disfrazado-de-feminismo-amlo.

3 "We all did it!"

him eventually hitting her. Finally, in October 2019, her boyfriend at the time, Jorge Luis González Hernández, was accused of femicide and condemned to forty-five years in prison. Berlín's case served as a catalyzer to reclaim State authorities to become implicated in femicide cases. At the end of March, a group of women has been occupying the main siege of the Comisión Nacional de Derechos Humanos (National Human Rights Commission) in Mexico City for almost seven months. Having demanded accountability for femicide and rape, and having denounced the austere measures that led to the dismantlement of women's refugees and childcare networks, they have decided to stay until their demands are met. In the meantime, they have established a refuge for women victims of gender violence, which has been exacerbated by the lockdown demanded by the COVID-19 pandemic.[4]

Without a doubt, the current forms the feminist(s) movement(s) have taken in contemporary Mexico would not exist with what precedes them. Historically, feminism was dissociated from Communism, as Communists took a stance against it because they considered it to be a bourgeois movement, giving it negative connotations. In 1953, a constitutional reform was approved to grant women the right to vote—legislation that came into effect in 1954 after a discourse had prevailed stating than women were more conservative than men. This prejudice had been an obstacle to acknowledging women's citizenship in the country, as well as President Andrés Manuel López Obrador's stance toward contemporary women's struggles. By the mid-1970s and early 1980s, feminist thinking and activism intensified as young university female students associated with the left began articulating demands linked to the body, sexuality, the legalization of abortion, reproductive labor, freedom of expression, and masculine violence. Among our predecessors are Amalia González Caballero, Elena Arizmendi, Hermila Galindo, Elvia Carrillo Puerto, Rosario Castellanos, Esperanza Brito, Patricia Mercado, and Marta Lamas, all of whom began to make demands for rights, education, economic, and political equality, as well as to lead a struggle against gender violence and for rights.[5]

---

4 See Irmgard Emmelhainz, "Pétroleuses and Mexican Morras," *The Funambulist* 34 (March–April 2021).

5 Gabriela Cano and Hilda Monraz, "Un recorrido por la historia del feminismo en México," *El Universal*, March 8 2020, https://www.eluniversal.com.mx/cultura/un-recorrido-por-la-historia-del-feminismo-en-mexico.

In the 1990s, as a result of the intensification of the femicide phenomenon, women in Tijuana and Ciudad Juárez organized to gain visiblity and demand accountability for the disappearance and murder of their daughters. These women sought help from state institutions to give justice to the victims or to search for the missing women, who were (and still are) mostly young, working class, or of Indigenous origin. An iconic figure of this movement was Marisela Escobedo Ortiz, who was able to find the murderer of her daughter by her own means and bring him to trial, where he was acquitted. She was eventually murdered while fighting for justice. Now femicide is a word crystallizing women's struggles in Canada, France, and elsewhere.[6] In the meantime, more privileged women live gender violence generally not as murder, but mostly as abuse and harassment.

We have been speaking for a long time, and now our stories are public. The debate that arose after the #MiPrimerAcoso in Mexico and the #MeToo global movements unleashed accusations of abuse across the world (with brackets in Hollywood and France) centered on men's freedom to conquer women. The #MeToo movement has been dismissed either as being prudish or as ignoring the quid pro quo behind certain forms of sexual behavior.[7] To transcend the easy victimization of women, however, we need to be aware of the distinction between predation and abuse and pit abuse against debauchery. Last February, beautiful French actress Adèle Haenel walked out from the Césars award ceremony in France in outrage as Roman Polanski's award for best director for his film *An Officer and a Spy* was announced. Only a few cheered on, perhaps seeing the irony behind the fact that Polanski had been given an award for a film he had made about an unfair and prejudiced prosecution against a Jewish man (Dreyfus) in nineteenth-century France. In an interview with Médiapart in November 2019, Haenel told the story behind her accusation of abuse as a teenager by Christophe Ruggia, the director of her first film. Her story is analogous to Samantha Gaily's, who was thirteen when Polanski raped her in 1977. In the Médiapart interview, Haenel

6 See Emmanuelle Walter, *Soeurs volées: Enquête sur un fémicide au Canada* (Montréal: Lux, 2014); and Megan Clement, "Sisters in Arms: The Families Fighting Femicide in France," *Aljazeera*, December 30, 2019, https://www.aljazeera.com/features/2019/12/30/sisters-in-arms-the-families-fighting-femicide-in-france.

7 For a brilliant historical account and discussion of this debate see Marta Lamas, *Abuso ¿Denuncia legítima o victimización?* (México D.F.: Fondo de Cultura Económica, 2019).

concluded that the difference between predation and debauchery lies on the fact that abuse inoculates self-hatred in women, along with the drive for self-destruction. As men have the capacity to derive pleasure from depredation, it has become clear that depredation has become the normative measure of behavior between men and women—a form of pedagogy of gender, and the basis upon which the whole of society is built. So, when we talk about gender violence and abuse, we are not discussing singular cases of abuse and harassment proliferating or coming to light. Rather, gender violence implicates the whole of society, and everyone must listen. We have to continue to fight, even while a virus has made speaking dangerous and our current struggle has been delegated as secondary by power (only in appearance).

At the end of March 2021, nature has been heard speaking back loudly for the past year, making it clearer than ever that our societies are erected not only on the depredation of women, but also of nature. Across the world, we are seeing leaders react to the Coronavirus crisis with extreme power grabs; for example, ruling by decree with no end in sight (e.g., Urban, Netanyahu, Trump's hint at postponing elections), the suspension of environmental regulations in the name of salvaging the economy (e.g., China and the United States), and attacks on our weakened democracies or Trump's threats against Cuba, Venezuela, and Panama.[8] In Mexico City, the government tried to seize extra power over surveillance, as cell-phone companies granted the government access to cell antennas for the military; oligarchs have taken extra power in business (especially pharmaceuticals); and the president pushed for debt schemes for small businesses as a solution to a lack of salaries and declared the dismantling of a variety of institutional trusts to produce a total of 25 billion pesos to rescue PEMEX from the COVID-19 crisis. The political measures taken to palliate the effects of the pandemic and quarantine are in complete logical continuity with neoliberal means to control subaltern bodies, to surreptitiously demand silence from the victims, and to intensify extractive capitalism. They also ignore the links between infectious viruses and industrialized animal farming and deforestation, as well as the role corporations

8 Naomi Klein, "Rising Majority Teach-In with Naomi Klein & Angela Y. Davis," *Now This Is Politics*, live on Facebook on April 2, 2020, https://www.facebook.com/NowThisPolitics/videos/1001197546941886.

such as Bayer, Monsanto, Singenta, Basf, Corteva, Cargill, Bunge, and ADM have as virus and death factories.[9]

In Silvia Federici's fundamental text, *Calibán y la bruja*, she describes how, during the transition from feudalism to capitalism at the beginning of the fourteenth century and in the aftermath of the black plague, the State (and the Catholic church) granted them free or easy access to sex as a means to co-opt young rebellious proletarians. This meant that, on the one hand, rape against working-class women went unpunished (becoming a kind of sport), and on the other, prostitution was institutionalized and condoned by both state and church. This paved the way for misogyny and the witch hunt, or genocide, that would last for the following three centuries.[10] The historical moment that Federici studies in her book, characterized by the institutionalized unleashing of unprecedented violence and women's degradation, is similar to our current era, which is characterized by the intensification of the implementation of neoliberal policies and laws that began in Mexico in the late 1980s. Both historical periods have in common the intensification of gender violence and femicide. This is why it has become key to concatenate all forms of violence that originate in privatization and capitalism: dispossession, displacement, gyoncide, and genocide, all of which speak for the mercantilization of life. Nowadays, the most visible figure and global voice in the fight against global warming is Swedish teenager Greta Thunberg. Last year, a disturbing drawing was brought to my attention: it displayed a nude woman seen from the back and slightly above, with two hands pulling her long braids from behind with the label "Greta." The image was accompanied by the official logo of the Canadian oil company called X-Site Energy Service, which claimed responsibility for the creation and distribution of stickers that depicted this sexualized and abusive image of Greta Thunberg. The image displays a direct relationship between gender violence and the depredation of the commons. It is acknowledgment that the same logic of depredation traverses this conjunction that women in Argentina in 2016 began the march and struggle that has now become ubiquitous in Latin America. This movement is intersectional and transversal, premised on the fact that depredation

---

9 Interview with Silvia Ribeiro by Claudia Korol, "No le echen la culpa al murciélago," *Página 12*, April 3, 2020, https://www.pagina12.com.ar/256569-no-le-echen-la-culpa-al-murcielago.

10 Silvia Federici, *Calibán y la bruja: Mujeres, cuerpo y acumulación originaria* (Madrid: Traficantes de Sueños, 2010), 70–75.

manifests in varying degrees of gender violence: femicide, harassment, abuse, and devastation of the commons. Depredation, moreover, materializes in heteropatriarchy, which is the social system underpinning a predatorial logic to relate to the world and others, which in turn is reproduced by nation-state structures.[11]

In the 1980s, the punk movement had declared "No future!" This prediction has become true: the modernist notion of a progressive future has been substituted by an apocalyptic feeling that the future is synonymous with global catastrophe at the financial, environmental, and urban levels.[12] In this regard, the Anthropocene thesis could be posited as the antithesis of neoliberal common sense that operates in the name of (individual) development and betterment: ours is the geological era of the sixth massive extinction, and its main cause is the transformation of earth by man under the rationality of industrial global capitalism, thus inaugurating a process of (self)destruction. Following Naomi Klein, our global economy is completely created and sustained by burning fossil fuels, and that foundational dependence of capitalism cannot be changed by neoliberal politics which presuppose that market mechanisms will be the solution, but, as Klein argues, through massive and immediate interventions.[13] That is to say, neoliberalism is a form of capitalist accumulation that puts life and the commons at its service and destroys them. The intensification of neoliberalism—what we can call post-neoliberalism or extractivism—is leading us to make the entire 80 percent of the world population redundant. Currently, 80 percent of land is held by 20 percent of the population, as 80 percent of profits are produced by 20 percent of employees. This means that the global economy will soon reach a stage in which only 20 percent of the workforce will have jobs because technological innovations will have made human labor redundant. The remaining 80 percent of the population will become irrelevant, without use or function, unable to be absorbed by sweatshops, tourism infrastructure, the service economy,

---

11 See Verónica Gago, *La potencia feminista o el deseo de cambiarlo todo* (Madrid: Traficantes de sueños, 2019).

12 Franco "Bifo" Berardi, *After the Future*, ed. Gary Genosko and Nicholas Thoburn (London: AK Press, 2011).

13 In fact, it is possible that it is already too late to take action; as Naomi Klein puts it, the situation with global warming is so bad that we should imagine that every alarm on every house on every street in the world is set off nonstop. Naomi Klein, *This Changes Everything: Capitalism vs. the Climate* (New York: Simon & Shuster, 2014).

or agroindustry. Before this landscape, which goes hand in hand with dispossession by accumulation, the main problems that should concern us are drought, poisoned land, devastated forests, sterile seeds, and mountains torn apart by mining companies or highways. The earth is being broken down from within, and the link between the destruction of the social tissue by violence and the destruction of the environment by extractivism is becoming clear; both mean the destruction of the communal capacities to sustain life autonomously through interwoven structures of reproduction in a war against life and the human capacity to make political decisions collectively. In this regard, struggles for territorial defense mean regaining autonomy against "modernizing" megaprojects undertaken by governments and corporations, which are grounded on the capitalist logics of scarcity and dispossession. Environmental devastation is inextricable from an economic model based on the orthodoxy of the free market and a frenetic drive toward economic expansion. In this regard, some prefer naming this era "Capitalocene" rather than Anthropocene.

One of the main forces that propelled the business model that led to globalization and extractivism, designed in the 1980s and the 1990s, was to allow multinationals to scour the globe, seeking the cheapest and most exploitable labor force. By the 1990s, the first sweatshops in Mexico and Central America had deterritorialized to China, where salaries were extremely low and unions were brutally repressed; the State had spent unprecedented funds in massive infrastructure projects (e.g., ports, highways, carbon electric plants, dams) to ensure that factories would not stop working. This is why the dream of a free-market businessman is the environment's nightmare, as there is an existing strict correlation between low salaries and low carbon emissions.[14] We must bear in mind, however, that this logic of finding the cheapest place to produce commodities has a precedent on the colonial scourge for primary commodities that began to be spoliated from Latin America in the sixteenth century. On the other hand, at the global level, food prices have not stopped increasing. This is partly because, following the colonial logic, now corporations, financial speculators, oligarchs, billionaires of the microchip industries, hedge-fund owners, and others are appropriating enormous tracts of cheap land to feed their people and to subject the food industry to financial speculation and, in the process, displacing, alienating, and bankrupting people by

14 Klein, *This Changes Everything*, 81–82.

creating unemployment and destroying cultures and forms of life[15]. Besides the fact that industrial farming and the current corporate system of food distribution are the main causes of climate change,[16] the problems of land misuse and distribution are rooted in the legacy of colonization. Developers that come to devastate the land impose calculations that are not sustainable; human gain is instantaneous, but profit in the long term is lost. Environmental destruction is a form of gradual and invisible violence—"slow," as Rob Nixon put it. It is caused by climate change, toxic-waste pouring, deforestation, and ocean contamination, and it constitutes a form of violence that underlies the lives of people considered expendable.[17] This form of violence, along with State violence and violence tied to organized crime and drug dealers, is directly tied to the systematic application of neoliberal reforms sustained in what is now considered *common sense*: acting on self-interest. This is part of a mechanism of subjection and subjectivation resulting in the fragmentation of the social tissue and environmental devastation, now intensified by the demand for energy, industrial minerals and metals, agroindustrial products, and other natural resources enmeshed in financial speculation, ultimately leading to the generation of extraordinary profits for extractive capital.[18]

The 2018 elections in Mexico mark the waning away of the hegemony of almost thirty years of progressive neoliberalism, which had been characterized by an alliance between the plutocrats, transnationals, and politicians with a liberal politics of recognition, freedom of expression, and investment without precedents in cultural production. This means that in Mexico, market liberalization from the State's heavy hand implied packaging neoliberal reforms in a progressive culturalized and democratic politics. In this context, the progressive forces of civil society were encouraged to disseminate the ethos of recognition, thereby establishing a democratic culture of freedom of expression, which was met with official tolerance. At the center of this movement were the ideals of "diversity," women's empowerment, LGBTQ+

---

15 Fred Pearce, *The Land Grabbers: The New Fight over Who Owns the Earth* (Boston: Beacon Press, 2012).

16 Silvia Ribeiro, "Comida que calienta," *La Jornada*, September 8, 2012, http://www.jornada.unam.mx/2012/09/08/opinion/019a1eco.

17 Rob Nixon, *Slow Violence and the Environmentalism of the Poor* (Cambridge, MA: Harvard University Press, 2011).

18 See the introduction to Henry Veltmeyer and James Petras, *The New Extractivism: A Post-Neoliberal Development Model or Imperialism of the Twenty-First Century?* (London: Zed Books, 2014).

rights, the recognition of Indigenous people's cultural rights, and environmentalist claims. In Mexico, therefore, the spirit of neoliberalism was tied to development, emancipation, cosmopolitism, multiculturalism, and progressive values. Soon enough, however, freedom of expression gave way to the endless showcase of violent deaths in the mass media and cultural industry under President Felipe Calderón (2006–2012) and to a ceaseless succession of political scandals. By the end of President Enrique Peña Nieto's regime (2012–2018), the progressive and hegemonic side of the neoliberal project had fallen into a crisis of legitimacy.[19]

In Mexico, it is generally perceived that the neoliberal state was an adulterated form of governing that failed to fix the evils of precarization, exclusion, inequality, and scarcity deepening inequality and increasing poverty. This perception is grounded, on the one hand, on the experience of the progressive dismantling of the welfare state by austerity measures and privatization policies that have been operating since the 1980s, and on the other, on the actuality of systemic corruption of political actors and public institutions. It is thus perceived that our adulterated (or in some cases "failed") state governs through omissions, indolence, and lack of action. This perception translates to a kind of "state fetishism" that considers the state to be an abstract homogenous entity responsible for all evils in the country—from disappearances to the ongoing crisis of food sovereignty, lack of water or fuel, and even environmental catastrophe. The problem with state fetishism is that it reinforces the central power of the state by obviating other operative forms of power, such as violence and racialization, that constitute our current neoliberal landscape but date back five hundred years. Another thing that state fetishism tends to obviate is the role national and transnational corporations, the financialization of capital, automatization and digitalization, and infrastructure have in giving shape to our existence, including our ("the citizens'") deep immersion in the global dispossession and destruction processes.

State fetishism, moreover, conveyed the feeling that the dogma of the democratic dream, whose grammar is grounded on democracy, elections, poverty, market freedom, corruption, drug trafficking, impunity, governability, income redistribution, had been vanquished. After four elections, "the elected president is the one we voted for." When President Andrés López Obrador came to power, a large portion of state infrastructure and federal property had

19 See Nancy Fraser, *The Old is Dying and the New Cannot Be Born* (New York: Verso, 2019).

been privatized or subcontracted. In this context, under President López Obrador's regime, a new post-neoliberal historical era was announced: "The Fourth Transformation." At its core, there is a redistributive agenda based on profound austerity measures seeking to correct the excesses of previous neoliberal regimes. President López Obrador has claimed to represent "the poor," giving priority to economic development, security, and peace, re-statizing the nation's economy beginning with PEMEX and CFE (Electricity Federal Commission), a revival of the welfare state (with hospitals "like in Denmark and Canada"), and a new moral, political, cultural, and intellectual hegemony. This hegemony is being slowly cemented on the president's daily *Mañaneras*, or morning addresses, in which he steers the political agenda and discussion, giving way to a new common sense in the Mexican political imaginary, grounded on class tensions, a fight against previous regimes' corruption. The current regime is characterized by a dismantlement of state institutions through austerity measures (the kind that would make International Monetary Fund (IMF) bureaucrats from the 1980s chuckle), a revolutionary cultural politics, a curious relationship between State and the Evangelical church, and daily polarization in the Mañaneras, including dismissal of opponents and criticism, especially feminists.

The main principle of the Fourth Transformation is to overcome neoliberalism and undo its evils, and it is thus grounded on a (populist) post-neoliberal governance and the intensification of an extractivist economy to the detriment of environmental policy. Climate change issues are not mentioned in the Plan Nacional de Desarrollo (National Development Plan), and thus there is no commitment to it.[20] Mexico, like the rest of Latin America, has become the site of major social conflicts over territorial rights to land, as well as water and natural resources, which is intensified by the current regime's post-neoliberal expansion of the extractive frontier. For the past twenty years, the State has facilitated multinational corporations' access to land, minerals, and other resources. Now that the model of neoliberalism is in crisis, a new economic model is being applied to Mexico through a public policy geared at national grassroots development through a kind of "developmentalist post-neoliberalism." James Petras and Henry Veltmeyer observed the unfolding of

20 Antonio Azuela, Julia Carabias, and Enrique Provencio, "¿Cómo está la política ambiental?" in *Balance temprano desde la izquierda democrática*, ed. Ricardo Becerra and José Woldenberg (México D.F.: IETD and Editorial Grano de Sal, 2020), 78–85.

this economic model in Bolivia, Ecuador, and Venezuela in the first decade of the twenty-first century—an economic growth strategy based on developmentalism, poverty reduction, the extraction of national resources, and the production of primary goods through open-pit gold, silver and copper mining, oil and gas, and agribusiness (transgenic soy). Corporations already control key segments of extractivist processes, but a new nationalism over resources is being implemented as resource extraction is posited as a catalyst for national development, taking advantage of the primary commodities boom in the world market. This "new extractivism" marks the end of the neoliberal era in Mexico and the return to nineteenth century capitalism grounded on free-market capitalism imposed by the IMF. A strategy is being implemented through left-wing populist discourse to reground the economy on fossil-fuel extraction and primary commodity exports as national development strategies through an interventionist State and regulatory regime.[21] Finally, the Fourth Transformation has been obliged to face the challenges of the COVID-19 crisis and waves of migrants from Central America crossing through Mexico to reach the United States.

The original *Tiranía del sentido común: La reconversión neoliberal de México* was written between 2010 and 2015 and encompassed an analysis of the effects of twenty years of neoliberal policies in the sensible regime and common sense in Mexico, focusing on key areas: urban planning, life and work, culture, social movements, and women's struggles. In the first version of *The Tyranny*, I posited neoliberalism beyond the political economy of market liberalization as the internalization of the objective conditions of the reproduction of capitalism in all areas of human and nonhuman life; in other words, neoliberalism as the marketization of every aspect of human and non-human lives that transforms and makes worlds, and that shapes imaginaries and subjectivities in different ways. Neoliberalism also means the intensification of state intervention in legislation to liberalize the market following World Trade Organization (WTO) and IMF structural adjustment policies and austerity regimes.

For the English edition, I have revised and substantially expanded my inquiry to encompass the developments of neoliberal common sense after Andrés Manuel López Obrador's ascent to power, as well as the implications of his "post-neoliberal" policies and the institution of a new hegemony. This

21 Veltmeyer and Petras, *The New Extractivism*, 37.

book is an interdisciplinary exercise of critical thought anchored in neoliberal Mexico with a global perspective. My purpose is to elucidate the neoliberal mechanisms that work from within subjectivities and that have become *common sense*, ruling all areas of life. I am interested in going beyond the postmodern idea that the subject is at the mercy of ideology and spectacle, behind which there is no absolute truth or reality: in the postmodern world view, reality is built with signs that constitute subjects. In contrast, I seek to posit the human as an element within the network of the reality that shapes the ways in which the world gives itself to perception through the neoliberal distribution of sensual reality, which is homogeneous, differentiated, and constituted by aesthetic and affective flows eluding definition and capture but which nonetheless mold it. More and more, the ways in which the world shapes itself to perception happens through singularized algorithms bringing about an era denominated by what Franco Berardi describes as neuro-totalitarianism. In conjunction with the mercantilization of every aspect of life and what is alive, as automatisms begin to slowly take over everyday life, the world presents itself to us as singularized bubbles of information, completely destroying our world in common.

As I will argue, neoliberal capitalism is deeply rooted in our lives, sensibility, and the distribution of the sensible. Specifically, what I explore in this book are the ways in which urban planning in Mexico City is geared toward spatial segregation, differentiating, and homogenizing the different socioeconomic classes, as well as the services and commodities to which each strata of society has access; the ways in which neoliberalism rules the logic of life, work, and subjectivation as means of social control; how culture and art production have obeyed the logic of the free market to become a showcase for democracy and vehicles for neoliberal sensibility that includes a twisted sense of empathy; and how the collective imaginary has been transformed by violence into a shared suffering, making urgent the emancipation of a moral vision of violence in order to enable the politicization of the collective toward anti-capitalist struggles. I also explore the ordeals of Indigenous peoples in Mexico under the light of the intensification of extractivism and massive repression of territorial defense struggles. In addition, I address the difficulties in representing these struggles due to the dissociation between urban (civil society) and originary populations' ordeals and what I call the colonial blind spot. In the chapter about culture, I include a new section on the "Cultural Revolution" currently undergoing in Mexico and its implications, as well as the relationship between the State and intellectuals and artists as it has evolved under neoliberalism. I also elucidate the implications of a sensible regime characterized by alienation and authoritarianisms, discuss the effect of alienation in empathy and solidarity, and inquire about the possible forms our common link to the world could take. I conclude by positing one of the political challenges of our era: to break through neoliberalism with models of autonomy for decolonizing, which also means destituting the legacy of modernity.

The current relevance of the women's march and strike lies precisely in its concatenation of capitalist and colonial violence, and thus in the fact that it is capable of transcending the Mexican political imaginary of state fetishism. It has become clear that politics is no longer articulated around contradiction or class struggle, and neither does it respond anymore to the strategic centrality of the proletariat; through state fetishism, it has been conceived as a counterhegemonic logic centered on the state. And yet we are living in the cadavers of the state and capitalism, which have begun to rot. Hegemonies have been broken. Indigenous peoples who are deserting from the nation-project organizing autonomies, arming themselves against state violence with "Communal Policing" *exist for real*. Current opposition in Mexico is not what is expressed on social media but what materializes in reality as "Congreso Nacional Indígena," "Consejo Regional de Pueblos Originarios en Defensa del Territorio de Puebla e Hidalgo," and "Prisioneros políticos indígenas por defender sus territorios." Without a doubt, a transformation will come from the imminent collapse of capitalism, and the most valuable forms of political imagination will be those grounded on empathy, non-injurious forms of interdependency, and our capacity to foresee concrete changes to the present situation. The desire for connection and togetherness, fueled by the uncertainty of the length of the social distancing to contain the pandemic, only needs to crystalize in continuing where we left off at the March 9 women's strike. The evidence is on the table: all toxicity is coming from the same source.

CHAPTER ONE

Neoliberal Sensibility and Common Sense

IN HIS 1993 NOVELLA, *La leyenda de los soles* (The legend of the suns), Homero Ardijis paints a sunken, deforested Mexico City with dead vegetation, the volcano scape destroyed, and trash everywhere. He describes it as a "boundless and foreign world," a city that underwent "gradual loss of soil, air and water . . . the loss of its own self."[1] The environment imagined by Ardijis for Mexico City in 2027 is dysfunctional and violent, the dictatorship exacerbated by indescribable forms of control and violence. He portrays a city scourged by evils perceived as being of the same kind: crime, corruption, pollution. On the background of Ardijis's apocalyptic visions of the city, akin to the ruined earth in *Elysium* (2013) filmed in Tijuana, are the neoliberal reforms promised in the 1990s: a road of prosperity for all that which became the answer to the problems of corruption of public service and bureaucracy, and the dysfunctional government body in the 1970s and 1980s. The "transition to democracy" heralded in 2000 when the PAN (National Action Party) took power after the PRI's (Institutional Revolution Party) seventy-year-long

1 Homero Aridjis, *La leyenda de los soles* (México D.F.: Fondo de Cultura Económica, 1993), 2.

reign, assuring the end of the perfect dictatorship and the beginning of real democracy: alternation, citizen participation, and an antagonistic struggle for consensus between civil society, the PAN, the PRI, and the leftist party PRD (Party of the Democratic Revolution).

More than twenty-five years after Ardijis's novel was published, I live in "CDMX," a branded Mexico City and a key locality in the economic and cultural map of globalization. With most of the public services privatized, it has become an archipelago of sophistication and wealth where the quality of gasoline blued the sky. We enjoy "first-world" infrastructure and services; there are police officers in every corner, including eventual checkpoints, and informal vendors and beggars have been removed from public spaces. Beautiful "public" green areas flourish—some of them kept by neighbors, corporations, or private businesses, instead of the municipality, under a program called "Adopta un área verde" by the city's government (Adopt a Green Area). The city I inhabit and the privileged areas in which I circulate are far from the dry, dark desert of violence that Ardijis imagined in his novella. After twenty years of privatizations, concessions, and the implementation of "zonification"—which means that every one of Mexico City's delegations or boroughs is oriented toward their optimal economic vocations—privileged territories, like in many cities throughout Latin America and increasingly all over the world, coexist side by side with misery belts or slums. That is to say, privileged areas in which the government and the private sector are present to protect and apply an array of techniques of governance, coexist with misery belts or zones of sacrifice of environmental devastation inhabited by populations that have been made redundant by neoliberal reforms, This creates relationships of injurious interdependency between both kinds of populations, the latter a by-product of the expansion of the scope of migration from the mid-twentieth century of the present, continuous migration of rural population to urbanized areas.

Under Felipe Calderón and Enrique Peña Nieto, Mexico came to be governed through a complex network of relationships and forms of power that complemented each other: violent state repression, government of opinion, and repressive tolerance, along with the criminalization of dissidence, labor precariousness and debt as forms of submission, and fear and insecurity caused by "organized crime" or "narco violence." In sum, a form of oligarchic totalitarianism was set up, supported by government legislation and surveillance, political forces that propelled a redistribution of wealth focused on the private sphere, media and cultural production in detriment to public infrastructure, and health and education systems. In this manner, neoliberal politics systematically exerted violence on bodies and forms of life, creating a form of sovereignty described as "deep power," comprised by decision-making behind closed doors by financial and political elites. That is to say, key choices concerning the economy came to be negotiated in secret within the limitless reign of capital, enclosing the space of political decision-making by shutting out the rest of the population.[2] Under this form of power, the government became the guarantor of the accumulation of capital hidden behind a smoke screen, where political processes foreign to issues of political decision-making were made public; for instance, cultural wars, corruption scandals, and human rights violations. At the global level, the new oligarchs had taken up the task to transform all nation states into servile instruments to enrich themselves and increase their power through neoliberal reforms and financial capitalism.[3] These elites are characterized by their lack of roots and alliances with nation states and carelessness about the injuries they could cause to workers or the environment. They tend to live inside gated communities and may float above traffic in otherwise congested cities, and they operate above borders, laws, and national and international regulations.[4] Thus, in order to legitimize the neoliberal politics that favored the elites while causing dispossession, extermination, and violence, state institutions were "hollowed out"—or rather, molded—to serve the interests of global capital in the name of "development" and "economic growth." A state of exception of permanent insecurity was normalized in which unprecedented and unthinkable levels of violence came to be part of the fabric of daily life and fodder to the Infosphere (the mass media

---

2 An example was the Trade in Services Agreement (TISA), which was ratified in May 2014. This treaty encompasses fifty countries and most commercial services in the world. It establishes rules to further the expansion of finance multinationals to other nations preventing regulatory barriers. The treaty prohibits regulation of financial services and promotes openness of the flux of information across borders (i.e., personal and financial information). When the treaty was signed, no one had heard about it.

3 Or the emancipation of money accumulation from industrial production of merchandise. See Franco "Bifo" Berardi, "Emancipation of the Sign: Poetry and Finance During the Twentieth Century," *e-flux journal* 39 (November 2012), http://www.e-flux.com/journal/emancipation-of-the-sign-poetry-and-finance-during-the-twentieth-century.

4 C. J. Polychroniou, "An Interview with Henri Giroux on Democracy in Crisis," *Counterpunch*, May 5, 2014, http://www.counterpunch.org/2014/05/30/an-interview-with-henry-giroux-on-democracy-in-crisis.

and the culture industry). The collateral damage of neoliberal predator capitalism expanded to destroy social ties and safety networks, relying on social Darwinism as a form of subjection and extermination, thereby legitimizing neoliberal politics of exclusion and violence.

One of the reasons for the normalization of extreme violence was the neoliberal institution—grounded on our colonial structures that remain intact from the past—of racialized disposability. This means that it no longer makes sense to think about the world as divided into "first" and "third"; rather, we are seeing modernized pockets of privilege and cultural sophistication coexist with enclaves inhabited by "redundant populations." This sector of the population has differential access to health care, citizenship, debt, education, and jobs. Some of them live in "zones of sacrifice," or the literal contemporary manifestation of coloniality. These zones are inhabited by communities surviving with the toxic load of our systemic need to consume fossil fuels undergoing slow violence,[5] and their common and sustainable autonomous forms of life are being destroyed in the name of well-being and development. Moreover, their destruction is de facto sustaining the privileges of people living in modernized enclaves who are denying, yet justifying, their annihilation under the logic of development and inclusion in global markets.

For the past forty years, people have been dispossessed and forcibly displaced to misery belts, rural cities, or to the north. Meanwhile, urban centers operate with measures like gentrification and the penalization of what are known as "quality of life crimes" such as: itinerant selling, homelessness, or vagrancy. There, "social cleansing" is the rule. Furthermore, the land of millions of people is being expropriated and given to private corporations in the name of "public interest" to create agroindustrial farms of Special Zones of Economic Development (SEZs), infrastructure projects like dams, highways, car manufacturing, growth of marihuana and poppy, or kitchens for chemically designed drugs; or they are transformed into extractivist zones. It is a fact that Mexico is a leading producer in silver, tenth in gold and copper and among the top ten in lead, fluorite, bismuth, and other minerals. Since 2000, the Mexican government has given hundreds of mining concessions to foreign companies, mostly Canadian.[6] The consequence: environmental

5 See Rob Nixon, *Slow Violence and the Environmentalism of the Poor* (Cambridge, MA: Harvard University Press, 2013).

6 Darcy Victor Tetreault, "Mexico: The Political Ecology of Mining," in *The New Extractivism: A Post-Neoliberal Development Model or Imperialism of the*

devastation manifesting as the rapid appearance of dead rivers, dry wells, bare mountains, toxic oceans, and deforested woodlands, all reflected on a damaged and impoverished social environment subject to precariousness and unthinkable levels of social violence.

It could thus be argued that neoliberalism is a form of ecological, social, and cultural reengineering that has destroyed the environment while reproducing a culture of consumption, stupidity, and illiteracy. As an intensified phase of colonial capitalism, the current manifestations of neoliberalism bring to light the fact that violence has sustained the system of Western supremacy by violence through extractivism exerted on Indigenous peoples' territories and bodies and specific forms of violence against women. Parallels may be drawn between the extraction of reproductive labor and financial exploitation and the capture of the sensible realm and vital forces by both financialization and automation; language has been expropriated by corporatized education, music by TV contests, flesh and sexuality by mass pornography, the city by the police and corporations, and our friends by Darwinist competitivity and precarious working conditions. Paul B. Preciado articulated the continuity of colonialism in the present in this manner: "If the annihilating workings of sixteenth-century colonialism hid behind the shine of Potosí silver, today, behind the screens are hiding the most extreme forms of neocolonial, technological and subjective domination."[7]

A lot of people have succumbed to the neoliberal limitation of autonomous action and have begun to think of themselves mainly as consumers or victims (of narco or state violence), and they are prey not only to the culture of hedonistic pleasure, but also of fear and violence. This is why one of the consequences of neoliberalism is the production of a collective existential crisis of agency. This crisis led to the current form of authoritarianism rooted in historical, pedagogical, and cultural Mexican traditions, which has taken further form as a net of control that proliferates, displaces, molds, and subjects under the guise of a neo-populist fight against corruption and petit bourgeois decadence (the 1% is invisible from this equation).

If the consequences of neoliberal policies have been so dire, I must ask, what has made neoliberalism prevail? One of the reasons I can think of is to

---

Twenty-First Century?, ed. Henry Veltmeyer and James Petras (London: Zed Books, 2014), 144–71.

7 Paul B. Preciado, introduction to Suely Rolnik, *Esferas de la insurrección: Apuntes para descolonizar el inconsciente* (Madrid: Tinta Limón, 2019), 9.

consider neoliberalism as the intensification of violence inherent to modern capitalist sensibility that manifests itself in our relationships to the world, nature, things, and beings, presupposing the creation of surplus value, unlimited growth, and development by way of the mercantilization of life and the marketization of human and nonhuman forms of life. Neoliberalism, moreover, has become the filter through which we now perceive and understand that which cannot be verbalized, a form of common sense that permeates our basic ability to understand and judge things based on a fear of others; it means existing in survival mode and having as goals hedonistic pleasure and generating surplus value. The neoliberal violence against the sensible, furthermore, means that sensibility and common sense are the battlefields on which individual options and collective forces of economics and politics are at play. From this point of view, "neoliberalism" designates at least three different things: the restructuration of capitalist social relations; a political party that at every juncture (it does not matter if left or right) tries to expand the free-market economic policy favoring corporations and the oligarchy; and governance through specific forms of coercion. The kind of neoliberal violence against individuals that subsumed desire to market forces, however, is no longer enough to sustain the neoliberal economic politics, which explains why neofascisms are being implemented worldwide. If neoliberalism had taught us to live according to free-market imperatives, now that it is in crisis, it is showing us its true, hostile face, attacking what remains of autonomous life forms and spaces with the intensification of extractivism, gender violence, intolerance, and militarization. The self-governing and governing techniques of coaching, repressive tolerance, and the promise of success and riches had been powerful tools of neoliberal subjection. But now that the incompatibility of neoliberalism and democracy is obvious, its "side effects" (such as environmental devastation, massive dispossession and displacement, and the COVID-19 pandemic, increased precarity and poverty) are impossible to deny. Therefore, the system needs to find other techniques like repression and the expansion of hatred against all who refuse to comply to the mandates of the free market. But what got us here is neoliberal common sense, the product of violence against the sensible at the basis of neoliberal subjectification.

Hannah Arendt described common sense as deriving from sensibility, or from the experience of the materially and sensually given world; it is the sense data that we share with others, enabling us to live and judge from a singular perspective in our common world.[8] Similarly, Suely Rolnik defines the sensible as the human capacity to perceive and feel to apprehend the world—what we denominate reality. The modes of existence or reality are articulated according to sociocultural codes that configure people, their places, and their distribution in the social field, which are inseparable from the distribution of access to material and immaterial goods, as well as from hierarchies and representations. Such codes orient the ways in which we apprehend the world; our perceptions and feelings are already associated to codes and representations that we project upon perception, which allow us to make sense of it.[9]

Therefore, common sense is shared meaning, with the potential to create a sense of belonging in social and political terms. Neoliberal common sense, however, is tied to a crisis of relationality, diagnosed by Félix Guattari in the 1980s, an exacerbated form of modern alienation. In Guattari's view, this crisis is due to the reduction of kinship networks to the bare minimum, the poisoning of domestic life by the gangrene of mass-media consumption, the ossification of family life by a standardization of behavior, and the reduction of neighbor relations to their meanest expression.[10] This crisis translates to a common sense of hostility toward public schools, social security, and other institutions focused on helping the weakest and administering the commons. Slowly, public institutions were privatized and government functions subcontracted, under the justification that they would be more competitive and offer higher-quality services. The mechanism for achieving this worked as follows: first, subsidies were taken away to make the organism or institution inoperative; then, unions were demonized and their independence and agency were limited. In order for the given public institution to stop being a disaster, people accepted privatization. Privatizations, however, do not make public institutions or services necessarily better; rather, they shift focus from providing a public service to making a profit.

The logic of privatization under neoliberalism, moreover, promoted that everyone could be a shareholder, owner, and entrepreneur. At the same time, it celebrated the creative visionary, the independent worker, and individual freedom of expression, and it proclaimed the autonomy of the economic,

8 Hannah Arendt, "Ideology and Terror: A Novel Form of Government," *Review of Politics* 15, no. 3 (July 1953): 324.

9 Rolnik, *Esferas de la insurrección*, 34.

10 Félix Guattari, *The Three Ecologies* (London: Athlone Press, 1989), 27.

political, and cultural spheres. The fetish verbs of the neoliberal era (almost always without direct object) are: to change, to reform, to move, to break away, to better, to participate, to interact. Everyone began seeking to exploit their human capital to modify some things and to preserve others; self-exploitation became the new conformism. Decisions, however, were being made by a minority, and public debt—the existential condition of the neoliberal citizen-consumer—continues to impoverish everyone. At a global scale, whether in public spaces or in the private sphere, we are always under surveillance. The Internet is the apparatus in which the vital infrastructure of millions of people from all over the world has been emptied out, and this has become available as a tool for the new government-corporate mechanisms of control.

Neoliberalism in Mexico

In 1979, the United States underwent two oil crises and a financial shock; in October of that year, Paul Volcker, chairman of the US Federal Reserve System, unveiled a new monetary policy aimed at making the American dollar the most sought-after currency in the world and began to force interest rates upward to combat inflation. Mexico defaulted in 1982 as the "Volcker Shock" was applied, and the United States secured rigid repayment at exorbitant fees. Capital flooded out of the country, while the Mexican peso lost 78 percent of its value and continued devaluating. As a solution to enable repayment, the Reagan administration found a way to assemble the powers of the US treasury and the International Monetary Fund (IMF) to roll the debt over in return for neoliberal reforms.[11] President José López Portillo's government cracked under the pressure and submitted the country to draconian austerity measures crafted by the IMF that encompassed an extensive privatization and deregulation program, as well as a series of reforms liberalizing the Mexican trade regime. The same year, and the last of López Portillo's presidency, banks were nationalized as a patriotic measure and as a means to solve the problems of speculation and capital flight, as well as a way to impose controls on foreign exchange. In his last presidential address, López Portillo announced the

11 David Harvey, *A Brief History of Neoliberalism* (Oxford, UK: Oxford University Press, 2005), 29.

decision, famously bursting into tears and sobbing: "It is now or never. We have been sacked. It is not the end of Mexico. We shall not be sacked again!"[12]

This episode marks the beginning of a severe restructuring of the Mexican economy, society, and politics, inspired by the ideology and operating framework known as neoliberalism, which generally implies a shift away from state-led industrialization and welfare state policies, and a move toward a market-led political economy. The banks were privatized between 1991 and 1992 under President Carlos Salinas de Gortari, followed by the ratification of the North American Free Trade Agreement (NAFTA) in 1993, which represented the continuation of Mexico's comprehensive trade liberalization and economic-reform programs that began in the early 1980s. Eliminating trade barriers between the United States, Canada, and Mexico was publicized as the best way to bring economic development to the southern country. According to Uruguayan writer Eduardo Galeano, politicians and technocrats promised that the trade agreement would finally allow the third world to become like the first world: "rich, cultured, and happy"; "We Can Be Like Them" was the mantra leading from underdevelopment to modernization.[13] The treaty covered aspects of investment, labor markets, and environmental policies. It was the first free-trade treaty signed between advanced countries and a developing economy, creating the world's largest trade area in terms of total gross domestic product (GDP); it is the second-largest in terms of total trade volume, after the European Union.[14] According to the official line presented by politologist and opinionist Luis Rubio, NAFTA is a strategic political instrument that has helped orient the country "toward the future and toward the outside," promoting economic development and establishing a regime of "political discipline." In Rubio's words, it also implied depoliticization in investment choices made by corporations and investment parties:

> Thanks to the treaty, the economy managed to enable Mexican exports to grow dramatically and prodigiously. In its 20 years of life, NAFTA has made

---

12 Gloria Leticia Díaz, "Quiso, no pudo . . . y se pudrió," *Proceso*, February 19, 2004, http://www.latinamericanstudies.org/mexico/portillo-pudrio.htm.

13 Eduardo Galeano, "To Be Like Them," in *Juárez: The Laboratory of Our Future*, ed. Charles Bowden (New York: Aperture, 1998), 121.

14 M. Ayhan Kose, Guy M. Meredith, and Christopher M. Towe, "How Has NAFTA Affected the Mexican Economy? Review and Evidence," *IMF Working Paper* WP/04/59 (April 2004), 6, http://www.imf.org/external/pubs/ft/wp/2004/wp0459.pdf.

> growth possible and now exports not only compensate for the *contraction that characterizes the internal market*, but it also provided a new horizon to the country's industrial development.[15]

According to Rubio, the new horizon of industrial development was related to an increment in Mexican corporations' productivity, having benefited from the comparative advantages that are characteristic of Mexico (e.g., cheap labor). Another positive consequence of NAFTA, according to Rubio, was credit growth (in consumption and mortgage credits) and the reduction of the real prices of consumer goods. These two factors, which are the basis of the myth of the emergence of the new Mexican "middle class,"[16] allegedly indicates the reduction of poverty in the past twenty years.

From a different point of view than the official, ten years after the treaty was signed, the promise of modernization had not yet been fulfilled—unless "modernization" is understood as massive access to cheap consumer goods and services through credit. Most foreign investment had gone toward *maquiladora* (assembly) factories, creating an export-oriented manufacturing and assembly-plant economy, severed from direct economic development in the rest of the country. Moreover, as China and other regions in Latin America were integrated into global trade networks, Mexico began to face competitive pressure, and some of the export sectors (such as textiles) shifted production elsewhere, where it was cheaper. Without a doubt, starting in 1994, the Mexican economy was weakened in favor of a subordinate and unequal "insertion" into international capital flows.

The agricultural sector was hit the worst. Between 1994 and 2004, the United States flooded the Mexican market with highly subsidized farming goods, forcing national producers to lower their prices and ultimately leading them to bankruptcy. By 2005, Mexico was already importing about 42 percent of the food it consumes. The production of basic grains, rice, sorghum, and soy was dismantled alongside the production of pork meat, milk, maize, and beans. As a consequence, in the past twenty years, almost two million campesinos were forced to leave their lands behind as Mexico lost its food autonomy. In addition to many other well-known problems brought about by the ratification of NAFTA, there has been a negative impact on natural

15 Luis Rubio, *Veinte años del TLC, su dimensión política y estratégica* (México D.F.: Fondo de Cultura Económica, 2014), 39. My emphasis.

16 Rubio, *Veinte años del TLC*, 58.

resources and worker's rights; moreover, wages and purchasing power have fallen for most Mexicans over the past thirty years, violating the Mexican constitution that guarantees a living wage.[17]

Almost forty years of neoliberal reforms imposed on Mexico have resulted in a remodeling of social hierarchies and an entirely new social landscape. Added to an already unequal society were geographically uneven urban and rural development, bringing about the simultaneous homogenization and differentiation of new, potentially politicized subjectivities. These include migrants, peasants, urban unemployed people, *ninis*,[18] public-school teachers, middle-class and poor victims of organized crime, anarchists, self-armed Indigenous defense groups, students of private and public universities, originary or Indigenous peoples fighting against transnationals' and government's megaprojects, miners, narco-insurgents, members of recently dismantled unions, and more. Drifting side by side, they have tried to speak out and to survive in a highly fragmented and violent social landscape.

In spite of the damage inflicted on the country and its citizens, subsequent treaties ensured the continuation and expansion of neoliberal reforms into other regions and institutional domains in Mexico. On November 30, 2018, US, Mexican, and Canadian leaders signed the United States-Mexico-Canada Agreement (USMCA) at the G-20 meeting, changing NAFTA in six areas: auto companies manufacturing (to create more US jobs), Canada opening up its dairy market to US farmers, Mexican trucks meeting US safety standards, Mexico allowing its workers to form unions, more protection for patents and trademarks (many of the intellectual property rights in the Trans-Pacific Agreement), allowing US drug companies to sell products in Canada and Mexico for up to ten years before facing generic competition, and finally, the new rule in which companies can no longer use Chapter 11 of NAFTA to resolve disputes with governments except for US oil companies. This last point was created in fear of the renationalization of Mexico's oil industry. Prior to USMCA, there had been the Puebla-Panama Plan (2001), later renamed the Mesoamerican Integration and Development Project (PPP-MIDP) in 2007; this agreement covers "development" projects in the area known as Mesoamerica, a hot spot rich in resources and biodiversity. There is also the Mundo Maya Project, conceived under Salinas de Gortari's

17 See "NAFTA's Impact on Mexico," *Sierra Club*, http://www.sierraclub.org/trade/downloads/nafta-and-mexico.pdf.

18 "Ni trabajan ni estudian" (neither do they work nor study).

presidency in the 1990s, but put into effect in 2011, a touristic development pole in the Southeast and Yucatán Peninsula. These projects seek to "promote connectivity and competition in the regions," opening them up for foreign investment and the exploitation of natural, mineral, and cultural richness, while at the same time, "integrating their economy with Central and North America."[19] The agreements were designed to advance Mexico's neoliberal economic, social, and political reform program and are currently transforming entire regions, forms of life, and ways of making a living. They follow an integration-fragmentation model based on dismantling small-scale productive activities at the national level in favor of massive foreign investment. While they include token production projects and assistance for the affected communities, they have devastated entire communities.[20] I must note here the continuity between previous regimes and Andrés López Obrador's "Plan Nacional de Desarrollo" made public in April 2019, which includes the "Tren Maya Project," an ambitious enterprise that if executed would definitely compete with Salinas de Gortari's and Calderón's projects in the region, geared at development of tourism infrastructure, having created the "The Mayan Riviera." López Obrador's "Tren Maya Project" will include 1,525 km of railroad with 15 stations across the states of Chiapas, Tabasco, Campeche, Yucatán, and Quintana Roo with the goal of promoting tourism, employment, and "sustainable development," as well as protecting the environment. The instruments used to conceptualize the project are territorial zoning and community consultation. The current regime, furthermore, envisions a similar development project with the purpose of boosting the economy at the Istmo de Tehuantepec, a 200-km area that comprises 76 municipalities in the adjunct states of Oaxaca and Veracruz, as well as the Mexican Gulf with the Pacific Ocean. The "Corredor Multimodal Oceánico" or "Multimodal Oceanic Corridor" would compete with the Panama Canal and would include an EPZ to attract private investment with lower taxes, cheaper fuel, state-of-the-art urban infrastructure, education and human-capital training, housing, and basic facilities for research and technological development. Apparently, approval of the originary Binnizá (Zapoteco), Ayuuk (Mixe), Zoque, Ikoots

---

19 Judith Amador Tello, "El proyecto Mundo Maya, 'salvajemente neoliberal,'" *Proceso*, July 30, 2011, http://www.proceso.com.mx/?p=277485.

20 Laura Carlsen, "Plan Puebla-Panama Advances: New Name, Same Game," *Americas Program*, September 10, 2009, http://www.cipamericas.org/archives/1834.

(Huave), Chontal, Chinanteco, Mazateco, Mixteco, Populca, Náhuatl, and Afro-American peoples inhabiting the region has been granted as of March 2019.[21] All these projects, however, have met huge resistance and mobilization, above all due to anomalies in community consultation procedures. The Tren Maya Project, moreover, has been highly criticized for potentially endangering originary communities and flora and fauna in the region, and it has been described as a project of "Border Reordering," aspiring to create yet a new globalized space for foreign investment and free market in an attempt to integrate and control territories rich in resources, which follows the current extractivist logic and seeks to contain migration from Central America as cheap labor.

In spite of its populist agenda of putting the interests of the "poor people" first and of fighting against corruption throughout the country, López Obrador's government seems to seamlessly continue his predecessors' neoliberal agenda. For instance, there has been no mention on the current or future status of Enrique Peña Nieto's reforms that enabled further entrenchment of neoliberal policies. In his inaugural speech on December 1, 2012, at Palacio Nacional in Mexico City, Mexico's symbolic seat of power, President Enrique Peña Nieto announced concrete reforms and plans to end the telecommunications monopoly in order to deeply transform Mexico's education system and energy sector. To that effect, the first actions of his government were to arrest Elba Esther Gordillo, the previously untouchable leader of the public school system's union (the biggest and most powerful in Latin America). The following day, he promulgated the education reform, and teachers who were members of the Education Workers Union (CNTE) organized protests in Mexico City, which were violently evicted from the Zócalo (Mexico City's main square in front of Palacio Nacional) on December 14, 2013, and were systematically demonized in the mass media. As an integral part of Peña Nieto's political program, and with the purpose of furthering Mexico's growth, the "Pacto por México" was put into action. This national agreement was signed by the three main political parties and implied an ambitious agenda of structural and institutional reforms promoting neoliberal political rationality: changes in labor law and reforms in the fiscal, public education, telecommunication industries, and energy areas, all of which were in favor of giving foreign corporations more freedom to hire and fire workers—hire them for

21 Plan Nacional de Desarrollo 2019–2024, https://lopezobrador.org.mx/wp-content/uploads/2019/05/PLAN-NACIONAL-DE-DESARROLLO-2019-2024.pdf.

extremely low salaries seeking to make the Mexican economy "more competitive" and controversially inviting foreign capital for investment in the oil, energy, and resource industries. As production costs and wages rose in China, efforts were made to position Mexico as the new China, or "Aztec Tiger," and draw manufacturing away from Asia, facilitated by the Pact for the rewriting of Mexico's 1970 labor laws.[22] Thus, Peña Nieto's Pact for Mexico, along with production innovations such as cloud computing and open-source innovation, were geared at attracting global investment in cars, aerospace, household goods, and even manufacturing drones for civilian use.[23]

From this point of view, the country's growth implied the return of the *maquiladoras*, as well as the continuation of attendant social policies: large-scale incarceration, mass surveillance, and permanent presence of the military in some regions of the country, under the guise of the "war against crime"; for instance, actions taken by the governments of the states of Morelos and Puebla against organized opposition to the Morelos Integral Project (PIM). The PIM is the alleged vanguard of the industrialization of Eastern Morelos and adjacent zones in Puebla and Tlaxcala at the skirts of the Popocatépetl volcano, a region that is also rich in gold and minerals like silver, copper, lead, zinc, and iron. The PIM was designed in the 1990s and envisioned the creation of two thermoelectric plants: a gas and water pipeline traversing 60 peasant communities, and an aqueduct to transport 50 million liters of water from the Cuautla River every day. The megaproject has put populations at high risk, creating opposition. Since 2014, however, social fighters and leaders mobilized against the PIM have been subject to harassment, threats, and arbitrary detentions, leading to the murder of Samir Flores three months into Peña Nieto's government and right before a referendum on the PIM. The results of the referendum—59.9 percent positive votes—were clearly marked by the murder of Flores. In López Obrador's daily morning address on February 25, he dismissed opposition and the boycott of the megaproject as "provocations," alleging that "contracts must be respected."[24]

---

22 Paul Imison, "The Ultimate Mexican Hype Machine: The Myth of the Aztec Tiger," *Counterpunch* March 29, 2013, http://www.counterpunch.org/2013/03/29/the-myth-of-the-aztec-tiger.

23 Chris Anderson, "Mexico: The New China," *New York Times*, January 26, 2013, http://www.nytimes.com/2013/01/27/opinion/sunday/the-tijuana-connection-a-template-for-growth.html?_r=0.

24 "Anuncia AMLO resultados de consulta: termoeléctrica y Proyecto Integral Morelos," *La Izquierda Diario*, February 25, 2019, https://www.laizquierdadiario.

Under Peña Nieto, repression had expanded to Indigenous campesino communities in the Sierra Norte in Puebla, opposing the "deadly megaprojects" that included eighty-seven mining concessions and more than ten hydroelectric and fracking projects. In addition, Puebla governor Rafael Moreno Valle proposed what is known as the "Ley bala" (Bullet Law), which enables police to shoot with firearms if a protest becomes violent; the law legitimized the use of force and weapons in detentions, emergencies, and natural disasters, as well as during public demonstrations. A similar law was also pronounced in Chiapas, which was denounced for its ambiguity and totalitarian and repressive undertones. Moreno Valle was accused of sending, through the "Ley bala," a social message to inhibit protests against these projects.[25]

Aside from the repressive policies tied to Mexico's intensified authoritarianism, since 2006 there has been a permanent military presence in certain regions of the country under the guise of the "war against insecurity and organized crime." According to Pilar Calveiro, the war against organized crime is a form of state violence that has a central role in the process of neoliberal reconfiguration; state violence is exerted by public and private organisms, is tied to global security policies and authoritarian domination, and has enabled the most radical forms of repressive violence. Permanent military occupation in certain areas in Mexico has been accompanied by reforms in the penitentiary system, resulting in the incarceration of more people, and for longer terms.[26] These measures serve as a means of social control to assure (or perhaps guarantee) the free traffic of (legal and illegal) merchandise within the country and toward the north, as well as the means to implement

---

mx/Anuncia-AMLO-resultados-de-consulta-termoelectrica-y-el-Proyecto-Integral-Morelos-van

25 See "Chomsky, Galeano, Sicilia y más intelectuales exigen a Graco (Morelos) y Moreno (Puebla) alto al acoso de activistas," *SinEmbargo*, April 25, 2014, http://www.sinembargo.mx/25-04-2014/973048; and Gilberto López Rivas, "Puebla: entre represión y el despojo neoliberal," *La Jornada*, April 25, 2014, http://www.jornada.unam.mx/2014/04/25/opinion/023a2pol; Sonia Corona, "Un Estado mexicano admite que la policía use armas de fuego en las propuestas," *El País*, May 20, 2014, http://internacional.elpais.com/internacional/2014/05/20/actualidad/1400613204_366357.html; and Gabriela Hernández, "Acusan a Moreno Valle de Infundir miedo a la oposición con la 'ley bala,' " *Proceso*, May 20, 2014, http://www.proceso.com.mx/?p=372718.

26 See Pilar Calveiro, *Violencias de Estado: la Guerra antiterrorista y la Guerra contra el crimen como medios de control global* (México: Siglo XXI Editores, 2013).

megaprojects of resource extraction or energy production (Aeolic parks, industrial farming, mines, hydroelectric plants, dams, etc.), which not only have negatively impacted the ways in which people live and make a living, but are also destroying the environment.

For many observers, Peña Nieto ended a cycle that started in the 1980s with the hurried reform of Articles 25, 26, and 27 of the Federal Constitution in December 2013, and he established a new political regime. With the energy reform, more areas of the public sector became profitable, and thus, a political regime, which consists in the coalition of hegemonic forces that have the purpose neither of governing nor administering the common good but rather of exploiting it, was secured. This new model of a state fragmented in autonomous sectors sought to gain from the commons and to compete at the international level as "state productive enterprises," bringing about a new relationship between the political class, corporations, and citizens. One of the consequences of this reform was that PEMEX and Comisión Federal de Electricidad (the former national enterprises of oil extraction and provision of electricity, respectively) ceased to be "commissions" with the purpose of offering a public service by providing energy to Mexican people. In turn, they took a profitable approach (owned by the State) and began to compete with transnational companies and sell their services for gain. In other words, Peña Nieto's reforms eliminated the articles that determined the State's exclusivity in energy management, and through a regime of contracts and concessions, both PEMEX's and CFE's autonomy were abolished, along with their bureaucrats and unions; the CFE's union was eliminated in 2010 with Felipe Calderón. The consequence of joining the free market is that both enterprises began to compete at the level of their foreign analogues, which happened to be protected by international treaties; NAFTA allows foreign investors to sue before international tribunals and to demand state compensation if its policies or domestic actions diminish the earnings they had expected. The details of the reform were ambiguous regarding the property of hydrocarbons: Is bestowing extraction "licenses" the same as "giving concessions?" And thus, do foreign companies not have the rights to own what they extract from under Mexican soil, yet have the ability to sell it?[27] As of March 2019, President Andrés Manuel López Obrador declared that contracts derived from the 2013 energy reform

27 David Brooks, "Deliberada ambigüedad en la reforma energética," *La Jornada*, 21 de diciembre de 2013, http://www.jornada.unam.mx/2013/12/21/politica/007n1pol; Laura Carlsen, "Mexico's Oil Privatization is a

would be respected.[28] In 2020, however, President López Obrador sought to limit access of the private sector to the production and distribution of energy, seeking to dismantle the 2013 energy reform. Private owners' connection to the public energy distribution network was suddenly threatened. Indeed, the government seeks to be in charge of the administration of the country's energy; the problem is that renewable energies are a collateral damage of restatization. Its aim is to provide cheaper energy produced by PEMEX through fossil-fuel burning in obsolete, inefficient, and polluting plants, in detriment of private renewable energy suppliers.[29]

Mexico, as of the first countries to implement a neoliberal state apparatus and its experience—along with other pioneering regions in Southeast Asia and China—served as a prime example of the effects of neoliberal structural economic reform. These included experimenting with the precarization of labor (or instituting precarious labor) and the relocation of dispossessed farmers. Its cities have served as social laboratories of repression and violence management, and its authoritarian state mechanisms have been emulated elsewhere; for example, the sexual harassment of women by police at the protests in Atenco in 2006, as well as at the 2010 G-20 protests in Toronto. Another example is the experimental militarization of fifty communities in the state of Guerrero undertaken in 2013, under the humanitarian disguise of Peña Nieto's hunger-relief campaign, *La Cruzada contra el hambre* [The crusade against hunger]."[30] A similar campaign has been implemented by López Obrador's regime, the "Sembrando vida" program, in which military forest nurseries expand through the southern and southeastern areas of Mexico. Experimental GMO corn crops were approved in the states of Sinaloa and Tamaulipas in 2010, putting at risk the country's important genetic food heritage (contaminating and destroying the environment). Transgenic seeds will soon be commodities patented by a few transnational companies, polluting

---

Risky Business," *Foreign Policy in Focus*, May 27, 2014, http://fpif.org/mexicos-oil-privatization-risky-business.

28 "Se respetarán contratos de la reforma energética," *Forbes*, March 18, 2019, https://www.forbes.com.mx/se-respetaran-contratos-de-la-reforma-energetica-asegura-amlo.

29 Fernando Tudela, "El cambio climático: balance temprano," in *Balance temprano desde la izquierda democrática*, ed. Ricardo Becerra and José Woldenberg (México D.F.: IETD and Editorial Grano de Sal, 2020).

30 Marcela Turati, "Militarización disfrazada de Cruzada contra el Hambre," *Proceso*, August 31, 2013, http://www.proceso.com.mx/?p=351609.

corn at its source of origin and eradicating the means for the autonomous production of food.[31] Transgenic soy fields are devastating the Yucatán Peninsula, whose economy, aside from tourism, is based on pig farming.

Moreover, neoliberal reorganizational alignments in the past forty years have caused the mass migration of individuals to the outskirts of cities and to the border, expelling people from their ways of life and of making a living, putting them in places where they are not wanted and where they are most vulnerable. The State manages and excludes portions of the population by selectively ignoring them, without investing or providing social and physical infrastructure, and governing by using a form of "graded sovereignty,"[32] which is discussed below in more detail. It is not only that the Mexican State has failed its citizens and that corrupt politicians are to blame. For example, poet Javier Sicilia's "Movement for Peace with Justice and Dignity" was problematically based on the apolitical premise of the idea that the government must be held accountable for violence and responsible for containing crime, and it was thus centered on an ethical critique of power as a form of politics.

Because of Mexico's history of colonization and repression, dispossession and racism are embedded in the DNA of Mexican people, and since its inception, the country has been ruled by a political culture that disregards laws. Neoliberal reforms were thus imposed on the country at very little political cost, facing meek (or effectively repressed) resistance. In this regard, governing as exclusion and exception was not a sign of corruption or failure, but strictly adheres to Bill Clinton's campaign catchphrase: "It's the economy, stupid." As Aihwa Ong has argued, the reconfiguration of the relationships between the governing and the governed, power and knowledge, and sovereignty and territoriality is integral to the neoliberal project. While the neoliberal state was shrunk or strengthened in certain strategic areas, techniques to exclude or reengineer citizen-subjects has proliferated.[33] Following Aiwha Ong, the neoliberal reconfiguration of relationships between those governed and those governing, power and knowledge, and sovereignty and territoriality are integral to the neoliberal project. Thus, while the neoliberal state shrinks or is reinforced in strategic areas (such as legislation), techniques

---

31 Silvia Ribeiro, "Químicamente tóxico," *La Jornada*, February 12, 2012, http://www.rebelion.org/noticia.php?id=144530.

32 Aihwa Ong, *Neoliberalism as Exception: Mutations in Citizenship and Sovereignty* (Durham, NC: Duke University Press, 2006), 96.

33 Ong, *Neoliberalism as Exception*, 96.

to exclude citizens proliferate; some through violence tied to crime and the war against crime, and others to reengineering techniques.[34]

Neoliberalism has also created particular ways of seeing the world, reconfiguring our common sense to justify destruction and dispossession with ideas of progress and development, and it has tried to solve economic precariousness with coaching, self-help, and permanent education.

In addition, it features the promotion of health regimes, such as Peña Nieto's national campaign to combat diabetes and obesity by taxing soft drinks and junk food as a regulative measure since December 2013 (when in reality huge amounts of tax money are returned to industrial food producers yearly). In continuity with this, the IMSS (Mexican Institute for Social Health) launched a policy to brand industrialized food products as the blame for the current epidemics of hypertension, diabetes, and obesity, giving way to Mexico's COVID-19 death rate of 12 percent.

The government has also promoted programs for the acquisition of skills, while private education institutions endlessly offer expensive *diplomados*, *certificados*, courses, master's degrees, and even doctoral degrees of dubious academic quality; there are public funds for the development of entrepreneurial ventures (there are state programs geared toward aiding the growth of small and medium entrepreneurial ventures, the PYMES), and other techniques of self-engineering and capital accumulation. As part of the Fourth Transformation, the program Jóvenes Construyendo el Futuro grants a scholarship to young men and women who want to be apprentices or interns in certain companies willing to teach them a trade. (I can't help but think of the 2005–2006 protests in France around a similar policy, the infamous *Contrat de première embauche*.) There are also the PILARES, which are cultural community centers disseminated across the country that offer programs of education, entrepreneurialism, and self-betterment. Furthermore, since the ratification of NAFTA, Mexican farmers and proletarians have been converted into *maquiladora* workers (virtually as slaves, because they earn below the minimum living wage), *sicarios* (hit men), entrepreneurs, consumers (or handicapped, indebted consumers), criminals, dead bodies, prisoners, and members of the permanently unemployed underclass. A term has even been coined to describe the eight million youths excluded from education and work: *ninis*.

34 Ong, *Neoliberalism as Exception*, 2, 14.

In this regard, *ninis* represent the very success of capitalism in producing unemployment and exclusion from the modernizing projects. Unemployment is in itself the most current form of capitalist exploitation, and thus of domination: "the exploited are not only those who produce or 'create,' but also those who are condemned not to 'create.' "[35] Domination is therefore inscribed in the very structure of the production process, which is why everyone can have personal freedom and equality—but only formal freedom and a graded equality, with many having no access at all to jobs, education, health care, housing, and other profit-generating enterprises, services, and goods. The current regime is attempting to generate inclusion through social programs based on cash handouts to students and vulnerable populations like the elderly or single mothers (in detriment of state-funded but privately run childcare centers, which have been dismantled). Inclusion here means making the redundant populations part of the market as consumers or debtors.

One of the main consequences of the implementation of neoliberalism in Mexico has been that life and death are now part of the economy, manifesting as a culture of violence, which both denigrates and gives life. The fact that more women have joined the labor market in places like Ciudad Juárez, where the *maquiladora* industry dominates, is understood as the reason why more and more women are being murdered there, and why this kind of death has been normalized and expanded to the rest of the country; in a traditional macho society such as Mexico, women's newly gained economic independence is perceived by men as a threat.[36] Following Sayak Valencia and Subhabrata Banerjee, the current period of neoliberal globalization can be characterized as *capitalismo gore* (slasher capitalism), or "necrocapitalism." In this regard, financial growth and economic accumulation are inseparable from the increase in the worldwide production of death.[37]

In short, the Mexican neoliberal experience shows what life looks like when institutional, material, and sensible forms of power operate the political

---

35 Slavoj Žižek, "Capitalism Can No Longer Afford Freedom," *ABC*, May 25, 2012, http://www.abc.net.au/religion/articles/2012/05/25/3511327.htm.

36 See Sayak Valencia, *Capitalismo Gore* (Madrid: Melusina, 2010); and Sergio González Rodríguez, *The Femicide Machine* (New York: Semiotext(e), 2011).

37 Subhabrata Banerjee, "Necrocapitalism," *Organization Studies* 29, no. 12 (2008): 1541–63, quoted in Marko Stamenkovic, "Radical Withdrawal: Necropolitics, *Capitalismo Gore* and Other Kinds of Life," *The Johannesburg Workshop in Theory and Criticism*, no. 6 (2013): 29–36.

economy, allowing transnational enterprises to control health, housing, agriculture, and the means of life in general. Neoliberalism thus created injurious forms of dependency on the State and on corporations, which in turn thrive on unprecedented levels of marginalization, violence, exploitation, displacement, dispossession, poverty, and death. In spite of President Andrés Manuel López Obrador's neo-populist agenda and anti-neoliberal discourses, his regime represents clear continuity with neoliberalism in its intensified extractivist version, and thus neoliberalism in Mexico seems to have no end within reach.

Neoliberal Sensibility

Our existence is always bound up with affective and aesthetic flows that elude cognitive definition and capture.—STEPHEN SHAVIRO[38]

With neoliberal policies, Carlos Salinas de Gortari's government (1988–1994) began waging a war against society in general, and against the poor in particular, at two levels: economic and social. At the economic level, it is what is known as privatization, which originates from the principle that every fragment and cell of the affective, biologic, and linguistic spheres needs to be transformed into a machine of surplus value production. The effect of this form of privatization is the impoverishment of everyday life, the loss of sensibility in the fields of sexuality, communication, and human relations; aside from having deepened social and economic inequality in Mexico, this creates a hyper-millionaire minority, an indebted middle class, and a dispossessed and redundant majority. At the social level, the war against the collective and the poor was waged by criminalizing and thus destabilizing the territory in order to dispossess citizens from their autonomous means of making a living. This had the purpose of enabling realignment of the country with global economic flows. The war against certain sectors of society also implied mental and physical occupation. The consequence of this occupation was that everyone is permanently preoccupied, if not downright anguished, about the insecurity caused by organized crime and incertitude inherent to precarious working conditions. What preoccupies us are uncertainty and fear; these

38 Stephen Shaviro, "Post-Cinematic Affect: On Grace Jones, *Boarding Gate* and *Southland Tales*," *Film-Philosophy* 14, no. 1 (2010).

expand in the environment we breathe, which is occupied by corporations and administered by the government. If fear used to be tied to specific events, nowadays everyone is constantly anxious and in panic. In this context, while the government imposed a fearful reality through the mass media and cultural production—in the realm of the sensible—it assured us that it is capable of maintaining its citizens' physical and economic safety by fighting against organized crime (which is, as I will argue, an excuse to militarize the country and to create a state of exception where state violence is exerted. As Dawn Paley has stated, neoliberalism is inextricable from war and state violence.[39] According to Paul Virilio, the consequence of a reigning environment of fear is that a "community of emotions" prevails over a "community of interests"; that is, fear creates a community of emotions synchronized, but with desires and interests that are out of sync.[40] The creation of an environment of fear while guaranteeing the citizen's safety reflects the effects of neoliberal government, characterized first by what I described above as the "deep state" from which the super-rich rule, the few people who direct powerful financial services, great corporations, the narco-elite, and the caste of politicians who act on behalf of their interests and who are well connected and politically powerful.

Taking this into account, my hypothesis is that the gradual implementation of neoliberal policies was inextricable from the introduction of neoliberalism as common sense and sensibility. This means that neoliberalism became not only economic policy, but violence against sensibility, and therefore the result of this violence led to the ways in which we apprehend the world and generate knowledge about it. This implies that pragmatism reigns in making decisions focusing on results, maximizing individual benefit. That is to say, I am not positing neoliberalism here as ideology in the classical sense: as an ensemble of ideas that partakes in the reproduction of the preestablished order and that contributes to maintaining domination and exploiting relationships. Rather, I understand neoliberalism as the production of common sense based on the rationality of self-interest and desire that not only maintains but also causes the proliferation of power relationships (a network of control). In other words, I understand neoliberalism as a sensibility that works upon our most intimate desires, colonizing our dreams, cannibalizing our ideals of freedom, and spitting them out as strategies of social control.

---

39 Dawn Paley, *Guerra Neoliberal: Desaparición y búsqueda en el norte de México* (México: Libertad bajo palabra, 2020).

40 See Paul Virilio, *The Administration of Fear* (New York: Semiotext(e), 2012).

The reasons why neoliberalism was so easily instituted in Mexico have to do, first, with the fact that it is a society traditionally and profoundly unequal in which socioeconomic colonial relationships still operate, along with pyramidal power relationships originating from a racial hierarchy (or pigmentocracy)[41]. Second, neoliberalism justifies instantaneous gratification and the search to realize individual interests. Within this framework, happiness and self-realization came to be considered as unalienable goals and rights. The consumerist invitation to enjoy—as Nike's slogan says, "Just do it!"—became the support within a complex process of subjectivation whose function is to ensure the acceptance of the basic neoliberal frame of domination: the fantasy of free trade.[42] Therefore, neoliberalism became a form of thinking, of producing and distributing antagonisms and enjoyment, by staging an eternally deferred promise of gratification, and power as a complex network of distribution of bodies immersed in the differential acceleration of sensual reality within their distribution in space. For instance, transnational corporations and the logic of marketing gave shape to our cities by changing and differentiating them radically (at the socioeconomic level), and homogenizing (at the sensible level) our surroundings. This is how neoliberalism operates in our sensual reality, working our subjectivities from within desire, sensibility, and affect, which in turn infuses art and culture, differentiating and homogenizing lives and desires, mistaking information with knowledge and communication with information, giving shape to space and thus to social relations, normalizing violence, creating forms of seeing the world from a notion of common sense that justifies destruction and dispossession with a belief in progress and development, and trying to give solutions to (precariousness) labor precarity with self-help and permanent education programs.

Neoliberalism is also a sensibility that established the terms of empathy and sympathy, delineating a new "Other." Configured as "social responsibility" or social work, "helping" the Other implies focusing on the "secondary malfunctions" of the current capitalist system and disseminating personal and administrative practices such as tolerance, showing respect, nourishing

41 See Federico Navarrete, *Alfabeto del racismo mexicano* (México D.F.: Malpaso, 2017); and Edward Tellez, *Pigmentocracies: Ethnicity, Race, and Color in Latin America* (Chapel Hill: University of North Carolina Press, 2014).

42 See Franco "Bifo" Berardi, "The Psychopathologies of Hyper-Expression," translated by Arianna Bove, *transversal texts* (June 2007), http://eipcp.net/transversal/1007/bifo/en.

dialogue, transparency, and social collaboration. In this regard, the Other is a "community to come," a "subject of rights," and the underclass; that is to say, those who are in reality permanently outside the processes of globalization, including access to education, jobs, and consumer goods as redundant populations, but who are incorporated into the system as potential entrepreneurs, debtors, consumers, or cheap labor. This Other became the main subject of President Andrés Manuel López Obrador's policies: his well-cited slogan, "¡Primero los pobres, por el bien de todos!" [The poor first, for everyone's well-being] is designed to counter the effects of neoliberal reforms and has justified budget cuts in culture, sports, health, and education, while serving to justify the regime's version of the welfare state—what he calls "grassroots modernity," an abstract "social below" (comprised of the dispossessed, oppressed, and discriminated). The main focus of President López Obrador's policies, he has stated, are those who have "traditionally been hit by the greater economic interests, ignored by the media, and deprived from their rights by political power." This social below is also the idealized carrier of pre-Hispanic cultural and social heritage that has supposedly resisted three hundred years of colonial rule and, of course, more than three decades of predator neoliberalism. For this social below, the regime has designed an array of programs that consist of the aforementioned handing out cash (between 1,275 and 5,000 pesos monthly, the equivalent of 60 and 250 US$) to mature adults, handicapped Indigenous people, poor children, *nini* youth, working-class students, and active peasants, as well as credits for urban or housing betterment and for small businesses.[43] This must mean that, if under neoliberal populism, the essence of democracy becomes obtaining benefits, and consumption is the only means of citizenship, then what is needed to solve the problems of the underprivileged is to shape all social relations through faith in the market. Those now excluded will be subject to manners, norms, values, and languages predetermined by neoliberal logic, thereby legitimating the further expansion of zones of economic, social, and civil death. Indebtedness, extractivism, and authoritarianism are behind President López Obrador's discourse of reversing neoliberal policies and "putting the poor first."

43 See López Obrador's Plan Nacional de Desarrollo 2019–2024, https://lopezobrador.org.mx/wp-content/uploads/2019/05/PLAN-NACIONAL-DE-DESARROLLO-2019-2024.pdf.

Neoliberalism and the Democratic Transition: The Tyranny of Common Sense

The incorporation of neoliberalism in Mexico must be understood in a broad sense: as the introduction of a new moral with new ideas on politics and about human nature. This is why it is necessary to recognize it as a phenomenon, and from an interdisciplinary point of view, because above all, neoliberalism is deeply a rationality; it is violence to sensibility, translated to common sense. That is to say, beyond merely being economic policy based on the free market, neoliberalism is an ensemble of ideas that are translated to institutions of political and juridical arrangements, to the ways in which we relate to the world, nature, assets, and human beings, all of this presupposing unlimited growth based on the liberalization of the market. As Fernando Escalante explains in *Historia minima del neoliberalismo*, in the 1970s this "civilizational turn" took place hegemonically, creating the new individualist society.[44] Neoliberal common sense, however, has deeper roots in Mexico. Following María Eugenia Romero Sotelo, in the 1930s, members of the financial elite in Mexico began a project to counter the economic and social nationalist measures promoted by President Lázaro Cardenas, seeking to give continuity to the nationalist economic project inspired in the Mexican Revolution. Through groups such as the Asociación de Banqueros (Banker's Association), the country's elite set out to create platforms to disseminate the Austrian School's ideas and to educate professionals who would influence the country's political economy and pressure the government to defend their interests. According to Romero Sotelo, neoliberalism was conceived in Mexico as an antithesis to interventionism and the government's nationalizing policies in the aftermath of the Mexican Revolution.[45] The legacy of this movement crystallized in education centers that formed a technocratic elite. Those elite administered and guided México for the past thirty years from the point of view of neoliberal common sense. In parallel, and to consolidate this project, a new cast of public intellectuals began to operate outside academia in the mass media, playing a crucial role in the dissemination of neoliberal common sense. Claudio Lomnitz points out in *La nación desdibujada* how,

44 Fernando Escalante Gonzalbo, *Historia mínima del neoliberalismo* (México D.F.: El Colegio de México, 2016).

45 María Eugenia and Romero Sotelo, *Los orígenes del neoliberalismo en México: La Escuela Austriaca* (México D.F.: FCE and UNAM, 2016).

after the debt crisis in 1982, the Mexican government reduced support to universities and channeled subsidies and aid to a "select firmament of 'intellectual stars.' " These liberal intellectuals focused their political project in "morally critiquing power" and in proclaiming a defense of a "transition to democracy" in the mass media, but without addressing the anti-state politics promoted by neoliberal governments, sometimes overtly supporting neoliberalism as did Octavio Paz, Enrique Krauze, Héctor Aguilar Camín, and others.[46]

The idea of the "transition to democracy" was one of the discourses embraced by the postrevolutionary neoliberal state. This system allegedly welcomed the country's ideological, cultural, and social plurality by building the institutional capacity to channel conflict, distributive battles, and power struggles. Intellectuals, academics, politicians, businessmen, opinion-makers, and civil-society organizations led the struggle to institute democracy; for instance, the Grupo San Ángel. On the eve of the 1994 elections, Jorge G. Castañeda, Demetrio Sodi, and Adolfo Aguilar Zínzer convoked eighty-one people with different ideologies and party affiliations linked to the candidates to create a group to lobby for democratic elections and to avoid turmoil. The group consisted of Carlos Fuentes, Teodoro Céserman, Alfreedo del mazo, Federico Reyes Heroles, Manuel Camacho, Lorenzo Meyer, Tatiana Clouthier, Vicente Fox, and Elba Esther Gordillo, to name a few.

The democratic transition was consolidated in 2000 with the downfall of the PRI and Vicente Fox's gesture of welcoming a caravan of the Zapatista National Liberation Army (EZLN) into the Zócalo in Mexico City. As I already mentioned, liberal intellectuals had a key role in this transition, along with specialists, experts, and opinionists who gave voice to the "citizen awakening" in newspaper columns, social media, and other forms of communication, as well as in social mobilizations and in open political opposition. In that regard, democracy brought spaces for the visibilization of antagonisms, deliberation, participation, and lobbying, resulting in a brief decline of the collective suspicion against state institutions and the discourse of the "State as the enemy." Democracy, however (which implies citizen participation, pacific coexistence of antagonisms, tolerance to dissidence, and visiblization of minorities), as it has been demonstrated by many theorists and thinkers, is empirically and theoretically incompatible with neoliberalism. Neoliberalism is based on the premise that, by nature, individuals are inclined to pursue their own

---

46 Claudio Lomnitz, *La nación desdibujada* (México D.F.: Malpaso, 2016).

interest in order to obtain the maximum possible benefit in detriment to the common well-being, thus justifying politics' functioning as a market. Market freedom is reflected by freedom of expression supposedly consolidating democracy through an opening up of objective and serious critique. Democracy and neoliberalism, moreover, are incompatible because every time there is a democratic assembly and government, antagonists will want to employ political power in order to redistribute wealth. But as Escalante points out, a fundamental part of the neoliberal political program consists in situating basic decisions about the economy *outside* the democratic game. That is why Enrique Krauze insists upon "ideological critique" against the State, insulting those he qualifies as "holy-water pissers" and "abusers of freedom of expression," and other forms of political action that are foreign to the mediatic-ideological apparatus that sustains his own voice as a "moral (apolitical) critic of power."[47] For its part, leftist neoliberal common sense abandoned inequality, income redistribution, and the production of public welfare as political goals, and instead focused its battles on individual preoccupations: freedom, authenticity, visibility, and the right to difference, or what I have called elsewhere the culturalization of politics. The result of the Mexican transition of democracy was democracy without demos (people), underscored by tolerant forms of power self-legitimizing through antagonism, yet hiding the gap between neoliberal possibilities of citizen participation (such as the vote) and the political decisions that are actually taken by a bunch of experts, representatives of the oligarchy, politicians, and transnational companies that are far from representing the interests of the majority of Mexicans. Gradually, it became evident that the total ensemble of neoliberal politics and reforms geared toward establishing a representative democracy failed in taking the majority toward prosperity. The result was the enrichment of a small minority, and for the rest, lives of precarious exploitation, marginalization, destruction of their territories, forms of life, and ways of making a living.

In this context, Alejandra Leal noted a change in the structures of identification and forms of making politics in the 1980s: the figure of the people as legitimate political actors was replaced by "civil society." This discursive and political transformation reflected incipient forms of the role of the State, the nature of society, and the relationship between both. In the 1980s, the idea that the State was "too" present came to prevail on the premise that its

47 Enrique Krauze, "Ensayista liberal," in *Democracia en construcción* (Penguin Random House, 2016), 17.

presence was ineffective; at the same time, the 1910 Revolution ceased to be the source of legitimacy of government policies. In parallel, the figure of the people started to vanish as the central actor of public discourse, at the time of citizen mobilizations, to rescue damaged persons from the earthquake on September 19, 1985. For many, these mobilizations signified the birth of civil society in Mexico that emerges as an autonomous collectivity to demand democratization.[48] A difference must be drawn, however, between a notion of civil society that is a belligerent subject in permanent confrontation acting within a "zone of antagonism" and whose strategy is permanent confrontation (as Carlos Monsiváis posited it back then), and the kind of civil society that was crystallized under the neoliberal discourse of the "democratic transition," which is defined as "groups of Mexicans who are neither rebellious nor submissive, act with specific objectives, and are dispersed when they have reached their objectives or expressed their disagreement."[49] These forms of citizenship have manifested in lobbying for private interests and as the national figure of the post-political victim claiming restitution and justice to the government.

One of the consequences of market liberalization in the 1980s was the radical change in the ways in which national imaginary and identity were deconstructed and reconstructed, bringing representation and representativity into a crisis in Mexico. For Claudio Lomnitz, this crisis begins with the unbreachable gap created between "an authentic national culture, based on Indigenous traditions materialized as a tortilla-eater people" against the "artificial dressing of Mexican identity by corporations in the hands of foreigners."[50] This dichotomy stems from the mythical part of Mexican identity of "two Mexicos," reflected in the struggle between "nationalists" and "neoliberals or technocrats" on the eve of the signature of the NAFTA treaty and on the brink of the PRI's political rupture and weakening of revolutionary nationalism, as well as the State's capacity to impose a hegemonic identity, which, as we have seen, the PRI and Televisa were attempting to do around this time.

Clearly, "the national" is a recurring figure in the collective imaginary, which has taken an array of different forms. By assembling an extraordinary archive of audiovisual and high art culture interwoven with an archive of

---

48 Alejandra Leal, "El despertar de la sociedad civil: sismo del 85 y neoliberalismo," *Horizontal*, September 24, 2015, https://horizontal.mx/el-despertar-de-la-sociedad-civil-sismo-del-85-y-neoliberalismo.

49 Krauze, "Ensayista liberal," 57.

50 Lomnitz, *La nación desdibujada*, 75.

historical memory and sociohistorical processes, along with key literary and film works and theoretical books and tendencies, Paola Vázquez Almanza has studied this shifting notion of national identity to look into political, social, cultural, and economic changes in Mexico since the 1990s. She points out that the basis of debates around national identity resides in the image a society has created for itself, and delivering a reality through explanations and solutions to "national problems."[51] On the eve of the neoliberal era, moreover, national identity came to be understood as a construct used by power that needed to be overcome or resignified. Still, some "national" traits remained, such as the myths of the "two Mexicos" or the "distant neighbors," by drawing contrasts between El Paso and Ciudad Juárez, or Tijuana and San Diego. In intellectual and artistic circles, the "dangers" of NAFTA in the cultural realm were discussed, while Carlos Fuentes, in *Nuevo tiempo mexicano* (1994), argued that hybridization was binational, and that it would have positive effects in Mexico. While in the 1980s, the trend of "neo-Mexicanism" in painting recovered folklore nostalgically as a critique of the heteropatriarchal State (Nahum Zenil, Enrique Guzmán, etc.), before the signature of NAFTA, a new national image of Mexico as essentially culturally rich and cosmopolite was manufactured and promoted through instances like the massive exhibition shown at the MET in New York: "Mexico: Splendours of Thirty Centuries" (1992), an official image that artists and intellectuals refused to contribute to disseminating. This is when antagonism to the State became a key element in the Mexican national imaginary, a seed that was planted after the 1985 earthquake, which many understand as the "birth" of Mexican civil society taking action in solidarity where the State failed to rescue the victims.

According to Vázquez Almanza, by the 2000s, national identity had become a personalizable and standardizable object embodying "a wish to return to an identitarian Aztlán wearing brand-new Nikes and bearing a portable CD player playing at full volume 'Las Flores' by Café Tacvba."[52] This means that the State's capacity to create a national hegemonic imaginary was hindered by the production of plural identities by way of the proliferation of audiovisual products and commodities. Throughout the twentieth century, a paradigm of national identity was established based on a narrative of "self-awakening" and consciousness toward the essence of the nation;

51 Paola Vázquez Almanza, *Aquellos que dejamos de ser: Ficción y nación en México* (México D.F.: Siglo XXI Editores, 2020), 10.

52 Vázquez Almanza, *Aquellos que dejamos de ser*, 334.

the question haunted intellectuals, writers, and visual artists. In contrast, neoliberal nationalism was a cultural product marketed by designers, specialists, intellectuals, and politicians in a network of transnational connections and consumer products. National identity came to be manufactured in the market, but it became state fetichism, or the gathering of civil society around the figure of victims of the State fighting for restitution and recognition, against corruption, defending democracy, and demanding that the State "do its job" properly.

In the global era of branded cities, moreover, as in Denmark, "Hygge" describes the essence of the Danish or Scandinavian experience, a positive and private feeling where everything is all right and thus denotes a fantasy-like element of national culture; what describes Mexico is "The Shit." In 2017, Anuar Layón designed jackets bearing the slogan "Mexico is the Shit."[53] Not only did the jackets sell out, but the slogan went viral. The jacket bears a manifesto inside, a declaration: "An opportunity to remind the world that Mexico is great, that everything that is made in Mexico is well done.... Mexicans throughout the world are changing global culture with their beautiful hearts and brilliant minds.... We are many and we are together, elevating standards, reminding the world that our voice matters. Mexico is the shit is a community, a support system and a movement that inspires love." In a kindred spirit, a video titled "Dedicate this to the haters," from 2018 and created by the marketing company Hunters based in Mexico City, celebrated Mexican entrepreneurs recognized globally, and acknowledged that while Mexico is "kind of fucked up" with its bad public infrastructure, racist proclivities, low national self-esteem, bad state funding for culture and arts, general mediocrity, and corruption—all residual effects of former Mexican "underdevelopment" that is "partially fixed" by the liberalization of markets and globalization—it is indeed possible to succeed.[54] The Mexican entrepreneur is known for facing a double challenge when seeking success: the "Mexican Shit" that can and has become "the Shit." And yet, this narrative largely obviates the deepening inequality brought about by market liberalization and privatization policies. It veils the fact that "success" is only available to a small portion of the privileged population; that "CDMX" is an urban enclave undergoing massive environmental problems such as lack of water, and yet it thrives from stealing water

53 https://www.instagram.com/p/BLroR9KFKnW.

54 The video can be seen here: https://josecardenas.com/2018/03/criticar-exito-mexicano-ve-este-video.

from surrounding states' originary peoples' water supplies (as in Hidalgo or Puebla). It also veils the fact that in Mexico City, culture (e.g., design, cooking, contemporary art, film, urban planning, music, dance) is only available to a few, and within and beyond the *cinturones de miseria* (misery belt, banlieue, favela) surrounding CDMX, a war is being fought against originary peoples and their territories that finds its reflection in the city in phenomena such as domestic violence and bullying in elementary schools. It is necessary to rescue forms of alterity from the violence of capital and its discourses, to point at the crisis of meaning and representation and the consequences, to denounce the imperialism of discourse that dictates the meaning of reality, and to understand the forces at play that are creating "redundant populations" inhabiting zones of sacrifice.

Again, the image of sophisticated Mexico is pitted against the "other Mexico," toward which the first has a historical debt. This is why the current regime, to oppose neoliberalism, represents "the other (marginalized) Mexico," recurring to the mythical Indigenous originary past, the yearning for the lost Paradise of originary essence in the current populist nationalism. This new sensibility is being promoted, for instance, in President Andrés Manuel López Obrador's defense of "his" notion of culture (mainly folkloric and linked to the country's precolonial roots), announced in an incipient official cultural program further analyzed in chapter 5. What our current neo-populist era faces is a kind of "post-national imaginary" based on nostalgia or certain signs: the viralization of the invitation to Rubí's *quinceañera* party in 2016, and the macro-party that the party became—televised, attended by celebrities, and sponsored by major brands—expresses nostalgia for a faraway "rural" Mexico that appears as exotic; the popularity of the Netflix series *Luis Miguel* (2018) set in the 1980s, or the imagery deployed (albeit in the background) in Alfonso Cuaron's *Roma* (2018) of a 1970s Mexico with welfare state, peasant land struggles, and "classic" state violence, are symptomatic in this regard.

In parallel to the imaginary designed by the mass media and the cultural industries (including Hollywood's "Day of the Dead Parade" for the opening scene of *Spectre*, the 2016-released James Bond 007 film, sponsored by the city's government), there is the image of Mexico as a gigantic mass grave on top of which political corruption scandals endlessly succeed each other. This image is part of the imaginary of the Mexican identity as a victim of violence or corruption by the State and thus the State as the enemy.

When we look at the traits of Mexican neoliberalism elucidated by Fernando Escalante, Enrique Krauze, Alejandra Leal, Claudio Lomnitz, and

María Eugenia Romero, it is evident that a neoliberal way to think about the State, politics, institutions, and citizenship has been instated, and that it gets confused with market logic; that we inhabit a social and political imaginary rooted in private interests and immediacy. As Escalante points out, some of the traits of neoliberal common sense had already been present as behavioral structures. They have been exacerbated, and I would add: we owe the lack of social contract, impunity, and the normalization of inequality and corruption to the legacy of colonialism. Escalante predicted that neoliberalism would survive as a dominant mode of sensibility and that there are no visible alternatives except the experiments of autonomy in rural areas that the "urban left" looks upon with a mix of condescendence, admiration, and skepticism. Autonomous practices, however, challenge the State, as they underline the obsolescence of the party system and the breach between representation and delegation of political powers. From here we can extrapolate one of the key points in critiquing neoliberalism: if neoliberal politics suppose a shrinking of state intervention in dismantling the welfare state, the new forms of politicization crystallized in the figure of "civil society" make evident that the neoliberal program needs a state that can function as an instrument for privatization. As Escalante points out, it is necessary that the State's modus operandi responds to the market and that it be protected by democratic institutions' inertia. From this we can infer that the neoliberal program does not mean that the state disappears—it is needed to legislate, produce, and feed markets—but it is a state that is consistently against the public in favor of the maximum expansion of the private sphere. What President Andrés Manuel López Obrador's regime is facing—and what it's attempting to undo, at least discursively—is the neoliberal configuration of a state strategically governing territories and populations differentially in order to connect them with global processes according to the logics of globalization, the free market, and a kind of restatization geared at an extractivist economy of primary resources destroying the environment; that includes populist cultural policies.

The Perfect(ed) Dictatorship

As we have seen, neoliberalism as an economic regime based on the liberalization of markets is inextricable from democracy—the political regime of participation based on the permanent negotiation of antagonisms and exclusions: a culturalized form of politics based on struggles for visibility and rights. One of the bases of neoliberalism is freedom of expression, and thus systemic criticism and scandal have prevailed in the mass media and cyberspace, and in the cultural realm. Freedom of expression, however, was guaranteed by democratic regimes as part of a policy of repressive tolerance, which brought about self-censorship, and that exemplifies how, under neoliberalism, production and consumption, and subjectivation and subjection, are intrinsically linked: the system of social control combines a militarized police regime with repressive tolerance, which implies combining the logic of securiziation with assuring and allowing freedom of expression and quality of life. Now things have slightly changed: President Andrés Manuel López Obrador began to ignore criticism and dissent against him or his regime. As he symbolizes the opposition—"the Other" Mexico—the president opposes his critics from a position of power, pointing fingers or being dismissive of opponents, polarizing society for capitalizing on the resentment.

The Institutional Revolution Party (PRI) that governed Mexico for more than seventy years (except for the brief pause between 2000 and 2012) earned the adjective "perfect dictatorship" by governing through a system of forced loyalties involving the use of unofficial rituals and institutions, secret negotiations, violent repression (on a small scale), media, and the co-optation of intellectuals to transmit their official version. When the PRI came back to power in 2012, it had undergone a mutation: the government had become a media empire with Berlusconian undertones,[55] serving corporate and financial interests, directing public action and attention through the mass media, social networks, and cultural production. *Wikileaks*' revelations right before

55 In the sense in which Alessandra Renzi posits Berlusconi as the emblem of differential accumulation of power through capital, encompassing connections between political power, economy, organized crime, and media empire. For Renzi, Berlusconi's presidency was characterized by capitalizing mediatic controls and public opinion in order to hollow out collective action and its social sense and political content. Moreover, Berlusconi supported his political power with a diversity of companies such as real estate, finance, insurance, entertainment, and publicity. Berlusconi is thus the emblem of savage neoliberalism, social Darwinism, and politics as action on behalf of self-interest, making alliances among financial institutions directors, state industry, and private entrepreneurs in order to generate secure investment niches, as well as exercising political power with bribes, nepotism, and corruption with the purpose of dominating the market through a capillary expansion in the economy's emergent sectors. See Alessandra Renzi, *From Collectives to Connectives: Italian Media*, doctoral dissertation (Universidad de Toronto, 2011), https://tspace.library.utoronto.ca/.../Renzi_Alessandra_201106_PhD_thes.

the 2012 election, regarding the contract signed between Enrique Peña Nieto and Televisa (Mexico's main TV station) to promote the candidate's image, inaugurate the logic of "celebrity representativity" and the student movement *#YoSoy132* [#Iam132].

The collaboration between Televisa and the PRI was not new, however. As I mentioned above, in the early 1990s, the PRI waged a war between "nationalists" and "neoliberals or technocrats," and the official Zeitgeist was expressed with the aid of Televisa. In 1990, the chain produced and disseminated a video starring Mexico's most beloved celebrities inspired by the USA for Africa 1985 campaign, "We are the world." Lucía Méndez, Cándido Pérez, Rigo Tovar, Lucía Mendez, Pandora, Timbiriche, Rocío Banquells, Daniela Romo, and Garibaldi sang: "Our enemy is poverty // solidarity is ours // with development, government, and people together are strong // the campesino and big businesses naturally united // Long live Mexico and let solidarity flourish in a new era // Green will be hope, white clean trust and red the boiling blood."[56] Government and television had united forces to build a neoliberal nationalism through celebrity culture based on the conceptual solidary alliance between empresarios and campesinos, which together would lead the country to progress.

On the eve of 2012, however, beyond the Televisa/PRI collusion, what the students also denounced was the transformation of politics into a world of appearances incarnating merchandises, fused with the celebrity world, and disseminated in the mass media and social networks. The logic of celebrity representativity was inaugurated when Arnold Schwarzenegger won the elections as the governor of California (in 2003 and 2006), becoming the paradigm of new power figures as celebrity politicians. These figures embody a gap between real politics and the public sphere (as the site for potential political action), now full with spectacle and cultural production, acquiring a new substitutive political function. The gap is created because, following Stephen Shaviro, cult celebrities are charged with affect: a celebrity seduces me, which means it is someone with whom, although I do not have an

56 In the original Spanish: "Nuestro enemigo es la pobreza // la solidaridad es nuestra // con desarrollo se demuestra // gobierno y pueblo hacen fuerza // el campesino y la gran empresa unidos por naturaleza // ¡Que viva México! y florezca solidaridad una nueva era // El verde será la esperanza, el blanco la limipia confianza y el rojo la sangre que alza."

intimate relationship with, I respond to intimately and I get obsessed with the distance between the figure and myself, because such a figure is unreachable.[57]

On the other hand, the new PRI was governed by capturing and managing attention, by violent repression, forced disappearances (on behalf of the State in cahoots with narco-paramilitaries) and strategic silencing in the media, linked to unprecedented economic investment in culture and symbolic production. One of the tools for capturing attention was an army of *peñabots*, the thousands of accounts that acted in a coordinated manner in cyberspace in order to position topics or counteract opposition in social networks. The *peñabots* were fundamental for the 2012 presidential campaign, and as the federal government burned in cyberspace (after a succession of scandals tied to conflicts of interest and state intervention in disappearances and murders of civilians), *peñabots* were soldiers in the virtual war of opinion.[58]

The film *La dictadura perfecta* (*The Perfect Dictatorship*, Televisa/CONACULTA, 2014) by Luis Estrada depicts the PRI's governing ways by means of capturing collective attention, while revealing the complex power structure behind it. The film is a popular satire that shows how power mechanisms work under the "new PRI." In the fiction, the headquarters of the largest broadcasting company (Televisa's doppelgänger) is the University Museum of Contemporary Art (MUAC) in Mexico City, and its sophisticated (criollo) director is surrounded by classical works of modern art (e.g., Jasper Johns, Jackson Pollock, Franz Kline, Barbara Hepworth). The form of power the director embodies, that of the puppet master pulling the strings behind the celebrity politicians through the mass media and social networks, is far above the power embodied by the *virreyes* (viceroys). The *virreyes* are the uncouth, provincial, mestizo, and uneducated governors, all of whom are tied to organized crime and keen on denigrating women in *machista* rituals decorated with naked table dancers. One of these governors aspires to become president, and thus hires the director of the television broadcasting company to help him build his celebrity power figure so he can win the next presidential election. Under this structure, the criollos have absolute power, because the neoliberal form of government, through images and social networks, is

57 Shaviro, "Post-Cinematic Affect," 54.

58 See "Peñabots del PRI #EstánDeLaGreña/ Que coman pastel / La guerra de nuestros tiempos," *SinEmbargo*, December 22, 2014, http://www.sinembargo.mx/opinion/22 12 2014/30192.

a government of opinion creating a dissident public, constituting a new style of authoritarianism based not only on social inequality, but also on media and cybernetic discrimination. Taking up a public discussion between Nina Power and Hito Steyerl, we could argue that there is a difference between the kinds of publics molded by power. There is, on the one hand, the public that mobilizes, occupies spaces, needs to be cautious in times of crisis. This is a "good public": alive, but silenced, unified by indignation and pain. There is, on the other hand, the destructive public, which breaks the public peace with violent outbursts—here we can evoke spontaneous violence not only in poor areas in London or in the Parisian banlieues in the past few years, but also in the government-infiltrated "anarchists" in recent protests in Mexico City or the feminist anarchic outbursts in 2019 and 2020. This public, which is more phantasmagoric than actual, is harmful, propagates fear and indignation, and serves to justify punishment of the "good" public.[59] Literally detained by the police in the name of the "bad public," the "good" indignant public, in shock, mobilizes alongside historical temporality, in a spasm of pain. The neoliberal distribution of bodies in the sensible realm translates to the resolution of an image: if the "bad" anarchist public is opaque and dark and its demands are merely translated to irrational gestures, *sicarios* (hit men) are low-resolution images and disabled consumers, who kill and destroy for hire so that they can consume semiotic products that could give them a better resolution.

The neoliberal form of governing through the sensible implies that images have crossed into reality[60] to deepen inequality, racism, and misogyny in the economic, social, and sensible realms. Exploiting the utopic potential of freedom of expression, limitless communication, participation, and reciprocity inherent to social and digital media as means of emancipation and alleged basis of democracy, the form of mediatic-corporate government under Peña Nieto was inextricable from the logic of the free market and citizenship as consumption. Under the light of Peña Nieto's government's capture of attention through scandal, frivolity, and corruption, it becomes clear how President Andrés Manuel López Obrador's election campaign and current

59 Nina Power, in conversation with Hito Steyerl at the Institute of Contemporary Art in London, March 28, 2014, https://archive.ica.art/bulletin/video/hito-steyerl-and-nina-power.

60 See Hito Steyerl, "Too Much World: Is the Internet Dead?" *e-flux journal* 49 (November 2013), http://www.e-flux.com/journal/too-much-world-is-the-internet-dead.

discourses are pitted against the legacy of the PRI's excesses, foreshadowing a new era for austerity and a crusade against corruption and the previous excesses of the political class. The current regime, however, as I will argue below, is in perfect sync with previous forms of celebrity representativity. Or rather, it is at the mass level, directly acting within the mass media and social networks, using it as a new political arena. It was not by chance that the president labeled social media as "holy" or *las benditas redes sociales*.

Another example of a magnified scandal under Peña Nieto is the case of the forced disappearances of forty-three *normalista* students (young men and women being trained to become teachers in the public-education system) from Ayotzinapa, Guerrero, on September 26, 2014, which has been the center of attention in the media, social networks, and public space under the motto: "They took them alive, we want them alive." The centrality of this case in the media rendered opaque and silenced voices that are also urgent, such as the police murders in Tlatlaya; river pollution by Grupo Mexico in one of their mines in Sonora; femicides all over the country, the disappearance of five hundred people in Allende, Coahuila, in 2011; repression and harassment of social leaders and activists in Puebla; and from the rest of the country, the escalation of food and gas prices (consequences of Peña Nieto's reforms). In the case of the disappearance of the forty-three students, the government opted to manage the tragedy in the media. The motto "We want them back alive" captured for many weeks the imagination of editorialists, web writers and publics. Debatably, Ayotzinapa's motto is not a signified that has been emptied in its incessant reiteration, but a signified that falls short in encompassing the anti-neoliberal demands of the citizens, limiting them to moral demands of accountability. This is due to the fact that the mobilization unleashed by the singularity of the event—a dead body count that finally mobilizes the "good" public—is insufficient as a catalyzer for the possibility of political subjectivation and the establishment of solidarity ties that would go beyond indignation and the divisions between city and country, social class, and race. This is why it is urgent to emancipate the population from the idea that the ailments of the country are provoked by organized crime and corrupt politicians: the violence prevailing in the country is the liminal manifestation of neoliberalism as necro-capitalism, the process of production and valorization founded in the destruction of life, the environment, heritage, and the commons. In the media, the idea that violence in the country is something external to neoliberalism is promoted, a distortion caused by blaming violence on Mexican cultural traits; local instances of violence, however, clearly respond to global processes that surpass them. Violence and inequality are mutually constitutive; violence is inextricable from neoliberal policies, as the free market's (invisible) hand is tied to the army's invisible fist, all interwoven in social events, political circumstances, cultural processes, and spatial transformations.

The previous regimes' forms of governing through mediatic power and the creation of publics were inseparable from the construction of a class of cultural producers through a funding system established by Carlos Salinas de Gortari's government: the FONCA (National Fund for Culture and the Arts), which was part of CONACULTA (the National Council for Culture and Arts), the state cultural apparatus. The function of this organization was to fund Mexican cultural production, either through scholarships for different categories like visual artists, writers, theater directors, dancers, screenwriters, and others or for concrete projects, exhibitions, publications, or symposia, who could receive three-year grants or lifelong creative pensions, depending on the relevance of their cultural production and age. Moreover, for the past decade or so, an unprecedented collusion between the private, corporate, and public sectors united to further support cultural production as a means to further democracy and counter violence in the country. One of the results was the creation of a class of cultural producers existing for and in itself to demonstrate the democratic health of the country (e.g., Mexico's 2009 Venice Biennial Pavillion drenched in blood and narco paraphernalia by Teresa Margolles, titled *What Else Could We Talk About?*). Debatably, cultural producers gave voice to neoliberal sensibility in favor of the elite's needs of legitimization, entertainment, and investment, self-censoring at times while informing the opinion of many at other times. In this context, criticism and protest occurred within the guidelines dictated by neoliberal decorum, or even giving voice to the conservative right, remaining vacuous and thus ineffective. An example of this is Enrique Krauze's homage to Lorenzo Zambrano, the *Regiomontano* (from Monterrey) businessman who owns CEMEX, the world's biggest cement company, in which Krauze narrates his career as a leading businessman, the history of the monopoly of cement in Mexico, and his prowess in technological and informational techniques and in business culture.[61]

---

61 Gabriel García Márquez used to call him "Lorenzo the Magnificent." Enrique Krauze, "La carrera de Lorenzo Zambrano," *Reforma* May 25, 2014, http://www.enriquekrauze.com.mx/joomla/index.php/biogr-retrato/99-biogra-de-la-sociedad-civil-y-la-ciudadania/874-la-carrera-de-lorenzo-zambrano.html.

Public opinion and knowledge were disseminated through an apparatus designed to transform them into reproducible and homogenizing one-liners—merchandises like any other.[62] The marketing of opinion was based on the claim of "cultural exception." That is to say, artists and intellectuals defended culture as a regime distinct from entertainment and communication, based on the critical autonomy of their opinions and in the apparent separation between culture and the economy. Following Maurizio Lazzarato, this position is weak before the current forms of production, socialization, and appropriation of knowledge and culture, which are not different from the ways in which wealth is produced, appropriated, and socialized. This is because intellectual production gives shape and direction to the organization of production and wealth. In other words, for Lazaratto, the "need for knowledge," the "love of beauty," and the "greed for the exquisite" are open roads for economic development. The use and value of cultural products, however, is guaranteed by the culture's alleged cultural exception within the economic regime. As a consequence, "public opinion" and culture are not adjacent to the State or corporations, but the media are part of the central mechanisms of the administration of consent and the channeling of antagonism. Just as any field of production, art, and culture had been subject to the logic of surplus value, they are not only one of the arms of power, but states and corporations invest in them because they are conceived as actual sources of economic wealth and as potential solutions to the devastation caused by neoliberal policies in the social tissue. As Jorge Volpi declared, "The horror that surrounds us proves that we live in imminently Shakespearian times. Art and culture are the sole balsam before barbarity."[63]

In this regard, museums, film festivals, art fairs, and other cultural initiatives helped to legitimize the government and corporations, while they also functioned as a supplement to manufactured public opinion in the mass media. Because art is symbolic power and a showcase for democracy, it is not necessary to censor what is "political" or "critical." The question that arose is,

62 Maurizio Lazzarato, "European Cultural Tradition and the New Forms of Production and Circulation of Knowledge," http://www.moneynations.ch/topics/euroland/text/lazzarato.htm.

63 Jorge Volpi is a writer and a public servant; the statement is from the inauguration of the Cervantino Festival on October 8, 2014, quoted by Abida Ventura, "Inauguran el Festival Internacional Cervantino 2014," *El Universal*, October 8, 2014, http://www.eluniversal.com.mx/cultura/2014/festival-internacional-cervantino-2014-inauguracion-1044447.html.

what role could intellectuals play in the neoliberal era, when the postmodern notion of political task to "speak truth to power" was perfectly incorporated to the market and embodies a benevolent form of power as repressive tolerance? Many intellectuals had given up on the struggle against neoliberalism, selling out to corporate and mediatic power, ceasing to vouch for important social subjects, or supporting social movements or using their knowledge to create a culture critical of the neoliberal model. Some even became ideological puppets, using their abilities to contribute to the destruction of the social contract, critical thought, and social institutions. Evidently, if an intellectual decides to put her talent to the service of power, she could acquire riches, prestige, and success, while at the same time convince herself that she can directly interfere in political processes. Incapable of perceiving her own ideological compromises, when she circulates her work in the market regime of intellectual and cultural production, her thought becomes a superficial defense of the status quo. Other intellectuals pled for *instituent* practices at the crossroads of a dialectic representation of power and resistance: a positive form of falling that also institutes. It is being: Melville's, Deleuze's, or Agamben's "Bartlebys."[64] Instituent practices instrumentalize institutions as tools of freedom of expression, platforms for visiblization, dissemination of information, or alternative proposals. The problem is that, following Pierre Bourdieu, the intellectual field is already predetermined by the position it occupies in the power field, which implies that socially determined agents occupy positions that the State has designated for them. This is why their positioning—albeit critical or progressive—is necessarily and objectively tied to the position that power has conferred upon them a priori.[65]

Andrés Manuel López Obrador, Durán Barba, and the Death of the Liberal Class

On July 15, 2020, a group of academics, analysts, intellectuals, and politicians denounced in the open letter "Contra la deriva autoritaria y por la defensa de la democracia" (Against the Authoritarian Derive and on Defense of Democracy) the stifling of pluralism in the Chamber of Deputies (López Obrador's party MORENA, the National Regeneration Movement, now has

64 Gerald Raunig, "Prácticas instituyentes: Fugarse, instituir y transformar," *transversal texts* (January 2006), https://transversal.at/transversal/0106/raunig/es.

65 Pierre Bourdieu, *Intelectuales, política y poder* (Buenos Aires: Eudeba, 1999), 33.

the majority of seats). The letter accuses the president of centralizing power in detriment of other state and federal powers and of destroying or deteriorating public administration and constitutional institutions, as well as making personal decisions, polarizing society into artificial bands, discrediting the authority of special organisms like INE (National Electoral Institute), and attacking all expressions not identified with his politics. They also denounce his suicidal austerity politics in the face of COVID-19 and his refusal to come up with a national agreement to responsibly reactivate the economy and save hundreds of jobs. Instead, they point out, the pandemic has been instrumentalized to accelerate the demolition of institutions that hold the State in check, and to take over more power. These "organic intellectuals" call for an opposition block—an alliance to give back to the Chamber of Deputies its role as institutional counterweight to the executive power, keeping the government in check to respect democratic plurality. In this regime, however, organic intellectuals belong to the same category as corrupt politicians, capitalism's cronies, and irresponsible privileged people.

This perception is perhaps due to the failure of the liberal class to articulate an alternative to profound inequality, but I also found answers in Jaime Durán Barba's books. Durán Barba is a political strategist and has been a consultant in dozens of electoral campaigns throughout Latin America over the past twenty years. In *Manual de relaciones legislativas con la prensa* (2002), he argues that a condition for the strengthening of democracy is that rulers maintain an adequate relationship with citizens through the mass mediatization of political communication. It is thus essential to do whatever is necessary to increase the government's press coverage addressing a specific audience, considering the context and headlines. Durán Barba is known to have invented President Andrés Manuel López Obrador's *mañaneras* (or daily morning addresses, akin to Donald Trump's tweets) when he was governor of Mexico City (2000–2005). In his *mañaneras*, López Obrador marked the political agenda every day on the radio, delimiting political discussions in the country, which enabled him to become the main opponent to Mexico's then-president Vicente Fox. The *mañaneras* now take place every day at 7:00 a.m. in a room at the National Palace, where about fifty journalists wait until the martial salute of a woman soldier is heard: "Good morning, Mr. President!" That is the signal that President Andrés Manuel López Obrador has arrived. Seconds later, the president climbs a pallet and stands before a lectern with a microphone, in front of a screen where a PowerPoint presentation is projected. He says, "Good morning. We will reveal information dealing with the government's plan of republican austerity." And thus the *mañanera* begins. For over an hour, the president announces his government's social programs, gives instructions to his collaborators, and sends political messages. The president is representing not himself, but his government, and he places journalists and actors right before the daily conjuncture. He jokes around, confronts his enemies, puts down journalists, makes personal statements, deploys his idiosyncrasy, comments on social media, dismisses criticism, and announces his political decisions. Many of his statements are outrageous and are echoed and criticized in social and mass media, giving way to shitstorms around specific topics, policies, or events. No one in the country has remained indifferent to his daily morning declarations, which have become the source of memes, jokes, endless commentary, memes, headlines, anger, outrage, and criticism.

I must note that "Mañanero" was the name of a TV political commentary program led by Víctor Trujillo "Brozo" between 1994 and 2019. Brozo's show was known for being satirical, critical, and ruthless against the political class, as well as for having exposed many political scandals. The name of Brozo's show and the president's daily morning address bears a double entendre: "(palo) mañanero" also refers to "morning sex," while "(cogida) mañanera" means "morning fuck." Both imply the normalization of misogynistic language in the public sphere, as in Paco Ignacio Taibo II's (the director of the Fondo de Cultura Económica, or the national editorial house which has recently edited the entire collection of his own police novels) stated "se las metimos doblada" or "we put it in folded," referring to López Obrador and his allies having "fist fucked" their opponents.

In another book Jaime Durán Barba co-wrote with Santiago Nieto, *Mujer, sexualidad, internet y política* (2006), they discuss the need for politicians to massify certain values and meanings. For them, it is key to address the "new voter," a figure with a specific political sensibility around whom they must construct a sociopolitical imaginary through mass communication; a political culture identifying with the right-wing or conservative right. This new voter is a consumer of communication—this is why the proposals need to be jazzy, armored against questioning. Ideology is thus recuperated through a false notion of politics: novelty, bombardment, and bombastic statements. Everything needs to become ephemeral and transitory, like the brief nationalization of private hospitals, which for a few months took in non-COVID patients from public hospitals, or like the short-term program to hand out credits to family business as a measure to help with the economic crisis. In the *mañaneras*, declarations are volatile and ephemeral, and they evaporate in the citizen-consumer's nonextant short-term, let alone history and memory.

Critical-intellectuals fantasize with changing society at their root, but they are in crisis: the "common people" no longer recognize them as superior beings and beholders of reason and consciousness. As Carlos Monsiváis noted, they ceased being moral referents for the Mexican people.[66] In the contemporary context, the president is imposing his agenda not without reason, but with passion. Passion has become the ruling value of the "new Latin American electorate," according to Durán Barba. In his view, the idea that intellectuals are right and are bearers of reason, and that the problems of the country will be overcome through their ideas and when the masses study sociology and learn to discuss and discern ideologies and government programs and speak their language, is wrong and a waste of public money. In this regard, a crusade against critical thought has been brewing in Latin America for the past twenty years. What criticism generates now is apathy, and that makes things worse. The attack against intellectuals, social sciences, and critical thinking parts from the strategy of the "art of winning elections."

Indeed, in the current contemporary imagination, images have annihilated words, and spectacle has replaced old discourses and programs. As we have seen, celebrity culture has taken over political communication generating, passions from staged authenticity, rather than genuine forms of recognition and belonging: a culture of the perpetuation of faux ecstasy. Now, words, discourses, and political programs and policy are a thing of the past. Durán Barba has prescribed to replace them with images, spectacle, and emotions underscored by the neoliberal values of individualism, apolitization, and personal idiosyncrasy.

Durán Barba did not bring President Andrés López Obrador to power, but former Mexico City's mayor seems to have learned the exercise of his communicational politics by heart. Ironically, it was Antonio Sola, the Spanish political consultant who supported Felipe Calderón's presidential campaign in 2006 and advised López Obrador's last campaign. I write "ironically" because Sola created in 2006 a campaign against López Obador crowned by the slogan, "AMLO is a danger to Mexico." For the 2018 campaign, Sola

66 Carlos Monsiváis, *Alusiones* (México D.F.: Anagrama, 2007), 44.

capitalized Mexicans' anger against organized crime, insecurity, and corruption, and he radically changed the figure of the president: he does not live in the official residency, he is paid less, he does not have bodyguards, he travels in tourist class on commercial flights, and he promised a peaceful strategy to eradicate insecurity and violence, pensions for the elderly poor, and scholarships for young men and women.

The figure of President Andrés Manuel López Obrador, however, is a perfect example of civil society's historical amnesia, as well as evidence that old PRI tactics have not been excised from Mexican politics. As candidate for governor of the state of Tabasco, he lost in 2004, and as a protest, he organized a march to Mexico City; some of his constituents took over oil wells and proclaimed his victory. He did not make it to governor of Tabasco governor, but in 2000 he was elected as mayor of Mexico City. As he took power, to demarcate himself from his predecessor Rosario Robles, he reduced government expenses he deemed unnecessary, like cell phones, consultants, and press offices with the goal of dedicating that money to social programs. Sound familiar? Back then, he was criticized for not making sure his people were following his rules of transparency and austerity; after a series of corruption scandals in 2004 around his party, the PRD, the Chamber of Deputies impeached him in 2005. Since then, he has begun to sell himself as an "uncomfortable subject" for power. His political strategy is sustained by the idea of a complot against him, which generates passions and divisions among citizens—something which he has evidently mastered.

"Organic intellectuals" are critiquing Andrés Manuel López Obrador's government for his positing himself as "caudillo" (chieftain) or "Messiah," but not by the principle underlying his government program, which echoes the 1990s Televisa "solidarity" celebrity music video: poverty as the enemy that can be defeated with the union of businessmen (oligarchs) and campesinos; no one is questioning the fact that López Obrador is not complying to the San Andrés Accords with the Zapatistas, who fight for a plurality of autonomous nations under the umbrella of the "Mexican Republic," or the fact that López Obrador posits the State as the only means of possible social transformation, or his tight relationship with the military. Journalistic research about his social programs is also lacking, but it is rumored that they are failing or have been halted due to improvisation and lack of viability; the financing for programs like public-rural universities, planting trees, scholarships for youth, and microcredits for the poor have been said to have come from arbitrary budget cuts (which are ongoing) and adjustments in vital projects, seriously affecting public institutions. He has ordered cuts in public realms like health (e.g., cancer patients now lack treatment in public hospitals), education, culture, and scientific research. But there is no journalism being written that could connect all the dots and paint a realistic picture of the relationship between the caudillo's promises and deeds.

In the context of global neonationalisms, the current regime is not an exception in creating a new identity discourse generated from within the state: a truly rooted nationalism grounded on the originary Indigenous past. This discourse is based on the goodness of Indigenous populations and an originary essential "communitarian democracy" that can realize the common good for all communities to overcome inequality. A society that becomes a community reflected through morality and rights, a "collective us" against an individual "I" that the president "governs obeying." This "communitarian democracy," led by President López Obrador, sounds very much like Luis Villoro's writings about Indigenous communities as an alternative and post-ideological form of political organization, and as a means to overcome inequality.[67] This discourse obviously contrasts with the current government's "development" programs in the South of Mexico. By many accounts, "modernization" is racism.

We are facing an extractive economy not only of resources, but also of data, cheap labor through budget cuts and megaprojects (EPZs and tourist infrastructure), more privatizations, and debt. None of these advances in capitalism could have been prevented by the cultural, journalistic, legal, or activist work of the liberal class, which is made up of artists, writers, journalists, researchers, activists, NGO workers, and advocates of human rights. Most of us have unquestioningly repeated the official "War Against Drugs" discourse in art, literature, and film, denouncing criminal violence, and unable to draw the links between organized crime, the myth of narcos, private armies, Blackwater, the Mérida Plan, the exponentiation of violence, and extractivism and dispossession. The war has been mostly denounced through the abstract umbrella of "violations of human rights," demanding that the "government do its job right."

During the past century or so, the press, universities, the labor movement, unions, culture, the Democratic Party, and NGOs have functioned as a defense against the excesses of power. According to Chris Hedges, however,

---

67 See Luis Villoro, *La alternativa. Perspectivas y posibilidades de cambio* (México D.F.: FCE, 2015).

for various reasons, the liberal class has collapsed as an effective counterweight to the corporate state. The most disadvantaged populations—the poor, the working class, migrants, even the middle class—no longer have a champion.[68] In the case of Mexico, the president has filled that void, positing himself and his policies as a defense of "the poor": a vague and obsolete concept that encompasses the lower and working class, students, and elderly, but not precarious workers, women, the non-exploited migrants, noncitizens, displaced and redundant populations, or victims of violence; "the poor" signifies Indigenous communities, but not those who are defending their territory against megaprojects. According to Hedges, this void has given way to a new terrifying political configuration: the gradual corruption and death of the liberal class, which no longer helps through institutions and the media to mitigate corporate control of politics, education, labor, the arts, and financial systems.[69] Now the post-neoliberal state is dismantling, without any barriers, the last vestiges of protection once put into place by the liberal class.

The way in which Chris Hedges's hypothesis applies to Mexico is easy to see but difficult to articulate. Since President Andrés Manuel López Obrador came to power, he has attacked and defunded students with scholarships studying abroad, scientists, academics, and the cultural sector. His attack has expanded to defunding the CONAPRED (the National Council to Prevent Discrimination), INE (the institution that keeps elections in check), and refuges for women suffering gender violence, but also major social sciences institutions like the CIDE (Centro de Investigaciones y Desarrollo Empresarial or Research and Business Development Center), the INAH (Instituto Nacional de Antropología e Historia or National Institute for Anthropology and History), and Instituto Mora. A massive transfer of wealth is taking place from institutions that produce and maintain the middle class as well as those that keep democratic mechanisms healthy (at least in a technocrat kind of way), but to where? To the regime's social programs? To handouts to "the poor"? To Dos Bocas (a new oil-extraction plant) and the Tren Maya, two of the regime's most prized megaprojects, for which oligarchs got contracts? To the Complejo Cultural Bosque de Chapultepec, which is being developed—for free—by conceptual artist Gabriel Orozco? It seems like what comes after neoliberalism is capitalism with Asian values like authoritarianism, Internet

68 Chris Hedges, *The Death of the Liberal Class* (New York: Type Media Center, 2010), 11.

69 Hedges, *The Death of the Liberal Class*, 17.

censorship, state control over certain sectors of the economy, a centralized cultural program, a new morality, and the intensification of the so-called War Against Drugs: the expansion of the apparatus of "amplified counterinsurgency," as Dawn Paley suggests. But I'm getting ahead of myself.

According to Hedges, the liberal class—*we* cultural producers, creative thinkers, artists, creative industry workers, journalists, NGO workers, activists, actors, researchers, professors—no longer have a place as moral authority. This is due to the rise of the corporate state and *our* inability to criticize unfettered capitalism, question the surveillance state, and boycott states or corporations against globalization and inequality. Indeed, opportunism and pretentiousness abound in the culture industry—at least that's the outsider's perception—with its caricature of appropriating marginal people's voices, of building modes of collective existing, of living together, of appropriating ancestral knowledges and radical subaltern gestures. Blind to extractivism and to the ethical nuances of participating in biennials and film festivals subsidized by oil companies, armament corporations, and corrupt governments. In an address at the 2007 Guadalajara Book Fair (FIL), Carlos Monsiváis discussed the novelty of "cultural empowerment" as an incipient form of nationalism. By this he meant that "our culture" had come to mean that "minorities believe in aesthetic complexity through faith and not by demonstration, they get excited with some poems and a bit of classical music and exhibit their astonished admiration before virtuously employed language that creates aesthetic reactions in unexpected places."[70] At the same time, Monsiváis points out, humanism has been expelled from education and delegated to the "iconosphere," or the realm of images. In the domain of high culture, he declared, what came to matter is a form of overloaded, delirious, and insane praise to convince everyone that the cultural product they are consuming is not a product, and that the praise is not marketing. In sum, for Monsiváis, neoliberalism signifies the encumbrance of a predatorial minority that despises humanism and adopts culture as adornment and education to disguise its technocratic ways. The tragedy for him is that cultural contexts and cultural referents came to be lost.[71] When pondering about this last line, I can't help but think that the rare meetings with my editor always take place at a corporate building where I need to pass three checkpoints to get in, and that the

70 Carlos Monsiváis, *Alusiones* (México D.F.: Anagrama, 2007), 46.
71 Monsiváis, *Alusiones*, 47.

image of Frida Kahlo has been sold to be placed on the labels of plastic water bottles and feminine pads.

When the official narrative critiqued the liberal class labeling us as *fifís* (or snobs), we were living comfortable lives working for the state or private-culture industries without fighting against the system. To be comfortable, we have had to compromise, self-censor, and accept the fact that the pillars of the liberal class (i.e., the media, the university, the arts) have been bought off with corporate money. Students are no longer educated to think critically but to make themselves helpful to the corporate state. We have been unable to stop—let alone denounce—extractivism and neocolonialism, living off the surplus in the economy that gets reinvested in cultural production. We are blind, unable to see the corporate structures that have made it impossible for most Mexican families to live with dignity (indebted to Coppel or Elektra with degraded access to health care through the Dr. SIMI chain, with decimated health by Maseca, Coca-Cola, and Bimbo, and minds bombarded by Televisa and now Netflix). We are blind to the neoliberal war: contempt with denouncing massive disappearances and violence against women as violations of human rights, as opposed to the continuation of colonialism and capitalism's systemic need to murder to thrive. In her newest book, *Guerra Neoliberal: Desaparición y búsqueda en el norte de México*, Dawn Paley argues that being unable to give signification to what we are going through is a brutal condition of demobilization, discord, and fear. We are trapped in that situation. According to Paley, an explanation of the current situation of violence in the country is beyond our grasp, because the framework for understanding it—"The War Against Drugs"—is obsolete, and giving the false impression that the Mexican State is waging a war against drug cartels who fight against each other, and that if innocent people die it's only collateral damage. Following Paley, however, the so-called War Against Drugs represents a change in the form of governing, in parallel with a deepening of the neoliberal processes throughout the application of what she calls "expanded counterinsurgent" war techniques. This form of war serves global capitalist interests and is occurring during a formally democratic moment, as opposed to yesteryear's military juntas or dictatorships. The War Against Drugs, or better called "Neoliberal War," is a depoliticized war without guerrillas, communists, and ideology, with state violence at the root, to dispossess private and common resources that sustain collective life and to hinder political capacities of resistance and struggle throughout Mexico. Two of the key tools of this war are forced disappearances and mass displacement of people; forced to abandon their businesses, lands, or homes by fear of extortion and death, serving the purpose of renewal of the primary accumulation cycle (extractivism). The form resistance is taking in this war is the organization of collectives of families of missing people who get together to find the remains of murdered people to hand them out to the police to run DNA tests, as does "Grupo Vida" in Torreón, Coahuila.[72]

While the Mexican State is painting itself as the physical and moral protector of the people, who among us is defying the corporate state and the power elite? What ideological alternatives are we going to put on the table? Our endless discussions on what makes art relevant to an unequal society, our pathetic defense to find support from civil society, banking on Mexican's (former) love for cultural figures and on the myth of aesthetic enthrallment falls short in envisioning what needs to be demanded right now: to stop extractivism, crony capitalism, the threats of Internet censorship, and the threat to native maize by T-MEC (or USMCA, United States-Mexico-Canada Agreement), to demand renewable energies and democracy by government reforms, the need to call for a rent and mortgage freeze, mutual-aid networks, counterinformation to tell the COVID stories the government is hiding behind data shoved down our throats nightly by the charming health care secretary, Hugo López Gatell. Unfortunately, art museums will go on conceiving their mission as being nimble stages for antagonism, putting in place a symbolic politics grounded on mere illusions, like poetic activism or poetic politics. In the meantime, enlightened cultural producers will go on believing that they are rising feminist, anti-racist children.

Thinking strategically, and not ethically, is how we are serving power. The current regime's critique and dismissal of the liberal class as *fifís*, as elitist and snobbish, closer to patrons and collectors than to the masses, is not too far off. Look at our history: Octavio Paz, Héctor Aguilar Camín, and Enrique Krauze vouched ferociously for neoliberalism as a means to develop Mexico. Against Carlos Fuentes, Paz condescendingly dismissed the Zapatista struggle, which Luis Villoro defended with the mystique of community and plurality. Not long after, and famously, while on tour, President Ernesto Zedillo was approached by an Indigenous woman who offered something for sale to him and he responded condescendingly: "No traigo cash." (I don't have any "cash" on me, using the word in English.) While market liberalization was at its peak, Jorge G. Castañeda and José Woldenberg worked on the country's democratic

72 Dawn Paley, *Guerra neoliberal: Desaparición y búsqueda en el norte de México* (México: Libertad bajo palabra, 2020), 14–17.

structures and "democratic transition," while the liberal class firmly believed in what is making us go extinct: technology, industrialization, capitalist production, free trade, development, and modernization; to be like the United States, to become European.

Mediocrity, opportunism careerism, and corporatism now invade democratic and cultural institutions that were envisioned to make the world a better place and give voice to the silenced. Neither have we protected the commons nor fought injustice (beyond likes and shares on social media). Claiming to speak on behalf of "universality" without defying the power elite is also how we lost our moral role in society, succumbing to the privileges that were offered to us. Workers did not become wealthier with neoliberalism (but became indebted or unemployed); the global market did not lift the developing world out of poverty (but renewed and strengthened colonial patterns of dispossession); trade barriers did not benefit citizens (but made them blind to global warming, mass migration, the fact that their privileges are sustained on war, dispossession, and violence). The final assimilation of corporate ideology into liberal thought is evident in the fact that artworks, films, and novels are conceived and disseminated in terms of marketing, as Carlos Monsiváis pointed out in Guadalajara.

Not having seen what was coming—a neo-populist régime that gained legitimacy by promising to undo the wrongs perpetuated by "neoliberal governments" but which would regardless continue with their extractivist and neoliberal policies—the liberal class voted for a government that does not represent us, but neither does it represent people undergoing hardship to survive due to climate change, women, migrants in Mexico hoping to cross to the United States, Indigenous populations whose territories are rich in resources fighting to defend them, the redundant populations, the families of victims of forced disappearance, people undergoing forced displacement through extortion or terror, and so forth.

Thus, what should the role of intellectuals be? I can think of whistle-blowing actions by Julian Assange, Anat Kamm, or Chelsea Manning. (The latter two have been jailed for their actions, and the former has been hiding in Ecuador's Embassy in London since July 2012 for fear he will be extradited and judged in the United States. In 2019, Assange was dragged out from the Ecuadorian Embassy in London where he had been taking refuge since 2012. He is now in a UK prison facing possible extraditions to the US where he will be indicted for violations of the US Espionage Act, facing 175 years in prison.) Instead of speaking truth to power, they revealed to the public what the "deep power" does not want us to know. In a recent article, Noam Chomsky argued that intellectuals have traditionally been caught between the conflicting demands of truth and power, because "the intellectual would like to see herself as someone who seeks to discern truth, speak truth as she sees it, and promote collective action to oppose injustice and oppression, contributing to give shape to a better social order."[73] For Chomsky, however, if the intellectual decides to go down that road, she will be a solitary, despised, or injured creature, just as whistle-blowers currently are. Before the urgency of the changes that need to be made in the socioeconomic model, without falling into leftist dogmatisms, the role of intellectuals and radical activists should be to try to persuade and organize, but above all, to avoid the temptation to join flanks with the repressive elite and to help create politics that could counteract the actual forms of authoritarianism.[74] In other words, there are two positions: either to work from the rotten, preexisting structures or from structures focused on a policy of profitable and tolerant democratic culture, or turning our backs to power to create other autonomous spaces, not in a (tolerated) confrontational relationship, but with autonomous alternative proposals. With regard to the massive mobilizations at the global level since 2011, it becomes evident that an uprising can occur at any moment. Intermittent occupation in ephemeral, yet more and more recurrent mobilizations, substitute yesteryear's union strikes; at the same time, we have witnessed the proliferation of self-defense and community police all over Mexico as efforts to contain organized crime's abuses and their complicity with the government, or to resist political powers auctioning off natural resources.[75] Currently, there are self-defense groups in Hidalgo, Puebla, Veracruz, Oaxaca, Guerrero, Michoacán, Tamaulipas, Quintana Roo, and areas in the Mexico State; even though many of these autonomous police organizations are recognized by Indigenous peoples' *usos y costumbres* (uses and customs) legislation, the government has started to criminalize them. Community police forces and self-defense groups (which are not the same thing) are conformed by citizens

73 Noam Chomsky, "Un movimiento genuino por el cambio social," *La Jornada*, December 7, 2014, http://www.jornada.unam.mx/2014/12/07/mundo/026a1mun.

74 Chomsky, "Un movimiento genuino por el cambio social."

75 This takes into account the negative legacy of self-defense groups in Colombia, formed by peasants and soldiers trained and financed by industrial farmers fighting against organized crime and corrupt militias in the 1990s, who ended up becoming criminal paramilitary associations.

who have organized and armed themselves to provide security to their communities, and once they achieve it, they disappear, become corrupt, or can be used by the government. Armed groups defending the interests of their communities are considered to be a political problem (of self-organization and government), as a sign of the lack of sovereignty of the State. As we will see, however, they are the result of problems that emerge directly from the economic model, before which communities see the need to construct non-state powers tied to their societies. As Raúl Zibechi points out, if the state is the monopoly of physical coercion exercised through a body separate from society (military and civil bureaucracy), with the non-state powers of self-organized Indigenous communities, power is dispersed and distributed through the whole social body and is subject to communal assemblies.[76] These forms of autonomy point to the urgency of the creation of autonomous spaces in which we could apply different rules to those imposed by the neoliberal system, to try to build radically different socioeconomic relationships, instituting communal property and resource-management regimes. An example is the *Ley de Reordenamiento Territorial* (Territorial Rezoning Law) in Cuetzalan, Puebla, which involves citizens' participation in zoning projects from the early stages of characterization and diagnosis.[77] In that regard, Cuetzalan's *cabildo* (chapter or town hall or town management) has had a recent victory through this law, establishing an institutional viewpoint to declare the town as free of mining, hydroelectric, or other resource-extraction projects that could damage the environment, as well as the possible concession to use and exploit water by private agents,[78] setting an important precedent in the struggle against neoliberal destruction and a model for autonomous organization.

76 Raúl Zibechi, *Dispersar el poder* (Quito: Ediciones Abya-Yala, 2007), 29.

77 Aurelio Fernández F., "Cuetzalan: defenderse y construir," *La Jornada*, April 8, 2014, http://www.jornada.unam.mx/2014/04/09/opinion/026a1pol.

78 Sandra Barillas, "El cabildo de Cuetzalan, en session abierta, oficializa el rechazo a proyectos mineros e hidroeléctricos," *La Jornada de Oriente*, November 6, 2014, http://www.lajornadadeoriente.com.mx/2014/11/06/el-cabildo-de-cuetzalan-en-sesion-abierta-oficializa-el-rechazo-a-proyectos-mineros-e-hidroelectricos.

CHAPTER TWO

Mexico's Neoliberal Conversion

Spatializing Political Economics or Neocolonial Extractivism

IN 2019, media mogul Ricardo Salinas Pliego, owner of Televisión Azteca and the Jalmolonga Hacienda in the state of Mexico, was in the midst of a scandal of dispossession and police repression. A legal battle had been ongoing since 2012 when a group of *ejidatarios* from Chalamita, a community adjacent to Salinas Pliego's estate, realized that the media mogul had rechanneled communal water sources toward his property, thus depriving the community of the vital resource. The conflict was taken to agrarian court, and although in early October 2019 a court resolution determined that the *ejidatarios* were to be granted access to the water source, it was intermittent and limited. A couple of weeks later, a Toulca agrarian judge changed the verdict, granting sole right to the source to Salinas Pliego. For three weeks, the *ejidatarios* protested day and night by Jalmolonga Hacienda's entrance. Salinas Pliego had built a structure made of chicken wire put under the custody of private guards to impede access. The *ejidatarios* tried to break in on October 26, but with the complicity of Governor Alfredo del Mazo, the media mogul deployed 2,000 bodies of the Security Secretary of the State of Mexico, who dissolved the protest.[1] Ironically (as two of the mantras of his campaign were to battle against corruption and crony capitalism), President Andrés Manuel López Obrador bestowed the concession of the "Bienestar Cards" to Banco Azteca and Electra, enabling people living in rural areas to cash out government social aid in financial and commercial establishments owned by Salinas Pliego.[2]

The case of water dispossession of the *ejidatarios* (or *comuneros*, communal land holders) in Chalamita (and the other six adjacent *ejidos* (communal lands) that also depend on the hijacked water source to raise their crops) illustrates the kind of power relationships that are in place in Mexico: a colonial condition that produces regional asymmetries and uneven distribution of resource control (at times through crony capitalism). Through this colonial matrix,[3] dispossession functions as a tool to enrich a few and produce misery for many, which is essential to social control and to maintain racialized hegemony, privilege, and inequality. These mechanisms of power and resource control create radically different economic realities that exist side by side, as do complementary movements of dispossession and zoning, development and underdevelopment (or zero growth, scarcity, incomplete modernity), prosperity and stagnation, and modernity and backwardness. This series of dichotomies gives way to the paradigm of "inequality," a political and economic discursive construct that serves as cover to the colonial matrix underpinning power relations in Mexico. The hegemonic paradigm of "inequality," moreover, is the basis for democratization and neoliberal policies that in turn cover the production of redundant populations I discussed in the previous chapter.

The hegemonic discourse of "inequality" in Mexico is articulated by academics such as Valeria Moy, who has argued that inequality in Mexico is based on differences in culture, food, tradition, nature, and geography, but also on radically diverging economic realities. In her view, these realities translate to

---

1 Rodrigo Vera, "Despoja Salinas Pliego un paraíso a Malinalco," *El Diario de Coahuila*, October 31, 2019, https://www.eldiariodecoahuila.com.mx/nacional/2019/3/31/despoja-salinas-pliego-un-paraiso-malinalco-803656.html.

2 Patricia Dávila, "Banco Azteca creará 'clientes cautivos' para Salinas Pliego," *Proceso*, March 19, 2019, https://www.proceso.com.mx/575944/advierten-que-reparto-de-subsidios-en-elektra-y-banco-azteca-creara-clientes-cautivos-para-salinas-pliego.

3 Aníbal Quijano, "Coloniality of Power, Eurocentrism and Latin America," *Nepantla: Views from South* 1, no. 3 (2000), 533–80.

the huge breach between the north and center of the country and the south: a Mexican region that grows and develops, contrasting with a region that stagnates and worsens. According to Moy, disparity and inequality are not based on five-hundred-year-old colonial relations and ongoing dispossession, as in the Jalmolonga estate, but on political-economic decision-making. Therefore, from her point of view, the solution to inequality is not to put a stop to spoliation, but to democratize economic growth and investment toward development.[4] From this technocratic point of view, prosperity—as a solution to inequality—is based on industrialization and linkage to US productive chains and processes, as is the case in the states of Bajío, Chihuahua, Nuevo León, Coahuila, Baja California, and Baja California Sur. In contrast, there is extreme poverty in the states of Chiapas, Veracruz, Oaxaca, Guerrero, and Mexico, and for Moy, this is due to a lack of access to education and poor-quality or insufficient infrastructure; although the southern region is rich in Aeolic fossil fuel and shale gas resources. For Moy, the formula to solve inequality in Mexico is "to connect the South, invest in infrastructure, to offer access to energy and technology and to seriously invest in education."[5] This is precisely the modernist developmental paradigm and extractivist agenda pursued by President Andrés Manuel López Obrador's regime, which by "putting the poor first" is conflating the categories of working-class citizens, Indigenous peoples, inhabitants of rural areas, and urban precarious workers, while celebrating the "cultural heritage" of originary populations. This celebration is in continuity with paternalistic and modernistic policies that justify dispossession by technocracy, zonification, and extractivism, ultimately covering the colonial matrix inherent to policies designed to better "poor" people's lives.

If we consider neoliberalism as a stage of capitalism and modernity as inextricable from colonialism, ours is an era of the intensification of the loss of nature and of its becoming territory in which the very notion of soil is changing through extractivism. As it has been conceptualized by neoliberalism, territory is no longer the milieu or background for human action, but like everything else (i.e., bodies, the sensible, life), it has become a function of valorization. Therefore, what is really at stake with this neoliberal spatialization of capital is not land property, but attachment—legal right to inhabit

4 Valeria Moy, "Desigualdad: La herencia regional," *Nexos*, July 1, 2018, https://www.nexos.com.mx/?p=38328.

5 Moy, "Desigualdad."

a territory and to have access to resources. As we feel the ground slip away from our feet, our means to make a living being taken away from us—a movement that began with the colonization of the Americas in which entitlement or belonging to the soil was predicated upon being foreign (male and white)—we are now seeing its most extreme form in forced migration. There is no longer an assured "homeland" for anyone. With homelessness skyrocketing in more privileged urbanized enclaves, the migratory crisis is not only exclusive to the south, but it has been generalized. And it is not only a question of attachment, but also of the universal lack of shareable spaces and inhabitable land. Following Bruno Latour, the modernity/coloniality matrix and their current manifestation as globalization have created a contradiction between two movements: to be attached to a particular patch of soil on one hand, and having access to the global world on the other.[6] This is why one of the challenges we face is the urgency to repoliticize what it means to belong to the land.

The question of a politicized notion of belonging to a territory is at the core of the battle for rights to water between Chalamita (the ejido) and Jalmolonga (Salinas Pliego's estate), as well as an exemplary instance of the pervasive mechanism of the concentration of land and resources in private, within the logic of extractivism. Macarena Gómez Barris defines extractivism as a form of extractive capitalism particular to the Americas that extends from the sixteenth century to the present, based on Eduardo Galeano's concept of the "Open veins of Latin America." This concept, according to Gómez Barris, denotes "an economic system that engages in thefts, borrowings and forced removals, violently reorganizing social life as well as the land by thieving resources from originary peoples."[7] In hegemonic reality, however, the reality of social and economic relationships of dispossession is veiled as State corruption and malfunction, and extractivism is posited as a means to democratize, develop, and modernize rural areas throughout the country. Its sequels are dramatic and dangerous material change to social and ecological life underpinning racialized capitalism. Mega-extractive projects such as large dams and mines, which require huge technological and resource feats, are justified with the imposition of modernity as a universalized mode of governance.

6 Bruno Latour, *Down to Earth: Politics in the New Climatic Regime* (London: Polity Press, 2019), 12.

7 Macarena Gómez-Barris, *The Extractive Zone: Social Ecologies and Decolonial Perespectives* (Durham, NC: Duke University Press, 2017).

State- and corporate-designed mega-development projects operate through an economic rationale without calibrating for the life forms that exist beneath the gaze of such grand schemes subjugating originary populations' to the new order of being.

Neoliberalized Mexico: Failed State or Exemplary Emerging Economy?

Thirty years of Washington consensus policies and market liberalization in Mexico brought about a general apocalyptic perception that Mexico is a dangerous country plunged in a loop of violence, and that things could only get worse. This perception coexisted with a view of a nation that, although unable to fully overcome its poverty, was untouched by the 2008–2009 global financial crisis and was gradually becoming a middle-class nation. In the media and the collective global imaginary, the country oscillated between a "failed state" and an exemplary emerging economy. The former implied that urgent corrective action was necessary, as a "failed" nation is:

> Utterly incapable of sustaining itself as a member of the international community [due to] civil strife, government breakdown and economic privation. . . . [Failed] states descend into violence and anarchy, imperiling their own citizens and threatening their neighbors through refugee flows, political instability, and random warfare.[8]

Journalist Sergio González Rodríguez embraced the "failed state" thesis, arguing that dominion of certain regions in the country by criminal groups implied the unsettling of the traditional division between public and private spheres and the deprivation of the population from their rights by their subjection to a regime of daily terror. In other words, for Sergio González Rodríguez, the thesis of the "failed state" implied absence of the rule of law due to the dysfunctionality of Mexican institutions. In that context, the State was considered a simulation because it had partially lost legitimacy in its own territory, implying a false rule of law and the construction of what he called an "an-State." For González Rodríguez, the "Mexican degradation" began at the heart of Mexico's institutions, because the narco-criminal machine was

8 Gerald B. Herlman and Steven R. Ratner, "Saving Failed States," *Foreign Policy*, June 21, 2010, http://www.foreignpolicy.com/articles/2010/06/21/saving_failed_states.

co-substantive with its political and economic institutions and with the United States' participation. The fact that the country's institutions have been corrupted or failed is also the conservative hegemonic opinion.[9]

In sum, the perception of Mexico as a "failed state" materialized in areas of the country in which the government had de facto suspended sovereignty, illustrating not a "failed state," but what Aihwa Ong has called "graded sovereignty." According to Ong, neoliberal governments treat populations differentially, creating a diversity of zones with regimes of exception. That is to say, there are some areas in which the State is very strong and protective, while in others it is nearly absent. This mechanism has the purpose of enabling areas to be either flexible with regard to markets—at the risk of rendering them structurally irrelevant[10]—or an obstacle for privatization and the free flow of (legal and illegal) merchandise, money, and people. For example, since 2006, the six Mexican states bordering the United States have been immersed in anarchy (with alternating periods of peace and spikes of violence), allegedly in a war among the cartels seeking to control the passage routes for illegal goods. It is known that gangs charge extortion and protection fees to citizens and force illegal immigrants deported from the United States to work for them. In addition to controlling smuggling routes, regional kingpins continue to hold sway over local business and governments. The maquiladora industry, however, has neither been affected by violence nor threatened by the gangs: in 2011, 10,000 jobs were created at 19 factories in Ciudad Juárez. Forty more opened in subsequent months. Despite the violence, foreign investment is pouring in, especially to the automobile industry.[11] As Valeria Moy wrote:

> To visit an automobile factory in the Bajío (center) or north of the country is like visiting it in any Asian country. Infrastructure is automated. It works with standardized processes; they are highly productive and there are few workers. Some of the cities where these factories reside grow, not always orderly but with first-quality-rate services. Corporative raise generating services demand like hotels and restaurants. There are more and more malls

---

9 Sergio González Rodríguez, *Campo de guerra* (Barcelona: Anagrama, 2014).

10 Aihwa Ong, *Neoliberalism as Exception: Mutations in Citizenship and Sovereignty* (Durham, NC: Duke University Press), 96.

11 "Violencia cierra pequeños negocios, pero no afecta a maquilas en Ciudad Juárez," *Milenio Jalisco*, July 27, 2011, http://jalisco.milenio.com/cdb/doc/noticias2011/43ce1154b9b35f5df68a76643e162d88.

that reflect the population rising acquisition power. There is infrastructure—highways, airports—and access to energy resources.[12]

In contrast, in states like Guerrero and Michoacán, *policías comunitarias* (community police squadrons) were created in 2013 to defend communities and agroindustrial farms against criminal organizations like the Caballeros Templarios. By mid-2019, deaths, decapitated or dismembered bodies, or corpses hanging from pedestrian bridges across cities and villages in the state have become normalized. Now the main enemy in Michoacán is the Cartel Jalisco Nueva Generación (the official efforts to dismantle the cartels by eliminating the leaders have led to the splintering and proliferation of criminal groups, it is said). Although President Andrés Manuel López Obrador has declared a policy of "abrazos no balazos" [hugs not gunshots], Michoacán inhabitants affirm that even though President Felipe Calderón first militarized the area in 2006, the community police are the only group capable of stopping the Cartel from controlling Michoacán.[13] But the problems in Michoacán go beyond territorial control for production and distribution of drugs: community police have been organized against deforestation to establish avocado plantations, known as "green gold." Around the Michoacán city of Uruapan, for instance, over a dozen groups are fighting to control avocado commerce, taking advantage of orchard owners, avocado gleaners, and drivers transporting the merchandise north to the United States. Orchard owners have founded their own vigilante armies to protect their avocado production, and the situation is blamed on the "absence of law enforcement."[14] Aside from the violence in Michoacán due to the avocado fever, we must underscore that it is part of the logic of the extractivist economy (as in Oaxaca, the mezcal fever) that will lead, in the midterm, to soil depletion.

Interestingly enough, in the states with heavy military presence, the government or corporations are developing energy infrastructure or

---

12 Moy, "Desigualdad."

13 Jacobo García, "En el corazón de la Guerra en México," *El País*, September 9, 2019, https://elpais.com/internacional/2019/09/08/mexico/1567906718_822056.html?ssm.

14 Kate Linthicum, "La guerra del narco para controlar la multimillonaria industria del aguacate en México," *Los Angeles Times*, November 21, 2019, https://www.latimes.com/espanol/mexico/articulo/2019-11-21/mexico-cartel-violencia-aguacates.

resource-extraction projects, both of which are severely damaging or even destroying the lives of the inhabitants of these regions. Symptomatically, phenomena such as Los Zetas, the huachicoleros (those who sell adulterated and possibly stolen gasoline), the Caballeros Templarios, community police, movements struggling against extractivist projects and dispossession across the country, forced mass deportation, and immigration are homogenized under the terms "organized crime" and "failed state." When organized crime is discussed, however, it is often ignored how it is not violence, but the presence of mining and megaprojects that have affected the social tissue, destroying entire communities by corrupting them or displacing thousands of originary and mestizo peoples from their lands and institutions (which have been rendered porous), and how privatizations and the liberalization of the market have radically changed the function of the State. The State has been hollowed out strategically; it has been depoliticized and transformed into the administrator and legislator of the country's commons (or in technocratic parlance: natural resources). And this is precisely the blind spot of the technocratic world view, for which people, territories, land, and the commons are abstractions apparently at the service of global markets. This omission, ignorance, or colonial blind spot is what is behind the visible patterns of violence across the country.

According to recent studies by journalists and academics, moreover, the forms of violence exercised in Mexico since 2006 constitute a new form of paramilitarism and subcontracted counterinsurgency that is benefiting the private sector and transnational corporations. That is to say, criminal organizations such as Los Zetas or Guerreros Unidos are the vehicle through which state and corporate economic interests are being assured.[15] According to Dawn Paley, for instance, the war against drugs is in reality an intensified form of the "shock doctrine"[16] that takes the form of a civil war, and of the counterinsurgent practice of forced disappearance[17] to generate panic and terror among the population and displace urban and rural populations, thereby generating changes in land ownership and facilitating the extraction and devastation of

---

15 Guadalupe Correa-Cabrera, *Los Zetas: Criminal Corporations, Energy, and Civil War in Mexico* (San Antonio: University of Texas Press, 2017).

16 See Naomi Klein, *The Shock Doctrine* (Toronto: Random House Canada, 2007).

17 Federico Mastrogiovanni, *Ni vivos ni muertos* (México D.F.: Grijalbo, 2014).

the commons.[18] Under this logic, the war is not about a "minimum of repression" or about maintaining the rule of law to connect the flows of capital from the Mexican territory to the rest of the planet. What we call the "war against crime" is about armed groups attacking citizens with the purpose of reinforcing their control over territories and perpetuating terror, exercising a form of "territorial cleanse" to facilitate the development of infrastructure and resource extraction by transnational and national corporations. An example where this pattern can be clearly observed is in the zone known as the Cuenca de Burgos that covers Nuevo León, Coahuila, Tamaulipas, and the North of Veracruz; its underground happens to contain the fourth-largest shale gas reserve, which is connected to the Texas reserve. This territory is completely controlled by the Zetas through extortion, forced disappearances, violence, and the cleansing of entire villages, after which come the installation of shale gas extraction companies.

Journalist Federico Mastrogiovanni makes a similar argument to Correa and Paley: he describes how many transnational companies extracting hydrocarbons globally are using the technique of supporting authoritarian governments to generate or disseminate high levels of violence and terror, resulting in the forced displacement of populations living in areas rich in hydrocarbons. In the specific case of Mexico, institutions are failing to solve cases of disappearance and extortion. According to Mastrogiovanni, this situation has led to a genocidal situation. If we do a Google search for "San Miguel de Aquila," "Valle de Juárez," "El Porvenir," "Práxedis," "Carrizalillo," and others, all of the information and testimonies will appear. It has become clear that economic agendas are the source of conflict in this dirty/civil war in a Mexico that, until 2018, was governed by a depoliticized system based on technocracy and expertise, unable to account for the tension between the two aspects of neoliberalism that govern it: the dynamic interaction between desiring and producing individuals who self-regulate in the market and the different means of control, corruption, and social cleansing that are necessary to make the first possible.

In her most recent book, *Neoliberal War: Disappearance and Search in the North of Mexico*, Dawn Paley argues that we are currently trapped in a situation in which we are unable to signify what we are going through:

18 Dawn Paley, *Drug War Capitalism* (Oakland, CA: AKA Press, 2014).

an epidemic of disappearance and violence. According to Paley, we are not being able to fully understand what is going on in a city, region, or country where disappearance of a loved one destroys a family's everyday life, leaving a void and bringing anxiety and endless pain of not finding the absent loved one. In her book, she takes up the task to explain how this situation is currently beyond our grasp, which first and foremost is obscured by the language used to describe it: "war against drugs," "failed state," "drug cartels." Rather, Paley establishes continuity with forced disappearances in the 1960s and 1970s throughout Latin America, within the frame of the Cold War's hunt for leftists and forced disappearance in contemporary neoliberal Mexico. For this, she coins the term "expanded counterinsurgency" characterized by (1) confusion of perpetrators, including members of state forces, people linked to organized crime and criminal networks, and nonorganized individuals; (2) the amplification of the category of insurgent to include more sectors in society; and (3) massive deployment of a complex of violence that goes from the public destruction and exhibition of bodies to the disappearance of people. That is to say, common people (working class, migrants, people in precarious jobs—in sum, the redundant population) are being treated as insurgents through subcontracted counterinsurgency instituting a labor discipline, social cleansing, massive population displacement, and the dissemination of fear as a form of control. Paley compares prisons in California and "expanded counterinsurgency" forced disappearance and massacres in Mexico as having a similar disciplinary and social cleansing function: to undo social cohesion, to repress. There is a lack of real insurgency, and cartels are paramilitary groups augmenting State power, while in truth, State and drug-war cartels are together waging a war against the people; there is huge confusion in terms of who is perpetrating the violence. Neoliberalization is inseparable from war as expanded counterinsurgency, and the civil response has come in the form of movements organized around the search of the remains of the disappeared in mass graves.[19]

As for what is at stake in the civil war that has been plaguing the country since 2006, it is territorial control. We should not be surprised that in spite of President Andrés Manuel López Obrador's declared policy of "abrazos no balazos" (hugs, not gunshots), the Mexican army reinforced its presence in certain regions in the state and city of Oaxaca as he came to power in 2018.

---

19 Dawn Paley, *La guerra neoliberal: desaparición y búsqueda en el norte de México* (México D.F.: Libertad bajo palabra, 2020).

In early 2019, the president further announced the creation of the National Guard, a controversial elite military body to prevent and fight against crime in the country. This has resulted in the perpetuation of militarization in police surveillance throughout the country, or in other words, the regularization of militarization in police functions.[20]

From this point of view, neoliberalization also needs to be understood, following urbanist Neil Brenner, not as a machine that produces inequality, but as a process of the regulatory restructuring of various spatial scales. The restructuring encompasses allocation of social resources and the commons for the sake of capital accumulation, translated to growth strategies and infrastructure. As we all know, this program has had devastating consequences for the commons. Therefore, we can understand neoliberalism as an intensification of processes of environmental destruction, assured through militarization and violence. If we understand the social and migratory crisis under the light of the ongoing dispossession, the intensification of extractivism across the globe, and neoliberalism as the spatialization of capitalism,[21] the image of underdeveloped and ungovernable Mexico from the technocratic imaginary is yet another resource to be exploited for the sake of the production of surplus value. This imaginary is also underscored by the colonial fantasy of there being vast extensions of territories with unlimited resources and cheap, uprooted, and willing labor hands to reconvert their life forms and make their living based on the demands of the global market. From this point of view (and the current regime under Andrés Manuel López Obrador is no exception), capitalism is the only means to value territories: as megaprojects and through the language of extraction and development, framed by narratives geared toward the production of surplus value. This is why poverty is conceived as an economic and social failure (or, under the current regime, as a result of corruption), and thus "the poor" (most of them originary populations) are conceived under a logic that is coherent with the role they have always been given in colonial Mexico: as subjects outside of the modern

20 Vanguardia, "Refuerza Ejército presencia en municipios de Oaxaca; mientras se discute la creación de la Guardia Nacional apoyan operativos estatales," *Grieta*, February 17, 2019, https://www.grieta.org.mx/index.php/2019/02/17/refuerza-ejercito-presencia-en-municipios-de-oaxaca-mientras-se-discute-la-creacion-de-la-guardia-nacional-apoyan-operativos-estatales.

21 Neil Brenner, "Neoliberalisation," in *Spaces of Neoliberalism: Urban Restructuring in North America and Western Europe*, ed. Neil Brenner and Nik Theodore (London: Wiley-Blackwell, 2002), 12–13.

nation that need to be incorporated through an array of techniques and policies, including violence and genocide.

Neoliberal Geno/ecocide and Resistance

Aside from the extractivist, displacement, and dispossession dynamics behind "organized crime," NAFTA rendered Indigenous populations even more vulnerable, as the treaty enabled foreign investors to fight, in foreign tribunals, local politics and actions, and thus they can demand compensation for politics that they consider threatening to the profit they expected to make.[22] Aside from being exposed to drug cartels' extortion, and to military subjection and repression, this has left Indigenous populations in a legal vacuum. Regardless, communities have organized against extractive or infrastructure megaprojects. Most notably, there is the eighteen-year-old struggle against the construction of the hydroelectric plant of La Parota, in Guerrero, or the ongoing Mazapil community struggle against Grupo Carso that has been exploiting an open mine (Tayahua in Salaverna, Zacatecas) at the cost of the destruction of their community. The mine is located beneath the village, and the corporation, in cahoots with the government, forced its inhabitants to relocate to the suburban development known as Nueva Salaverna. The common strategy for mining or other types of extractive missions is to put pressure on communities until resistance collapses. In spite of the literal and spiritual collapse of the community (the community was corrupted and broken from within throughout their ordeal, and the mine severely damaged their homes), they organized to struggle via legal means. The mining has been stopped because the corporation has, until today, been unable to prove ownership of the land.[23]

---

22 Public Citizen, "NAFTA at 20: One Million Lost U.S. Jobs, Higher Income Inequality, Doubled Agriculture Trade Deficit with Mexico and Canada, Displacement and Instability in Mexico, and Corporate Attacks on Environmental Laws," press release, January 2014, http://www.citizen.org/documents/NAFTA-at-20.pdf.

23 Sergio Elías Uribe Sierra and Grecia Eugenia Rodríguez Navarro, "Salaverna, el pueblo que no quiere morir: una experiencia de megaminería a cielo abierto," *REMA (Red Mexicana de Afectados por la Minería)*, July 6, 2019, http://www.remamx.org/2019/08/salaverna-el-pueblo-que-no-quiere-morir-una-experiencia-de-megamineria-a-cielo-abierto.

Another exemplary case is the Comité de Reordenamiento Territorial (Territorial Reorganizing Committee)[24] in Cuetzalan, in the northern mountains of Puebla, which in 2011 impeded the construction of a Walmart that sought to capture the 500 million pesos that flow yearly into the region to sustain its autonomous economy. In 2019, the town of Cuautepec in the state of Guerrero, through the Consejo Regional de Pueblos Originarios en Defensa del Territorio de Puebla e Hidalgo (Originary Peoples Regional Council for the Defense of Territory in Puebla and Hidalgo) won a legal protection warrant against the construction of the Tuxpan-Tula oil duct by Transportadora de Gas Natural de la Huasteca (TGNH), a subsidiary from TransCanada. The judge ruled out that the project, insofar as it involved the use of explosives and deforestation, would affect the right to land and territory of originary communities in the states of Veracruz, Puebla, and Hidalgo.[25] Hundreds of struggles like these proliferate across the country, their leaders' murders barely making it to the national news: Mexico is the sixth most dangerous country in the world for leaders of environmental and territorial struggles, and in 2018 alone, 164 were murdered in the country[26].

Yet the most iconic case of territorial defense that went on for twenty years in San Salvador Atenco in the state of Mexico, a few kilometers away from Mexico City. In 2001, President Vicente Fox announced that Atenco was meant to be the site for the New Mexico City Airport on expropriated *ejido*. Resistance, state repression, and violence began, and the Atenco community created an organization called Frente de Pueblos en Defensa de la Tierra (FPDT, or Front for Peoples Defending the Land), who began to struggle by various means. In July 2002, they took over the Texcoco highway. Arturo Montiel Rojas, then Mexico state's governor, ordered six hundred armed police to "liberate" the highway. After a four-hour-long confrontation, the police were dispelled and Vicente Fox canceled the megaproject, causing

24 The committee is a legal tool crafted by activist Erwin Slim Torres and approved at the municipal level which enables civilians, as well as civil, social, and political organizations, to partake in any decisions that the government may make concerning territorial arrangements in the region.

25 Gabriela Hernández, "Comunidad indígena gana amparo contra gasoducto Tuxpan-Tula," *Proceso*, February 11, 2019, https://www.proceso.com.mx/571364/comunidad-indigena-gana-amparo-contra-gasoducto-tuxpan-tula.

26 Alberto Pradilla, "México, el sexto país más peligroso para defensores del medio ambiente," *Animal Político*, July 29, 2019, https://www.animalpolitico.com/2019/07/defensores-medio-ambiente-asesinatos-mexico.

criticism against the federal government from real estate groups and politicians who had lost a business opportunity. According to journalist Diego Enrique Osorno, the State violence that unfolded on May 3–4, 2006, in Atenco was revenge by the political class against the group of *comuneros* that had said "no" in 2002. In 2006, a few days after adherents of the Zapatista Army of National Liberation's Other Campaign had traveled to San Salvador Atenco at the urging of Subcomandante Marcos, leader of the Ejército Zapatista de Liberación Nacional (Zapatista Army for National Liberation), to hold a meeting there. A confrontation broke out between police and inhabitants of Texcoco and Atenco, following a badly planned police operative to relocate informal flower vendors in Texcoco. According to Carlos Montemayor and John Ross, behind this confrontation was a counterinsurgency campaign to subjugate the *comuneros*' rebellion in the region. Ultimately, 3,000 armed state and federal police killed two people and arrested 209, including 47 women who reported having been raped or sexually abused under police custody. Those arrested, according to John Ross, included farmers and women, human rights observers, lawyers, alternative reporters, non-Mexicans, and Zapatista adherents.[27] Although the FPDT achieved international visibility and support after the 2006 attack and the megaproject had been put to a halt, in 2014, President Enrique Peña Nieto (responsible for the 2006 repression as Mexico state's governor) gave approval to restart the project, accelerating a legislating process of land-use change in 2,000 ejido hectares through illegal assemblies. Although the human and environmental damage caused by the airport had been widely publicized, and opposition was ongoing,[28] an architecture contest was launched, contracts were allotted, and construction began. When President Andrés Manuel López Obrador took power, the population was invited to vote for or against the airport through a referendum. Although a large percentage of the airport had already been built, the environmental damage—not only in Atenco and Texcoco, but also in adjacent communities—had already been done. According to Al Dabi Olvera, when President López Obrador launched the referendum, discussions about the Nuevo Aeropuerto

---

27 John Ross, "The 'Dirty War' Returns to Mexico," *Narco News Bulletin*, May 18, 2006, http://www.narconews.com/Issue41/article1831.html.

28 No sólo están desplazando gente que vive allí pero habrá consecuencias medio ambientales importantes una vez que el aeropuerto esté funcionando. (Not only inhabitants are being displaced but there will be important environmental consequences once the airport is functioning.)

Internacional de la Ciudad de México (NAICM, or New International Mexico City Airport) were reduced to corruption around the assignation of contracts, the commitment of resources, and the bad image of Mexico if the project were to be canceled, covering the extent of the damage done in the region. A wall 31 km in length now surrounds the half-built NAICM as a metaphor of the conflict that arose among the communities living there. Extensive mining has been done to extract *tezontle* stone to build the airport; the remains of the lake are gone, and an example of the kind of destruction that took place in the adjacent communities of Tequesquinahuac and San Luis Huexotla is the 4 million cubic liters of mud containing boron chlorine, sodium, and carbonate that was extracted from the bottom of the lake they were dumped into.[29] Under the current regime, the new airport project has been moved to Ṣanta Lucía, while the CONAGUA (National Waters Commission) is in charge of transforming the carcass of the Texcoco airport into an ecological, self-sustainable park.

Graded Sovereignty: Modernized Enclaves of Privilege

Areas such as Michoacán, in which the rule of law and state institutions are nearly absent or act against the people's interests (as in Chalamita), the resistance to transnational megaprojects and living with the environmental and social damage seen in Atenco, contrast with first-world luxury enclaves protected by state-of-the-art private and public security technologies that have access to high-end (private) services, jobs, entertainment, health care, and education. In a 2013 *New York Times* editorial, Thomas Friedman frivolously and superficially wrote that Mexico was likely to become a dominant economic power in the twenty-first century, reporting that corruption, crime, the weak rule of law, and drug-related violence are seen as a condition to be lived with and fought, but not as things that define the country or its economy.[30] As I mentioned in the introduction, NAFTA promised to fulfill "a

---

29 Al Dabi Olvera, "Detrás del muro del Nuevo Aeropuerto: la historia que nadie ve," *Pie de página*, June 18, 2018, https://elecciones2018mx.periodistasdeapie.org.mx/2018/06/13/detras-del-muro-del-nuevo-aeropuerto-la-historia-que-nadie-ve.

30 Thomas L. Friedman, "How Mexico Got Back into the Game," *New York Times*, February 23, 2013, https://www.bajacallcenters.com/about/news/how-mexico-got-back-into-the-game.html.

desire for development," and twenty years ago, megalopolises in the South were the "great cities of the North viewed through a warped mirror."[31] That is, before NAFTA was signed, modernization in Mexico was perceived as a distorted version of developed countries: dirty and full of smoke, noise, and toxic fumes; walking around the streets was perceived as risky.[32] Nowadays, fortified buildings and gated communities prevail, and some of the more affluent areas such as Polanco, Anzures, Cuauhtémoc, Condesa, and Roma in Mexico City—with their enhanced surveillance, gentrification, and social cleansing—even became pedestrian-friendly. In these neighborhoods, the city's collective transportation system came to include bike lanes, as in some European and North American cities. Santa Fe, an urban hub for corporate headquarters, office buildings, and luxury residential housing, conveys the impression of living in a North American city, or somewhere in Southeast Asia—if one overlooks the intermittent areas of extreme poverty. And San Pedro Garza García, the richest district of Latin America, in Monterrey, Nuevo León, resembles a wealthy Texan suburb, surrounded by buffering hills and accessed via a single tunnel, therefore isolated from the violence ruling the north of the country.[33] San Pedro Garza García's mayor between 2009 and 2012, Mauricio Fernández Garza, famously created an intelligence body, financed by the affluent inhabitants of the district, with the purpose of combatting and defending themselves from organized crime. As part of his public-safety politics, he created a controversial database of the district's domestic employees as a preventive measure for kidnappings and thefts. Today, some areas of the city and the country remind inhabitants and visitors alike of European and American cities, similar to the way Bucarelli Street and Reforma Avenue did at the turn of the nineteenth century. In this regard, contemporary urban planning and architecture, as we will further see below, are geared toward isolating elites from the poor, conveying the false impression—fueled by writers like Friedman—that they live in a homogenous city within a prosperous country. The areas in which the rule of law and state

---

31 Eduardo Galeano, "To Be Like Them," in *Juárez: the Laboratory of Our Future*, ed. Charles Bowden (New York: Aperture, 1998), 123–27.

32 Galeano, "To Be Like Them."

33 See David J. Danelo, *Toward a U.S.-Mexico Security Strategy: The Geopolitics of Northern Mexico and the Implications for U.S. Policy* (Philadelphia: Foreign Policy Research Institute, 2011), 16, https://www.fpri.org/docs/Toward_a_US_Mexico_Security_Strategy_Danelo.pdf.

institutions are absent or manifest as counterinsurgency against resistance to transnational megaprojects and self-defense groups contrast with these first-world luxury enclaves protected by high-end private security technology, with access to the best private education and health services, as well as jobs, entertainment, and so forth.

These opposing perceptions of neoliberal Mexico cannot be reduced to President Peña Nieto's efforts to change the image of Mexico from "Drug War Zone" to "Free Trade Poster Child,"[34] but should rather be attributed to the differentiated reality of the country. The refrain "the world has never been better" is not exclusive to a one-sided view of Mexico. As Žižek notes, such a view of the world invaded the (right-wing) mass media and finance publications worldwide after the 2008–2009 crisis and is an example of the unevenness of neoliberal development and progress.[35] "Progress," in turn, appears as the incomplete realization of a social and economic project. In Mexico, a token of progress—as well as the obstacle to political and economic progress, according to Jorge G. Castañeda, as we will see below[36]—is considered to be the presence of the middle class. In September 2012, as his term was about to come to an end, President Felipe Calderón stated that Mexico had become a middle-class nation: "Mexican families have improved their possibilities of access to housing, cars, goods like computers and electronics, health and education and entertainment services—basic products that characterize the middle class worldwide."[37] Calderón's statement was echoed by an online World Bank publication, which reported that from 2003 to 2009, the middle class (defined here as people who are neither poor nor vulnerable, but not rich, and schooled up to 12 years of age) grew by 50 percent. This means that 17 percent of the Mexican population would have joined the middle class

---

34 Paul Imison, "The Ultimate Mexican Hype Machine: The Myth of the Aztec Tiger," *Counterpunch*, March 29, 2013, http://www.counterpunch.org/2013/03/29/the-myth-of-the-aztec-tiger. See also Jenaro Villamil, "Bienvenido a la recesión, Sr. Peña," *Proceso*, October 1, 2013, http://www.proceso.com.mx/?p=354274.

35 Slavoj Žižek, "The World Has Never Been Better," *The Guardian*, February 17, 2013, http://www.guardian.co.uk/commentisfree/2013/feb/17/free-market-fundamentalists-think-2013-best.

36 See his *Mañana Forever: Mexico and the Mexicans* (New York: Knopf, 2011).

37 Felipe Calderón, quoted in Jorge Ramos, "México se convierte en nación de clase media: FCH," *El Universal*, September 25, 2012, http://www.eluniversal.com.mx/notas/872400.html.

in the past decade (and that neoliberal policies had, of course, succeeded).[38] But where is this new middle class? A *New York Times* article published at the end of 2013 published reports on the middle class from the Bajío (a region that comprises the states of Aguascalientes, Jalisco, Guanajuato, Querétaro, San Luis Potosí, and Querétaro) that emerged as the car industry flourished in the region. Ultimately, 100,000 jobs were created, and 30 percent of them were for young people who had been educated in universities specializing in engineering, aeronautics, and biotechnology. Alluding to the displacement of the car industry from the US Midwest to Mexico's Bajío, the article also underscores how the educated or white-collar workers at General Motors, Ford, Chrysler, Honda, Mazda, Nissan, Audi, and Volkswagen were employed based on merit, thanks to international business and the liberalization of markets. The article concludes that although these white-collar employees are making a fraction of what their equivalents in the United States used to make, they have now joined the middle class.[39] But how substantial or precarious is the status of that emergent middle class in the Mexican Bajío?

One of the contention points of the renegotiation of NAFTA was precisely the car industry. The Trump administration disparaged NAFTA, and after difficult negotiations, in 2018 it was replaced by USMCA, the United States-Mexico-Canada Agreement. The key point (one of six) dealt with the car industry and was driven by Donald Trump's policy of "making America great again" by bringing back manufacturing jobs to the United States. Modifications in the original trade agreement were made in order to incentivize automakers to increase the amount of North American parts they use in their cars and light trucks. USMCA also mandated that automakers manufacture 40 percent of their motor vehicles in factories where assembly workers are being paid US $16 an hour. In sum, to increase manufacturing in the United States, USMCA will have raised production costs for North American automakers, and the dreamy Mexican middle-class life at the Mexican Bajío is under threat because automation has reshaped North American manufacturing and the work force. For instance, San Luis Potosí, the Bajío's automation hub, runs

38 "La clase media mexicana creció en la última década," *Banco Mundial*, November 13, 2012, http://www.bancomundial.org/es/news/feature/2012/11/13/mexico-middle-class-grows-over-past-decade.

39 Damien Cave, "In Middle of Mexico, a Middle Class Rises," *New York Times*, November 18, 2013, https://www.nytimes.com/2013/11/19/world/americas/in-the-middle-of-mexico-a-middle-class-is-rising.html.

the risk of getting squeezed between leading automation countries that can offer more advanced manufacturing and countries that can offer lower costs and labor. As Amy Guthrie points out, the impacts of automation in the work force were not integrated into the USMCA negotiation. As robots are getting cheaper and easier to integrate into production, Mexico risks losing many of the car-industry jobs it has gained thanks to low-cost labor.[40]

This is why it is very possible that the newly middle-class Mexican citizens born under President Felipe Calderón's regime were incorporated into the economy not as workers, but primarily as consumers—and debtors.[41] This is highlighted by Calderón's definition of the middle class: to be middle class means to have access to housing, all kinds of goods, (private) education, and health care. Following Aditya Nigam, development implies a "global hypermodernity" as a plentiful utopia of shopping malls, casinos, and superhighways, where consumption and debt are the rule.[42] In neoliberal societies, there is thus an elaborate network of systems, processes, apparatuses, and relations that work to produce individuals as middle-class consumers (albeit, nominally) by forming their desiring subjectivities in the Western image—and Mexico is no exception.

As I mentioned above, in the official Mexican narrative, progress is embodied in, and yet hampered by, the very middle class of newly indebted consumers that the State, under Calderón, boasted of having created through neoliberal policies. As numbers under Enrique Peña Nieto contradicted the narrative of the emerging middle class, President Andrés Manuel López Obrador's election campaign was precisely designed for the urban politicized middle class (precarized by neoliberal policies and with leftist sensibility) primarily concentrated in the country's capital. President López Obrador's main slogans were grounded on leading a war against corruption (especially against corrupt politicians and the oligarchy) and against the decadence of the ostentatious political class and the elite. He further promised to boost economic growth, to cease crime and violence, and to establish a referendum and a truth

---

40 Amy Guthrie, "While Negotiators Talk NAFTA, Mexicans Grapple with a Automation," *The Wilson Quarterly* (Summer 2018), https://www.wilsonquarterly.com/quarterly/the-grinding-gears-of-north-america/while-negotiators-talk-nafta-mexicans-grapple-with-automation.

41 See Andrés Lajous, "Verse en la clase media," *Nexos*, February 27, 2014, http://andreslajous.nexos.com.mx/?p=1802.

42 Adita Nigam, *Desire Named Development* (New Delhi: Penguin Group, 2011), 3.

committee for two of the most controversial political cases under Enrique Peña Nieto: Atenco's ongoing struggle against the airport and the murders of the forty-three students from Ayotzinapa in Iguala, Guerrero, in 2014.

We should note that the middle class that brought Andrés López Obrador to power had been conceived by the previous regimes as the main obstacle for national progress. In his 2011 book, *Mañana Forever? Mexico and the Mexicans*, right-wing intellectual Jorge G. Castañeda attempts to answer a question that has intrigued Mexican male thinkers, from José Vasconcelos, Alfonso Reyes, and Octavio Paz, to Samuel Ramos and Carlos Monsiváis: the nature of the Mexican national character. Based on interviews, polls, and statistics, Castañeda explores the "nature" of the nation's middle class and concludes by defining the essential traits of Mexicans: an aversion to market liberalization (a view held by the urban politicized left middle class who voted for Andrés Manuel López Obrador), corruption, and the incapacity of participating in community action. Moreover, he argues that the Mexican middle class despises conflict and suffers from a dysfunctional anti-American individualism that ignores social participation and likes to negotiate behind closed doors, as opposed to seeking consensus. These tendencies, according to Castañeda, clashed with the pressing need (under Felipe Calderón) to open up the economy to the globalized world and impede the consolidation of a plentiful and effective democracy. Mexico's main obstacle, in his view, was therefore the national, inborn aversion to conflict and competition. For Castañeda, the problem is that the middle class believes in protectionism and subsidies—the very welfare state that the current regime is apparently in the process of reviving—but demonizes privatization. Therefore, in Castañeda's view, the middle class benefited from economic liberalization (following Felipe Calderon's discursive line), but they were averse to the open market, private initiative, and foreign investment; supposedly, this was the result of citizens having cultivated an irrational and anachronistic character, and it had been the main obstacle for the country's progress.[43] In the context of Jorge Castañeda's arguments of the regressive middle class—a position that is echoed by President Andrés Manuel López Obrador, who accuses critics of budget cuts, populist policies like cash handouts, or those highlighting the ongoing waves of violence of being "conservative"—Mexican official

43 Isabel Turrent, "Reseña de *Mañana o pasado. El misterio de los mexicanos* de Jorge G. Castañeda," *Letras Libres*, August 11, 2011, http://www.letraslibres.com/revista/libros/el-caracter-nacional.

intellectuals and academics dictated that, because of Mexicans' "love" of stagnation, a Deng Xiaoping figure was needed to direct the country toward development, carrying out necessary reforms in order to assure growth. Thus, after thirty years of neoliberal reforms, Mexican technocrats, official intellectuals, and the corporate class envisioned and promoted a Mexican version of "Capitalism with Asian Values"—defined by Žižek as a dynamic and efficient form of capitalism functioning within an authoritarian state[44]—for the supposed sake of the country's prosperity.[45] And this might be what we have voted for in 2018. As in many other places in the world, President Andrés Manuel López Obrador's policies and public discourse do appear to be a version of left-wing authoritarian capitalism, in which the former neoliberal technocratic rhetoric has been supplanted by a discourse of development, restatization of the economy, and revival of the welfare state not by reconstructing its institutions ravaged by neoliberalism, but mainly through cash handouts. We now have a version of neoliberalism grounded on "authoritarian capitalism with left-wing values" (as in Argentina, under the Kirchners, for instance). Now the middle class is too expensive, and it serves an obstacle to rescuing the poor from "grassroots development" based on extractivism of primary resources promoted by the current regime.

It must be noted that in a different context, official intellectuals' assessment and critique of "Mexican backwardness" (posited as the incapacity to undertake the changes required to grow economically due to the rejection of institutional reforms that would assure those changes) at the turn of the twenty-first century echoed not only the prescriptive recommendations of the IMF and World Bank—as a surreptitious infiltration of market-driven truths into the domains of culture and the media[46]—but also the late-eighteenth-century Bourbon Reforms of Mexico City. In late-colonial Mexico, revisions

---

44 Slavoj Žižek, "Capitalism with Asian Values," *Aljazeera*, November 13, 2011, http://www.aljazeera.com/programmes/talktojazeera/2011/10/2011102813360731764.html.

45 Lorenzo Meyer, "Por sus frutos la conoceréis (a la economía)," *Reforma*, June 6, 2013; and Isabel Turrent, "Reseña de *Mañana o pasado*."

46 See Yevgeny Kuznetsov and Carl Dahlman, *Mexico's Transition to a Knowledge-Based Economy* (Washington, DC: The World Bank Institute, 2008); and M. Ayhan Kose, Guy M. Meredith, and Christopher M. Towe, "How Has NAFTA Affected the Mexican Economy? Review and Evidence," *IMF Working Paper* WP/04/59 (April 2004, http://www.imf.org/external/pubs/ft/wp/2004/wp0459.pdf.

were imposed on the municipal framework in the name of improving health and welfare for all city residents. Back then, however, the problems faced by the population were somewhat different: disease, waste and garbage, limited access to water, poorly paved and flooded streets, and dirty markets. The renovations program carried out by city officials, according to Sharon Bailey Blasco, reflected the anxieties of the emerging elite, surrounding the fact that rich and poor people coexisted intimately, and that there was no separation between the public and private spheres. In this context, the reforms were geared toward reshaping plebeian culture, as the elite blamed the ills of the city on the "unruly and polluting activities of the lower classes," such as public drunkenness and nudity, defecating on the streets, and a lack of personal hygiene. Therefore, the city's reorganization project was inseparable from a re-education of the urban poor, changing their "traditional" or backward behavior into "modern" behavior, both productive and nonthreatening.[47]

Specifically, Castañeda's description of the backwardness of the Mexican middle class—potentially remediable, as he pointed out—resonates with the colonial elite's perception of "those below" and the discursive aspects of the reforms they imposed on them (attended by physical punishment if they were noncompliant). Nowadays, notions of "democracy," "development," "betterment," "security," "efficiency," "sustainability," "design," "autonomy," "creativity," "green urbanism," and "self-sufficiency" are the excuses used to model new ways of life and imply a similar behavioral "correction"; the results, as I mentioned above, include (self-)exploitation, slavery, and death. These concepts, moreover, revolve around the surreptitious privatization of government services and functions and the systemic and ongoing nationwide process of displacement and dispossession behind extractivism. The reason why Jorge G. Castañeda chose to posit the middle class as a token for Mexican identity is twofold: it implies that the middle class comprises the majority of the country (which is clearly not the case, despite his, Calderón's, and the World Bank's assessments), and it makes sense in this age of social control, by way of what Gabriel Tarde and Maurizio Lazzarato call "the public(s)." For them, as public opinion is increasingly fabricated by the corporate media and addressed to the middle class, the receptors bear the potential to influence other minds; the fundamental problem here is the creation of consensual subjectivities acting upon one another. For example, I have often heard the

47 See Sharon Bailey Blasco, *Constructing Mexico City: Colonial Conflicts over Culture, Space, and Authority* (New York: Palgrave Macmillan, 2010).

following description of people from Oaxaca: "They like their old ways, they do not like progress, they are not interested in modernity, they are backward." In this sense, "improvement" and "development" are measures serving to lubricate the system and the perfect means to condition citizens as subjects aspiring to become middle-class (and indebted) consumers.[48] In a society in which privilege is inherited, moreover (at the end of 2012, the poor were 53.3 percent of the population), the gaps between the poor, the "middle class," and the rich are wider than ever. The 1 percent live in a social and material universe entirely distinct from the rest, rendering redundant notions of equality and democratic access. Indeed, many have defined neoliberalism as a form of class warfare, and the ongoing assault on organized labor in Mexico—including the dismantling of the National Electricity Company's Union in 2010, the Mining Union Section 65 in Cananea in 2013, and Enrique Peña Nieto's efforts to destroy the Public School Teacher's Union—is the result of the systemic drive to segregate the working class from the rest of society and the economy. Under President Andrés Manuel López Obrador, the center of Mexican policies are "the poor" and "Indigenous populations," both figures that are highly idealized and still subject to the same neoliberal (and colonial) measures of betterment as before.

Neoliberal Mexico City: Zones of Graded Sovereignty

Despite the fact that, with the introduction of neoliberal policies, the Mexican industry began shifting its center of gravity away from the center of the country, the Federal District (or now CDMX) is still the political, media, cultural, and educational core of the country. The past thirty years of neoliberal reforms have influenced its politics, society, and culture industry, creating new city sites that accurately represent the reforms; for instance, by optimizing the conditions for the easy flow of people, goods, and money, thus translating the neoliberal logic into spatial and sensible terms. The districts (*delegaciones*) are governed differentially, with securitized enclaves of privilege coexisting side by side with misery belts.

48 See Maurizio Lazzarato, "De las sociedades disciplinarias a las sociedades de control," *Revista Euphorion*, no. 5, (July/December 2009), 46, http://revistaeuphorion.files.wordpress.com/2012/05/euphorion_5_cerebro_y_estetica_julio-dic_2009.pdf.

The neoliberal logic also expresses itself in the organization of everyday life by excluding and creating regimes of exception and displacement disguised as policies of optimization, development, and betterment. Leftist mayors (e.g., Andrés Manuel López Obrador, Marcelo Ebrard, Miguel Ángel Mancera) implemented apparently progressive city policies, such as gay marriage and populist urban attractions, like the massive free ice-skating rinks in the Zócalo and in three of the city's districts, artificial beaches during spring break in poor districts of the city, bike lanes, and affordable bike rentals as a supplement to public transportation in affluent areas of the city. There was also the memorable Timbiriche concert (a pop band with children singers popular in the 1980s who have reunited sporadically as grown-ups to perform concerts) to celebrate the Mexican revolution on November 20, 2018, at the Zócalo. But these policies have merely served to whitewash or hide the fact that urban space had become an object of massive surveillance, restriction, gentrification, displacement, and social cleansing. Indeed, a private superhighway, the "Supervía Poniente," was built on forcibly expropriated terrain and on an ecological reserve, to the detriment of a much-needed expansion of green areas and the public transportation system. This megaproject prompted a struggle against land expropriation in the La Malinche neighborhood in La Magdalena Contreras district, northwest of the city. The government announced the expropriation of over one hundred homes in the area by issuing a decree in 2010. The neighbors created the Vecinos del Frente Amplio contra la Supervía Poniente (Neighbors of the Ample Front against the Supervía Poniente), mobilizing against the loss of their properties.[49] But in spite of the pacific civil resistance, works for the highway began in 2010. The movement responded by setting up a camp occupying the expropriated lands, but riot police were sent in January of 2011 and in July and November of 2012 to attack the occupiers. In the last attack, the protesters were forcefully expelled by 300 riot police and 500 workers with heavy machinery who forcefully continued the construction of the Supervía. Major Marcelo Ebrard justified the attack as a "legitimate use of public force," earning the accusation of "authoritarian left"

---

49 See Miriam Alfie, "Supervía Poniente: conflicto social y visión urbano-ambiental," *Estudios demográficos y urbanos* 28, no. 3, (September/December 2013), http://www.scielo.org.mx/scielo.php?script=sci_arttext&pid=S0186-72102013000300735&lng=es&nrm=i&tlng=es; and "La Supervía, cueste lo que cueste," *Proceso*, (August 2010 https://www.proceso.com.mx/80993/la-supervia-cueste-lo-que-cueste.

by movement leader Cristina Barrios. In the last confrontation, homes were razed with caterpillar trucks, Israel-Palestine–conflict style.

Other developer-driven megaprojects geared toward changing the fabric of Mexico City with upscale mixed-use areas, housing complexes, and entertainment areas were Campus Biometrópolis,[50] a medical research center in the southern part of the city, designed by Norman Foster, that did not get built; the New Polanco Masterplan, or the "Mexican Manhattan," which includes about forty-two development projects including Plaza Carso, designed by Fernando Romero; the Alameda Central in the historic downtown; the Súper Arena, an entertainment complex in Atzcapozalco, opened in 2012; Ciudad Jardín Bicentenario, a mixed-use district (sports and commerce) built on an ancient waste deposit in Ciudad Nezahualcóyotl and opened in 2009, and others.[51] These urban projects were built by subcontracted or private companies, justified on the one hand by the presupposition—pushed forward by corporations, private interests, and official intellectuals—that the government is too overwhelmed to be able to manage and supply Mexico City, and that the aid of civil society and private investment is thus necessary. On the other hand, the government of the city, through a scheme in the Fiscal Code termed "contribution to betterment measures," has sought to transfer the cost of urban renovation to the citizens. A concrete case is the rehabilitation of President Masaryk Avenue in Polanco, half of which was expected to be covered by the 2,700 neighbors and business owners around the avenue. The project under Mayor Miguel Ángel Mancera included installing hydraulic concrete as pavement, rehabilitating sidewalks, a fountain in the Arquímides roundabout, subterranean electric and Internet cabling, new urban furniture, security cameras, and the substitution of streetlights and signals for new ones. Some of the inhabitants refused to pay because they considered it to be an additional tax to the "predial," or property tax, and demanded to be exempted from participating.[52] In spite of the opposition encountered, the scheme will

---

50 This project was suspended in 2012. See: Arturo Páramo, "Biometrópolis, el proyecto que no prosperó," *Excélsior*, October 14, 2012, http://www.excelsior.com.mx/2012/10/14/comunidad/864232#imagen-1.

51 See Ivonne Santoyo Orozco, "The Apparatus of Ownership," *Scapegoat Journal 06: NAFTA/Mexico City*, no. 6 (March 2014).

52 Laura Gómez y Alejandro Cruz, "Analizarán esquemas para concluir obra en Masaryk, ante la negativa vecinal a pagar," *La Jornada*, February 20, 2014, www.jornada.unam.mx/2014/02/20/capital/038n1cap; Rocío González, "En Polanco desconocen que deberán pagar remodelación," *La Jornada*, January

be implemented in other areas of the city, justifying it with the argument that the winners are the owners whose real-estate properties prices rise with the renovations. Initiatives like these have intensified the progressive erasure of the distinction between private and public in the spatial organization of the environments we inhabit.[53]

According to Jamie Peck and Adam Tickell, in the past two decades, cities have become incubators for the major political and ideological strategies that have helped maintain neoliberal dominance.[54] As Mexico City has become globalized, some of its areas have been transformed into strategic economic spaces, concentrating material and immaterial flows necessary to global processes of production, creation, and exchange; for example, as providers of services needed by corporations, such as insurance or accounting. In this regard, the transnationalization of corporations has meant the homogenization of the city through the creation of office districts (e.g., Santa Fe, the Reforma Financial Corridor, Cuicuilco), residential spaces (e.g., Nuevo Polanco, Interlomas, Casas Geo), and spaces for entertainment and consumption (from Tlalpan, Satélite, and Cuauhtémoc to Ecatepec, Las Águilas, Tacubaya, Chalco, and Mixcoac). The historic downtown has been rebuilt and partially gentrified, and the Condesa, Colonia Roma, San Miguel Chapultepec, and San Rafael boroughs, which may be considered the city's "creative zones," have undergone processes of intense gentrification. These transformations simply mirror similar processes—as well as modern and minimalist architectural styles—that have materialized in other parts of the world over the past two decades. The transformations the city has undergone obey the perceived

---

30, 2014, www.jornada.unam.mx/2014/01/30/capital/037n1cap; Laura Gómez, Alejandro Cruz, and Raúl Llanos, "Tesorero: impuesto por mejoras, sólo en las zonas de alta plusvalía," *La Jornada*, January 29, 2014, www. jornada.unam.mx/2014/01/29/capital/037n1cap; and Alejandro Cruz, "Pagarán vecinos de Mazaryk (Polanco) las renovaciones al área," *La Jornada*, January 24, 2014, www.jornada.unam.mx/2014/01/24/capital/033n1cap.

53 Israel Rodríguez y Alejandro Cruz, "Ofrece Mancera seguir apoyando a constructores, para evitar pérdidas," *La Jornada*, 21 de Mayo de 2014, www.jornada.unam.mx/2014/05/21/capital/037n1cap. There is even a new law and official program of Public-Private Associations. See the website of the PIAPPEM (Programa para el Impulso de Asociaciones Público-Privadas en los Estados Mexicanos) or Program for the Support of Public-Private Association in Mexican States: www.piappem.org.

54 Jamie Peck and Adam Tickell, "Neoliberalizing Space," *Antipode* 34, no. 3 (July 2002), 390.

necessity to face and solve urban problems in order to be able to characterize the city as a global city. Mexico City has important multinational corporate presence and prestige based on the concentration of artistic and scientific elites. These traits, according to anthropologist Néstor García Canclini, make CDMX high in concentration of economic and cultural capital, comparable with global cities such as Barcelona, Brussels, New York, Paris, and Hong Kong. According to Canclini, the problem is that, because development in the city has been "uneven," the city is stuck between disintegration and globalization. That is to say, the city is not safe enough, and neither does it provide efficient services or fast connections, which make productivity abate due to heavy traffic on the streets. In this manner, for Canclini, the city exists between its potential as a global city and its deficient realization.[55] Evidently, urban development projects in the last twenty years have focused on compensating for those shortcomings. The problem of the dichotomy established by Canclini is that "deficient" aspects of the city will be eternal subjects to betterment. That is to say, deficiencies are the direct result of neoliberal policies, because in the global world, enclaves of privilege inevitably coexist with those of poverty.

An example of an effort to solve the "failures" of the city was Andrés Manuel López Obrador's (who was mayor of Mexico City between 2000 and 2005) decision, with Carlos Slim, to renew the Centro Histórico. In 2003, López Obrador and Slim hired New York City's former mayor Rudolph Giuliani for an assessment on security problems and solutions, following the premise that "security attracts investment." Giuliani recommended attacking crime at the root of "quality-of-life" crimes: *limpiaparabrisas* (or car window cleaners) in Reforma, prostitutes at La Merced, poor children hanging around public buildings, ambulant sellers, and more. The Penal Code was modified, and theft of merchandise worth as little as one peso was made punishable by jail.[56] In the name of development, and with the purpose of inserting Mexico City in global processes, poverty was criminalized, and social cleansing was justified. In this regard, Washington consensus policies of graded government intervention and trade expansion have transformed not only how Mexico City looks and functions, but also the ways in which people live and work.

55 Néstor García Canclini, "Mexico City, 2010: Improvising Globalization," in *Other Cities, Other Worlds*, ed. Andreas Huyssen (Durham, NC: Duke University Press, 2008), 49–53.

56 John Ross, *El monstruo: Dread and Redemption in Mexico City* (New York: Nation Books, 2010), 22.

After six years of construction, the price of real estate in the area had considerably risen (Slim owns between seventy-two and one hundred and sixty buildings in the Centro).

As in other global cities, urban planning and design had become major: while they materialize to furnish spaces for neoliberalism to thrive in, they create ready-to-consume modes and forms of life, inseparable from signs circulating in the sensible regime that have hypostatized in the hypermodern global utopia of consumption. The homogenization of the environment, brought about by corporatization, coexists with spatial differentiation, as urban space is more and more polarized, introducing new spatial legibilities and regimes of exception: slums and illegal settlements, or misery belts, in Ciudad Neza, Chalco, Santa Fe, Ecatepec, and Jaltenco; hyper-securitized luxury enclaves for the rich in Interlomas, Pedregal, San Ángel, Lomas de Chapultepec, Santa Fe, Valle Escondido, and Bosques de las Lomas; for the upper-middle and middle classes, Coyoacán, Tepepan, and San Jerónimo; and for the working class, what I call "subcontracted mass social housing," conceived as city dormitories and named after the companies that build them—Casas Geo, Urbi, Ara, Sare, Homex, and others. Mexico City's public version of this kind of housing is called *Ciudades Bicentenario* (Bicentennial Cities). Under President Carlos Salinas de Gortari, a portion of the working class was transferred to minuscule isolated boxes throughout Mexico, without infrastructure, and considerably far away from the big cities. The price for easy access to a mortgage was tolerating long commutes to the workplace and lack of access to basic services. Built quickly on cheap land and with inadequate materials, these projects are the result of a mere impulse to make profit. Construction and subcontracted construction companies delivered suburban-like environments that are now falling apart and too far from cities, jobs, and basic services. Many of these "massive social housing" developments have become uninhabitable and are now a social problem at a national scale. In the past few years, over five million houses were abandoned either because the quality of the construction is faulty, because they are in environmental high-risk zones, or because the families were unable to pay the mortgage.[57] At the same time, these projects gave shape to a new form of life for the working class living in precarious conditions. Relocating them to peripheral zones, having "cleansed" the city, the working and precarious class was transferred to these

57 Patricia Muñoz Díaz, "5 millones de casas abandonadas," *La Jornada*, September 4, 2013, www.jornada.unam.mx/2013/04/09/sociedad/039n1soc.

new places, sterilized of references to popular traditions, urban social movements, Indigenous cultural resistance, and more. "Massive subcontracted private housing" consists of grids of houses measuring 93 square meters, each with approximately 50 square meters of built area and about 6 meters of street façade. These "neighborhoods" were conceived around an idealized and aestheticized single-family dwelling, translated into a spatial calculus of maximized profit and following an aspirational model.[58] Surrounded by walls imitating upper-class gated communities, the neighborhoods have one or two entrances in which a docile and orderly working class lives. Like their middle- and upper-class counterparts, health and happiness are intrinsically linked to security and control.

According to Ivonne Santoyo Orozco, who has extensively studied this form of urban development particular to Mexico, there is a paradox inherent to the policy for fulfillment of a social promise—the constitutional right to housing, as the means of providing housing have often run counter to the very principle of guaranteeing such a thing in Mexico under neoliberalism. The INFONAVIT (Institute of the National Fund for Worker's Housing) was created in 1972 as a financial mechanism to encourage home ownership, under the principle that the extension of property rights was crucial for ameliorating poverty. With neoliberal reforms, housing was financialized, shifting from being a social concern to becoming an administrative, technical, and financial one. Private construction companies such as GEO, ARA, and HOMEX became partners with INFONAVIT, amalgamating private development with state-administered housing. According to Santoyo Orozco, under neoliberalism, housing became a means of "financial inclusion," with debt serving as an instrument for government management. Housing, in other words, became both a device for the expansion of new markets and a device to construct power relations.[59] Under the regime of President Vicente Fox, money was poured into the sector and vast housing tracts began to mushroom outside many major Mexican cities, following the dominant model of cheap housing. The fact that INFONAVIT (a public institution) provided a steady stream of funds to private developers meant a transfer of wealth from the public sector

---

58 Ivonne Santoyo Orozco, "From the Right to Housing to the Right to Credit: The Drama of Ownership in Mexico," in *A House is Not Just a House: Projects on Housing*, ed. Tatiana Bilbao (New York: Columbia Books on Architecture and the City, 2018), 117.

59 Santoyo Orozco, "From the Right to Housing," 117.

to the private, and exploitation of the indebted poor, and made the social promise of housing an instrument of financial volatility.

In the spatial differentiation logic, modernization, however, has meant that the city has barely changed since the nineteenth century. According to Michael Johns, by 1890, Mexico City had acquired the principal geographic feature that defines it to this day: a division into rich West and poor East.[60] Fragmenting even further the landscape of civil society, those governed as citizens coexist with the underclass, who are governed as noncitizens with a different set of rights and possibilities to access (e.g., credit, health care, education, food). This, alongside the proliferation of physical barriers, surveillance, and the exclusion of the majority, has further fragmented the landscape of civil society, while allowing for the emergence of new types of apolitical insurgent actors; for example, the recent figure of the narco-insurgent,[61] or the "ninis." Inequality, as we have seen, is a matter of fact, an endemic to the kind of development brought about by neoliberal policies, which have not only given shape to how people live and work, but also to the ways in which people are being actively dispossessed, their lives and livelihoods rendered precarious. The socio-spatial differentiation that characterizes Mexico City is mirrored in urban and rural regions in the rest of the country, where new development areas have been created, enhancing the "natural economic vocation" of distinct regions that have different roles to play in the Mexican economy; for instance, the conurbation of Tijuana-San Diego, which is grounded on economic integration between both cities supplying complementary economic activities. San Diego specializes in high-tech activities, while Tijuana is oriented toward low-skill labor manufacturing and services. Consequentially, there is a marked difference of income and infrastructure. Tijuana, moreover, is known to be a hybrid city in which a state of exception reigns with continual permissiveness as a site for sex, drug, and pharmaceuticals trade. US citizens also visit the city for cheap health care or retirement homes. While the San Diego economy is characterized by high productivity and technological development, the economy of Tijuana is based on maquiladoras (assembly

---

60 Michael Johns, *The City of Mexico in the Age of Díaz* (San Antonio: University of Texas Press, 1998).

61 See Ioan Grillo, *El Narco: Inside Mexico's Criminal Insurgency* (New York: Bloomsbury Press, 2011); and John Ross, "The Next Mexican Revolution," *Coutnerpunch*, September 21, 2010, http://www.counterpunch.org/2010/09/21/the-next-mexican-revolution.

manufacturing plants), services, and tourism. The city was established as a Special Economic Zone (SEZ) in the 1960s and contrasts highly with San Diego economic clusters, which are agglomerations of interrelated industries and businesses (i.e., entertainment, tourism, high-tech communications, aerospace, biotechnology, and biomedical products). In Tijuana, the maquiladora activities are oriented to the manufacture and assembly of temporarily imported inputs to be re-exported to the United States.[62] The region is characterized by extreme contrasts—more than those present across the country. In the canal known as "el bordo," which constitutes the dividing line between Mexico and the United States, deportees have built precarious living structures, known as "ñongos," as a waiting area before they try returning to the United States. These informal settlements are prey to regular police raids, who destroy these already precarious homes for the inhabitants of the canal, which are assembled with recycled material, trash, tarps, rugs, plastic, cables, cloth, and wood. The inhabitants of "el bordo" are Mexicans without documents deported from the United States (Obama's government deported over two million people). They find themselves in a situation of homelessness, unemployment, social disconnection (many of them do not even know Spanish) and are prey to addiction and crime, as depicted in the 2015 documentary by Ricardo Silva, *Navajazo*.

Tijuana has also been a victim of the same inefficient housing schemes that came out from the public/private association between the Instituto Mexicano del Seguro Social (Mexican Institute for Social Welfare) and corporations like URBI, Casas Geo, and others. The city was direly affected by the 2008 economic crisis, and when the housing market crashed, it left a trail of ruined social housing that had boomed in Tijuana since 2000 to provide affordable housing in the periphery of the city. Visual artist Mónica Arriola created a series of photographs, *Social Disinterest* (2013), documenting these obsolete urban models, incomplete serial housing, or abandoned homes in ruins.

By means of treaties such as NAFTA, the Mesoamerican Integration and Development Project (PPP-MIDP), and the Pact for Mexico, the national economy was further fragmented into urban and regional industrial systems.[63]

62 Jorge Eduardo Mendoza Cota, "Economic Integration and Cross-Border Economic Organizations: The Case of San Diego-Tijuana," *Estudios Fronterizos* 18, no. 35 (January–April 2017): 22–46.

63 Neil Brenner and Nik Theodore, "Cities and the Geographies of Actually Existing Neolibrealism," *Antipode* 34, no. 3 (July 2002), 370.

The multiplication of differentiated zones of economic production, as well as variegated governance policies across the national territory, promotes the differential regulation of populations who can either be connected to or disconnected from the global circuits of capital. Moreover, certain regions are characterized by being flexibly managed so that corporations can have strong indirect influence over the political conditions of citizens with goals of enhancing the "predetermined economic vocations of each region";[64] this is also known as "zoning."

For example, the "economic and industrial vocation" of Mexico City has been said to be the creative economy, which implies exploiting human capital by developing talent to trigger productive and living activities that would attract applied technology.[65] Another instance of "economic vocation" can be found in the six northern states: the fact that they share a border with the United States, the area's semi-arid climate with limited water resources (which restricts other productive activities), and the availability of cheap labor make maquiladora industrialization the "natural economic vocation" of the North. Similar to the urban conglomerate constituted by Guangzhou-Shenzhen-Hong Kong—in which the first two cities are devoted to production and the latter to high-end services such as logistics, finances, legal, design and marketing services, and distribution—there are several emerging, binational conurbations, such as San Diego-Tijuana, El Paso-Ciudad Juárez, and Matamoros-Brownsville along the Rio Grande-Bravo. Some 3,700 maquiladoras have mushroomed on the Mexican side under the regime of Export Processing Zones or Special Economic Zones (SEZ), characterized by federal law exemptions regarding taxes, quotas, and labor in order to make the goods produced there globally competitive.[66] According to Valeria Moy, the purpose of SEZs is to generate development in specific areas or industries as a solution to decrease growth inequality and contribute to development in

---

64 Ong, *Neoliberalism as Exception*, 77.

65 Simón Levy Dabah, "Nacionalidades creativas y capitalismo chilango," *Animal Politico*, October 23, 2012, http://www.animalpolitico.com/blogueros-el-chino-taliban/2012/10/23/nacionalidades-creativas-y-neocapitalismo-chilango/#axzz2ijsZhLdo.

66 See "Special Economic Zones: Performance, Lessons Learned, and Implications for Zone Development," *The World Bank Group* (Washington, DC: FIAS, 2008), 26, https://www.wbginvestmentclimate.org/uploads/SEZs%20-%20Performance,%20Lessons%20Learned%20and%20Implications%20for%20Zone%20Development.pdf.

backward states. Some of the SEZs are located in geographic regions that are difficult to access, and in order to entice investors to those places, incentives must be offered, like infrastructure expenses and fiscal benefit.[67] Insofar as these spaces can be considered to be global economic infrastructure (they exist in China, the Middle East, and Central and South America and are expanding throughout the world), they function as laboratories for political policy because they are often jurisdictionally independent from their host nations. According to Keller Esterling, these zones (created in the 1970s at the Mexican-American border) are morphing and becoming towns and cities outside of the restrictions of the State and are built through repeatable formulas, creating homogenous spaces anywhere in the world. The construction of infrastructure evokes networks for transportation, communication, or utilities, a hidden substrate of grids, pipes, and wires, but also pools of microwaves beaming from satellites. For Easterling, the Zone is "a quintessential apparatus of the neoliberal state" that represents a form of extra-state administration. President Andrés Manuel López Obrador's megaprojects, such as the Tren Maya in the Yucatán Peninsula, the Istmo Tehuantepec Development Project that includes the Corredor Multimodal Interoceánico connecting the Istmo with the ports in Veracruz, or the Programa Zona Libre de la Frontera Norte (15 km of the Export Processing Zone (EPZ) from Ensenada in Baja California all the way to Tamaulipas), are tools to further economic liberalism and economic rationalization, operating shadow economies within SEZs in which the State serves as its proxy, or camouflage.[68]

As mentioned above, anarchy and lawlessness often reign in the areas surrounding SEZs—but without affecting the production. Moreover, the violence is not simply a result of war among narco-cartels, but it is intrinsically tied to the fact that in the past decade, Mexico lost competition to Asia, and thousands of workers lost their jobs, forcing them into the circuits of narco-capitalism. This was the cause of the explosion of violence.[69] In Ciudad Juárez, for instance, a combination of volatility and precarity prevails, and

67 Valeria Moy, "Zonas Económicas Especiales: ¿Un paso hacia el desarrollo?" *Foreign Affairs Latinoamérica*, August 29, 2016, https://revistafal.com/zonas-economicas-especiales-un-paso-hacia-el-desarrollo.

68 Keller Easterling, *Extrastate-Craft: The Power of Infrastructure Space* (London: Verso Books, 2016), 30.

69 Ed Vulliamy, "Ciudad Juárez is All Our Futures," *The Guardian*, June 20, 2011, http://www.theguardian.com/commentistree/2011/jun/20/war-capitalism-mexico-drug-cartels.

the cartels and the maquiladoras both follow the same free-market business logic. As Charles Bowden has pointed out, Juárez has always been the "laboratory of the future": not a breakdown of the social order, but *the new order* in which massive unemployment and violence coexist within the fragile maquiladora economy.[70]

According to Easterling, the Zone, which she terms "Extrastatecraft," has transformed urban development into infrastructure development, establishing the rules for governing everyday space by creating parking spaces, skyscrapers, garages, streetlights, driveways, airport lounges, highway exits, strip malls, cash machines, tract housing, container ports, industrial parks, call centers, golf courses, and suburbs.[71] The Zone became a repeatable formula, moreover, that generates most of the space in the world; for instance, in the Special Controlled Development Zones (ZEDEC in Spanish) created for the privileged populations in Mexico. The ZEDECs are corporate, residential luxury zones exemplified by Santa Fe and Atizapán, west and north of Mexico City respectively, but also by Interlomas (north of Santa Fe), Puerta de Hierro in Zapopan, Jalisco and Lomas in Puebla, and the entire district of San Pedro Garza García in Monterrey. The ZEDECs are zones of high real-estate development that embody an upper-class utopia where the poor are rendered invisible. A kind of exurbs, they are modeled both after SEZ and after the small cluster of cities that constitute Orange County in California or Hudson Yards in New York, and their design seeks to convey a sense of the highest efficiency, safety, and the idea that "it's good business to live here." For instance, Zona Esmeralda in Atizapán is considered to be the "safest zone in Mexico City," and together with Lomas del Valle and Lomas del Valle Escondido, they constitute a cluster of upper-middle and upper-class housing developments (sixteen gated communities in total), which include shopping, entertainment, and educational complexes, along with an ecological reserve, two golf courses, and an airport. This and other privileged zones of Mexico City constitute concentric zones traversed by a hierarchical division of labor and degrees of access to services: Atizapán, the former village whose arable lands were expropriated to build this housing cluster, has now expanded into a small city that lacks everything a city usually has. More like a misery belt, it

---

70 See Charles Bowden, *Murder City: Ciudad Juárez and the Global Economy's New Killing Fields* (New York: Nation Books, 2010); and Charles Bowden, ed., *Juárez: The Laboratory of Our Future* (New York: Aperture, 1998).

71 Keller Easterling, *Extrastate-Craft*.

largely houses the cheap domestic labor employed in the gated communities to the West. A newspaper ad for Lomas in Puebla expresses, and/or constructs, people's desire to live in such isolated, homogenous, urban conglomerates:

> To live in Lomas means that you, your children, and your parents will recover your freedom; it means that you will be able to go out to the streets without a worry, that you will know that your children are playing in the park, safely riding their bikes on the bicycle path; it means coming home and listening to their stories about their adventures in Lomas. It means that you will be able to relax on a Sunday morning, listening to the sound of water falling, the laughter of people, knowing that you are surrounded by nature, that a coffee is within walking distance, or that you can go shopping without leaving Lomas. It means that you will be able to go jogging or walking at any time of the day you desire, so you can take a break; it means that you will know that you live in a unique place in Puebla.

For intellectual José Steinsleger, these developments are "Bantustans for the rich," comparable to recent projects in Guatemala and Honduras, which he posits as cities "without God, State or law," administered by magnates and ruled by the principle of "security." In Guatemala, there is Paseo de Cayalá, which represents the new, gated urbanism; like the North American suburbs that many of these projects tend to emulate, Paseo de Cayalá is characterized by New Urbanism's nostalgia for village life with its pedestrian-friendly streets. While it offers a cosmopolitan lifestyle, the National Guatemalan Police need a warrant to enter the city, and all of the community's problems are dealt with by an "Owner's Association," who make decisions inside a building inspired by the Lincoln Monument in Washington, DC, and the Parthenon.[72]

Like Paseo de Cayalá, Mexico City's Western Cuajimalpa/Santa Fe district is also premised on modifications of the law. It emerged as part of a larger project under Salinas de Gortari, who established ZEDECs as a legal tool to regulate land use and allow for partnerships between the city's government and private investors or real-estate developers. In this regard, urban planning has legitimized the imposition of controls and decisions to the exclusive benefit of the residential and corporate enclave—to the detriment of most

72 José Steinsleger, "Guatemala y Honduras: ¿Bantustanes para ricos?" *La Jornada*, January 23, 2013, http://www.jornada.unam.mx/2013/01/23/opinion/025a1pol.

citizens' needs.[73] These new developments have greatly exacerbated mechanisms of social exclusion, as populations live under the illusion of existing in a homogenous society.[74]

The legal tool represented by the ZEDECs was Miguel Mancera's (mayor of Mexico City from 2012 to 2018) child-poster project of "Economic Development Zones," or ZODEs (another kind of Extrastatecraft, in Keller Easterling's terms). This project of "strategic urbanism," which has not yet come to fruition, implies the creation of thematic neighborhoods and involves a partnership between the government, civil society, corporations, and academia. For the project, areas of the city would be redesigned, repopulated, and rehabilitated according to five specific economic "vocations" and themes, anchored in specific main buildings: Future Technology City, Creative or Cultural City, Agribusiness City, Government or Administrative City, and Health Care City. World-renowned architects Herzog and de Meuron were hired to design the project. The aim was to create spaces where people would be able to live, hang out, study, work, and have access to culture and entertainment in specific areas—without having to go through the cumbersome ordeal of displacing themselves to other parts of the city to that effect.

Furthering the tendency to segregate and homogenize the population through urban planning, as I mentioned above, the Mesoamerican Integration and Development Project (PPP-MIDP) is a treaty geared toward transforming the southern part of Mexico (and extending to Belize, Colombia, Costa Rica, Dominican Republic, El Salvador, Guatemala, Honduras, Mexico, Nicaragua, and Panama) into a region of megaprojects devoted to tourism, agribusiness, the production of biofuel, hydroelectric plants, and resource extraction. The treaty's purpose, proposed by Vicente Fox in 2001 and launched in 2008, was to better the already existing infrastructure (highways, ports, electricity infrastructure, etc.) in the region, which would allow for the smooth and quick flow of goods and services throughout and toward strategic centers—all within a "competitive" framework. Along with the Plan Mérida (a US-led counter-narco-insurgency plan modeled on the Plan Colombia), the treaty takes into account regional security and implies territorial reordering in order to

---

73 Alfonso Valenzuela, "Santa Fe (México): Megaproyectos para una ciudad dividida", *Cuadernos Geográficos*, 40 (2007–2011), 53–66, http://www.ugr.es/~cuadgeo/docs/articulos/040/040-003.pdf.

74 Margarita Pérez Negrete, "Santa Fe: A 'Global Enclave' in Mexico City," *Journal of Place Management and Development* 2, no. 1 (2009): 33–40.

"liberate" strategic zones, so that transnational corporations can develop their megaprojects, thus displacing farmers, peasants, resisting communities, and drug dealers. It also involves changes in land use, financed by governments and private and transnational entities such as the World Bank.[75] What the PPP-MIDP envisioned for the population is their transfer to "Rural Cities," suburban-like villages (another form of Extrastatecraft) where dispossessed farmers and peasants were (with partial success) relocated to the states of Chiapas and Puebla. The Rural Cities Program was also an experiment in "co-participation" between the public and the private sectors. The program was comparable to the "Prawer Plan," according to which Israel sought to relocate 40,000 Bedouins from the Negev into townships with few municipal facilities. Similarly, the Mexican State intended to concentrate members of isolated communities scattered throughout rural areas, promoting their relocation under the discourse of "access to services" and "quality of life." The motivation behind the Rural Cities Program, however, was evidently more economic than social, and the proposed network of rural integration centers has the ultimate purpose of achieving a more efficient territorial organization by expropriating land from farmers. Once living in Rural Cities, farmers would certainly cease to grow crops for their own consumption, and be forced to work for the mining, agribusiness, or biofuel industries. The "productive conversion" aspect of the program implies that entire communities would and have been obliged to change their forms of life and ways of making a living, lose control over their mode of production, and shift from a position of autonomy to one of dependency on corporations and the State; the suspicious participation of Elektra, Banco Azteca, and BrainPOP education in the program makes it evident that the plan for the inhabitants of rural areas is to incorporate them into the so-called upcoming national middle class of indebted consumers. Evidently, the Rural Cities Program has a counterinsurgency objective as well, echoing Guatemalan "Model Towns" from the 1980s, which relocated communities displaced by the civil war to so-called development poles.[76] Rural Cities are merely another chapter in the ongoing

---

75 Mariela Zunino, "Integración para el despojo: Proyecto Mesoamérica, o la nueva escalada de la apropiación del territorio," *CIEPAC*, no. 584, June 8, 2010, http://www.ciepac.org/boletines/chiapasaldia.php?id=584.

76 Japhy Wilson, "La nueva fase del Plan Puebla-Panamá en Chiapas," *Boletines del CIEPAC*, no. 562, May 30, 2008, http://www.ciepac.org/boletines/chiapasaldia.php?id=562.

history of the dispossession of Indigenous communities; while in the past they were expelled from valleys and fertile lands and pushed to arid mountains, now they are being forced to relocate because their lands are rich in mineral resources, oil, and water.[77] The first Rural Cities were built in Chiapas, and two more were planned for the Sierra Norte in Puebla, but many of them have not been built at all; or, like the "Casas Geo," they have been abandoned or are falling apart. Projects such as Export Processing Zones, Rural Cities, and "Casas Geo" (as well as housing developments geared toward more affluent populations) are social laboratories that normalize the violence embedded in these spaces by determining citizens' terms of subjectivity, survival, and livability; according to Judith Butler and Athena Athanasiou, subjection here implies a sensible subjectivation and a distribution of vulnerability.[78] The application of neoliberal policies in Mexico, therefore, implies that citizens are not only being dispossessed of their traditional modes of life, but they are also being subjected to injurious State and corporate dependency, as well as other modes of sensible subjugation. Moreover, these zoning projects are evidence of the government's policy of selectively reinforcing institutions at the national and local levels, adjusting political space to the demands of global capital, and ensuring their total regulation of spaces only partially linked to or severed from global markets.[79] The articulation of different Extrastatecrafts driven by global production and financial markets in Mexico are examples of how the spatialization of capital subjects populations and communities to political, military, legal, and criminal violence, forcing them into new forms of life ("productive conversion"). Their forms of life, as well as the sensorial and affective perception of the places they inhabit, are thus shaped by corporate interests and values, tending toward both architectural homogenization and socioeconomic differentiation, in many ways normalizing the modes of apprehending and inhabiting landscapes.

The government-led and seemingly unstoppable corporate conversion of rural areas throughout the country somewhat contradicts President Andrés Manuel López Obrador's government policies toward Indigenous communities. In truth, his is a State that reproduces old paternalism toward them,

---

77 José Gil Olmos, "El despojo interminable de los pueblos indígenas, *Proceso*, October 12, 2013), http://www.proceso.com.mx/?p=355293.

78 Judith Butler and Athena Athanasiou, *Dispossession: The Performative in the Political* (Cambridge, UK: Polity Press, 2013).

79 Ong, *Neoliberalism as Exception*, 78.

denying their potential status and their right to become collective political subjects *as communities*. When the president stated, "We have reached out to 9 out of 10 communities,"[80] it meant that the word "community" had been reconverted into a propaganda tool to feed a new institutional Indigenism centered around the historical demands established by the San Andrés Accords:

> Indigenous communities are entities with public rights and districts which recognize themselves as belonging to an indigenous community shall have the faculty to associate freely in order to coordinate their own actions. . . . [Thus] competent authorities will transfer resources in an orderly and timely manner, so they can administer the public funds assigned to them.[81]

If, throughout history, their political condition had been denied, they are recognized as autonomous cultural entities, losing all possibility to have agency in the ways that they and the State and are linked. Reduced to mere cultural subjects, current political policy is not the result of dialogue between communities and the government. At the same time, the machinery of the State has been put to work to intensify their dispossession from their lands, forests, waters, and forms of living and of making a living, resisting being reduced to "extractive zones," and thus to capitalist resource conversion.

The Xico Valley Community Museum: A Tale of Resistance[82]

As I drive away from the Museo Comunitario del Xico in the outskirts of Mexico City, I feel overwhelmed, humbled, and disquieted. I have in my mind the seemingly endless landscape of cement and pollution unfolding from the museum's courtyard, and the image of a sculpture that hangs there from a tree: an anthropomorphic figure suspended from an egg-shaped cage made out of wire and branches, standing on top of random discarded objects—a pile of trash. A sun, made also of wire, is suspended on top of the faceless

80 On September 19, 2019, in his first government report, https://politica.expansion.mx/presidencia/2019/09/02/21-datos-del-primer-informe-de-gobierno-que-presento-amlo.

81 Signed on February 16, 1996, in Chiapas, http://www.cedoz.org/site/content.php?doc=400.

82 An earlier version of this piece was published under the title, "Chronicle of a Visit to the Xico Valley Community Museum Or: Cultural Solidarity in the Globalized Neoliberal Age" in *Afterall* 43 (Spring–Summer 2017).

figure, and I cannot help but think about the sculpture as an allegory of the people of the Chalco Valley.

A century ago, the area was farming land, artificially fabricated by having desiccated the Lake of Chalco—a project that began in the sixteenth century and materialized in subsequent efforts by the Spanish Colony to dry out and channel the lakes upon which the Aztec City Tenochtitlan and adjacent cities were built (which comprised five connected lakes: Zumpango, Xaltocan, Texcoco, Xochimilco, and Chalco). In the 1970s, immigrants from the countryside, looking for opportunities, and modern subjectivities began to settle in the Valley of Chalco on stolen, bought, or appropriated land. Gradually urbanizing the farmland, this migration gave leeway to what today is an incommensurable underclass urban sprawl, named under Carlos Salinas de Gortari's regime in the 1990s, "Valle Chalco Solidaridad." The urban conglomeration of which Chalco is part (along with Iztapalapa and Neza, where the scene of the judo lesson takes place in Alfonso Cuarón's acclaimed *Roma*) has been described as the "biggest slum in the world".[83] Most of its inhabitants work in precarious conditions in the service and informal economy in Mexico City; this means exhausting daily commutes in deficient public transportation, absolutely no labor rights, and access to low-quality credit, infrastructure, housing, commodities, healthcare, education, and food (cancer and diabetes abound). In this region, the State has made itself strategically present since the 1990s: most of Xico lacks basic services like water, education, work, electricity, and health care,[84] but corporate chains of pharmacies, supermarkets, shops, and Christian temples have a strong presence there. In the 1990s, the federal government "invested" there, implementing reforms and laws mostly geared toward favoring the interests of private real-estate projects, water concessions, and other forms of territorial exploitation. Chalco Solidaridad gathers thirteen municipalities and a complex network of grassroots councils, including originary peoples, neighborhood councils, *núcleos ejidales*,[85] communities,

---

83 See Michael Waldrep, "Scenes from Neza: Mexico's Self-Made City," *National Geographic Online*, March 26, 2015, http://voices.nationalgeographic.com/2015/03/26/scenes-from-neza-mexico-citys-self-made-city.

84 Gustavo Magallanes, Atzin Bahena, Amanda Ramos, and Fiorella Fenoglio, "La rebeldía del Valle de Chalco: La lucha contra las aguas negras y el mal gobierno," *Revista Rebeldía*, no. 7, http://revistarebeldia.org/revistas/numero70/06chalco.pdf

85 "Ejido" designates in Mexico communal lands owned and worked by local people, the land commonly distributed equally among them.

NGOs, universities, and various political organizations mobilized around various struggles; a few kilometers nearby is San Salvador Atenco, a town in which a movement of resistance against the construction of a new airport received strong media attention after an unprecedented degree of gendered state violence was applied by then DF Governor Enrique Peña Nieto in 2006 to repress the movement.

In this context and territory, the Xico Valley Community Museum was created twenty-plus years ago in a collective effort of care, and following the values of reciprocity and communality, the museum has resisted against eviction, relocation, lack of funds, and efforts of appropriation by private interests or public organizations. I arrive on a cold January morning with my daughter, and we are greeted by the museum's team: art workshops coordinator Mariana Huerta Páez, librarians Giovanni Veracruz del Angel and Juan José Ayala Fonseca, tourism liaison Ana Laura Lira Huerta, cultural promoter Diana Ivete Espinosa Hernández, design and social networking coordinator Juan Neri, and the museum's director and Xico's official chronicler, Don Genaro Amaro Altamirano. As they generously share with me their lives' project and describe the museum's collection and programs, we have a *rosca de reyes* and coffee.

The Community Museum was created by the Neighborhood Council for the Preservation of Cultural Heritage of the Chalco Solidaridad Valley, with the goal to upkeep and preserve the archaeological vestiges of the Xico archaeological site. The museum opened in July 1996 in a small locale in the town of Xico, exhibiting a collection of pieces donated by the inhabitants of the valley. The museum holds 5,000 pre-Hispanic artefacts, 1,000 of which are currently on display along with local contemporary art. Aside from preserving and documenting the collection, they organize community-related activities such as Día de Muertos (Day of the Dead), posadas, *tertulias*,[86] and other festivities. The Xico Valley Community Museum, moreover, has served as a catalyzer for initiatives such as the reactivation of a *chinampa* in Tláhuac, or resistance against real estate and megaprojects in the area.[87] The museum is known for lodging the Zapatista Caravan every time it passes through, for having hosted

86 "Día de Muertos" is a Mexican celebration to commemorate those who have passed away. "Tertulia" is often used to refer to informal meetings or gatherings. As for "posadas," it refers to a nine-day festivity that takes place during the Christmas season.

87 Chinampas are manmade islands used for cultivation purposes on lakes.

meetings for the recently dismantled Federal Electricity Commission Union (because of privatization), and for the Policía Comunitaria (Community Police) from Guerrero. Along with art workshops, the museum has created a project to write and teach the history of the Xico from its inhabitant's point of view. A grant from a Finnish NGO has guaranteed training and salaries for three historians who either teach history workshops in public schools or hold them in the museum's headquarters. The museum has also produced a series of thirty-five booklets, which are taught and distributed in public schools in the region, and regularly offer painting and drawing classes. The first Saturday of every month, they also host a gathering where they share artistic, literary, and musical work from the people of Xico. Recently, they have devoted a considerable portion of their space to show local contemporary art, and when I visited, local artist Stephanie Bringas was having a solo show.

In 1997, the museum relocated to the Hacienda of Xico, built on a pre-Hispanic platform from the Teotihuacán era, on the edge of one of two adjacent extinct volcanoes, and vestiges of a sixteenth-century ranch owned by Hernán Cortéz.[88] The building suffered partial damage during the Mexican Revolution, has undergone modifications since the twentieth century, and is actually being restored with a budget of 20 million pesos provided by the Xico Municipality.[89] The Hacienda is the symbol and site for Xico's identity and history, and it is obviously a complex—yet not unique—palimpsest of Mexico's history of colonization, dispossession, and dreams of modernity. Xico was the bigger of the two islands in the Chalco Lake, and what is particular to the area is that it lodges traces of *all* pre-Hispanic and modern eras of the history of Mexico.

Between 1885 and 1903, with the support of dictator Porfirio Díaz, Spanish entrepreneur Iñigo Noriega Laso embarked on a megaproject to dry out the lake, with the purpose of transforming it into arable lands. During this period, thousands of the Chalco Valley's inhabitants were violently removed by Iñigo Noriega Lasso's private army or forced to work for his feud. The Hacienda was considered to be the epitome of modernity and progress of pre-revolutionary Mexico, with a train that went from Xico to Atlixco in the adjacent state of Puebla, connecting all of Iñigo Noriega Lasso's properties. In 1913, Iñigo

88 "Hacienda" refers to an estate or a farm, and the term dates back to the colonial period.

89 Ignacio Ramírez, "Arrumban Museo Xico por obra," *Mural*, November 21, 2015, http://www.mural.com/aplicacioneslibre/articulo/default.aspx.

Noriega Lasso's Xico Hacienda was occupied, and the lands were transformed into *ejidos*. In the decades that followed, the land was gradually transformed into urban space, and in the 1980s, an aquifer began to emerge and is now a considerable lake named Tláhuac-Xico.[90] As a matter of fact, every rain season, the lake comes back to flood the entire valley—a vestige of which is on display at the museum: a dead refrigerator bearing the muddy watermarks of a devastating flood in 2000 that made it obsolete before its time.

In a key recent book, influential architect and theorist Eyal Weizman, who is concerned with elucidating the power dynamics inherent to spatial, architectural, and urban arrangements, explains how the Negev Desert is a movable frontier that advances in response to agriculture, colonization, displacement, urbanization, and climate change. In his view, all these processes are tied to dispossession, and thus colonialism and climate change are intrinsically linked. While climate change is generally understood as an unintentional effect of modernity for Weizman, from the point of view of colonization, climate change has never been collateral damage, but rather a declared goal; making the desert bloom, in the case of the Negev, is changing the climate. This story linking colonization and global warming can be linked to Chalco, as another case study. Like Iñigo Noriega, who sought to expand arable lands during Porfirio Díaz's regime, Israeli governments sought to expand the limits of arable land and to place the nomads under the control of the State. In Chalco, as in the Negev, climate change and the displacement of originary populations has gone hand in hand.[91] From land degradation to the destruction of fields and forests, pollution, and water diversion, the conflict has reciprocal interaction with environmental transformation.

Aside from periodic flooding, also caused by the overflow of the La Compañía Channel, which carries much of the former lake's water, the region has been affected by the lowering of the lake bed. The drainage of the lake, combined with the pumping of groundwater, caused the water table to drop, and this desiccation of the soil is causing topographic changes we see as subsidence: the "lowering of the lake bed." As the lake bed sinks as a result

90 Following theorist and researcher Seth Denizen, Lake Chalco and the aquifer need to be carefully distinguished here because they are not necessarily connected. For instance, it is possible for the lake to re-emerge and the aquifer to be depleted at the same time. The dense clays of the former lake bed can prevent water from moving into subterranean aquifers.

91 Eyal Weizman, *Erasure: The Conflict Shoreline* (Göttingen: Steidl Verlag, 2016).

of subsidence, it also grows closer to the sinking water table, sort of chasing it downward. Unlike the sunken topography, the water table can rise again. During the rainy season, the water table rises and the first moment in which it intersects the topography is the base of the sunken former Lake Chalco, and it fills this topography once again.[92] The pumping of the water is not only polluting the aquifer of clean water below, but it has also caused the land to sink down: by 2013, the ground had sunk 12 meters from its level 20 years prior. A collateral effect of the gradual sinking of the Chalco Valley has been the continuing collapse of the Xico Hacienda.

The history and current challenges faced by the inhabitants of the Valley of Chalco have given this territory a special status. For the past decade, an array of architects, urban planners, cultural producers, transnational think tanks, environmentalists, government officials, doctoral students, biologists, civil rights organizations, activists, and experts of every kind attached to an array of different institutions have proposed policies, projects, symbolic histories, and plans to bring the water back, to make the area sustainable, and to provide infrastructure—for instance, much-needed drainage systems and the culverting of La Compañía Channel. For example, in 2011, the Urban Development Department of Mexico's Valley Commission made a "Hydrological Plan" to identify all the problems that the region is undergoing, like lack of clean water, pollution, drought, floods, and sinking, cracking, and erosion of the soil. There is also the Water Caravan, a study to implement a master plan to rescue the Chalco Lake and Xochimilco basins, and the "Vuelta a la ciudad lacustre" (Return to the lake city), an ambitious ecological and urban project by a team of architects, biologists, philosophers, engineers, and politicians (gathered under the aegis of architects Teodoro González de León, Alberto Kalach, Gustavo Lipkau, and Juan Cordero) to bring the lake back by building water-treatment plants and creating new public spaces and solutions to the irregular urban sprawl. This initiative has a precedent in the 1964 Save the Texcoco Lake Project (adjacent to Chalco) by Mexican engineers Nabor Carrillo and Gerardo Cruickshank. All remain unrealized; some proposals due to their utopian nature, and others because they either represent transient palliatives or are the locus of water rights and land-use disputes. Many are also tied to infrastructure and real-estate projects (like privatized

92 As explained to me by Seth Denizen.

social-housing projects like Casas Ara or Geo) backed up by corporate and state neoliberal interests.

Bearing this background in mind, and within the context of global solidarity and environmental justice furthered by cultural initiatives, the Xico Valley Museum was the subject of an international controversy. In 2012, artist Maria Theresa Alves exhibited dOCUMENTA, a project developed in collaboration with the Xico Museum. The exhibition showed dioramas describing the history of the place and included a portrait of Iñigo Noriega Lasso burning in flames, symbolizing past and ongoing dispossession, destruction, and exploitation of Chalco. There was also a section about the "heroes" of the region's history, and another one about the axolotl, a near-extinct amphibian made famous in a short story by Julio Cortázar and by Roger Bartra's positing of the creature as an allegory for modern Mexico: neither tadpole nor reptile, it is forever caught in between evolution and stasis. The project included an invitation to Don Genaro to visit the Immigration and Indian Archives in Colombres, Spain, lodged in Iñigo Noriega Lasso's estate, to deliver a history book written from the point of view of the people of Xico in a gesture of counter-history. In this regard, Alves's project—in its weaving of a net of memory from the nineteenth century in relationship to the neoliberal politics of accumulation, is a very-much-needed exercise of counter-history and restitution. Evidently, memory is a crucial part of the current war waged against megaprojects and resource extraction everywhere.

After dOCUMENTA, Mexico City's MUAC (University Museum of Contemporary Art lodged at the UNAM or the National University) exhibited in 2014 a second edition of Alves's *The Return of a Lake*, in collaboration with the Xico Museum. A selection by Don Genaro from the Xico Museum's collection was shown at MUAC, and a series of roundtables in which representatives from Chalco's thirteen municipalities were able to discuss their local environmental, political, and economic problems took place. In turn, MUAC organized workshops, lectures, and tours engaging Xico's community in the Valley. A few months after the exhibition, under the excuse of restoring the Hacienda, the Xico Museum's headquarters were forcibly relocated to an adjacent building. In their attempts to gain financial and institutional support from MUAC and other arts people and institutions, the Xico Valley Museum administrators were kindly discouraged from directly contacting MUAC's directive staff. Instead, they were offered money collected among the museum's employees; together with a donation from the Kurimanzutto Gallery, they were able to minimally habilitate the building where the museum is currently located.

Under the light of the eviction from the Hacienda, and MUAC's and Mexico City's art community's lackluster response and lack of solidarity, art historian and critic Paloma Checa Gismero questions the ethics and politics of Alves's intervention/collaboration with the Xico Valley Community Museum.[93] Checa Gismero argues that collaborations such as this one tend to bring together dispositives, whose publics and actors are worlds apart of difference, and thus "activate an aesthetic and ideological torsion that alienates publics from the real problematic originally addressed by Alves: an environmental and social crisis in a Mexican town." The "impossibility" of MUAC and the art community to genuinely engage with the Xico Museum's struggle precisely demonstrates the fact that the power relations created in these exchanges are never at stake; structural inequality remains untouched, and restitution can only happen at the symbolic level, shedding light on the dissymmetry in publics and executors that characterizes intervention work.

In response to the urgency of addressing this kind of asymmetry, and in a radical exercise of decolonial institutional repurposing, the Wood Land School: Kahatènhston tsi na'tetiátere ne Iotohrkó:wa tánon Iotohrha project took place in Montreal, Canada, in 2017. Following curator Cheyanne Turion's description, for the year, Montreal SBC Gallery's (directed by Pip Day) institutional identity and resources functioned wholly in support of the Wood Land School. Theirs was an experiment in what it means for settler-colonial infrastructures to work in service of Indigenous imperatives. The experiment was also an exploration of power relations and their possible reconfiguration from an initial perspective of Indigenous self-determination.[94]

Back in Mexico, after two years of works in the Hacienda, the funds to restore it provided by Xico's Municipality have run out, and the date of the collection's relocation to the renovated headquarters is nowhere in sight. The building where the museum is currently housed is a former industrial trash deposit, and a third of the space is occupied by an enormous pile of rubble

---

93 Paloma Checa Gismero, "On *The Return of a Lake*," *Field Journal*, no. 1 (Spring 2015), http://field-journal.com/issue-1/checa-gismero.

94 Cheyanne Tourions, "Woodland School *Kahatènhston tsi na'tetiátere ne Iotohrkó: wa tánon Iotohrha*," January 16, 2017, https://cheyanneturions.wordpress.com/2017/01/16/wood-land-school-kahatenhston-tsi-natetiatere-ne-iotohrkowa-tanon-iotohrha.

that the museum's team has been patiently cleaning out for the past two years. The building has thin metal sheets and canvas as its ceiling; and more than the humidity and dust felt inside the space, the carefully mounted pieces on discrete Styrofoam plinths and the wobbly wooden vitrines containing them are eloquent about the survival conditions of the museum. Community museums are a figure formalized in the 1990s by the INAH, Mexico's Institute for Anthropology and History. Thanks to a provision given by the INAH to Don Genaro, he has been able to fend away all previous threats of eviction and destruction. It has become evident that the museum's autonomy efforts and social initiatives pose a threat and are prey to appropriation of foreign agents for cultural capitalization. In this context, the Xico Museum resists by existing, and its condition of possibility comprises different modes of being and belonging, and new economies of giving, exchange, obligation, and reciprocity are at work in the museum's program and objectives, and in Don Genaro's ethics of directing it.

Differently than state or private museums, community museums are developed in consultation with the community, and the space responds to its needs. Museums of this kind are geared toward channeling communal action and organization, to strengthen identity through endogenous knowledge and interpretation of their culture. In practice, community museums generate projects to ameliorate the quality of life of communities by offering courses and training to cover an array of needs, seeking to support cultural traditions, to develop new forms of expression, and to generate tourism controlled by the community. They also serve as bridges for cultural exchange with other communities, to build alliances, and to integrate networks through joint projects.[95] There are about fifty community museums throughout Mexico supported by the INAH (although hundreds just in Mexico City, making it a special culture and tradition of community museums) concentrated in the states of Oaxaca, Yucatan, Veracruz, Morelos, Tlaxcala, Hidalgo, Guerrero, Querétaro, and Puebla. The INAH provides the museums with recognition, along with workshops, small budgets in select projects, and support in conservation and archiving.[96]

---

95 From their website: http://www.museoscomunitarios.org/que-es.

96 "Museos comunitarios preservan la memoria e identidad," http://www.inah.gob.mx/es/boletines/4434-museos-comunitarios-preservan-la-memoria-e-identidad.

The Xico Valley Community Museum is part of this vulnerable network of instituent efforts to build counter-histories, autonomous identarian narratives, and initiatives for sustainability and recovery of traditional forms of communal life. There are indeed contradictions operating at the heart of these projects, as one of the main tasks they have is to decolonize the very structures of knowledge, categorization, classification, and periodization, even the concept of a "museum." This is the work for generations to come, but examples such as the Xico Museum are an inspiring start. Art historian T. J. Demos posited Alves's project as serving a socioenvironmental politics of justice and compared "its struggle for local self-determination, return to subsistence, greater autonomy, community solidarity, and ecological sustainability" to the Zapatista movement; although, in his condescending view, "the Museum is no revolutionary withdrawal from the State."[97] It is evident that for now, it is impossible to go beyond the State or institutions as means to do politics—the museum would not exist without the INAH provision—but what is actually being done is the beginning of building an autonomous historical horizon, taking into consideration the contradictions and ambiguities of social relations of domination within the capitalist system we inhabit. Furthermore, *we* ("we" on the side of privilege) should no longer deny the way underprivileged populations are being negated by the kind of social relations imposed by capital and bureaucracy, operating their interests through well-intended betterment and restitution projects. It should be made clear that such interventions are neither neutral nor horizontal, and that exogenous reforms and interventions of all kinds have nothing to do with autonomy, solidarity, or democracy, and the power of the people. This is because current forms of power are embedded not in what we do, know, talk about, or see, but in what infrastructures we operate.

A question that remains open is whether a project such as the Xico Valley Community Museum can be emancipatory. Beyond uprising and mobilization, exercises in autonomy open up perspectives to think about "other" means to organize, preserve, self-preserve, and reproduce. In this context, the common horizon of communal emancipation is not a series of explicit and systematic objectives to be achieved, but as Raquel Gutiérrez argues, it is an ambivalent and open process, a trajectory protagonized by multiple

97 T. J. Demos, "*Return of a Lake*: Contemporary Art and Political Ecology in Mexico," https://tjdemos.sites.ucsc.edu/wp-content/uploads/sites/374/2016/08/Demos-Alves-MUAC-copy.pdf.

groups, by men and women. Bearing this in mind, the relationship between state-centered politics and autonomous politics is not one of opposition, but one of disjunction, of the confrontation of incompatible differences and perspectives.[98]

The Xico Museum's efforts of autonomy and its links to a national network of community museums have further global resonance in Mark Fisher and Nina Möntmann's proposal to potentially enable clusters of small-scale institutions throughout Europe to build a transnational network that would combine the autonomist emphasis on the network with the Gramscian emphasis on institutions. They envision a cluster containing hubs of activation, with the task of building publics and collectivities pitted against market interests. The cluster would serve, organizationally and aesthetically, as an international infrastructure combining aspects of exchange and mutual support of small-scale institutions, with a debate on decentralized internationalism.[99] The Xico Museum and the Wood Land School would be nodes in this international hub, adding a perspective toward decolonizing cultural spaces and practices, bringing awareness that knowledge and cultural infrastructures have been built upon the negation and silencing of originary peoples.

Moreover, the Xico Valley Community Museum is an instance of a new paradigm of political organization emerging at the surface of the social level, within Indigenous and underprivileged communities throughout Latin America. These exercises are creating the possibility of living in dignity at the margins of the capitalist markets and neoliberal states, enabling subjects to begin to recognize themselves as autonomous entities that resist by surviving, conscious of the appropriation of their own political practice. They are characterized by dignified and gracious distrust against anything that may smell of or have a hint of disciplining, subjection, or foreign capitalization, and by elegant suspicion of prescriptive and universal statements that speak from the site of the imposition of power. What is needed is to begin to project a road in common, displacing thought and debate, pitting reform and

98 See Raquel Gutiérrez Aguilar, "Los Ritmos del Pachakuti. Reflexiones breves en torno a cómo conocemos las luchas emancipativas y a su relación con la política de la autonomía," in *Hacer política para un porvenir más allá del capitalismo* (México: Grietas editores, 2016).

99 Mark Fisher and Nina Mönntman, "Peripheral Proposals," in *Cluster: On a Network of Visual Arts Organizations*, ed. Binna Choi, Maria Lind, Emily Pethic, and Nataša Petrešin-Bachelez (Berlin: Strenberg Press, 2014), 171–82.

revolution against emancipation, in awareness that social relationships cannot be transformed because they occur within the very system that denies that anything was ever broken—and is still being broken—by (neo)colonialism. It is that structure, the standpoint from which colonialism makes sense, that is limiting our ability to find each other. According to Moten and Harney, today it is neither useful to speak truth to power, nor to recognize; what is pressing is to *inhabit* the language of the other, which has been rendered as a nonentity by colonialism. To show the sovereign's space and time that makes itself present as absence, as death, as things which *are* not.[100]

---

100 Fred Harney and Stefano Moten, *The Undercommons: Fugitive Planning & Black Study* (New York: Minor Compositions, 2013), 15.

CHAPTER THREE

Subjectivation and Governmentality

Life, Work, and Imagination under the Neoliberal Sensible Regime

Tomorrow these trade winds begin moving in reverse.
Blowing goods back to their factories.
Blowing people back to their homes.
Blowing their homes back to their countries.
Blowing their countries back to their assumed origins.
Blowing full-grown adults back into wombs.
—BRIAN KUAN WOOD, Weather for *Liquidity*

TO THESE WONDERFUL LINES by Brian Kuan Wood that delineate a post-neoliberal utopia of the end of market liberalization, the redistribution of work and wealth, giving citizen status to all migrants and refugees, the rigorous separation between life and work, to basically allow humanity to start over, we should add one about the situation lived by peasants in rural areas: "Blowing peasants back to cultivating their lands." The massive new wave of Mexican and Centro American peasant migration that began in the 1990s toward cities in their home countries and toward the north to the United States as one of the effects of NAFTA (as well as a side effect of US counterinsurgency policies from the 1960s on[1]) was due to the fact that neoliberal reforms made working in their land unprofitable. Direct producers lacked the technology or the distribution networks to deliver to the market the goods that began to be demanded; the prices offered for Mexican produce, moreover, were undervalued due to the cheap imports of US agroindustrial products (such as maize). The campesino sustainable and autonomous form of life became thus obsolete, leading way to massive migration while bringing about radical changes in the function and morphology of the countryside. While they became gradually urbanized, rural subjects gained access to consumer goods, cable TV, and Internet, resulting in new subjectivities. It could be said that the Mexican originary populations formerly portrayed throughout the twentieth century as exotic objects of anthropology or signs of cultural and economic backwardness in Mexico dressed in *manta* (raw cotton ethnic gear) and sandals were seriously abated. They had been subjected to a neoliberal reconversion. Market liberalization brought new opportunities of personal progress as well as cultural hybridization, subjectivation choices, and the progressive disappearance of ethnic identities, which was understood as modernization. The cash flow prompted by remittances, for instance, materialized in the construction or betterment of homes in rural areas, reflecting the new urbanized status of people living in them.[2] The originary populations were reconverted in reality and in the national imaginary into narcos, sicarios, (successful or unsuccessful migrants), maquiladora workers, or cheap and precarious labor hands as masons, domestic help, in the service industry, and so forth. In turn, throughout the 1990s, middle- and upper-middle-class urban youth were reconverted, getting degrees in international business or law, administration, economics, or tourism. They were preparing to become

1 See, for instance, Julian Borger, "Fleeing a Hell the US Helped Create: Why Central Americans Journey North," *The Guardian*, December 19, 2018, https://www.theguardian.com/us-news/2018/dec/19/central-america-migrants-us-foreign-policy.

2 The deep change in rural areas brought about by neoliberalism has been, for example, portrayed in *La arquitectura de remesas* (Remittance Architecture), a photograph exhibition and book about remittance architecture in Guatemala, Honduras, and El Salvador, presented in the Centro Cultural de España in Guatemala in 2010, curated by Walterio Iraheta. See http://arquitecturadelasremesas.blogspot.mx.

the new technocrats and white-collar workers (or *godínez*[3]) in corporations and enterprises that would eventually come to operate in the country. Fluent in English and literate in standardization, optimization and logistics norms, social responsibility, and cultural openness, they learned to be sensibilized to neoliberal lingo and practices. In both cases, in rural areas as in cities, a generation of subjects who grew up watching Hollywood films and US sitcoms came of age dreaming of the lifestyles and merchandise there portrayed.

Amid efforts to promote relations among the three countries that are members of NAFTA, a policy was established to subsidize the education in North American universities of a new Mexican elite of cognitive workers confident in intercultural diplomacy, international law, ISO 9000 quality management systems, and international negotiation, as well as versatile in the lingua franca of modern global art, design, film, and literature to furnish, decorate, and illustrate the new enclaves of sophistication and privilege in Mexico. Once the grantees came back to the country, they became academics, prime ministers, government bureaucrats, technocrats, corporate lawyers, bankers, and cultural producers, helping to open up the country's economy to global corporations and cultural institutions to tourism. While Mexico is de facto one of the most dangerous countries for journalists, under the regimes of Carlos Salinas de Gortari through Peña Nieto, it became one of the best places for cultural producers and academics. Through a policy of supporting graduate education, science (through the CONACYT or Science and Technology National Council), and culture (through the SNCA or National System for Art Creators), President Carlos Salinas de Gortari's regime established a middle class of cultural producers that allowed intellectuals, writers, artists, and academics to live comfortably and to share their work across the world. A few years later, the government opened up to the private sector collaborations in culture, allowing Mexico (or rather, Mexico City) to achieve global relevance as a high-end center for contemporary art, design, and cultural production.[4] The three phenomena I just outlined—the reconversion of Indigenous peoples and campesinos into migrants, narcos, or cheap labor hands; a new middle and upper middle class of professionals becoming

3 A "godín" or "godínez" is Mexican slang to refer to the office worker, someone who lives the nine-to-five lifestyle.

4 Malú Huacuja del Toro, *Salinato Versión 2.0: reflexiones desde el periodismo cultural sobre el retorno de Carlos Salinas al poder* (México D.F.: Plaza y Valdés, 2013).

white-collar workers in transnational corporations; and a US-educated elite working in key sectors in the country (including researchers and cultural producers)—were underscored by the unquestionable normality of market rationality, decision-making based on the maximization of the production of surplus value, and the efficiency and maximal optimization of resources and human capital.

As we will see, neoliberalism is intrinsically tied to post-Fordist labor reforms, which implies that the form, content, and working conditions of all sorts of workers changed radically, becoming indissociable from the new forms of collective subjectivation and forms of life. Labor reforms (legal and other kinds) also became a means of neoliberal subjection, insofar as subjects stopped defining themselves from the point of view of salaried relationship, ceased to identify as a social class, and instead, subjectivities came to be based on imaginary identities offered by the mass media, the consumer market, and the working regime. These imaginary identities originated in the principle of devoting one's life to self-realization through work, creating an understanding of precarity, and self-exploitation as the necessary cost to succeed or to achieve one's dream. Self-realization also became the basis of the administration of one's own life and took over precedence of family values, the general interest, and the common good.

Subjectivation and Forms of Life in Post-Fordism/Cognitive Capitalism

Post-Fordism implies a change from industrialized societies and standardized mass production to diverse and flexible production. At the end of the 1970s, mass industrial (Fordist) production of developed countries entered a crisis due to the new economic developments, aside from the rights achieved by workers' struggle at the global level, which changed the conditions of industrialized production. Many companies began to reorganize production processes and salary contracts by introducing flexible working systems, subcontracting, team work, multitasking, and multiskilling, what is known as flat management, transferring, and thus deterritorializing production to countries and regions where work laws were lax or inexistent,[5] among them Mexico, where the Volkswagen factory was established in 1964 in the periphery of the city

5 Sebastian Budgen, "A New 'Spirit of Capitalism,'" *New Left Review*, no. 1 (2000).

of Puebla. Manufacturing companies were seeking new markets, consumption systems, and production methods; diversification in merchandise and specialized or targeted market niches were thus introduced. Expert workers in any component of the production process were substituted by flexible production methods, enabling both machines and workers to quickly adapt to the tasks demanded by the changing merchandises. With post-Fordism, moreover, capitalism became a decentralized global network dominated by great corporations, with a diversified system of production and consumption. Post-Fordist production forms, along with neoliberal reforms, brought about the precarization of labor. To the work force, this meant a change in having fixed and assured salaries, as well as a pension, creating incertitude about where the next check will come from. This creates the need to embrace strategies characterized by novelty and perpetual self-reinvention. To be successful in precarious working conditions also came to imply virtuous performativity of a self in social media and encounters, through a kind of self-branding and permanent education.

Under industrial capitalism, the worker would sell his own qualified labor for a minimum salary, determined by basic individual and family needs, and the welfare state would protect society against capitalist exploitation, covering or subsidizing key areas by investing taxes in education, housing, and health. Under neoliberalism, bosses no longer hire individuals, but rather acquire packages of work time that are separated from the executors and their bodily needs. This depersonalization of work time from its social existence is put to the service of the free market: the boss is no longer obliged to grant rights nor to listen to workers' demands. As a consequence, aside from precarity having become a generalized working condition, self-exploitation is one of the conditions to enter the working market. This is how neoliberal capital subjects and dominates life, entering into direct conflict with it; for instance, by forcing subjects to eat and sleep poorly, unable to sit down at the table and share a meal, living in perpetual stress and illness, children improperly cared for by parents, and so forth. The fact that life and work are hardly distinguishable has also brought about identities constructed through over-identification of the working realm, which in turn serves to justify increasing self-exploitation. In order to palliate the effects of self-exploitation, the pharmaceutical industry now offers antidepressants, stimulants, and symptom suppressors in order to enable the worker to fulfill their workday. These are some of the reasons why we can no longer think about "class struggle," which is the confrontation between the proletariat and the bourgeoisie that could push history forward by demanding equality and better working conditions. Another of the aspects of post-Fordism is automatization, which is the substitution of a process executed by a single person, by a technological apparatus that replies the logic and function of humans. For Franco (Bifo) Berardi, this substitution has two goals: (1) to increment productivity of workers, and (2) to subject their political force. With post-Fordism, the machine and the digital network expanded to increment productivity, and the new forms of automatization drastically changed cognitive activity (attention, memory, language, imagination) to situate it as a basic condition of Semiocapitalism, and to capture it introducing automatisms in social existence. For Berardi, the automatization of cognitive activity has devastating consequences, taking the place of political decision-making and the possibility of making conscious or voluntary choices. Now sociopolitical action is less and less the result of autonomous organization, and more and more the result of automatic chains of cognitive elaborations and digital social interaction.[6] Automatization and technology have further created a racialized division between cognitive and manual workers and a territorialized division of labor: cognitive workers inhabit enclaves and spaces of privilege and the latter do not, often working in dire conditions. We are clearly living in an era of power relations and complex mechanisms that differentiate and hierarchize lives as more or less valuable, more or less vulnerable, more or less protected, with more or less access to goods and services (and of varying qualities), and more or less exploited or merely excluded and therefore redundant, struggling for a territory in which they can survive.

Neoliberal capital, moreover, has directly conflicted with life, because subjects live with the expectations of consumption as portrayed in the mass media. In that regard, the free market is a mise-en-scène of the deferral of the promise of self-realization and the fulfillment of our needs and desires by the market. According to Slavoj Žižek, one of the dead points of contemporary consumerism is rooted in the Lacanian distinction between pleasure and enjoyment. For Lacan, pleasure is mortal excess that goes beyond enjoyment and is moderate by definition. Nowadays, consumerism materializes both. On the one hand, there exist the illuminated hedonists who calculate their pleasure, seeking to prolong their fun without damaging their health,

6 Franco "Bifo" Berardi, "The Neuroplastic Dilemma: Consciousness and Evolution," *e-flux journal* 60 (December 2014), https://www.e-flux.com/journal/60/61034/the-neuroplastic-dilemma-consciousness-and-evolution.

by consuming decaf coffee, cigarettes without nicotine, nonfat chocolate, and so forth. On the other hand, there are those who enjoy, ready to consummate their existence in the mortal excess of jouissance. This distinction gives way to two forms of consumers: one who protects themself against health threats, and the drug or alcohol addict inclined toward self-destruction.[7] In either case, everyone has the obligation to enjoy themselves. Armed with credit cards, consumers are invited to do, to consume, to experience more, to reinvent again and again their identity (through consumption of lifestyle choices). In this regard, consumers' identities are as volatile and dynamic as market fluctuations.[8] Lifestyle and work therefore converge in perpetual reinvention cycles underscored first by embedded obsolescence, and second by the eternally deferred goal of self-fulfillment. In periods of crisis, workers are forced to migrate or acquire new skills or knowledge to reconvert themselves and adjust their life form, skills, and competencies according to market demands, without forgetting a new form of branding themselves.

Self-branding and lifestyle are inextricable and have direct ties (and come from) cultural production, and both feed onto the knowledge economy. This means that virtuosism and creativity, which are values traditionally linked to the arts and cultural production, are now at the center of the production of surplus value and work processes. In that regard, post-Fordism implies an opening toward cognitive or intellectual work, because nowadays, we are no longer buying material things, but rather the signs they project or the experiences a consumer good or service offers. We buy material and immaterial merchandise to give shape to our lifestyle and branding. According to Baudrillard, the revolutionary struggles from the nineteenth and twentieth centuries culminated in the myth of "the rights of man": the right to equality and the right to happiness. The latter needed to be measured in terms of objects and signs. Throughout modernity, the "phantasmagoria of equality" is reflected in the struggle against the "exclusivity of signs" (signs of social power and prestige), which gave leeway to the proliferation of consumable signs. For instance, for Baudrillard, imitations, fakes, and pirated products

7 Slavoj Žižek, "Fat Free Chocolate and Absolutely No Smoking: Why Our Guilt about Consumption Is All-Consuming," *The Guardian*, May 21, 2014, https://www.theguardian.com/artanddesign/2014/may/21/prix-pictet-photography-prize-consumption-slavoj-Žižek.

8 Jodi Dean, "Enjoying Neoliberalism," *Cultural Politics* 4, no. 1, (2008): 47–72.

challenge the exclusivity of privilege signs and social power.[9] This implies that the exchange value has taken precedence over use value, understood as the basis of merchandise fetishism. In other words, the *usefulness* of merchandise is subjected to its exchange value. For Marx, use value is tied to the physical properties of merchandises and their material uses; that is to say, how we put them to work and how they satisfy human needs. Commodities' usefulness is measured in terms of money, and a third term comes into play between use value and exchange value: symbolic value. Exchange value is the use value, because for Marx, money hides the merchandises' true value (its use value), and this is why it becomes fetishized, because there are other things that come into play in the valorization of merchandise (symbolic value). Let's remember that demand is based on the desire for the commodity.

Under industrial capitalism, while working more implies producing a more valuable commodity, commodities actually freeze within themselves the labor time it has taken to produce them. In post-fordist capitalism, efficiency in the production process—translated to lowering costs and automatization—has rendered difficult the quantification of a commodity's production value (it can be the product of slave labor, unlegislated work or subcontracted, etc.).[10] Therefore, under neoliberalism, production value is dissociated from exchange and symbolic value. Exchange value is based on offer and demand and on the desirability of the product, embedding the value in the sign and dematerializing the commodity. In that regard, more than objects, we acquire signs of "equality," "happiness," "modernization," "well-being," and "self-realization" in order to construct our own lifestyles. Together with the generalized acceleration of the consumption cycles, commodities now fulfill *desessities*. A striking, often cited passage from Don Delillo's *White Noise* describes our relation to commodities, marketing, and branding as *desessities*:

> We added Murray's single lightweight bag of white items to our load and headed across Elm in the direction of his rooming house. It seemed to me that Babette and I, in the mass and variety of our own purchases, in a sheer

---

9 Jean Baudrillard, "Towards a Critique of the Political Economy of the Sign," *SubStance* 5, no. 15 (1976): 111–16.

10 For a crucial study about industrial means of production in sweatshops in the Third World during the post-industrial era, see Naomi Klein, *No Logo* (Toronto: Random House and Picador, 1999).

plenitude those crowded bags suggested, the weight and size and number, the familiar package designs and vivid lettering, the giant sizes, the family bargain packs with Day-Glo sale stickers, in the sense of replenishment we felt, the sense of well-being, the security and contentment these products brought to some snug home in our souls—it seemed we had achieved a fullness of being that is not known to people who need less, expect less, who plan their lives around lonely walks in the evening.[11]

The fact that capitalism construes *desessities* means that the consumer is also manufactured, designed by the product. As Baudrillard declared, objects are no longer merchandise or signs whose messages we can appropriate and decipher, but are rather tests that interrogate us. The answer is already included in the question commodities ask us, and thus they operate under the circular logic of code verification. Like referendums, they manipulate and create sameness and homogeneity.[12] The commodity looks at us and we find ourselves in it, and this is how branding is indissociable from *self-branding*. For instance, I acquire spiritual enlightenment in yoga retreats, I model my body at the gym, and I model my public persona in restaurants, where I will come across the group of people I want to be associated with.[13]

Signs and meanings, desires, and projections are in the market because the economy is based on fulfilling consumers' *dessessities* by manufacturing experiences, signs, and information. Creativity is the center of the knowledge economy (also known as communicative capitalism), and this is why the qualities of aesthetic production have become hegemonic and have transformed working and consumption processes alongside aesthetic experience. As Eva Illouz argues in *Cold Intimacies*, emotions have been shaped by capitalism, by their introduction into production as well as into consumption processes.[14]

Not only have sensations and feelings been trivialized by being packaged and sold, but disinterest—the basis of aesthetic experience—has also disappeared, because now everything, even art, is subjected to the ultimate goal of the production of surplus value, either in the market, politically, or as

11 Don Delillo, *White Noise* (New York: Penguin Books, 1985), 20.
12 Jean Baudrillard, "Towards a Critique of the Political Economy of the Sign," 114.
13 Slavoj Žižek, "Fat Free Chocolate and Absolutely No Smoking."
14 Eva Illouz, *Cold Intimacies: The Making of Emotional Capitalism* (Oxford, UK: Polity Press, 2007).

corporate or state investment.[15] This is the result of what Shaviro describes as the ruthless capitalist capture of cognition of sensation, aesthetic feelings which have been transformed into information, exploited as forms of work and sold as novelty, as exciting life choices, or as socially responsible cultural activities.

Commodity design also involves cognitive production, a form of labor that produces informational and cultural content as the commodity. This form of production implies exercising communication, language, memory, sociability, aesthetic, and ethic sensibility, as well as the capacity for abstract learning, which are work as well as non-work.[16] In this context, the labor market values, above all, qualities associated with creativity. For instance: "Thinking outside of the box," to be able to work independently, to bring in extravagance into the work place, horizontal relationships instead of vertical at work, and so forth. Furthermore, when we buy signs for "equality," "happiness," "belonging," "well-being," "practicality," "efficiency," "competitivity," "sophistication," and "self-realization," we are not only constantly consuming signs, but we are also producing them, as we are all now part of what is known in post-workerist theory as the social factory. The factory is social in the sense that it produces knowledge that is available to all. Social knowledge production could have emancipatory potential, or it could function as the glue that binds a community together. The problem with the current formations of the social factory is that the knowledge it produces is being captured, resold as merchandise, and modeled through social media: it circulates, simplified and focused on the construction of a spectacular "I." Another worrisome aspect of the neoliberal social factory is that the industrialized factory as a site of discipline has been extended to all of society, now organized around the same principles of domination and production of value as traditional factory work. We are all now workers at the social factory, producing a hybrid of material and immaterial content linked to social media and productive networks, in highly developed cooperative modes in which we have no agency. At the same time, we are subjecting ourselves to techniques of self-betterment

---

15 Steven Shaviro, "Accelerationist Aesthetics: Necessary Inefficiency in Times of Real Subsumption," *e-flux journal* 43 (June 2013), https://www.e-flux.com/journal/46/60070/accelerationist-aesthetics-necessary-inefficiency-in-times-of-real-subsumption.

16 Rob Horning, "Social Media, Social Factory," *The New Inquiry*, July 29, 2011, https://thenewinquiry.com/social-media-social-factory.

that involve molding our psyches and lives to the demands of the market; for instance, through coaching.

Entrepreneurship and Neoliberal Governmentality

The basis for neoliberal capitalism's capture of life and social processes is language. According to Arundhati Roy, neoliberalism is characterized by deploying words that mean the opposite of what they really mean, like "deepening of democracy," "free market," "women empowerment," "development," and "aid."[17] Neoliberalism has coined its own keywords that serve, according to John Patrick Leary, as instruments to perpetuate destructive neoliberal dynamics and patterns. Examples of neoliberal lingo are: "innovation," "lean," "personal brand," "collaboration," "artisanal," "best practices," "brand," "choice," "coach," "collaboration," "empowerment," "excellence," "free," "leadership," "maker," "meritocracy," "resilience," "share," and "sharing," among others. According to Leary, neoliberal keywords describe the extra-economic realms of spirit requisitioned for the sake of private profit, transforming the internalization of the will to profit as an intrinsic human trait. The neoliberal keywords enlisted and defined by Leary circulate broadly in both mass media and specialist discussions of working life and the economy, evidencing how surveillance and labor discipline shape not only assembly-line work and retail jobs, but also the so-called sharing economy, gigs, and even life outside work.[18] A crucial aspect of the neoliberal capture of language is how it has embraced dissent and heterodoxy, thus governing by deeply transforming subjectivities by propagating new forms of feeling, thinking, fantasizing, and living: common sense.

Neoliberal governance traverses subjectivity, conducts, work, and individual forms of life on the basis that the individual is "an entrepreneur of herself" or *homo oeconomicus*, the final product of a process of subjectivation and subjection. As "human capital," the subject implicates all their activities affective and cognitive, as well as material resources, with the goal of becoming a "better version of self," to adjust themselves to the demands

---

17 Arundhati Roy, *My Seditious Heart (Collected Nonfiction)* (Chicago: Haymarket Books, 2019), xix.

18 John Patrick Leary, *Keywords: The New Language of Capitalism* (Chicago: Haymarket Books, 2018), 22.

of the market[19] through self-investment in each one of the spheres of their existence, in order to strengthen their competitive positioning and to appreciate their value to attract investors. As human capital, the *homo oeconomicus* seeks to augment the value of their actions in all domains of their life. According to Wendy Brown, under neoliberal rationality, human capital is our *being* and our *duty*, because we are human capital not only for ourselves but for the company, the state, our partners, or our workplace.[20]

In turn, the government functions as facilitator of the administration of (human and material) capital, through what Foucault calls governmentality (*gouvernmentalité*). This mechanism conceives the political as a field of administration, strategies, techniques, and procedures through which a variety of groups attempt to maximize their programs, integrating subjects to the objectives and trajectories of nation-states, companies, universities, and so forth.[21] In the public realm, for instance, governmentality expresses itself in programs such as the PYMES or the Entrepreneur Support Network, a government initiative that provides assessment to those who wish to start a business or to consolidate it and see it grow. Under President Enrique Peña Nieto, this network operated through a website, a 1-800 phone line, and a service window in each municipal state economy department, as well as stands all across the country.[22] President Andrés Manuel López Obrador's government has created a similar entrepreneurship program through the PILARES (Innovation, Freedom, Art, Education, and Knowledge Points) or community centers in marginal areas across the country. Three hundred are planned by Mexico State Governor Claudia Sheimbaum, and they offer cyber-school, workshops for cultural development, and sports, as well as an entrepreneurship program. In the private sector, schools for middle, upper middle class, and the elite offer what is called "entrepreneurship education," teaching children entrepreneurship as a civic and personal value grounded on imagination, creativity, and curiosity, thus breeding autonomous individuals built from kindergarten, "with the mindset that their potential can only be realized

---

19 Maurizio Lazzarato, "Neoliberalism in Action: Inequality, Insecurity and the Reconstitution of the Social," *Theory, Culture & Society* 26, no. 6 (2009): 109–33.

20 Wendy Brown, *Undoing the Demos* (New York: Zone Books, 2015), 38.

21 Brown, *Undoing the Demos*, 127.

22 José Antonio Román, "Pospone Peña Nieto el envío de la reforma energética," *La Jornada*, August 7, 2013, https://www.jornada.com.mx/2013/08/07/politica/003n1pol.

in the struggle for wealth accumulation and whose creativity can only be productively exercised for profit."[23] Children's education is oriented toward profit, as they are embedded language forms that imagine and make things to be grounded on neoliberal values. Under neoliberalism, all individuals are therefore summoned as actors and entrepreneurs in all spheres of life, under the premise that they act "freely" based on self-interest and according to market rationality. A "badly administered life" becomes an excuse to depoliticize neoliberal governmentality. It means that whoever is not "profitable" does not count, because the main theme of the political economy is competition. Neoliberalism thus produces a modern form of social Darwinism that subdivides society into powerful and nonpowerful, winners and losers. This model promotes competitive behaviors in the name of self-interest, elite consciousness, and struggle, instead of cooperation.[24] Perhaps this is one of the reasons why (alongside the ubiquitous cult of money) it has become so difficult to eradicate corruption.

During the industrial era, man was subject to the machine as a piece of the machinery, with the function of guaranteeing its proper functioning. Subjectivity was defined by work, alienated and disciplined by the factory spaces in which bodies circulated: schools, hospitals, prisons, work. Disciplinary subjectivity coexisted with the possibility of cultivating a private and liberating subjectivity, what Foucault called "care of self."[25] In his fundamental text, "Postscript on the Societies of Control," Gilles Deleuze describes how disciplinary societies had been substituted by control societies. For Deleuze, the incipient dispositives for control functioned through modulation, changing in form and content from one moment to the next, giving shape to the soul, "like a gas" formed by its container. This idea was taken up by Foucault, who then proposed that the means of control after disciplinary societies were based in biopower and biopolitics; they are imperceptible and have the task of conducting conducts by subjecting life and its mechanisms to the reign of calculation. As a consequence, knowledge becomes an agent of technical transformation of human life. The rationality of control implies

23 Leary, *Keywords*, 28.

24 Christoph Nutterwegge," Neoliberalism as a Variety of Social Darwinism: Ten Million More Unemployed," *Indymedia LA*, April 16, 2013, https://la.indymedia.org/js/?v=cont&url=/news/2013/04/259574.json.

25 Gilles Deleuze, "Postscript on the Societies of Control," *L'Autre journal*, no. 1 (1990).

that we ceaselessly need to transform ourselves to better shape the world and to make correct, optimal, and ethical consumption choices. To be flexible also implies to be able to optimize our "dead" or "free" time, incorporating it to the temporality of limitless productivity, putting all our skills at the service of capital. This includes nonreproductive sexuality—so we can become more profitable ourselves. This Taylorization of the self[26] is the new form of objectification or colonization of something through a gaze; its being put to work or alienation implies that all subjective dimensions have been colonized by capitalism: humans have become their talking CVs. As Nina Power posits it, however, objectification implies that there is something remaining within the subject that resists capture, which is a minimal subjective difference. In the workplace, however, we are mandated to completely expose personality and private life, and thus the personal has ceased being political, instead becoming absolutely and entirely economic. This is another way in which life and existence have been colonized by the new forms of domination that go beyond how we used to understand objectification.[27]

For his remarkable master's thesis at the Colegio de la Frontera Norte in Tijuana, Uriel Gudino Terán developed a study based on ethnographic analysis of coaching in the border city, focusing on how coaching affirms a series of hegemonic values of dominant groups such as entrepreneurialism, whiteness, and heteropatriarchal roles.[28] The teachings of coaching have been disseminated since the 1990s in an array of platforms, from religious groups such as Unidad Cristiana and Iglesia Ancla, whose pastors' sermons are full of coaching rhetoric of human development and leadership, to private companies such as "discovery seminars and coaching" or "KDL Comunicación" (all in Tijuana), to elite groups such as NXIVM, which was led by the infamous Keith Raniere. According to Gudino Terán, "coaching" is a multilayered

---

26 Taylorism refers to the division in different tasks of the process of production within the organization of work. It was a method of industrial organization elaborated by Frederick Taylor, with the purpose of augmenting productivity and avoiding the control the worker could have in production times.

27 Nina Power, in conversation with Hito Steyerl at the Institute of Contemporary Art in London, March 28, 2014, https://archive.ica.art/bulletin/video/hito-steyerl-and-nina-power.

28 Uriel Gudino Terán, "¡Sólo hazlo! *Coaching, training* y sujeción: sobre la producción de subjetividad neoliberal y la nueva masculinidad hegemónica en Tijuana, B.C.," Tesis para la Maestría en Estudios Culturales, Colegio de la Frontera Norte, agosto 2020.

method that combines business administration, organizational development, fitness psychology, self-realization, and self-help jargon, plus positive psychology or happiness science, in the format of Alcoholics Anonymous group therapy. It is grounded on the figure of the sports coach as "carrier," working through the emotional and physical optimization of an athlete.[29] Coaching is supposed to lead the individual to become an autonomous leader of themself, with authority to delegate even under duress; to control their emotions with resiliency and flexibility; to be able to overcome limits and to commit to excellence. Through coaching, the subject will become self-confident, better at communicating, to be able to reach qualitative objects, and to maximize performance, as well as to devote themself to their passion, to take risks, and to reinvent themself all in a path toward success, in which the "I" becomes a life project.[30] Gudino Terán discovers, moreover, that beyond "self-betterment," coaching affirms hegemonic values pitted against sloth, unemployment, vice, obesity, poverty, sexual debauchery (thereby normalizing inequality), entrepreneurialism as virtue, the subject as human capital, and success as happiness. This "aspirational telos" is racialized and gendered, hiding logics of discrimination perpetuated by pigmentocracy, as whiteness is indeed an advantage in today's labor market.[31]

Subjectivities produced by coaching and other self-help techniques such as mindfulness, together with the new control apparatuses, coexist with ancient forms of coercion, guiding behaviors, and molding desires and values. The current control apparatuses have the quality of being perpetually stable, because they invariably rise up above all challenges; as they are always in crisis from within (like capitalism), they are constantly being subjected to reforms, remakes, look changes, or prizes. Differently than disciplined subjectivity of the industrial era, social subjection is centered on the social, urban, and domestic tissue, on the individual psychological landscape, and on the collective means of communication, including the entertainment industry. The latter, for instance, has radically changed toward the notion of "productive consumption." In the world of children's entertainment, for instance, this implies introducing productivity and development as "pedagogical entertainment" or edutainment. For example, *Dora the Explorer* or the *Umizumis* are cartoons in which children learn a second language and mathematics,

29 Gudino Terán, "¡Sólo hazlo!," 52.
30 Gudino Terán, "¡Sólo hazlo!," 11.
31 Gudino Terán, "¡Sólo hazlo!," 12.

respectively. In Mexico, however, there is specific case in which edutainment and neoliberal subjectivation operate together. Kidzania (when opened to the public, it was known as "La ciudad de los niños," or the City for Children) is an entertainment complex first created in Mexico City, with branches in London, Malaysia, Tokyo, Delhi, Mumbai, Cairo, Istanbul, Lisbon, Seoul, Portugal, Indonesia, UAE, Chile, Thailand, India, Doha, Johannesburg, New York, Paris and Kuwait, and there are eleven more envisioned in the next few years. Called "signature interactive edutainment experiences," most of them are built inside malls, established as mini-cities with airports, police stations, stadiums, theatres, shops, universities, banks, concessions to restaurants and other services, their own newspapers, passports, and money. When children enter, they receive a check with the option of spending it on merchandise, food, and/or services, or putting it in the bank, getting a job, and accumulating more money. The activities children can participate in range from flying an airplane, making hamburgers or pizzas, putting gas in their cars, or becoming firemen, judges, or postmen, to learning fashion design at H&M, administering hotels, and so forth. The stroke of genius of its creator, Mexican Xavier López Ancona, was to have invited established corporations to lend their brands to create miniature versions of them at Kidzania. The argument in favor of this kind of edutainment is that it prepares children for the real world, empowering them to make their own decisions. In that regard, the participating brands like Nestlé, Coca-Cola, Mitsubishi, Johnson & Johnson, Unilever, Nike, Bancomer, Pizza Hut, Cemex, Corona, Bimbo, Domino's, DHL, and others give "authenticity" to the game. The whole concept of Kidzania, however, fuels the fantasy that good things can be obtained from capitalism, creating blindness about the real forces behind the market, like dire and precarious working conditions or the fact that the children are being conditioned to brand fidelity. Now, merchandises no longer seduce their consumers from the TV screens: liberated, they can now put themselves directly at the reach of children's hands as "pedagogical toys." Kidzania, moreover, is a kind of hyper-reality model in the sense Jean Baudrillard defined it, transforming children into entrepreneurs of themselves, administering their human capital.[32] Differently than Disneyland, in which the imaginary materializes in fantasy and virtual reality,[33] Kidzania captures the real world,

32 Jean Baudrillard, "Disneyworld Company," *Libération*, March 4, 1996, https://www.liberation.fr/tribune/1996/03/04/disneyworld-company_166772.

33 Baudrillard, "Disneyworld Company."

integrating it to a synthetic universe devoted to monetary and consumption transactions, reducing social and playing relations to a monetary one. In Kidzania, reality is not a spectacle like in Disneyland, but a dispositive for subjectification under the law of capitalism and the free market. Kidzania is a hallucination of the real, without the distraction and the distance offered by the Disneyland experience, because as an apparatus, it enters into children's minds to drive them to naturalize decision-making based on monetary value and self-interest. In sum, Kidzania is a mental universe in which children are productive nodes within an omnipresent and ubiquitous network of market relationships, who join in offering their human capital. This is one of the means through which neoliberal governmentality is imposed at an early age, along with a hegemonic discourse that imposes a single possible world with a sole way of interpreting it: as a relationship of production and consumption. Another Mexican invention that furthers this interpretation of the world is the brand *Distroller*. Created by Amparín, *Distroller* offers girls ages two through twelve a world of collectible dolls to be adopted at the store under different guises with fun names: *Neonatos* (Neoborns), *Ksimeritos* (Almostborn), *Pimpollo*, *Chamoys*, *Alushes*, and *Chikihadas*. Girls take their *Neonatos* home after they have been vaccinated by a nurse; these stuffed amorphous characters come with a variety of accessories, from cribs, strollers, and feeding devices, to clothing. The brand has been highly criticized for furthering right-wing values, as the *Ksimeritos* are in reality fetuses in bright colors: thus, little girls nurture toy fetuses unconsciously, absorbing an anti-abortion stand. The brand also comes with a line of home, jewelry, purses, and other kinds of accessories, bearing a cartoon version of the Mexican catholic icon of the Virgin of Guadalupe. Each commodity embodies a prayer: "Virgencita plis," the objects read (Please little virgin). The brand is characterized by sprinkling fun slogans across all its merchandise, appropriating common sayings in Mexico, also using misspelling and English transliteration to Spanish ("plis" for "please," "distroller" for "destroyer"). The consumer it molds has fun being naughty—*Alushes* come with "fart spray" and with a checkbook of sorts, through which children can bargain potential mischief with their parents. What made me want to write about this brand in particular was the *Distroller* musical, one of the most successful mises en scène in Mexico in the past few years (2018–2020), which struck me for its direct product placement strategy. Like Disneyland, but instead of appealing to a world of common sense, *Distroller* disseminates its own nonsense through a narrative in which *Chamoys* are placed. *Chamoys* are archetypical dolls representing Mexican bilingual upper class—racialized culture, of sorts. For instance, there is "Berinice Rilouded" (Very Nice Reloaded), the exquisite or posh *Chamoy*, who is obviously blond and white. The "reloaded" *Chamoys* are interactive, as the young consumer can modify the doll's "Mud" (or mood).

Having grown up "playing" in Kidzania, children will not dream of the Playboy Mansion or Las Vegas (places for adult entertainment), but of cities like Hong Kong and Dubai; these are cities in the post-democratic global world that do not produce anything, but are rather nodes of international financial fluxes advocated toward sheer consumption of material and immaterial luxury goods.[34] If Disneyland is an amalgam of traditions, myths, stories, and visual regimes presented in a synchronic plane that eliminates the past, present, and future,[35] in Kidzania, the cultural elements are not atavic, but rather they simulate corporate culture in the temporality of the eternal present, as does *Distroller*, offering a world of ready-made myths to consume while furthering right-wing upper-class values. Under neoliberalism, cultivating self-efficiency is added to the possibility of nurturing an emancipatory subjectivity exercised through consumption. When we involve our intelligence and knowledge, behavior, tastes, opinions, dreams, and desires—when language and communication (the sensible) are captured for the purpose of the extraction of surplus value—this means that capitalism not only has reified everyday life and colonized vital time, but also operates affectively, causing deep changes in subjectivation and forms of life, dissociating language and sensibility. One of the consequences of the dissociation between language and sensibility is automatization, which means the decomposition of the linguistic function, the liquidation of meaning, and the source of psychopathologies like panic and anxiety.

The decline of disciplinary and control structures brought about new techniques of individuation, exemplified by a culture centered around personal identity, flexible modes of authority, ubiquitous networks, and ruthless branding of the most intimate aspects of subjective experience,[36] reflected in the call for individuals to self-express. Language, transformed into

---

34 Thorsten Botz-Bornstein, "A Tale of Two Cities: Hong Kong and Dubai," *Transcience* 3, no. 2 (2012): 1–16.

35 Baudrillard, "Disneyworld Company."

36 Jodi Dean, "Collective Desire and the Pathology of the Individual," in *The Psychopathologies of Cognitive Capitalism: Part One*, ed. Arne De Boever and Warren Neidich (Berlin: Archive Books, 2013).

communication between technological devices, has mutated to a sphere that is isolated from control through techno-biological automatisms ceasing to reveal, making communication opaque, and exterminating common sense, and substitutes it with redundancy, repetition, prefabricated intimacy, and intransitive communication. The mutations in the soul are caused by the semiotic fluxes that affect subjectivity, as they transform ways of seeing, feeling, desiring, enjoying, thinking, perceiving, inhabiting, dressing, and so forth, and thus propagate homogenization, extreme control, paralysis, and alienation. Capitalism, moreover, constantly molds governmentality by rendering flexible its means of subjectivation and subjection while vampirizing the labor time of workers, as well as all the aspects of life, psyche, and human sensibility.[37]

Wendy Brown explains that "best practices" or "benchmarking" are forms of "soft power," because they are focused on marking marketable spheres that previously were not subject to surplus value processes. "Best practices" mean executing internal reforms to maximize a company's competitive advantage and success by establishing goals, consensus, and ethics.[38] Among best-practice techniques, we can highlight giving form to the road toward a solution before a problem springs up; that is to say, to propose a previous script toward resolution, or to translate goals to concrete behaviors to solve problems.[39] Another example is the administrative techniques practiced at Zappos, an online shoes and clothing store located in the state of Nevada that has the goal of creating a special and unique workplace in order to make the workers happy by promoting a familiar working environment in which extravagance, creativity, and blurring the boundaries between being at home and at work prevail. Aside from clothes and shoes, Zappos declares to also sell "experiences."[40] In the realm of state control, what comes to mind is the organization of a

37 Franco "Bifo" Berardi, *The Soul at Work* (Los Angeles: Semiotext(e), 2009).

38 Brown, *Undoing the Demos*, 140.

39 Chip and Dan Heath, *Switch: How to Change Things When Change Is Hard* (New York: Crown Business, 2010).

40 The values of the Zappos family are: To deliver WOW through service; to welcome and to push for change; to create fun and a bit of weirdness; to be adventurous, creative and open; to seek through growth and learning; to create open and honest relationships through communication; to create a positive team and family spirit; to do more with less; to be passionate and determined; to be humble. See http://about.zappos.com/our-unique-culture/zappos-core-values.

quinceañera party as part of the pacification program—seeking to recuperate state control of thirty-eight favelas dominated by "organized crime"—at the favela Cerro-Cora by the Rio de Janeiro Military Police, a program established in Rio in 2014. The *quinceañeras* party took place at the Ilha Fiscal castle, where thirteen teenagers, some of them single mothers, lived for a night a fairy-tale story organized by "fairy godmothers" from the Unidad de Pacificación Policial (UPP, or Police Pacification Unit). With donations from the Copacabana Palace Hotel, from designer Monique Gracielle, and from Aquim's catering, the teenagers were made to feel like royalty for one night. In spite of the reputation the police have for acting violently against favela inhabitants, the girls' dance partners were members of the police corps.[41] Here is where neoliberal common sense applies, because what prevails is fulfilling the teenagers' desire to be "normal girls" for one night, although members of their families are routinely aggressed by the UPP.

The Conflict between Self-Interest and the Sustainability of Life

Before coaching, aerobics and bodybuilding were the individual activities for physical and mental self-betterment, emblematic of the 1980s and 1990s. They complemented a working regime that became more and more demanding and euphoric around the dot-com bubble, the liberalization of markets, and the mandate to self-model physically and mentally. On the eve of the twenty-first century, following the values of self-management, geared at utmost efficiency and performance through coaching ideology, yoga and jogging began to take over physical activities. Aside from relaxation and well-being, the first offers spiritual illumination, while the second works as an alternative to Ativan, Rivotril, or other meds that offer a daily dose of endorphins required by workers under the neoliberal regime. At the jogging track in the Tlalpan Park in Mexico City, every morning there is a mass of differentiated uniformity: dozens of Nike checkmarks and some triangles (if we were in a different part of the city, we would see Lulu Lemon and Alo) displayed on clothing of various styles tailored to an array of tastes, each body singled out in a dense crowd, moving like the Periférico during rush hour. On weekends,

---

41 Flora Charner, "Brazil's Favela Fairy Tale: When Prince Charming Packs Heat," *Aljazeera America*, November 24, 2014, http://america.aljazeera.com/multimedia/2014/11/debutantes-ball-riodejaneirofavela.html.

mothers can be seen running, dragging behind them children between the ages of three and five, cheering them on to keep up with them. And I wonder if perhaps they have no choice but to make them run behind because they have no one to help them look after their kids when they exercise. I have also seen couples identically dressed, pushing matching strollers, alternating pushing hands rhythmically in tandem. Sometimes there is a group of people wearing shirts with printed logos of the main entities governing the country: Bimbo, TV Azteca, Barcel, Grupo Salinas, SEMARNAT, and the legend, "I am helping to keep the park clean." They are members of the "Limpiemos nuestro México" (Let's clean our Mexico) brigade, a campaign that gathered 8.5 million volunteers who have picked up 138,000 tons of trash across the country.[42] Every weekend, this brigade visits public parks to clean them up. They believe they are providing a service to their community, but in fact, these concerned citizens unsuspectingly collaborate with politicians and functions previously covered by the State. Public parks, which are maintained by public funds, are periodically invaded businessmen to privatized marathons or other kinds of sports events subsidized by corporations that actually trash them with publicity and marketing. These forms of partial privatization of Tlalpan Park create a condition shared by other public spaces and roads throughout Mexico City, which is typical of neoliberalism. With the increasing presence of the corporate sector—and with there being more cars than public transportation, privatization of public roads, and the omnipresence of publicity—and the extension of market relations to every nook of the public sphere, the image of maximal individualization or collective atomization at the park is emblematic of privatization and self-cultivation, in detriment of the public in common, collaboration, equality, and interdependency. The rights of citizens to education, to health, or access to public spaces are slowly being substituted by other interests: to stay healthy, to be educated, and to be well-informed.

According to Brian Holmes, one of the consequences of autonomy and self-interest predominating in social and market relations is blindness, as well as the invisibilization of collateral damage.[43] Collateral damage implies the increasing need to depend on the market to access resources and services no longer guaranteed by the State. As subjects and markets become self-sufficient,

---

42 See http://www.limpiemosnuestromexico.com.

43 Brian Holmes, "Neoliberal Appetites," 16 Beaver Group, 2009, www.16beaver-group.org/drift/readings/bh_neoliberal_appetites.pdf

both inequality and monopolies become naturalized. It is now a common belief that those who are not self-sufficient have bad decision-making or investment habits, or who did not make enough of an effort, just like merchandises, are not good enough quality because they cannot compete, or they fail in creating and satisfying consumer needs. Holmes uses food as an example.[44] In order to maximize profit, agroindustry, which tends toward monopoly under the rule of Monsanto and Cargill, sells us products with genetic and transgenic modifications, sometimes contaminated with chemicals that damage our health. Agroindustry therefore sells bad-quality food. Acting on behalf of self-interest, consumers, conscious of the negative role agroindustry has in global warming and of the bad effects of industrially produced food on our health, choose to consume organic food. The optimization of markets and self interest in this sector, however, operates in detriment of the common good: there is no good-quality food at available prices for everyone, and in spite of the global food crisis, individual benefit (staying healthy) is above any possible political demands against damage to our bodies caused by the agroindustry sector.

Life is essentially vulnerable and interdependent, and the self-sufficiency ideal is not universalizable. According to Amaia Pérez Orozco, the self-sufficiency ideal is only achievable by creating exploitative (or injurious) forms of interdependency.[45] By putting social and life relationships at the center of the socioeconomic structure, life enters into conflict with capital because it has become the raw matter for production and accumulation processes. Life needs to be sustained both materially and emotionally—through what is known as reproductive labor, generally feminized—and the accumulation of capital depends on the exploitation of reproductive work and other forms of nonremunerated work, creating a structural tension between the accumulation of capital and the sustainability of life itself. The State, which is the organism that could mediate that tension, or that had attempted to mediate and palliate that tension as a result of many decades of political struggles, established the existence of collective responsibility in order to sustain life and regulate the working market, working rights, and business companies' contributions to social security.[46] Through what is known as the "Welfare State,"

44 Holmes, "Neoliberal Appetites."

45 Amaia Pérez Orozco, *Subversión feminista de la economía* (Madrid: Traficantes de Sueños, 2014).

46 Pérez Orozco, *Subversión feminista de la economía*, 161–76.

the State took charge of a number of dimensions of the sustainability of life—transportation, education, housing, pension, and health—with the purpose of collectivizing the responsibility of dealing with vital needs. Neoliberalism, however, implies the sustained dismantling of the collective structures that assure the sustainability of life, privatizing that responsibility.

Alongside life, bodies and their biological functions have become the raw matter of capitalism, fomenting a new form of alienation. For Marx, capitalist alienation implies that we feel human only during animalistic functions like drinking and eating. To this form of alienation conceptualized by Marx, we can add an extra neoliberal dimension: "lifehacking." Lifehacking consists of liberating the self from certain needs like eating, sleeping, or changing clothes, in order to be able to devote oneself fully to productive activities. An example is Soylent, a food substitute that solves the problem of the "loss of time" that implies the biological and recreative need to eat, which reflects the conviction that daily routine can and must be optimized.[47] On the website *Lifehacker*,[48] advice is shared about how to optimize activities and maximize productivity. For instance, it is suggested to buy five identical shirts and wear one many days in a row, every night putting it in the freezer to eliminate odors, avoiding having to wash and iron them. Lifehacking is thus a tool for self-Taylorization as an aid to deliver under pressure and to get through long and demanding workdays. It is also an example of how workers are restructuring themselves around corporate logic, in which life literally becomes work, and the ethos of the neoliberal self is its incorporeal existence in the market. This means that we live in an era in which all necessary labor to sustain life—reproductive labor—is ruthlessly subsumed to efficiency, profit, and productivity, becoming a direct threat to life. As a meme circulating in social-media states, internalized capitalism looks like: feeling guilty for resting, basing your self-worth on having a successful career, placing productivity before health, believing that hard work equals happiness, or using busyness as a way to avoid one's needs (@therapywithlee).

Under neoliberal logic, vital and bodily functions have become raw matter for production, and there are forms of life that are not profitable at all, especially the lives of the underclass, described by Bauman as those who inhabit

---

47 Jeff Sparrow, "Soylent, Neoliberalism and the Politics of Life Hacking," *Counterpunch*, May 19, 2014, www.counterpunch.org/2014/05/19/soylent-neoliberalism-and-the-politics-of-life-hacking.

48 See www.lifehacker.com.

the blank spaces in maps—blank because they are disconnected from the global markets, and thus dysfunctional from the point of view of productivity.[49] Naomi Klein has denominated these spaces "sacrifice zones," or those areas rich in "resources" that are more valuable than the work time that their inhabitants can offer, having thus become redundant, and giving way to what is known as necropolitics.[50] The redundant populations are also being produced by automation: human labor is slowly becoming redundant, and many will not be required to participate in (or be remunerated for) productive activity in the near future.

Amaia Pérez Orozco has reconceptualized Judith Butler's notion of "non-mournable lives," which implies a series of social rhetorics and practices that frame the loss of lives as either mournable or non-mournable. Non-mournable lives have become targets for exclusion or annihilation, with the purpose of maintaining the status quo of the lives that are considered to be "worthy of living";[51] Pérez Orozco speaks of "lives worthy of being lived." In her view, the socioeconomic system establishes varying levels of life that deserve to be lived, mourned, or rescued. What would a life look like, if worthy of being lived, in spite of state violence, dispossession, food crisis, impoverishment, forced migration, and pollution undergone by exhausted, tired, and ill bodies? Under the neoliberal scheme, well-being is measured by one's capacity for consumption. How can one flee the enslavement of salaried work? How can we create autonomous spaces where life can exist, and where we can take our bodies back, to promote dignified lives with different rules to those imposed by the neoliberal system as common sense?[52]

4. Neoliberal Imaginaries for Subjectivation

In order to sustain the necessary unreality it needs to function, neoliberal democracies are grounded on the visualization and discourses that organize attention and desires toward its own goals. For instance, through cinema and cultural production, neoliberalism operates directly on the collective

49 Zygmut Bauman, *Globalization* (New York: Columbia University Press, 1998).

50 See Sayak Valencia's interpretation of Achille Mbembe's concept of "necropolitics" in *Gore Capitalism* (New York: Semiotext(e), 2018); and Achille Mbembe, *Necropolitics* (Durham, NC: Duke University Press, 2019).

51 Judith Butler, *Frames of War* (London: Verso, 2009).

52 Pérez Orozco, *Subversión feminista de la economía*, 35–73.

imaginary. Examples of programmatic movies would be the hundreds of films that were produced and screened during George W. Bush's regime, dedicated to everything that happens before, after, and around a wedding.[53] There are also Hollywood narratives devoted to apocalyptic themes, populating cinema screens since 2000. Clearly, the spirit transmitted by these kinds of narratives reaffirms the hegemonic tendency to make it easier to imagine the end of the world rather than the end of capitalism. There are also films that purport the myth of the successful entrepreneur, from Martin Scorsese's *The Wolf of Wall Street* (2013) to its "third-world" version in Danny Boyle's *Slumdog Millionaire* (2008). But the ground archetype for the myth of the entrepreneur is conveyed in John Wells's *The Company Men* (2010), a film in which Bobby (Ben Affleck) loses his job at CTX when the corporation decides to downsize due to recession. Bobby loses everything but manages to reinvent himself, working as a carpenter for his (much less successful) brother-in-law, and after a long purgatory, which involves giving up his many cars, his wife, and his mansion, he gets right back on track to the top. Dozens of movies depicting stories of entrepreneur musicians, dancers, finance wizards, lawyers, and others have populated our screens in the past fifteen or so years. There is even an indie version of this narrative: in Noa Baumbach's *Frances Ha* (2012), we see a young woman (Greta Gerwig) in New York City struggle to achieve her dreams living a deeply precarious life, following the mandate to succeed in the city.

To this imaginary, we can add the Mexican critique against the system through the circulation of fictions like *La ley de Herodes* (1999), *El infierno* (2010), and *La dictadura perfecta* (2014), all by Luis Estrada; there is also Fernando Naranjo's *Miss Bala* (2011), *Heli* (2012) by Amat Escalante, *La jaula de oro* (2014) by Diego Quemada Diez, or documentaries like *En el hoyo* (2006) by Juan Carlos Rulfo, *¡De panzazo!* (2012) by Carlos Loret de Mola, and *Colosio: The Murder* (2012) by Carlos Bolado, among others. All of these films make visible, to a certain degree, the mechanisms of corruption in the country, giving voice to the general feeling of discontent with the PRI (the National Revolution Party) and its legacy in our political culture and practices. These critical fictions would seemingly enable civil society to put in check the governing regime by making sensitive information public. But just as apocalyptic films make it easier for us to imagine that everything will remain the

53 Between 1950 and 2000, the total of films with that subject was 164. Between 2000 and 2019, a total of 110 were planned.

same till doomsday, they naturalize corruption as inherent to the Mexican character. While fear and collective victimization are activated, empathy is shut down. According to Steven Shaviro, digital moving images that surround us are *expressive*: this means that they are both symptomatic and productive, insofar as they give voice (sound and image) to a kind of sensibility that floats in the air, permeating our society, and that is not attributable to any subject in particular. This implies that audiovisual production does not represent social processes, but rather, it actively participates in them by helping to constitute them, generating affect and extracting surplus value from it. The fluxes of affect catch us and take us away from ourselves in the form of emotions. This is why movement images do not represent but actively construct and stage social relations.[54] In other words, images, aside from being part of reality, act upon it, giving it shape. For instance, the first sequence of *La dictadura perfecta* begins with an interview at Palacio Nacional between the Mexican President and the US ambassador. The meeting occurs in front of a few journalists, and the Mexican president is vouching for a migratory reform in the United States that would favor Mexicans, because "Trabajamos más que los negros" (We work harder than Negroes).[55] The president's racist slip is an object of immediate transformation into a meme that becomes viral in social media. When the image of the president making the politically incorrect declaration becomes autonomous—that is, neither politicians nor the mass media have control over it—the directors of "Televisión Mexicana" (Televisa's doppelgänger) decide to apply the "Chinese Box," a method designed to distract the masses by creating another trending topic: a greater political scandal that will neutralize the previous one, turning attention away from the president's indiscretion. Ironically, Enrique Peña Nieto's regime was characterized by an endless succession of scandals, and now with President Andrés Manuel López Obrador, as I will further discuss in chapter 5, shitstorms on the Internet as a form of governing have become the rule. After Franco Berardi, power is no longer constructed by silencing the crowd, for instance, through censorship, broadcast media, or political discourse, and neither is it grounded on repressive tolerance. It is now based on the intensification of noise. For Bifo, social

54 Steven Shaviro, *Post-Cinematic Affect* (London: Zero Books, 2010).

55 In fact, President Vicente Fox made that statement in 2005. Rosa Elvira Vargas, "Realizan mexicanos trabajos que ni los negros quieren: Fox," *La Jornada*, May 14, 2005, https://www.jornada.com.mx/2005/05/14/index.php?section=politica&article=008n1pol.

signification is no longer a system of exchange and decoding of meaning, but saturation (a neural hyperstimulation). This is the basis of "post-political" power, along with having control over the shitstorms in the Infosphere. Power stimulates collective expression, controlling the data emerging from the noise in the world: white noise is the current social order.[56] Evidently, technical transformations have changed the conditions of mental activity and forms of interaction between the individual and the collective sphere.

In the second decade of the twenty-first century, the mindscape and the social scene are flooded by flows of unhappiness and violence. Ignacio Sánchez Prado elaborates on the presence of fear as a form of life as embedded in neoliberalized subjectivities, through its presence in the collective imaginary. Fear and pain are present in narratives, both in the mass media and cultural products that privilege violence, as well as in the social dynamics behind such scenarios. According to Sánchez Prado, these imaginaries negotiate the rupture of the social contract from the Welfare State that linked revolutionary nationalism with modernization. According to Sánchez Prado, the cultural narratives of the first half of the twentieth century predominated imagined migrant subjects coming to the city to incorporate themselves to the newly industrialized Mexican reserve. An allegorical relationship was thus established between individual and nation, enabling the territorialization of marginal subjects to material structures (like worker unions and campesino organizations linked to the PRI). "Mexicaneity" then meant citizenship. Sánchez Prado further argues that neoliberal sensible production registers the loss of the horizon of citizenship and modernization, narrating subjectivities no longer linked to the nation-state subjectivation machine, but to neoliberal precarization machines. Alejandro González Iñárritu's *Amores perros* (2001), Alfonso Cuarón's *Y tu mamá también* (2001), and Alejandro Gerber Biccecci's *Viento aparte* (2014) all register forms of life whose relationship to Mexican culture's symbolic and citizen structures have been rendered precarious. The imaginaries of the precarization machinery are processes of political and juridical de-subjectivation that enable the efficient incorporation of bodies to the new regimes of sovereignty and labor: vulnerable, racialized bodies pullulate in these new imaginaries of violence, uprooting, and displacement like *La jaula de oro*, Luis Mandoki's *La vida precoz y breve de Sabina Rivas* (2012), or *Miss Bala*. Unable to be part of the neoliberal economy as productive entities,

56 Franco "Bifo" Berardi, *Breathing: Chaos and Poetry* (South Pasadena, CA: Semiotext(e), 2018).

the characters in these films are rendered precarious through different forms of brutality like rape, ending up in the monetization of their bodies.[57]

A parallel imaginary to that of political and juridical de-subjectivation originates in the "war against drugs," an official narrative stemming from the resignification of the "red threat" of the Cold War that posited drug trafficking as a global threat. According to Oswaldo Zavala, a "ghost" of organized crime was created through the myth of powerful drug traffickers waging a war against each other for territorial control, while defying Mexican State violence. The work of writers such as Juan Pablo Villalobos, Yuri Herrera, or Élmer Mendoza constitute narco-narratives, which, according to Zavala, are the indirect result of the imaginary disseminated by official sources since the 1970s, creating a discursive matrix that imposed the rules of enunciation and narrative functions of "narco," creating a habitus of meanings about this phenomenon.[58] Journalism by Sergio González Rodríguez, Alejandro Imazán, Diego Enrique Osorno, Anabel Hernández, and Edgardo Buscaglia further disseminated this discursive matrix to explain violence across the country, validating official discourse.

While the government has used the discursive matrix of the war against drugs to further its policy of militarization as a means to securitize the country, the push toward development has left a trail of destruction, and the poor are free-falling toward their own redundancy (and death). As do the narratives of precarization, the politics of safety prioritize personal comfort, bringing the potential of political subjectivation to a standstill. And what is beneath this discourse of security is racial violence, because the populations affected are originary or mestizos from rural or urban areas that constitute the working class of the country. According to Jackie Wang, the underside of security is racial violence. She writes: "White civil society has an investment in the erasure and abjection of bodies onto which they project hostile feelings."[59] A racializing logic is behind who is considered acceptable to be killed or raped, and the links that are woven between our lives and the generalized

57 Ignacio M. Sánchez Prado, "Máquinas de precarización: afectos y violencias de la cultura neoliberal," in *Precariedades, exclusiones y emergencias: Necropolítica y sociedad civil en América Latina*, ed. Mabel Moraña, and José Manuel Valenzuela (México D.F.: UAM Iztpalapa y Gedisa, 2018), 98–106.

58 Sánchez Prado, "Máquinas de precarización," 98–106.

59 Jackie Wang, *Carceral Capitalism* (New York: Semiotext(e), 2018), 287.

atmosphere of violence, following Wang, is submerged in a complex web of institutions, structures, and economic relations that legalize and legitimize this ceaseless repetition of violence.[60] This web of relationships determines who may be murdered or assaulted; there are, of course, exceptions of "morally agreeable cases," based on standards of legitimate victimhood[61] like state violence exercised in Atenco (2006) and Ayotzinapa (2014), or femicides. In these cases, the inherent precarity lived by racialized and gendered subjects serve as instruments for emotional relief for privileged populations, which clearly live in a separate world in which different rules apply: legal processes and police authorities bend the rule of law to protect and accommodate them (as they do to render the lives of the redundant populations precarious or to eradicate them). This is how the global capitalist legal system is not only a continuation of colonialism, but corruption itself legalized. As sensible imaginaries that justify and perpetuate this state of affairs prevail, we could argue that culture is no longer an exception that makes visible something to illuminate spectators and potentially change things, but is more and more a central ingredient of our mainstream "real" economy and governmentality. In a way, cultural production conceals what I call the "double bind, or *pharmakon* of modernity"; it serves the purpose of evidencing and thus concealing the colonial carnage necessary for modern progress to advance, even as it strategically reveals this same carnage for the purpose of accruing cultural capital. The modern *worlding of the world*—which includes the production of objective reality by experimental science, knowledge, and design—coincides with the ruthless elimination and instrumentalizaton of certain creatures by others. This blind spot is the "habit" of coloniality. Habit, according to Elaine Scarry, either closes down sensation entirely or builds up perception as its own interior. Habit creates sentience by either opening or closing the world.[62] The habit of coloniality is ingrained in the Western unconscious, predicating universality, progress, betterment, and growth on the eradication of alterity. This is the condition of modernity itself, even as it furnishes the resources for a critique of such systemic destruction. As Rolando Vázquez argues, "The narrative of salvation of modernity was built on the denial of the genocidal violence

60 Wang, *Carceral Capitalism*, 287.

61 Wang, *Carceral Capitalism*, 294.

62 Elaine Scarry, *Thermonuclear Monarchy: Choosing Between Democracy and Doom* (New York: W. W. Norton, 2014), 377, 378.

of colonialism."[63] The first mass colonial genocide was the early expression of a system geared toward the consumption of human and nonhuman life—that is, the consumption of the earth.[64]

In Mexico and Latin America, the ordeals of Indigenous peoples are currently known as "environmental conflicts." Their source is the neoliberal strategy of expropriating "natural resources," or rather, "the commons," through extractive projects across the country. This strategy has been implemented through the introduction of industrialized agriculture, a system that excludes small producers and destroys sustainability. Such extraction and exploitation of the commons is evident, for example, in mining concessions and in the construction of infrastructure projects like highways, ports, tourist enclaves, trash dumps, and dams designed to centralize energy in big cities, and to connect territories rich in "resources" and "cheap labor" to the flows of global exchange. In the past 15 years alone, the Mexican government has granted 24,000 concessions for open-pit mining. Under agreements such as NAFTA, transnational corporations are entitled to file lawsuits against local governments who fail to stop local interference with their resource-extraction efforts.[65] To block these neoliberal processes of capital accumulation, new forms of resistance are emerging. These seek access to and control of the means of subsistence (like land and seeds) and are accompanied by new forms of communal recomposition. Mina Lorena Navarro explains these efforts to defend territory across Latin America as a new sensibility of peoples and their environment, and as the actualization of "nonpredatory" life worlds against capitalist and extractivist relationships.[66]

---

63 Rolando Vázquez, "Precedence, Earth and the Anthropocene: Decolonizing Design" *Design Philosophy Papers* 15, no. 1 (2017): 77–91. https://doi.org/10.1080/14487136.2017.1303130.

64 Vázquez, "Precedence, Earth and the Anthropocene."

65 Two recent examples in Colombia are Gran Colombia Gold against the Colombian government for the Marmato project and South African miner Anglo Gold Ashanti, struggling to retain access to 33 million ounces of gold at their La Colosa site. See Luke Taylor, "Canada's Gran Colombia Gold Files $700 Million Lawsuit Against Colombia Over Marmato Project," *Financial Post*, April 10, 2017, http://business.financialpost.com/news/mining/canadas-gran-colombia-gold-files-700-million-lawsuit-against-colombia-over-marmato-project.

66 Mina Lorena Navarro, "Luchas por lo común contra el renovado cercamiento de bienes naturales en México," *Bajo el volcán* 13, no. 21 (September 2013).

The Habit of Coloniality and the Double Bind of Modernity[67]

In April of 2017, the Juan Rulfo Foundation withdrew from its plan to participate in the ninth annual Book and Rose Fair at the Universidad Nacional Autónoma de México. The Foundation objected to Cristina Rivera Garza's scheduled presentation of her new book on Rulfo, *Había mucha neblina o humo o no sé que* (There was a lot of fog or smoke or I do not know), which it considered to be "defamatory." Garza's book offers Juan Rulfo as an embodiment of modernity's double bind. Known primarily for *El Llano en llamas* (The plain in flames), a short-story collection from 1953, and his novel *Pedro Páramo* from 1955, Rulfo also worked for Goodrich-Euzkadi, a transnational company responsible for expanding the tourism industry in Mexico. He was also an advisor and a researcher for the Papaloapan Commission, the state organization charged with extracting "natural resources" from Southern Mexico; most notably, the commission installed the Miguel Alemán Dam in Nuevo Soyaltepec in Oaxaca. Rulfo legitimized the emblematic projects of Mexican modernity in the mid-twentieth century, even as he memorialized the very peoples whom his work risked erasing in his writing and photography.[68] Rivera Garza compares Rulfo's vision to that of Walter Benjamin's Angel of History: a retrospective gaze that observes—even relishes—all the details of the disaster caused by the winds pulling it toward the future.

Modernization and memorialization coincided in Rulfo's position as the head of publishing at the Instituto Nacional Indigenista (INI or National Indigenous Institute), a state institution created to look after the needs of all Indigenous Mexicans. Founded in 1948 with the goal of integrating Indigenous peoples into "national" culture by "acculturating them," and thus "elevating their condition," INI's policies were characterized by a homogenization of Mexico's "ethnic" groups. This understanding of Indigenity as a problem to be solved is what links Goodrich-Euzkadi, the Papaloapan Commission, and the INI, which combined to threaten autonomous life and community work in the name of development and modernization. In the 1950s, the euphemism

---

67 A version of what follows appeared as "Fog or Smoke? Colonial Blindness and the Closure of Representation" in *e-flux journal* 84 (May 2017), https://www.e-flux.com/journal/82/134265/fog-or-smoke-colonial-blindness-and-the-closure-of-representation.

68 Cristina Rivera Garza, *Había mucha neblina o humo o no sé que* (México D.F.: Random House, 2017).

reacomodo, which means "rearrangement" or "reshuffling," was coined to designate Indigenous extermination while obscuring the colonial matrix.

That Rivera Garza's contradictory portrait of Rulfo would be considered defamatory is in itself representative of modernity's colonial blind spot, which, like Freud's neurotic, cannot bear to hear its past openly or honestly discussed. An active agent of the Mexican State's modernization project and a passionate believer in progress, Rulfo's reports to the Papaloapan Commission amplified 1950s attitudes about Oaxaca as one of Mexico's "backward" regions, whose natives were seen as primitive and thus nonexistent. Their territory was officially qualified as "virgin" (or empty). Describing the living conditions of Chinantecos and Mazatecos in the Soyaltepec Valley region, Rulfo took an active, firsthand role in their *reacomodo,* helping to justify the government's efforts to displace and dispossess them. Nevertheless, Rivera Garza also portrays Rulfo as an advocate working in solidarity with Indigenous communities, looking melancholically at their ruin and misery though his photographs that document the imminent loss of vital Indigenous material culture. This tension is apparent in Rulfo's other works as well, such as his short story "Talpa" (1953), in the script for *La fórmula secreta (Coca Cola en la sangre)* (*The Secret Formula: Coca-Cola in the Blood*, 1965), and in *El despojo* (*The Plunder*, 1976).[69] "Talpa" is a confessional monologue that describes the narrator's travels with his brother, Tanilo, and his wife, Natalia, to see the legendary Virgin of Talpa in the hopes that she will heal Tanilo's terminal illness. The narrator describes Tanilo's mutilated body in detail as it disintegrates during the pilgrimage through arid, hot, and dusty land. The trip becomes an aimless voyage toward nothing but guilt: the narrator and Tanilo's wife are in love, and both know that Tanilo will not survive the trip. Yet they press him onward, secretly desiring to "finish him off" forever. Tanilo's death march in search of the savior Virgin becomes an allegory for Indigenous *reacomodo.* The displacement justified by the "progress" of modernity and the benefits of a nation-state is in fact an aimless, self-destructive trip toward annihilation.

In a sequence from *La fórmula secreta*, we see Indigenous people in three distinct contexts: first as peasants; then in the baroque Santa María Tonanzintla church in San Andrés Cholula, Mexico (alluding to the hybridity of pre-Hispanic and Spanish culture in the country); and then wearing modern

---

69 Published in *Revista de América*, January 1953.

clothes and suspended from a ceiling. The sequence poses a question: How will originary peoples be figured or represented by the modernizing process? How will they be figured, that is, once they have "Coca-Cola in the blood"? What place or role will modern Mexico offer them? The film ends with a long list of transnational companies that were besieging Mexico in the 1960s. Although animated by a belief in a modern future for all, Rulfo's literary and cinematic work depicts the suffering and abjection of Indigenous peoples' social and cultural deaths.

These forms of political subjectivation stand in direct opposition to capitalism. Still, they remain *other*, either because the habit of coloniality perceives them as nonmodern, as stubborn remnants of a residual world, or—in what is the opposite valence of the same judgment—because they are romanticized and identified with the "noble savage" by way of this same projection of "prior-ness." From the romantic point of view, Indigenous struggles are regarded as "a road to the future," because in fighting corporate-led environmental catastrophe, Indigenous people are fighting on behalf of all of us.[70] But this picture of originary peoples helping to "save the future" and shape new forms of worldly cohabitation is highly problematic. Part of the problem is that "environmental justice" struggles remain localized and culturally specific. Connections among and between them are precarious. As a result, to the extent that struggles for territory defense are grounded in "environmental identities," environmental injustice goes hand in hand with cultural loss. Because the prevailing counterhegemonic framework amalgamates cultural identities, ways of life, and self-perception into a metaphysical connection between given communities and their physical environment, environmental struggles remain unlinked to the responsibilities that privileged inhabitants of urban areas have as the main consumers of "resources" such as real estate, food, and fossil fuel.[71] The result is a revived pastoralism, where these same communities are used as prestige resources available for exploitation, and as

70 Noam Chomsky, "Los pueblos indígenas están salvando al planeta de un desastre ambiental," *Ecoosfera*, March 2017, http://ecoosfera.com/2017/03/noam-chomsky-activismo-ambiental-indigena-latinoamericano-video.

71 Robert Melchior Figueroa, "Indigenous Peoples and Cultural Losses," in *Climate Change and Society*, ed. John S. Dryzek, Richard B. Norgaard, and David Schlossberg (Oxford, UK: Oxford University Press, 2016).

a salve for colonial guilt. Perversely, the "enlightened" metropolitan subject uses those most victimized by the historical Enlightenment to reconfirm their commitment to those same values of freedom, justice, and equality.

What is at stake in Indigenous peoples' struggles is decidedly not freedom, equality, or justice, but rather the short-to-mid-term survival of their communities and of humanity at large. This is what makes these struggles so difficult to represent outside of their own local specificities. When Indigenous communities mobilize to defend their lands from narco-exploitation or from megaprojects like mining and hydroelectric plants, repression and killing are the rule. The state has beaten, tortured, imprisoned, and murdered many of those who have fought against pollution, land theft, deforestation, and the destruction of rivers.[72] In the territories of Indigenous people—regarded by neoliberal common sense as "markets"—an apparatus of dispossession and a state of exception are imposed. Mina Lorena Navarro writes that this apparatus is built on institutional consensus and legitimacy, cooptation and capture, disciplining and normalization, and criminalization and counterinsurgency—and evidently racialization. The apparatus operates on a continuum of material and representational violence that crescendos as the state becomes the guarantor of the accumulation of capital.[73] The apparatus is accompanied by transnational legitimization tools like NAFTA, and US-led antidrug campaigns like the Plan Mérida which are really just forms of neocolonial war, genocide, and ethnocide.[74] The habit of coloniality lurks behind the symbolic and discursive efficacy of the apparatus of dispossession.

---

72 Margarita Warnholtz Locht, "Represión en Michoacán," *Animal Político*, April 7, 2017, http://www.animalpolitico.com/blogueros-codices-geek/2017/04/07/represion-en-michoacan.

73 Claudia Composto and Mina Mina Lorena Navarro, "Claves de lectura para comprender el despojo y las luchas por los bienes comunes naturales en América Latina," in *Territorios en Disputa: Despojo capitalista, luchas en defensa de los bienes comunes naturales y alternativas emancipatorias para América Latina*, Claudia Composto y Mina Mina Lorena Navarro, Compiladoras (México D.F.: Bajo Tierra Ediciones, 2014).

74 Santiago Arbolez Quiñonez, "Plan Colombia: Descivilización, genocidio, etnocidio y destierro," in *Territorios en Disputa: Despojo capitalista, luchas en defensa de los bienes comunes naturales y alternativas emancipatorias para América Latina*, ed. Claudia Composto and Mina Mina Lorena Navarro (México D.F.: Bajo Tierra Ediciones, 2014).

The A-Representability of Originary Peoples' Struggles

Climate change is generally understood as an unintended effect of modernity. Modernity is blind to its colonial habit, and this is one reason why most environmental struggles lack a framework that connects coloniality to the Anthropocene. For instance, members of the Mexico City–based Cráter Invertido Collective have done counter-information work in solidarity with the community of Ostula, in the state of Michoacán. The inhabitants of Ostula are currently defending their sovereignty and way of life against narcos, the military, and illegal deforestation. Symptomatically, the young artists of Cráter Invertido Collective have been unable to draw a link between their political activism in Ostula and political work in the city, or a project of decolonization. And yet, the struggles in which the collective has engaged remain present in their fanzines, posters, and drawings. In 2015, a communality congress took place at a university in Puebla, gathering academics from all over Latin America to discuss the links between decolonization, environmental struggles, and new forms of community organization. Somehow, the word "communality" was substituted for "socialism" as the new politically correct ideology to which progressive researchers must now subscribe. The obvious question—how to translate "communality" into urban contexts—was absent from the discussion. Another example of the blind spot inherent to the double bind of modernity is the celebratory conversation that took place around Norman Foster's Mexico City airport project. As we saw in the previous chapter, the airport was meant to be built in Atenco, an expropriated ejido (plot of communal land) where local resistance had taken place since President Vicente Fox announced the project in 2006. That year, resistance was followed by massive repression, including the pervasive use of gendered violence. The group Frente de Pueblos en Defensa de la Tierra (FPDT or Front of Peoples in Defense of the Land) gained international visibility for its fight against the Atenco airport, but the struggle and its repression have since been forgotten. The creative class lobbied for Foster to consult FPDT as he developed his plan for the airport, and the privileged sector of the population rejoiced at how the airport would make life easier for everyone in the city. But the airport would have inflicted heavy human and environmental "collateral damage," especially on the local communities (it already has, as a large percentage of the infrastructure was built before President López Obrador canceled it in 2019), and this was conveniently forgotten in the rush to praise the project. In its neoliberal manifestation, coloniality embodies a new cycle of dispossession in Latin America, based on the belief that the lands where Indigenous peoples live are more valuable than the labor their inhabitants can provide.

For Eyal Weizman, climate change has never been an unintended side effect of colonization, but rather its declared goal. In his important recent book *Erasure: The Conflict Shoreline*, he develops a hypothesis that connects colonialism to environmental changes. Weizman's chief case study is the "battle for the Negev" in which the Israeli State has sought to uproot Bedouins from the Negev desert in order to plant forests and expand the forestation line. Weizman studies the Negev's movable frontier as it advances and recedes in response to colonization, displacement, urbanization, agricultural trends, and climate change, all phenomena intrinsically tied to dispossession. In the Negev, "making the desert bloom" is, in effect, changing the climate.[75] In Mexico, Lake Chalco exemplifies a similar historical link between displacement and global warming. As we saw in the previous chapter, in the nineteenth century, under the regime of Porfirio Díaz, Spanish entrepreneur Iñigo Noriega Lasso sought to expand arable land by draining Xico, the lake adjacent to Chalco and Xochimilco on the outskirts of Mexico City. Similar to Israel's displacement of the nomadic Bedouins, Noriega Lasso forced the lake's originary peoples to work as peasants in his hacienda. In the Negev, as in Chalco and Atenco, climate change and the displacement of originary populations go hand in hand.

In 2003, Juan Rulfo's Instituto Nacional Indigenista became the Comisión Nacional para el Desarrollo de los Pueblos Indígenas (CDI, or National Commission for the Development of Indigenous Peoples), premised on the idea that Indigenous groups have the right to preserve their ethnic identity and should participate in the planning of development projects. Although CDI's task is to recognize Indigenous cultures and the plurality of Mexico (correcting for INI's homogenization of Mexico's ethnic groups), the organization only undermines the cultures and bodies of Indigenous peoples, insofar as it reinforces their status as beings apart. In the eyes of CDI, Indigenous peoples "have things of their own"—like traditional customs, religious beliefs, and medical remedies—that need not only be recorded and admired, but mined for corporate patents. Difference is relativized, and it continues to justify a relationship of inequality. Having been made vulnerable by neoliberal international agreements, how can Indigenous peoples protect themselves, their

75 Eyal Weizman, *Erasure: The Conflict Shoreline* (Göttingen: Steidl Verlag, 2016).

lands, and their knowledges as political, not cultural entities, as I discussed in the previous chapter?[76]

If modernity figured Indigenous peoples and their lands as the foundational (re)source of nation-states, neoliberal common sense has turned them into maquiladora laborers, *sicarios*, kidnappers, and "illegals" deported from the United States. In this schema, the local technocrats functions as the broker between transnational corporations and the natives as resources to be exploited. Here, equality, as we have seen, means inclusion as debtors and consumers, and those who remain outside circuits of consumption and debt—the "other" of *homo oeconomicus*—are systematically criminalized. New versions of the 1950s *reacomodo* have emerged in the form of efforts to displace Indigenous peoples to "sustainable rural cities."

From literature and philosophy to politics and the arts, discourses about Mexico's native populations are still dominated by a mentality of colonization, slavery, and dispossession. This means that Indigenous populations continue to appear as other, as spectacle, as subjects of anthropology and ethnography, and, more recently, as markets to be exploited. With the rise of neoliberal globalization, Indigenous peoples have passed from being a "problem" that must be dealt with through modernization and civilization, to redundant populations that must be managed through repression, displacement, and genocide, or by being "modernized" by imposing on their lands agroindustry, infrastructure projects, or Special Economic Zones. They are still targeted for elimination, but less through physical death (although this is still tragically common) than through exclusion, confinement, and resource extraction. The war against underdevelopment is a war against the redundant populations of twenty-first-century capitalism.

Toward Radical Imaginaries of Relational, Decolonizing Representation?

It is telling that in their struggles against "projects of death"—that is, extraction and infrastructure projects—Indigenous peoples are figured as faceless. Recall the iconic balaclava of Subcomandante Marcos, who declared, "We are all behind the mask." This facelessness makes clear that the disappeared Indigenous body is only visible through capitalist colonialist relationships.

---

76 Linda Tuhiwai Smith, *Decolonizing Methodologies* (London: Zed Books, 1999), 27.

We must remember that while the original epoch of colonization is over, colonizing relationships persist. Government and corporate projects to transform Indigenous territories into profitable markets bring Indigenous groups into contact with NGOs, researchers, and development agencies that view these projects not only as emancipating oppressed communities from underdevelopment, but also as serving the greater good of humanity as a whole. This is why Indigenous knowledges, cultures, and languages remain sites of anticapitalistic struggle—albeit struggle that is culturally specific and territorially bound, and thus unable to build bridges to struggles elsewhere. For instance, the inhabitants of Cherán, Michoacán, dismantled state political institutions complicit with the deforestation of their territories. A new precarious politicized subject emerged, but one that was still perceived as other, nonmodern, foreign, and unrepresentable. This failure of representation is closely bound up with the habit of coloniality.

A recent version of the double bind of modernity has posited design and the arts as the means to reinvent life, defend autonomous zones, and protect the environment. In this framework, cultural transformation is thought to direct new forms of political organization and bridge the gap between grassroots action and government policy. As T. J. Demos has written recently, "Creative ecologies of collective resistance [can create] new combinations of images and stories, music and participation, solidarities and sacrifices . . . [enabling] a 'Great Transition.' "[77] The problem with this approach is that it remains confined to cultural representation (as opposed to political representation) and is thus prone to the fascist essentializing of culture. Moreover, as Linda Tuhiwai Smith has argued, if the West's concept of culture remains the only legitimate form of emancipatory politics—easily universalized and not really "owned" by anyone—it will merely reaffirm the West as the center of all legitimate knowledge and action.[78] This idea of culture will lead to a new imposition of Western authority over all aspects of Indigenous struggle.

In the face of the urgent need to neutralize the extractive model, block accumulation by dispossession, and end environmental degradation and the destruction of human beings, liberals still navigate the double bind of modernity in the melancholy style of Juan Rulfo; we are just as sad, just as beautiful,

---

77 See T. J. Demos, "The Great Transition: The Arts and Radical System Change," *e-flux journal* (April 2017), http://www.e-flux.com/architecture/accumulation/122305/the-great-transition-the-arts-and-radical-system-change.

78 Tuhiwai Smith, *Decolonizing Methodologies*, 66.

just as ineffective. We must break out of this trap and realize that modernity's way of worlding the world is by annihilating worlds. This devastating impulse is behind Eduardo Abaroa's *Total Destruction of the National Anthropology Museum* (2012), an installation that comprises a detailed hypothetical plan on how to physically destroy the building. Abaroa's project (first shown at the Kurimanzutto Gallery in Mexico City) underscores the narrative of the Mexican modern nation based on the obliteration and then on the museification of pre-Hispanic and originary cultures reduced in complexity. Their destruction and dispossession is the premise of the wealth of a few in the country. Abaroa's piece anticipates more recent discussions in Europe around the repatriation of colonial spoils as decolonial gestures.

A nonfascist, anticolonial form of aesthetico-political representation would encompass the counterknowledges produced in Indigenous struggles, and it would ultimately lead to the dissolution of representation in favor of relation. According to Rolando Vázquez, relationality is a mode of realization that recalls and foregrounds, that sustains and gives, that is before the before. It is a coming-into-presence grounded in precedence, as opposed to representation (which always has a blind spot). Noncolonial representation acknowledges the other of modernity and colonization, and it challenges the tenets of modernity itself.[79] This is the aesthetic, political, and intellectual task at hand.

According to Lebanese philosopher Jalal Touffic, the long-term effects of material and social destruction remain in the depths of the body and psyche as traumatic latent effects that become genetic codes. Anhishnaabeweke (ojibwe) activist and academic Winona LaDuke has explained how her people, after having suffered colonization and living as third-class citizens in the United States, live subject to corrupt leadership and an epidemic of PSTD. LaDuke's community—with the highest suicide rate in the United States—is one of many across the world living with the genetic memory of catastrophe, trying to survive. Other consequences of displacement, dispossession, and military and colonial occupation are eradication of identity, as well as cancelation and destruction of a world of moral belonging. There are, thus, entire communities surviving the end of their world in conditions of senselessness and solitude. These populations are trapped living in intolerant worlds, at a time in which the intolerable is no longer considered to be serious injustice, but

79 Vázquez, "Precedence, Earth and the Anthropocene."

has become everyday banality. How can these populations reject the conditions under which they live? The imaginaries that circumscribe and racialize their life forms, communities, subjectivities? How can they elect a life worthy of being lived? How can they become strong in order to rise up?

For his exhibition at Lawndale Art Center, "There is Nothing Left for Us in the Thickness," Saúl Hernández-Vargas takes up the task to explore means to invoke the energy of his Oaxacan pre-Hispanic ancestors along with the life world that was destroyed by colonization and by nation-state's official history. In a decolonizing effort and creating a true-false (or false memory) archive, he seeks to unveil, through a specific case study, the ways in which Mexico's nationalist narratives have implanted succeeding mestizo identities on the Oaxacan peoples, transforming them into "Mexicans." Although in the nationalist narrative the Mexican independence of Spain meant liberation from the colonial yoke, colonial patterns are still present through the racialization of originary peoples who exist merely as a tourist attraction, as opposed to potential political entities (which are unfailingly criminalized) and whose lands are being targeted for destruction as transnational resource-extraction or touristic sites. In tandem, the progressive de-Indigenization of Mexico's originary peoples has been executed through the ideology of "mestizaje,"[80] which has meant the Hispanization, Christianization, homogenization, and modernization of originary peoples and their transformation into folklore, but also into cheap labor hands, consumers, and subjects to "development." Mixe writer Yásnaya Elena Aguilar explains that originary peoples are not the mythical root or origins of Mexico, but that their role in national consciousness as archeological curiosities means their constant negation. For Yásnaya, moreover, "mestizo" is not a racial category but a political project by the Mexican State, and the fact that originary peoples identify as "mestizos" means the triumph of the colonial nation-sate over them.[81] In the Mexican official narrative, every mestizo is the inheritor of the great archaeological patrimony safeguarded by the nation-state. This homogenized material Indigenous heritage is found and preserved through the national science of archeology, and archeology has therefore been one of the main mestizaje tools used by the

---

80 Or "hybridization" between pre-Hispanic and Spanish cultures.

81 Pablo Ferri, "Interview with Yásnaya Elena Aguilar: Los pueblos indígenas no somos la raíz de México, somos su negación constante," *El País*, September 9, 2019, https://elpais.com/cultura/2019/09/08/actualidad/1567970157_670834.html.

Mexican State. This is why the starting point of Hernández-Vargas's exhibition is the mise-en-scène of the discovery of Tomb No. 7 in the archaeological site of Monte Albán, Oaxaca, in 1932 by archeologist Alfonso Caso. Taking up this historical event as case study and prime matter, Hernández-Vargas creates a counter-archive against the politics of official memory that has captured the past as something inexorable, which can only be told from a singular and hegemonic perspective, reiterating the truth of colonial violence as the imposition of a given universe of sense that conceals nonhegemonic realities. Through varying means, Hernández-Vargas's counter-archive reveals that the jewelry discovered in Tomb No. 7 was a shrewd fabrication by an astute governor in cahoots with the elites as major players to turn attention to Oaxaca. The relevance of Alfonso Caso's finding, however, must not be underestimated: In the classic pre-Hispanic era, Monte Albán was a flourishing Zapoteco city, but the findings of the tomb reveal historical, sacred, and cultural links to the Mixteco culture. It turns out that the burial had taken place after the Zapotecos had left Monte Albán, which was then ruled by a Mixteca tribe (1325–1521) who were highly skilled artisans based in Zaachila, near Monte Albán. Tomb No. 7 is one of the greatest discoveries in American archaeology, and the most important tomb. The way in which the objects and human remains were found, neatly arranged, speaks of an analogy to a complex cosmic order at the center of which was a gold disk representing a human heart. Surrounding it was an extraordinary ensemble of gold and other precious objects like beautifully carved crystal rock cups, thousands of shining beads, gold pectorals and bracelets, a human skull covered with turquoise plaques, a translucent alabaster urn, ear pieces, rings, fake nails, and more than 3,000 pearls scattered in the area; there were also many loose bones that do not constitute full skeletons or primary burials, but which were probably part of sacred bundles. Tomb No. 7 was built on top of a classic Zapoteco tomb, which was probably reused by the Mixtecos in the post-classic as an underground sanctuary for the cult to the ancestors. Among the findings there are also engraved pictorial texts on bones of jaguars and eagles that tell the story of the Mixteco peoples.[82]

With a great sense of humor, Hernández-Vargas unveils the fact that a year before the discovery of Tomb No. 7, in 1931, an earthquake had shaken Oaxaca to ruins, along with hunger and a cholera epidemics. The fabrication

82 Maarten Jansen, "El oro en la Tumba 7 de Monte Albán. Contexto y significado," *Arqueología Mexicana*, no. 144 (March/April 2017).

of the discovery, shock-doctrine style, was therefore designed to turn national and international attention to Oaxaca as a site rich in unknown cultures, and thus as a main touristic destination and investment site. A twist is added to Hernández-Vargas's true-false archive by the fact that he has a personal connection to the story: Alfonso Vargas Sánchez, his maternal grandfather, was a goldsmith who, in the 1960s, began to fabricate copies of the jewelry found in Tomb No. 7 that were meant to be exhibited in site museums and sold as souvenirs for tourists to promote the treasure. Vargas Sánchez modified the scale and graphic vocabulary of the pieces to make them circulate in the widest range of market circuits possible. According to Hernández-Vargas, Tomb No. 7 became a brand. Furthermore, he wrote, "My grandfather turned those objects that touched the inert body of the Mixtec elites into delicate pieces especially designed for the bodies and tastes of white tourism roaming Oaxaca."[83] The molds of the pieces and wax detritus in the goldsmith's workshop became part of the family archive, and Hernández-Vargas decided to use them as means of instilling life back into the pre-Hispanic pieces, away from their branding by the Mexican nationalist narrative.

Hernández-Vargas's project began with two Wikipedia interventions, in which the artist added a paragraph to the Tomb No. 7 entry speculating that Alfonso Caso may not have been responsible for the colossal archaeological discovery, but in truth, a mere collaborator with Oaxaqueño politicians who staged the discovery with political intentions. Two fake-found videos[84] followed, along the lines of Walid Raad's Atlas Group's work: *XipeTotec que llora* (Crying XipeTotec), found at the Geisel Library at USCD, shows Cornado Martínez (none other than Hernández-Vargas's alter ego) discussing the discovery of Tomb No. 7 as a political montage, directly related to the earthquake that devastated Oaxaca exactly a year before the archaeological discovery, with the aim to rebuild the city and give the state an economic boost. In a second video, we see the spokesperson from the Clandestine Revolutionary Committee Angry Xipe-Totec announcing his future project NineWind. Zapatista-style, the Committee addresses the "Fourth Transformation" and

83 In an unpublished text by Saúl Hernández-Vargas, "Alfonso Vargas Archive: Specters of January 14, 1931."

84 *Xipe-Totec que llora* is available here: https://saulhv.cargo.site/xipe-totec; and *Nine Wind* is available here: https://saulhv.cargo.site/ninewind.

the INAH[85] rejecting the findings of Tomb No. 7. The committee is made up of third-generation Zapotecos living in Los Angeles who claim the patrimony of Tomb No. 7. Therefore, the NineWind project contemplates the creation of "authentic replicas" of the Monte Albán jewels approved and legitimized by their own peoples. The videos and the Wikipedia interventions could be understood as prequels for the pieces shown at the Lawndale Art Center, which include drawings from the series *Archivo negro* (*Black Archive*), which are carbon paper drawings, and a note from Saúl's mother in which she names the people who allowed his grandfather to make replicas for the Tomb No. 7 jewelry at the National Museum in Oaxaca. There are also clay plates intervened with tiny objects, which are nothing other than the wax molds for the jewelry pieces Saúl collected from his grandfather's workshop. The clay plates function as "taongas," or amulets that store the energy from the mountains from which they belong: the Oaxacan valley adjacent to Monte Albán. In Hernández-Vargas's narrative, not only did the earthquake have agency in the discovery of the Tomb, but the clay plates also had agency in possibly resurrecting his grandfather's wax molds that replicate the tomb's jewelry (by means of direct contact). The plates were created together with local craftsmen and were allowed to naturally crack and fragment before they were cooked. They embody—not represent—a live connection with the past-present and bring to the fore the true life world that has been gone and that is materially alive in them, in spite of the mestizo identities that have buried this connection.

Again following Yásnaya E. Aguilar, identity traits are determined in a complex network of power relationships. The Mexican nation-state was erected by monopolizing originary peoples' identities, determining an ensemble of "normal" traits in terms of languages, symbols, hymns, dances, history, folklore, and gastronomy. Patriarchal, racial, and capitalist systems have hierarchized these traits, generating artificial identities monopolized by the State. Originary peoples' stories were silenced through mestizaje and they were transformed into "Mexicans."[86] In the context of this history of relent-

85 The "Fourth Transformation" or "Cuarta transformación" is the name given to President Andrés Manuel López Obrador's anticorruption and pro-Indigenous policies. "INAH" is the acronym for Mexico's National Institute for Anthropology and History.

86 Yásnaya Elena Aguilar Gil, "Ëëts, atom. Algunos apuntes sobre la identidad indígena." *Revista de la Universidadd e México*, September 2017, https://www.revistadelauniversidad.mx/articles/f20fc5ef-75e2-44d0-8d5b-a84b2a87b7e3/eets-atom-algunos-apuntes-sobre-la-identidad-indigena.

less pillage, President Andrés Manuel López Obrador has declared that under his government, Indigenous peoples will receive "special attention" and that the Mexican narrative of mestizaje pride will be pitted against an allegedly pernicious mestizaje.[87] Skepticism abounds before the State's recent measures to continue the destruction of orginary peoples' lands through the Mayan Train project in the Yucatán peninsula, as well as other megaprojects. Against the nationalistic grain, the premise of Saúl Hernández-Vargas's *forensic poetics* is that the past cannot speak through the objects (the jewel, the mold, the wax detritus), but that they require shamans or artists to invoke the specters from the past in them. This is because they are sensors or agents in which complex relationships operate, granting them agency. The forensic poet-artist thus rejects hegemonic historical discourse to recuperate the future as the past and the past as ahead of our present, living in the material and live heritage of the originary Zapoteco peoples of Oaxaca and elsewhere, such as the Zapoteco community in Los Angeles.

---

87 Alida Piñón, "El mestizaje que creó el nacionalismo es pernicioso," *El Universal*, May 10, 2019, https://www.eluniversal.com.mx/cultura/el-mestizaje-que-creo-el-nacionalismo-es-pernicioso.

CHAPTER FOUR

Neoliberal and "Post-Neoliberal" Culture Policy

Farewell to Autonomous, Committed Art?[1]

FOR THE PAST COUPLE OF DECADES, artists' voices have been thought to be important in giving shape to society, and art is considered to be useful. The "usefulness" of art is related to a social function of culture, as corporations, states, and arts patrons have put into practice the principle that there can be no development without culture, and there can be no cultural development without freedom of debate. This means that the public expects from both culture and art rigorous accountability, critical questioning, democratic access, dialogue, and openness, as well as equal representation in the visual regime (and this is posited as the road to development). Culture is perceived to be "a basic need." Art's power to critique is taken for granted, and thus is its (alleged) capability to change the world when exercising critique (including

1 A version of this section was originally published as "Art and the Cultural Turn: Farewell to Committed, Autonomous Art?" in *e-flux journal* 42 (February 2013), https://www.e-flux.com/journal/42/60266/art-and-the-cultural-turn-farewell-to-committed-autonomous-art.

self-critique). The state, the private sector, and society, on one hand, are attributing to art a decisive political role, as they are investing in purpose with the goal of generating political and economic surplus value. On the other hand, art and cultural practices are now part of the same network of strategies and questions, as social movements are (in the Infosphere as, we will see in chapter 5). In a context in which the creative, political, and mediatic fields are intrinsically linked, contemporary cultural practices point toward a new social order in which art has merged with life, privileging lived experience, collective communication, and performative politics. In turn, the commodification of culture and its use as a resource, as well as the fusion of art, politics, and media, have had a significant impact on the way in which capitalist economies operate. A consequence has been the predominance of immaterial or cognitive labor over industrial production. Not to say that industrial production has ceased to exist; on the contrary, for the most part it has been transferred to third-world countries. The prevalence of cognitive or immaterial work in contemporary capitalism implies that the main source of surplus value is the production and dissemination of signs. In other words, " 'creative' work" has been injected into all areas of economic life. Immaterial labor also means the production of social life—as lifestyles and forms of life—and a new form of the common at the center of which culture is located.

In this context, the production of contemporary art, as Brian Kuan Wood and Anton Vidokle point out, has been foreclosed by a network of protocols dictating the forms and means of production of art circulating in exhibitions, galleries, biennials, and fairs. And while artists may address exhibition politics as a theme in their work, they are limited in terms of producing something outside of the consensual barriers placed on exhibition politics. This is due to the existence of a systemic enclosure that extends well beyond the consensus of the art world. Art is fused with political sensibilities that exploit art's diplomatic potential, as these political sensibilities consider culture to be a form of social capital, a resource. Thus, a lot of money is at stake.[2] While governments and collectors have invested in cultural production and unprecedented quantities of funding in the past twenty or so years—as art is considered to be an asset that promises investors to benefit from a growing market, while it

2 Anton Vidokle and Brian Kuan Wood, "Breaking the Contract," *e-flux journal* 37 (September 2012), http://www.e-flux.com/journal/breaking-the-contract.

confers glamour related to money in free tax ports[3]—art is intrinsically tied to financial speculation processes, production, consumption, and power. This is why the neoliberal restructuring of wealth determines what kind of art and artists enter the hegemonic networks of exhibition and circulation, and what is at stake at the intersection of these networks. In this regard, politicized art is a kind of art that is tied to power: the conditions of its production are not even a peripheral topic of debate, and neither are they something that a lot of globalized artists, critics, or cultural producers with interests differing from the hegemonic ones have taken upon. In what follows, I will analyze the conditions of production of contemporary art and culture under neoliberalism in Mexico, elucidating the role that "political art" plays in power relations and neoliberal ideology, and questioning whether there could be room for autonomous committed art in this context.[4] I must note that a discussion of contemporary art in Mexico is necessarily global, as Mexico City has been a key hub in contemporary art and culture production globally for the past couple of decades. I conclude this chapter with an exploration of the "post-neoliberal" conditions and implications of cultural production under the current regime of President Andrés Manuel López Obrador.

Politicized Contemporary Art and "Sensible Politics"

From the point of view of materialist realism, some aesthetic practices have sought to map out the fluxes of capitalism: working and living conditions under globalization. For instance, Allan Sekula's *Fish Story* (1996) and *The Forgotten Space* (2010) sought to break with the abstraction inherent to the processes of global capitalism. For Sekula, containers came to embody the material condition of the possibility of global capitalism, and thus he took up the task to examine the flux of merchandises around the world linked to maritime commerce and ports. There is also *Remote Sensing* (2002) by Ursula Biemann, a topography of global sex traffic tied to women's migration and

---

3 Ben Davis, "On Art and Investment," *art-agenda*, March 25, 2014, http://art-agenda.com/reviews/on-art-and-investment.

4 The term "autonomous, committed art" refers to Theodor W. Adorno's retort to Jean-Paul Sartre's text on the autonomy and commitment of art in his essay, "What is Literature?" in *What is Literature? And Other Essays*, ed. Steven Ungar (Cambridge, MA: Harvard University Press, 1988). See also Theodor W. Adorno, "Commitment," *New Left Review* I/87-88 (September/December 1974): 75–89.

exploitation. In her *Timescapes/B-Zone* (2005–2006), Angela Melitopolous maps out the construction of Europe's infrastructure with the purpose of communicating Europe with other regions, in order to insert itself in the global flux of merchandise, people, and capital. There is also Martha Rosler's photographic series, *In Place of the Public: Airport Series* (1983–1994), which visualized the new forms of social interaction and experience, transformed by the privatization of public space exemplified by airports. Airports are highly controlled environments designed with a modernist aesthetic turned to consumption, and in a way, they are the blueprint for our current corporate private-public spaces around the world. Through cognitive mappings, Sekula, Biemann, Melitopolous, and Rosler sought to visualize the material condition and the bases for the new politicized discourses and practices about globalization. Another example of materialist realist aesthetic is Harun Farocki's exploration on how images look at and touch us in an era in which they are intimately tied to neoliberal control and destruction processes. These works are autonomous and exist in a qualitatively different space from social movements, in the materialist tradition of Bertolt Brecht, Dziga Vertov, Jean-Luc Godard, and others.

In the past two or so decades, a vein or niche parallel to materialist realism emerged in contemporary art and cinema geared at participating actively in social processes, with an array of manifestations belonging to realms outside of cultural production. The emergence and proliferation of "politicized art" could be explained by the fact that it has been assumed that art, in one way or another, could serve as a catalyst for political action or participation, as it can reveal capitalism's "hidden contradictions." An example is Artes Mundi Foundation's mission statement, an international art organization based in Wales that recognizes and supports contemporary visual artists who "are engaged with the human condition, social reality and lived experience."[5] And while the present is always opaque, art is given the task of teaching us how to see or perceive things in a different way—it is considered to be training, an act of observation, or exegesis. Exhibitions and biennials in the past decade have addressed questions that are perceived to be "political"; for example, labor, poverty, exploitation, violence, globalization, war, and exclusion. Examples of exhibitions in Mexico whose titles underscored the politicization of their content included "For the Love of Dissent" and "Exercises of Resistance" (MUAC,

5 See their website: http://www.artesmundi.org/about-us.

2012), "The Redeeming Institution" (SAPS, 2012), and "Resisting the Present" (Amparo Museum-Puebla, 2011). In 2012, two exhibitions at the Modern Art and Digital Cultural Center Estela de Luz in Mexico City addressed the way power interferes with the flows of information and representational codes, as well as the blurring distinctions between art, action, social movements, and media and semiotic ownership. At the international level, there was Manifesta 9 in Genk, Belgium, the European biennial for young European art curated by Cuauhtémoc Medina entitled "The Deep of the Modern." The exhibition dealt with the political and economic history of the city of Genk from the point of view of the heritage of its coal mines. Works in the show addressed the realities of the coal miners' work, and of the production and business of coal mining; an iconographic study of coal in modern art and a display of mining paraphernalia was also included. The politicized nature of this exhibition was justified through Walter Benjamin's dialectic materialism, insofar as the exhibition incorporated material traces of Genk's industrial past in order to renegotiate them in the present. In this case, the art shown illustrated a curatorial framework that signaled the conditions and production relations of a specific historical moment—the age of industrial capitalism. Another example was the 2012 Berlin Biennale for Contemporary Art, which invited the Occupy movement to participate and camp out in the show's most important site (Kunstwerke). A small group, also related to the Occupy movement, was welcomed by dOCUMENTA curator Carolyn Christov-Bakargiev after the group set up outside the Fridericianum. Occupy interventions borrowed techniques and tactics from contemporary art and offered a participatory, anti-elitist cultural practice, as indicated by one of the signs hung by Occupy members in one of the Kunstwerke showrooms: "This is not our museum, this is your action space." In 2013, the Jumex Foundation exhibited in its Ecatepec venue "The Corrupt Show and the Speculative Machine" by the collective Superflex, which sought to evidence, through a series of actions and objects, speculation and corruption at the center of the current economic system and how corruption is contagious.

Linked to similar politics as the Occupy movement or the Superflex show in this context, there is also what has been termed "semiautonomous" art, a manifestation that goes beyond the confines of studio practices to focus on being active in the social field. Artists working in this vein follow an ethics of action and commitment outside of the art world, seeking to intervene in urgent topics in the complexity of the public sphere. Traces of these manifestations are occasionally exhibited in museums or conducted within the framework of other cultural institutions. This fusion of art and life presents new forms of collective civic experience and is based on communication and exchange. It is known as "relational art," "participatory art," "community art," or "socially engaged art," among other names. According to Claire Bishop, socially engaged art opposes, in principle, political and aesthetic "spectacles," favoring social participation as a guiding strategy. Beginning with the premise that "contemporary capitalism produces passive subjects with very little agency or empowerment,"[6] participatory works seek to stimulate the public and turn them away from the passive, private consumption of spectacle in favor of creating a shared space for collective social engagement through constructive or symbolic gestures that have social impact and create new alternatives.[7] These works propose solutions for short-term improvement, unlike more traditionally politicized art that opposes the status quo and reveals contradictory social truths.

During the past decade, an alliance in the field of cultural production between the State, corporations, the art market, and the private sector was consolidated. In this context, the politicization of art may imply a search for openings in order to affirm the (rapidly dwindling) public character of cultural institutions defending their autonomy (which they don't really have) from the marketplace and from corporate patrons. An heir to what's known as "Institutional Critique" is a recent project by visual artist Jonathan Hernández, which was vetoed by the head of the Tamayo Museum in Mexico City. Hernández's proposed contribution to "First Act" (2012) consisted of making available to the general public information about the museum's remodeling costs and the exhibition production budgets. Blurring the line between civic duty (demanding transparency) and institutional critique (revealing the hegemonic interests behind the politics of the museum's exhibitions), interventions of this kind seek to exacerbate the tensions between institutions, public opinion, and the art world at large.

What does this have to do with art's autonomy? As we will see, with postmodernism, art and culture had been put at the center of social, political, and economic processes, and they are now inseparable from work, production, consumption, and subjectivity. Under neoliberalism, art in particular,

---

6 Claire Bishop, "Participation and Spectacle: Where Are We Now?" in *Living as Form: Socially Engaged Art from 1991–2001*, ed. Nato Thompson (New York, 2012), 34–46.

7 Bishop, "Participation and Spectacle," 34–46.

culture in general, and creativity as tools, aside from having a predominant role in production and consumption, are actively used as means to compensate the side effects of neoliberal policies or as betterment measures. On the other hand, political work has been transformed into codification, as mediatic forms are used with the purpose of creating a sensible realm for political acts, an "activist imaginary" made up of political fields conformed by images. Political action lodged in cultural forms thus implies making things public through signs, under the premise that the act of visibilization—of antagonisms, minorities, testimony, and so forth—is political. This "sensible politics" is a niche in contemporary art and cultural production that has taken up the task to "codify unstable political acts in mediatic forms."[8] Some examples could be Trevor Paglen's photographs of ultra-secret governmental sites, the documentation of protests, documentary cinema in general, the audiovisual component of social movements, Sharon Haye's mise-en-scène of protests and slogans from the 1960s, Superflex's *Guaraná Power* project,[9] *Penetrados* by Santiago Sierra (2010), and *Dining in Refugee Camps: The Art of Saharahui Cooking* (2013) by Robin Kahn.

A branch from "sensible politics" operates under the logic of intervention. Defined by Michel Foucault in 1979, intervention is manipulation of the social in order to introduce an ensemble of liberatory devices seeking to produce freedoms, along with economic development and cultural emancipation. The problem is that interventions run the risk of falling exactly into the opposite that they pretend to, becoming a tool for control. The logic of intervention in the military realm, for instance, implies "doing good elsewhere," bringing economic development and infrastructure, as the contentious US interventions in Iraq and Afghanistan claimed. Under the premise of doing (unquestionable) "good" elsewhere, moreover, site-specific interventions in the realm of culture have been one of the predominant modes in aesthetic practices under globalization. For instance, biennials here and elsewhere are characterized by implementing "liberogenic" cultural devices in the short term in public places. It is not by chance that "InSite," the biennial that instituted the model of interventionist cultural practice in the 1990s, was created at the Tijuana-San Diego border when the NAFTA treaty was signed. Krzysztof Wodiczko's *Tijuana Projection* (2001), produced in this context, is as iconic of

8 Megan McLagan and Yates McKee, introduction to *Sensible Politics: The Visual Culture of Nongovernmental Activism* (New York: Zone Books, 2012), 9–22.

9 Marc-James Leger, *The Neoliberal Undead* (New York: Zone Books, 2013).

this branch of cultural production as it is problematic. Wodiczko parted from the premise that technology is emancipatory, and thus he created a device with headphones and a camera, connected with a 60-meter-diameter projection. With this device, Wodiczko sought to give voices to women working in enslaved conditions for sweatshops at the United States-Mexico border. Wodiczko's device enabled women to give testimony of having been abused at work, sometimes sexually, aside from living in dysfunctional families where alcoholism and violence predominated. Their testimonies were projected live in the public square in front of the Tijuana Cultural Center. In this manner, Wodiczko was hoping to create an emancipatory platform for these women, through which they could denounce their problems. The discursive position from which they spoke was as victims. Their voices were addressed to a virtual form of power and a co-present viewer, from absolute affective proximity. The problem with the piece is that the enunciative position of the victim given by Wodiczko to the women alienated them as victims, thereby transforming them into aesthetic objects in a cultural circuit foreign to themselves, hindering their potential for political subjectivation. It is known that after the artist left Tijuana, the women who took part in the project suffered backlash from their employers. As they listened and watched, spectators accepted the ethical terms and the demands made by the images. And yet the spectators, as they belonged to a more privileged class than the workers, were complicit with their enslaving working conditions at the macro level, as they are consumers of cheap electrodomestics assembled by women like them. Wodiczko's intervention, moreover, makes evident the enormous and problematic gap that exists in how artists tend to position themselves vis-à-vis nonegalitarian and exploitative conditions of global capitalism: they denounce them through art in networks of consumption and distribution of art that thrives in inequality and exploitation, for example, as art and culture are subsidized or collected by corporations or governments of corrupt oligarchs.

In a way, sensible politics has adapted political action to cultural production, and neoliberal tastes to humanitarian sensibility and general depoliticization. Erasing the frontiers between everyday life, political reality, and creative intervention, this kind of artwork tends not to have a political program. Sometimes they are soaked in sad passions (cynicism, impotence, melancholia) and remain short in expressing or transmitting solidarity. Another problem with sensible politics is that what it represents remains vague, transforming political action into a matter of expression. This form of politics in the realm of signs is a reductive version of Jacques Rancière's definition of politics: "Politics is first and foremost an intervention in the visible and sayable."[10] In that context, *visibility* and *recognition* have become a problem. How did we come to this? We are informed of the horrors, abuses, human rights violations, and power abuses all over the world. On the one hand, to be informed has become a form of politicization in itself, and thus it becomes a way of normalizing injustice, debasing our ethical and political standards, making us accomplices with the neoliberal barbarity. On the other hand, sensible politics represents politics in an abstract and distanced way, while it disseminates a form of political action without previous theoretical analysis. Mistaking "artivism" for "micropolitics," sensible politics is a form of politics that is not willing to pay the price for real political struggle. It is worth mentioning here Renzo Martens's self-reflective *pornomiseria* film, *Enjoy Poverty* (2009). The film transmits impotent moral indignation regarding the economy of the production of images that testify to the conditions of extreme misery in which the inhabitants of Congo live. The film is a critique of "concerned" artists in particular, documentarists, and photojournalists in general who exploit the Western belief that things can be bettered if suffering and abjection of developing countries is visualized. The film also shows how poverty can be a fixed asset in underdeveloped regions because it has the specific function of making privileged people believe they can change things. Martens's film, as his project to introduce "cognitive labor" to Congo, however, is problematic in that they remain soaked with sad passions, contributing to keeping us impotent, stuck in the *années d'hiver* (winter years). Art historian T. J. Demos categorized *Enjoy Poverty* as part of a series of "concerned" contemporary artworks that deal with the specters of colonialism present in current unequal relations between North and South. For Demos, this category of works seeks to confront Europe's conscience with her colonial past and with the fact that the colonial era has not ended, but is ongoing. From his point of view, the political task of this category of art conjures up the ghosts of modernity against amnesia and lack of recognition, aligning art politics with the struggle against forgetting.[11] While Demos's distinction between North and South is obsolete, as we have seen, because the world is now divided into enclaves of privilege and sophistication embedded in the former "Third World," and enclaves of exclusion and misery within

10 Jacques Rancière, "Ten Theses on Politics," *Theory and Event* 5, no. 3 (2001).

11 T. J. Demos, *Return to Postcolony: Spectres of Colonialism in Contemporary Art* (Berlin: Strenberg Press, 2013).

the First, Demos's modernist melancholic framework maintains this kind of intervention, trapped within a moralizing cry to recognize the excluded, eluding the possibility of seeing them as equals, and thus as entities who can potentially self-determine politically and aesthetically, without the possibility of rewriting their own stories of colonization through the lens of the present.

One of the problems made evident by the ubiquity of sensible politics is that in our post-political actuality, the gap between aesthetic and political representation is wider than ever. To *represent* implies "to make present the absent," a task that is always incomplete because it is impossible to reproduce a totality. We should also consider that representation works in two senses: as *Vertreten* (or political representation), which implies putting oneself in the place of others to speak on their behalf, and as *Darstellen* (or aesthetic representation), which is the form of representation that implies describing others in the first person. In the 1960s, both forms of representation were brought into a crisis, accused of hiding the fact that the speaker occupies the place of the represented; workers and minorities were, in fact, encouraged to speak in their own name and in the first person. Nowadays, the gap between political representation (*Vertreten*) and aesthetic representation (Darstellen) is wider than ever because whatever it is that codified political actions represented in mediatic forms is unstable. Politics has become unstable and thus impossible to represent, partly due to a lack of stable political subjects: instead of Modern political abstract figures of "the worker," or "the campesino," politicized subjectivities are collective enunciations in a constant process of "becoming."[12] "Expressive" politics is valued over representation because it "embodies rebel subjectivities expressing themselves without delegation and they do it through formal and symbolic richness."[13] The problem is the lack of common ground to universalize the multiplicity of singular struggles and social movements scattered throughout the world, which exist more like scattered archipelagos.

---

12 Michel Goddard, "Media Ecology, Political Subjectivation and Free Radios," *The Fiberculture Journal*, no. 17 (2011), https://seventeen.fibreculturejournal.org/fcj-114-towards-an-archaeology-of-media-ecologies-%E2%80%98media-ecology%E2%80%99-political-subjectivation-and-free-radios.

13 Marcelo Expósito, "Lecciones de historia. El arte, entre la experimentación institucional y las políticas del movimiento," paper presented January 30, 2009, at the VIIth International Symposium of Theory of Contemporary Art (SITAC) *Sur, sur, sur, sur*, http://marceloexposito.net/pdf/exposito_sitac.pdf.

This has given way to an ensemble of sporadic isolated forces and demonstrations of discontent, and antagonism without signifiers, that could encompass all the topics concerning us collectively. Ironically, the old left's internationalist perspective was substituted by the murderous titans of capitalism. A new plutocracy of liberal mentality took up charity and social responsibility, seeking to change the world, applying the same formulas that made them rich in the first place. This new plutocracy, made up of oligarchs directing corporate global monopolies and other players from financial institutions, emerged thanks to the transformation of state capitalism by the neoliberal policies of market liberalization. The new forms capitalism has taken have forced us to devise new forms of politicization beyond class divisions, decolonization, or anti-imperialist struggles, in order to account for the new forms of power, subjection, and exploitation, as well as the new wave of primitive accumulation and extractivism.

From this point of view, the actual discourse of exclusion, for instance, is too weak to offer a social base to confront the system. The exploited are not only those who produce or create, but also those condemned *not* to create. Domination is therefore inscribed in the structure of the production process, and this is why everyone can have freedom and equality (formal and graduated), but without having access to work, education, health services, housing, credits, or commodities. In this context, art and culture have been placed at the center of neoliberal processes, as they are being instrumentalized as tools of betterment and development, counterinsurgency, pacification, and even as agents for globalization. In a way, the neoliberal cultural project ended the idea of political militancy, as today the only acceptable solutions to political problems elsewhere are the Western version of democracy and neoliberal capitalism, while revolutionary ideas, if they are not used as clichés for cultural marketing, are considered to be utopian and even criminal. Anyone who resists to be lectured on the moral of armed struggle or liberatory violence is marginalized in the name of security and rights. Paradoxically, transnational wars—against drugs and terrorism—are being waged in the name of security and human rights. In this context, sensible politics exists as a niche for its own public of cultural producers with liberal political sensibilities. Cultural infrastructure functions as a platform for sensible politics in which curators, museum directors, and board members (who mostly represent corporate interests) select and contextualize art that presents certain events and social actions circumscribing the limits of political thinking in the public sphere.

Contemporary Art and the Democratization of Culture

Being "contemporary," art exists in the same temporal space as culture, and it has therefore been integrated into it. Culture is the social process through which we communicate meaning in order to understand the world, build identities, and define our values and beliefs. In the late 1990s, theorist Fredric Jameson argued that the social space was completely saturated with the image of culture.[14] This is because, in our professional and daily activities, as well as in the various forms of entertainment we enjoy, society consumes cultural products all the time. This characterizes the postmodern "cultural turn" diagnosed by Jameson, which was further elaborated by George Yúdice upon observing (in 2003) that the uses of culture had undergone an unprecedented expansion, not just in the marketplace, but also along social, political, and economic lines. According to Yúdice, since the State and corporations already utilize culture as a tool as they search for economic and sociopolitical betterment—for instance, in peacefully resolving violence and crime, reconstructing the social fabric, transforming society, creating jobs, increasing civic participation, and so forth—culture has become a resource.[15] In Mexico, for example, one of the priorities of the National Action Party (PAN) was "the development and democratization of culture." The government invested an unprecedented amount of money in producing, disseminating, and managing culture; inviting and even facilitating the participation of corporate and private sponsors; collaborating with the art market by investing in the Zona MACO art fair; and, in general, implementing an official program to guide the symbolic development and satisfy the demand for cultural and creative assets.[16]

---

14 Fredric Jameson, *The Cultural Turn: Selected Writings on the Postmodern, 1983–1998* (Brooklyn: Verso, 1998), 111

15 George Yúdice, *The Expediency of Culture: Uses of Culture in the Global Era* (Durham, NC: Duke University Press Books, 2004).

16 Carlos Lara González, "Un año de gestión cultural y perspectivas para el desarrollo de la política cultural del sexenio," *Revista Bien Común* 153, September 2007; Leonor Flores, "Política cultural ineficaz pese a mayors recursos," *El Economista*, May 17, 2013, https://www.eleconomista.com.mx/artese-ideas/Politica-cultural-ineficaz-pese-a-mayores-recursos-20110517-0177.html; Javier Aranda Luna, "No más cultura de utiliería," *La Jornada*, June 21, 2012, https://www.jornada.com.mx/2021/03/10/opinion/a04a1cul; *Conaculta Cuaderno 13: Patrimonio cultural y turismo gestión cultural: Planta viva en crecimiento* (Guadalajara: Encuentro Internacional de Gestores y Promotores Culturales, 2006).

In the realm of culture, the return of the PRI (Partido Revolucionario Institucional or Institutional Revolutionary Party) in 2012 implied a continuation of the PAN's cultural policies, following the model of the culturalization of social problems as the solution to social tearing and violence. For instance, in January 2014, Peña Nieto inaugurated the "Programa Cultural para la Armonía" (Cultural Program for Harmony) in the state of Michoacán, with the objective of reconstructing the social tissue and transforming public spaces through art.[17] In general, Peña Nieto's government considered culture as an essential part of the general development it promoted. In that regard, Rafael Tovar y de Teresa, president of CONACULTA or the National Council for Culture and Arts (1992–2000 and 2012–2015), and who would then become the first secretary of culture (as the dependency was created in 2016), sought to offer a perspective of social inclusion through cultural action parting from the following axes: to promote dialogue between State and intellectuals; to promote equality through culture; to conserve and profit from the already existing cultural infrastructure and patrimony in Mexico; and to expand dialogue and cultural exchange between Mexico and the world.[18] To privilege culture as a site in the social field, to transform society, to highlight the "social" dimension of culture,[19] and to execute cultural work with a social perspective are all policies that evidently consider culture to be a tool for social, economic, political, and even touristic transformation. In this context, the PRI's cultural politics implied to take action and to invest in social, educational, and cultural programs to transform the violent reality of the country. The Colombian city of Medellín was an example to follow as a city that vanquished violence through culture.[20]

The tendency to "democratize culture" is not exclusive to Mexico, and it is inspired by the definition of culture proposed by the UNESCO Universal Declaration on Cultural Diversity. According to this declaration, culture plays a crucial role in social and economic development, since the cultural and

---

17 "Peña Nieto lanza programa de cultura en Michoacán por la paz," *La Jornada*, January 18, 2014, www.jornada.unam.mx/2014/01/18/cultura/a02n1cul.

18 "Peña Nieto lanza programa."

19 "Cultural policy is a privileged field for the social field: Rafael Tovar," *La Jornada*, December 17, 2013, www.jornada.unam.mx/2013/12/17/cultura/a05n2cul.

20 Michael Kimmelman, "A City Rises, Along with Its Hopes," *New York Times*, May 18, 2012, www.nytimes.com/2012/05/20/arts/design/fighting-crime-with-architecture-inmedellin-colombia.html.

creative industries generate jobs and income, and attract investment.[21] The directives of the global consensus on the functionality of culture as a democratizing entity establish a link between cultural freedom, cultural promotion, and democracy, with goals of expanding individual choices, encouraging the active participation of the people, respecting other cultures, and promoting the freedom to choose one's own identity (and to respect the identity of others), among others. Despite the high expectations we might have regarding the value of culture, however, the effects and benefits of showing politicized art and organizing cultural discussions and exchanges are unpredictable.

The relationship between the cultural and political spheres (i.e., the instrumentalization of culture in the name of politics) is nothing new. Yet, according to Yúdice, UNESCO's cultural projects, globalized civil society, governments, NGOs, the market, cultural managers, and those who work in cultural and creative industries have brought about an unprecedented transformation in our understanding of culture and what we do on its behalf.[22] This transformation brings up a well-worn contradiction between the trivialization of cultural products to serve the mass consumer market, which is seen as something negative, and the process of cultural democratization, which is seen as something positive. In transcending this contradiction, I am interested in explicating why art (subsumed to the demands of the cultural and creative industries, subsidized by the State, market, and corporations) is considered a privileged field of politicization and even an integral part of political action and voice when it comes to antihegemonic practices. What is the implication of this for committed, autonomous art?

Art and the Neoliberal Order

Generally, in the realm of art production, neoliberalism has signified privatization or the collusion between public and private sectors to subsidize art. In the past couple of decades, neoliberalism played an important role in the investment in culture. This is because institutions and corporations "have sought to have a visible role in communicating the corporation's perspective

---

21 See "Plan Nacional de Desarrollo 2007–2011," 3.8, Objetivo 21, http://pnd.calderon.presidencia.gob.mx/igualdad-de-oportunidades/cultura-arte-deporte-y-recreacion.html.

22 Yúdice, *The Expediency of Culture.*

in a variety of critical public themes."[23] According to Gregg Sholette, corporate influence in art has motivated the transformation of public cultural capital into private economic capital. As State support for the arts parted from the premise that culture was an asset to the nation, nowadays, corporations have appropriated this function, as in time, they generate economic surplus value through marketing and public relations; they sponsor and judge art contests, offer prizes, and collect art, aside from promoting their own perspective on critical themes.[24]

The logic of the symbiosis between corporate and aesthetic sensibility was described in a 1998 article by art historian Chin-tao Wu, who underscores how corporations have appropriated the concept of innovation (from the vanguard) to redefine its meaning in corporate terms. Wu quotes a declaration by John Murphy, Philip Morris Inc.'s CEO, with regard to sponsorship by his company to the decisive 1969 exhibition "When Attitudes Became Form," which broke ground in art history by presenting the European version of conceptual art: "We feel it is appropriate to take part in bringing these works to the public, because there is a key element in this 'new art' that has a counterpart in the business world. That element is *innovation*—without which it would be impossible for any segment of society to progress."[25]

This declaration marks the beginning of an era in which corporations, the economy, and critical/vanguardist art began to share the base value of innovation, known also as "disruptive innovation" or "creative destruction." This implies that the critical modernist vanguard was imbued with marketing, finance, and consumption. In 2013, "When Attitudes Become Form" was recreated in a Baroque palace in Venice sponsored by the Fondazione Prada, curated by Germano Celant, the original curator of the exhibition, in dialogue with artists Thomas Demand and Rem Koolhas. The modern Kunsthalle's exhibition rooms were reproduced in the Venetian palace from documentary photographs of the original exhibition. What is at stake here? The affirmation of the status of conceptual and minimal art as the genesis of

23 Gregory Sholette, *Dark Matter: Art and Politics in the Age of Enterprise Culture* (New York: Pluto, 2004), 259, www.gregorysholette.com/wp-content/uploads/2011/04/05_darkmatterw01.pdf

24 Sholette, *Dark Matter*, 260–61.

25 Chin-tao Wu, "Embracing the Enterprise Culture: Art Institutions since the 1980s," *New Left Review*, no. 230 (1993), 31.

global contemporary art, understood as a design and leisure commodity, the flattening of its critical and theoretical aspects, and the consolidation of corporate sponsorship of arts tied to glamour and the fashion industry.

With this in mind, the transformation of Mexican culture under neoliberalism was characterized by a gradual passage from state to a combination between state and private sponsorship, or in some cases, only corporate funding. An example of the fusion of both forms of state sponsorship is the case of collector Andrés Blainstain, who was invited by the UNAM in 2007 to show his collection to the public in the Tlatelolco Centro Cultural Universitario (University Cultural Center). Subsidizing art became a gesture that is as financial as it is spiritual by privileged citizens who began to give back to their community by offering democratic access to their art collections. This was not motivated by disinterest, but by the belief that culture is vital to accrue in the "human capital" of the country. Art is thus conceived as a privileged asset to invest in. The two museums in Plaza Carso and the New Polanco facing each other could not be more different. The Soumaya Museum (2011), which hosts a portion of telecommunications tycoon Carlos Slim's Mexican and European art collection, is housed in a daring and ostentatious building. It is free to access and is thus populist in spirit. In contrast, the Jumex Museum (2013) is discrete, refined, and elegant; it lodges Eugenio López's international contemporary art collection and can be visited by paying an entrance fee of 40 pesos.[26] Both are examples of private museums linked to the corporate missions of the companies that fund them. This is underscored, for example, by the use of identical typography in the lettering of the Soumaya Museum and Sanborns, which has a restaurant, pharmacy, and store chain, also owned by Carlos Slim. The physical presence of Telmex, another one of his companies in the museum through the Telmex Digital Classroom, offers to the public the coexistence in the same register of commodities sold by Slim's corporate image and art collection. In contrast, for the Jumex Museum, to make a direct visible link between collection and company would be distasteful, although the practice of drinking Jumex Juice in the offices is common. Without a doubt, the Jumex Museum is at the vanguard of corporate art collections, as it adheres to a preestablished international protocol and code of professionalism and work ethic, which includes maintaining a discrete distance between the corporation's subsidy of art. If Slim's collection is indistinguishable from

26 As of 2020, the minimum wage in Mexico is 126.22 pesos a day, according to the Diario Oficial de la Federación.

his companies, reflecting the character of his cultural philanthropic mission, the Jumex Collection symbolizes a unique philosophy reflected by the good taste and aesthetic sensibility of the owner. No public or private institution possesses an equivalent acquis to the Jumex Museum in Mexico, focused on minimalist and conceptual art since the 1960s. In that regard, the Jumex Collection adheres to the new form of thinking about corporate art collections—as private—and their relationship to the public. Aside from historical pieces from the 1960s, the Jumex Museum lodges a collection of young and living artists, and it has its own body of specialists and aesthetic vision standards, which are up to date with regard to market aesthetic vanguards recognized at the global level in the art world.

Differently than nation-state museums, whose mission is to disseminate, exhibit, and educate about art, parting from a narrative that can be mythical, historical, identity-based, or canonical, to reinforce the metanarrative that unites the people as such, private museums tend to be used strategically to develop the identity and image of a company. They are also sites for channeling funds, because aside from direct subsidies offered by the state when it comes to corporate tax exemptions, to corporations that collect art, it is considered to be an asset just like gold or real estate, as it offers stable yields in the long term. In that regard, alliances between collectors strengthen the international market, showing that art acquisition is a guarantee for protecting money that they otherwise would not know how to invest.[27] While every museum is a place in which memory and the relationship to memory is organized, tangible objects and exhibitions in private and corporate museums reflect the interests of the owner or company. According to art advisers, the main propeller of the acquisition of art is the "emotional value" (84 percent), although 61 percent refers to social value (status, prestige, relationships) and 60 percent refers to exclusivity.[28] In that regard, the main objective of a private museum is being an instrument of public relations and marketing. The vocation of the Soumaya Museum was announced by Slim himself:

27 Leticia Gasca Serrano, "Todos coinciden: invertir en arte es Buena opción," *El Economista*, February 13, 2012, http://eleconomista.com.mx/entretenimiento/2012/02/13/todos-coinciden-invertir-en-arte-es-buena-opcion.

28 Leticia Gasca Serrano, "Arte en México, ¿cómo se compra?" *El Economista*, February 13, 2012, http://eleconomista.com.mx/entretenimiento/2012/02/13/arte-mexico-como-se-compra.

> We believe in the importance of making this museum part of the Mexican population, of bringing the building and the collection at the disposition of the city council and of the country, with the purpose of engaging in contributing to the formation and development of human capital, with the goal of enriching and sharing art history, world history and Mexican history. A great deal of the works in the Soumaya Museum are European, we want to make available works of European great masters, to those Mexicans who have been unable to travel outside of the country so they can enjoy them.[29]

According to the website, the museum receives an average of 3,500 visitors a day, among them 300 schools, as well as groups from elderly homes and orphanages who also receive breakfast, guided visits, and pedagogical workshops for free at the museum. The Telmex Digital Classroom within the museum is a space endowed with resources, tools, and devices to "innovate learning processes and to favor integral development of the school community."[30] The museum was designed by architect and designer Fernando Romero, who is also Carlos Slim's son-in-law. Dressed with hexagonal aluminum mosaics, it could be mistaken for an eccentric monument reminiscent of a corset or nuclear reactor cooling tower. It was a project Romero proposed to Beijing, but it was never realized. Its brave ostentation contrasts with the conservative approach to the way in which art is exhibited within its walls. The pieces in the collection are of uneven qualities, among which only a few are exceptional. The objects in the collection are further tainted by the horrid vitrines lodging some of the objects, the reed roof, the neon light illuminating most of the rooms, and the general unkemptness of the space. Slim's "philanthropic sensibility" in culture is complemented by his contribution of billions to foundations, but never to programs against poverty, because according to him, they create dependency.[31] The Soumaya Museum has two branches: Plaza Loreto, home to Slim's collection of Rodin sculpture casts, and the Guillermo Tovar de Teresa House—the former secretary of culture who passed away in 2016, leaving a premodern Mexican art collection housed in a beautiful nineteenth-century house in the Colonia Roma, now administered by the Soumaya Museum. Slim also owns the Broadway-playing Telcel Theatre in Mexico City and the US journal *The New York Times*. Perhaps Slim's cultural

---

29 See www.telmexeducacion.com/proyectos/Paginas/aula-telmex.aspx.

30 See www.telmexeducacion.com/proyectos/Paginas/aula-telmex.aspx.

31 Rodolfo Acuña, "The Age of Billionaires," *Counterpunch*, December 12, 2013, www.counterpunch.org/2013/12/27/the-age-of-thebillionaires.

philanthropy attests to the validity of trickle-down theory: if rich people's horses have abundant fodder, they will always leave a few grains in their manure. In a way, the Soumaya Museum opens up its gates to the masses, who are mindless on whether they stroll through a Sanborns or an art collection; the museum has also served as a diplomatic showcase and business room. In 2011, Argentinian President Cristina Fernández was entertained there in a business dinner offered by Slim, to whom she paid a visit even before the mandatory official visit to President Calderón while passing through Mexico.

The Jumex Museum could not be more different. It is an enclave of power that hosts the local elite, thirsty for the kind of refinement and exclusivity offered by contemporary art. At the same time, the Jumex Museum is the showcase of the company's ambition of positioning itself at the global level economically, socially, and artistically. For the museum's opening, a party for 3,000 guests was offered, among which 700 of them—curators, gallerists, and collectors—were flown in from all corners of the world. These guests had the role of assuring that the artists Jumex are backing up will be a good financial investment. The party took place at the Estado Mayor Presidencial (Presidential Military Staff Headquarters). According to the chronicles, the staircase to access the grand salon was covered with gold leaf, the party cost three million dollars, and the salon was designed by Etienne Russo, producer of fashion runways for Channel, Jean-Paul Gautier, and Dries van Norten. Among the guests were directors and curators from the Guggenheim, LACMA, MoMA, PS1, and the New Museum; London Serpentine Gallery's board; critic and curator Hans Ulrich Olbrists; gallerists Paul Schimmel and Monika Sprüth; Lorena Jáuregui, FONCA's director; collectors from all over the world; and artists like Anri Sala, Thomas Demand, Adam McEwen, and Lari Pittman.[32]

With its restricted elegance, the Jumex Museum's building was conceived by British architect David Chipperfield. The building is generous, but not monumental. If the Soumaya Museum's architecture is clumsy and bold in its attempt to seem like postmodern architecture, the sophisticated and refined neomodernism of the Jumex Museum recalls Mies van der Rohe, I. M. Pei, Luis Barragán, and Ricardo Legorreta. Walls and floors are covered with travertine and the rooftop features raised triangles, reminiscent of saw teeth and evoking the manufacturing heritage of the area, which also bathe the art

32 Linda Yablonski, "Creative Juices," *artforum*, November 25, 2013, http://artforum.com/diary/id=44217.

exhibited inside with natural light. The museum was inaugurated with an exhibition of seven sculptures by Fred Sandback, installed among fifty pieces from the collection. The title of the exhibition, "A Place in Two Dimensions," evokes the existence of parallel realities, perhaps the differentiated realities coexisting in the country: that of those who visit the museum, those who exclusively visit the museum across the street, and those who do not visit museums at all. The museum houses artworks that underscore its ludic and formal aspect, highlighting the tendency to favor design, neo-conceptualism, and neo-minimalism. The curatorial script of James Lee Byars's retrospective (2014) posited art as an object of contemplation to underscore perfection, beauty, and balance (all secularized spiritual values). Transforming into museographic fetishes objects like the garments Byars made to link two or more people (with resonance to Lygia Clark's experiments), the Jumex retrospective neutralized the political and social character of Byars's work. Both exhibitions were the unfortunate result of prefabricated curatorial formulas from imperial museums with works chosen from the art market (the 2019 Koons/Duchamp blockbuster was hardly an exception). It would seem that the focus of the Jumex Museum's exhibitions is to contribute to discussions in the artworld encompassing art students. With few exceptions, exhibitions at Jumex are not academic, and neither are they inserted in a global dialogue about recent art history. Rather, they give shape to the way in which publics can approach art to enjoy and discuss it as mere amusement.

A comparison between private or corporate cultural politics with state cultural politics in Mexico reveals that while state cultural institutions instrumentalize culture as a means to reestablish the social tissue, foment social plurality and democracy, and revitalize dialogue with the intellectual and cultural community, private cultural institutions function as an "alternative" luxury niche in which privileged classes can enjoy the feeling of exclusivity and of being cultivated with art made irrelevant by its exhibition context. Inevitably, corporate museums bring to the table discussions about how privatization is modifying public space. In the realm of culture, moreover, privatization implies naturalizing relationships of dominance by normalizing the oligarchy's sensibility and making it hegemonic, consolidating corporate power structures in the world of culture, as well as new power spaces and forms of organizing life, and promoting elitism and capitalist social forms. Damián Ortega's description of the piece he made as a commission by the Jumex Museum for its front yard at the time of inauguration, titled *Cosmogonía doméstica* (Domestic Cosmogony), describes this new public corporate/privatized space: "The public space as metaphor of outer space, cosmic . . . a perpetual movement, a moving choreography that reconfigures space by producing ephemeral associations amongst the elements that compose it and the public itself";[33] that is to say, a public space made up of privatized space elements, in perpetual search for its own balance, perfection, and beauty where there are no antagonisms, but rather passing (unequal) productive alliances. The sculpture consists of five concentric circles spinning on the ground, sustaining a table standing on one leg around which a teakettle, dishes, cups, and kitchen utensils spin around. The "publicness" of the sculpture in the yard contrasts with the everyday and intimate aspect of the objects in Ortega's sculpture.

Aside from the privatization of culture and its consequences in the context of reforms and neoliberal sensibilities, there is a global tendency to subject contemporary art to the politics of culture administration. This implies "democratizing culture," making it accessible to the masses and using it as a tool for society's well-being, as well as for healing a community that has experienced violence. In other words, cultural institutions subsidized by corporations and individual patrons apparently put forward progressive agendas promoting politicized art, or socially "responsible" art. For instance, Creative Time in New York—founded by NYC Culture, Lambent Foundation, Ford Foundation, Bloomberg Philanthropics, Art Works, The Standard, fleursBella, and NYSCA—supports public and community art, with the purpose of politicizing social space with cultural intervention. For instance, Creative Time financed Tania Brugera's "International Immigrant Movement" in Queens in 2011, which materialized as a long-term flexible community space and a sociopolitical movement that included workshops, actions, and alliances with immigrant organizations. Brugera described her project as "useful art."

In that regard, privatized cultural spaces or museums that function with private-public funds have become institutional bastions for democratic self-expression and sites for social reconciliation and self-help (a case in point would be the MUAC or University Museum of Contemporary Art housed at the UNAM, or National University). Due to the current inoperative status of democracies under neoliberal regimes, this implies an ethical, political, and ideological devolution. Theoretician Oliver Marchart argues that the insertion of private funds in art of this kind (relational, semiautonomous, participatory,

---

33 Damián Ortega quoted by Oscar Cid de León, "Alista el Museo Jumex su inauguracion," *Reforma*, October 26, 2013.

etc.) is a step toward dismantling the welfare state, which offered some of these services to the citizens.[34] While corporate support and the establishment of antagonistic spaces or practices that seek to facilitate or repair social links are institutionalized by society, the questions that arise are the following: To whom does cultural capital belong to, who has the right to use it, and who benefits with its use and with the dissemination of certain discourses or pseudo-politicized programs?

Art and Culture at the Center of Neoliberal Bellicose Projects

In the globalized world, art and culture are at the center of neoliberal processes as agents for globalization—as tools for betterment and development, counterinsurgency, and pacification. An extreme example is the occupation of Iraq that has been "fortunate in cultural terms." Nato Thompson (the director of Creative Time) recounts how General David Petraus wrote a field manual addressed to changing the attitude of people to the US occupation in Mosul: ""A story about counterinsurgency, community organization, about getting to know a people not as an occupation force but as neighbors. It is the story of the military accessing the terrain of that which is known as culture."[35] Thompson compares the US military occupation of Iraq as a "cultural approach" to community and social artistic practices, as all instances deal with getting to know people to be able to change landscapes of life and power; the problem is that in the case of the citizens of Mosul, this is done by obviating their experiences under attack and occupation. The cultural turn in the US army's machinery took place a few years after Frederic Jameson famously diagnosed a cultural turn in capitalism, arguing that social space had been completely saturated by an image of culture. This is because in our daily and professional activities, as well as in many of the entertainment forms we enjoy, society consumes cultural products all the time. The diagnosis of the "cultural turn" by Jameson and elaborated by Júdice implies that culture has become a resource and an apparatus of compensation for the ravages caused by neoliberal policies in

---

34 Oliver Marchart, "Art, Space and the Public Sphere(s)," *transversal texts* (January 2002), https://transversal.at/transversal/0102/marchart/en.

35 Nato Thompson, "The Insurgents Part I: Community-Based Practice as Military Methodology," *e-flux journal* 47 (September 2013), http://www.e-flux.com/journal/the-insurgents-part-i-community-based-practice-as-military-methodology.

the social tissue: both give meaning and symbolic representations, mourning mechanisms, and tools for reinvention and betterment. Nato Thompson's comparison attests to the ways in which the lines between public and military programs and social art or relational aesthetics are being blurred.

Mexican examples would be the disarmament program by Mexico City's mayor Miguel Mancera and his "Pink Ladies Brigade,"[36] or the appearance of President Felipe Calderón at the US border under the legend "No More Weapons" and Pedro Reyes's project *Palas por pistolas*, sponsored by Mexican corporations Coppel and Trupper. "Calderón demands US to stop traffic of armament with a mural at the border" was one of the headlines of newspaper *La Jornada* from February 17, 2012, illustrated with an image of the president looking at the billboard he had had made at the border, turned toward the United States with the legend, "No more weapons." The billboard was 8 meters high by 21 meters long. It was built by soldiers from the Secretaría de la Defensa Nacional (National Defense Secretary) with 3 tons of assault weapons confiscated from criminals, melted down and transformed into bricks. In the inaugural ceremony, Calderón invited the United States (in bad English) to stop sending weapons across the border: "No more weapons! Dear friends of the United States, Mexico needs your help to stop this terrible violence we are suffering." According to *La Jornada*, during his trip to Ciudad Juárez, Calderón participated in the destruction of 6,000 weapons seized from criminals, and he also planted a tree at the Felipe Ángeles El Retiro Community Development Center. Calderón's propagandistic gesture in Ciudad Juárez is reminiscent of the language of contemporary art interventions, and particularly of Pedro Reyes's *Palas por pistolas* (Shovels for weapons) project executed within the frame of an artist commission on behalf of Culiacan's Botanical Garden in 2008. *Palas por pistolas* consisted of organizing a voluntary donation campaign of privately owned weapons, for which TV and radio commercials were broadcast, inviting citizens to give up a gun to be exchanged for home appliances. Reyes collected 1,527 weapons, which he took to a military zone to be melted down in a public act. Adding another symbolic twist to his intervention—which ended in a collection object—Reyes had the molten metal pieces transformed into 1,527 shovels with an engraving telling their own story. The shovels were distributed among art institutions

36 Gabriela Romero Sánchez, "Un éxito, el desarme voluntario: Mancera," *La Jornada*, December 22, 2013, http://www.jornada.unam.mx/2013/12/22/capital/036n2cap.

and public schools in which adults and children planted 1,527 trees. For Reyes, the action had the pedagogical purpose of teaching a people how "an agent of death can become an agent of life." The message of Calderón's actions in Ciudad Juárez announces the army's "effectiveness" in confiscating assault weapons, while it points a finger at the United States as responsible for the drug trafficking and violence plaguing Mexico. Calderón's action is similar to Reyes's in that both make public a weapons purge through symbolic rituals while they exercise paternalism from above: those who donate their weapons are rewarded and those from whom they were confiscated are punished. Both actions ended with the planting of trees and with a clichéd symbology; both actions simplify the problem of violence while contributing to propagating blindness of its real causes. We must note that Calderón preferred to execute this series of public actions instead of officially protesting as state leader to the US government right after the "Fast and Furious" operation became public. From 2006 until 2010, agents of the ATF Bureau (Alcohol, Tobacco, and Firearms) attempted to identify leaders of weapon trafficking by allowing the weapons to flow freely into Mexico. The problem with the ATF's strategy of "letting guns walk" was that they were found in more than 170 crime scenes across Mexico, but since the ATF scandal was made public, there has not been a formal accusation on behalf of the Mexican government against the United States, and neither has there been a call from this country to take more effective measures and cease the influx of weapons from the United States to Mexico. The parallel between Calderón's action in Ciudad Juárez and Pedro Reyes's *Palas por pistolas* in Culiacán (which was also executed in Ciudad Juárez the same week of Calderón's visit on February 2, 2012) could be interpreted as a case in which official language has appropriated the language of contemporary art. The analogy between both sensible realms is no more than an example of how all realms (politics, mass media, cultural) operate in the realm of symbolic and perceptive—semiotic—fields of design, information, and creativity. Cosmopolitan artists, as well as Calderón's image designers, work as social designers through "interventions." "Intervention" is the act of finding a space to interact in the sociopolitical field so that the protagonist (be it an artist, marketing agent, or politician) takes up the role among the community to build social consciousness in order to reveal a potential area for "political" activation and/or collective preoccupation. An acknowledgment of these specific situations is achieved through investigation and documentation. The purpose is to reveal areas of potential action and to involve the community in participating in the creation of an apparatus for interaction for sharing signs. This is how the mise-en-scène of a social situation is executed, but in a different context in order to make it better, facilitating the interaction between the artist, the community, and the social field (in the cases mentioned above, the army also takes part). We must also acknowledge the link that is drawn between socially committed artistic projects and forms of life, as sometimes social practices function as prescriptions for "forms of life." In the cases I have described, to be against violence implies adopting a form of life with a pro-life ecological consciousness—as trees are being planted. If before, participatory marketing was hardly distinguishable from participatory art, now the latter gets confused with participatory state propaganda. The gesture of gathering and recycling assault weapons to offer society a positive message, within the actual panorama of political violence, is nothing other than a demagogic gesture full of pedagogic condescendence. The struggle among different social sectors within unstable power relations (between narcos and the government) have fueled a culture of coexistence imbued with violence in an environment of fear and paranoia, in which the elite locks itself in its security bunkers of entertainment and culture. In the latter, violence is culturalized, along with structural inequality of the neoliberal system, which is the real source of violence. The problem is that we are made to believe that violence can be solved through culture or by pointing a finger toward the North. That is neoliberal demagogy characterized by soft anarchism, based on "objective" truths and freedom of expression—expression that is executed in the creative market as a prescribed form of life.

Art with Political Purpose: Art and Social Movements

In her 1968 essay "The Crisis in Culture," Hannah Arendt argues that true art has no purpose and is useless, and therefore it is not a part of political action.[37] According to Arendt, art and politics are two separate spheres, since political action or "speaking out" necessarily implies means or ends, while art is autonomous and needs no justification. When art has political aims, it becomes propaganda (e.g., socialist realism under Stalin's regime). For Arendt, what art and politics have in common is that both are carried out—to use a term posterior to Arendt—in the public sphere. With the advent of industrialized culture, however, once mass society became interested in cultural values and

37 Hannah Arendt, *Between Past and Future: Eight Exercises in Political Thought* (New York: Viking Press, 1968), 197–226.

began to monopolize culture for its own ends, transforming cultural values into exchangeable values, a fusion between art and politics occurred in the greater cultural sphere.[38] From this moment on, modernism's political project of transforming the world by means of criticism, subversion, transgression, transformation, and negativity took its place within postmodernism at the very center of society.

The fusion of art and politics in the cultural sphere takes place within the domain of the Infosphere (also referred to as the "media landscape" or the "field of perception"), which can be defined as the layers of communication that comprise the social system. These include the Internet, society, culture, means of mass communication, and symbolic and affective regimes. Within the Infosphere, cultural currents flow across cultural space, changing the language and forms of self-representation and the meaning of reality.[39] Culture is, therefore, a significant sphere of production that manages to multiply meanings by mobilizing a whole system of overlapping cultural references and generating, on one hand, economic surplus, and on the other, social life—its forms and styles. In the context of the Infosphere, it has been said that political activism implies spreading and sharing the desire to change lifestyles, and that social movements are the vehicles for spreading desires and implementing changes.[40]

Neoliberal policies tend to erode ways of life. For this reason, contemporary social movements haven't been triggered by problems of wealth distribution or antagonism between the working and wealthy classes (as was the case in the previous century), but rather by concerns regarding the grammar of forms of life: quality of life, equality, individual self-realization, democracy (participation and transparency when it comes to both the media and the government), human rights, the environment, anti-globalization, security, and so forth.[41] With this in mind, Brian Holmes observed that social

---

38 Arendt, *Between Past and Future*, 197–226.

39 Tiziana Terranova, "Communication Beyond Meaning: On the Cultural Politics of Information," *Social Text* 22, no. 3 (Fall 2004): 51–73.

40 Brian Holmes: "Eventwork: The Fourfold Matrix of Contemporary Social Movements," in *Living as Form: Socially Engaged Art from 1991–2001*, ed. Nato Thompson (New York: Creative Time, 2012), 73.

41 Jürgen Habermas, "New Social Movements," *Telos*, no. 49 (September 1981): 33–37. A project we can evoke here is Tania Bruguera's "Immigrant Movement International" in Queens, New York, sponsored by Creative Time and the Queens Museum of Art. It consists of a long-term project in the form of a sociopolitical

movements necessarily incorporate a matrix of four convergent elements: art, scientific research and critical theory, media, and politics (self-organization). This implies that social movements are built within society's cultural sphere. On the one hand, creativity and culture lie at the heart of the struggles that social movements engage in, because their primary means are information and communication technology, which are instrumental when it comes to challenging existing power structures and creating alternative means of dialogue. On the other, we have to consider that politics has become a question of epistemology, a means of expression, and a technique for making certain topics intelligible—topics which gain relevance the more visible they are in the media and in sociopolitical fields, enabling them to mobilize emotions such as fear, insecurity, indignation, and anger. Political work involves not only the creation of new forms of life, but also the modification of what is visible in the Infosphere in order to shape political "forms of consciousness" (adding, deconstructing, denouncing, diverting signs, codifying, and decodifying). While being "counterhegemonic," however, these interventions favor the power structure. How? If we consider Jodi Dean's crucial distinction between politics practiced in the Infosphere and politics exercised institutionally, the distinction brings to light the abysmal disconnect between committed criticism and national strategy, between politics as a means of circulating content and politics as official policy. It could even be argued that politics as a means of circulating content benefits the power structure under the logic of repressive tolerance (freedom of expression is a sign of a healthy democracy): messages are contributions to the circulation of content, not actions seeking answers, and the exchange value of messages overtakes their use value.[42] On

movement initiated by the artist, whose venue is a community space in the largely immigrant neighborhood of Corona, Queens. Bruguera subscribes to the principle of "useful art," which aims "to transform some spaces in society through art, transcending symbolic representation or metaphor and meeting with their activity some deficits in reality." A complimentary project is the "Immigrant Party," which functions as a political party. Bruguera's problem with action—other than (provocatively) referring to art as merely utilitarian—is that the political formation of both the immigrant and the political party are obsolete forms of political representation. In this sense, I believe the task that Brian Holmes entrusted to social movements (to propose and implement new forms of life) is more akin to the current historic and socioeconomic moment (though not unproblematic).

42 Jodi Dean, "Communicative Capitalism: Circulation and the Foreclosure of Politics," *Cultural Politics* 1, no. 1 (2005): 51–74, https://commonconf.files.wordpress.com/2010/09/proofs-of-tech-fetish.pdf.

the other hand, in terms similar to those used by Brian Holmes, Chris Kraus suggests that the consequence of fusing art with daily life is that art is the final frontier for vindicating the desire to live differently.[43]

Nevertheless, conceiving of social movements and politicized art as vehicles for changing forms of life is problematic because it implies the subsumption of social and economic criticism into art criticism in proposing solutions for short-term improvements. It runs the risk of reducing politicized art to a simple beautification program in gentrified neighborhoods, museological factories, and corporate parks. Changing forms of life is not about creating a reality that is antagonistic to the prevailing one, because it perpetuates the blockage of what could be. To modify forms of life instead of building a distinct reality—negating the established way of life, its institutions, its material and intellectual culture, its liberal morality, its forms of work and entertainment—is self-repression. Constructing a reality that differs from the current one requires opening an enabling channel for society to intervene directly in political matters, the ability to veto the government's neoliberal plans, and the ability to offer alternatives to the current social orders of exploitation and political and economic exclusion.[44] The problem is that the bourgeois state of law and its institutions—which are the pillars supporting prevailing neoliberal economics and ideology—are the sacred cows which remain untouchable. What must be taken into account is that some recent social movements have been fighting to *maintain* their ways of life—their privileges—rather than to change them.[45]

For a Committed, Autonomous Art

Besides artistic production that is at the center of social movements (along with communication, critical theory, and self-organization, as we have seen), there is autonomous art—that is, art that is not created specifically to serve

---

43 Chris Kraus, *Where Art Belongs* (New York: Semiotext(e), 2011).

44 See Raquel Gutiérrez, "The Rhythms of the *Pachakuti*: Brief Reflections Regarding How We Have Come to Know Emancipatory Struggles and the Significance of the Term *Social Emancipation*," *South Atlantic Quarterly* 111, no. 1 (2012): 51–64.

45 Slavoj Žižek, "Capitalism," *Financial Times*, October 8, 2012, http://foreignpolicy.com/2012/10/08/capitalism.

social movements or causes. More than other forms or expressions (with the possible exception of film and theater), art that is produced for museums or biennials occupies a privileged space of politicization, while simultaneously being intimately linked to neoliberal processes. By this I mean that today art plays the twin roles of compensating and reducing the effects of neoliberalism, while at the same time actively participating in the new forms of predatory economics and geopolitical power distribution, thus contributing to the transition to the New World Order.[46]

How so? By being at the center of population displacement processes in impoverished urban areas in order to renovate them and generate capital (in other words, gentrification), and by abetting speculation and urban marketing, branding, and cultural engineering. Cultural engineering embodies corporate and government interference in the design and form of living spaces, because it means developing projects with the goal of constructing realities in which culture acts as a fundamental element of innovation, dynamism, and individual and social welfare. For example, culture has been used to revive economically depressed areas, develop educational strategies, and design social spaces. By being present in every corner of the world as an instrument of intervention and improvement—and to promote liberal values—contemporary art also helps normalize neoliberal policies. A recent example of this is the extension of dOCUMENTA (13) to Kabul.

In this case, "culture" came before the fighting ceased, before the NGOs and other foreign companies arrived to rebuild and install civil infrastructure, fiber optics, and security and surveillance devices, among other things. This sort of thing is possible because cultural expressions are easily integrated into the global panorama of states of emergency, militarized zones, and eternal war, which have become the norm in the early twenty-first century.

When it comes to contemporary art, we must also consider that the bourgeois order that sustains the economy—along with the internal conditions of producing, exhibiting, and consuming art—are strictly taboo: untouchable by even the artists considered most radical.[47] This is because contemporary art is a playground for corrupt opportunism, speculation, and manipulation, a

46 Hito Steyerl, "Politics of Art: Contemporary Art and the Transition to Post-Democracy," in *The Wretched of the Screen* (Berlin: e-flux journal and Sternberg Press, 2012).

47 Steyerl, "Politics of Art."

place where Darwinist competitiveness has created a workforce that will never achieve solidarity.[48] In this context, the profile of the artist as an antisocial radical has softened, giving way to a new, affirmative image of an enterprising artist in and of himself, able to solve problems in a nonlinear, creative manner.[49] As such, the contemporary artist embodies the figure of the precarious, entrepreneurial worker, the manager of his own human capital, freelancing from project to project. We must also take into account that society disproportionally rewards A-list artists, curators, and other cultural producers in a way not unlike how it rewards managers or CEOs of massive corporations, conferring on them direct membership in the new oligarchy.

We could consider politicized art, as Hito Steyerl argues, as art that focuses not on what art shows but on what art *does* and *how it does it*.[50] To paraphrase Jean-Luc Godard, it's not a question of making political art or film; it's about making art or film politically. With regard to the politics of the field of art, however, what prevails is the diluted and domesticated version of 1970s institutional critiques—for example, Jonathan Hernández's rejected piece, or the phrase coined by the Tercerounquinto art collective, "No artist can resist a $50,000 cannon blast," which was supposedly carved into a wall at the Museo Amparo. Another example is Adriana Lara's 2006 *Artfilm I: Ever Present—Yet Ignored*, which shows several young people meandering through an art gallery while hearing a voiceover reflecting on the conditions of producing contemporary art (it is a consumer's market; it is not politically effective; artists today are mainly interested in their own emotions). These two works arose through the ironic self-reflexivity of the conditions of producing art, reiterating the predominance of an enlightened false consciousness and propagating the ideology of cynical reason: "they know very well what they are doing, but still, they are doing it."[51] It becomes clear that the state of contemporary art is quite different from what gave rise to institutional critique in the 1970s, which was focused on examining the subjection of art to ideological

---

48 Steyerl, "Politics of Art."

49 Gregory Sholette, "Speaking Clown to Power: Can We Resist the Historic Compromise of Neoliberal Art?" http://www.gregorysholette.com/wp-content/uploads/2011/11/Speaking-Clown-to-Power.NOCROP.pdf.

50 Steyerl, "Politics of Art."

51 Slavoj Žižek, "Cynicism as a Form of Ideology," in *The Sublime Object of Ideology* (London: Verso, 1989), http://www.egs.edu/faculty/slavoj-Žižek/articles/cynicism-as-a-form-of-ideology.

interests.[52] Unlike forty years ago, institutions today are more opaque, more exclusive, and they share objectives intrinsically linked to corporate, neoliberal agendas (to the point that those agendas have become invisible). Cultural institutions are the administrative organs of the dominant order, and cultural producers actively contribute to the transmission of free-market ideology across all aspects of our lives.[53]

In the September 2013 editorial of *e-flux journal*, the authors declared that art is produced within a double bind: while art can be accomplice to or instrumentalized by power, its autonomy is localized in an imaginary space. What does this mean? First, that art in order to be *seen* depends on a platform—on an institution—and thus it needs to be part of some art world. Second, that the autonomy of art—as a separate regimen or an isolated sphere from society—is a fantasy. In order to be able to consider art outside of this double bind, Clement Greenberg tied art's autonomy—as art for art's sake—to the vanguard, situating criticality within the discipline of the medium of art in itself. Clearly taking a position against social-realist painting and the debates in the 1930s about the relationship between art and politics—represented, for instance, by socialist realism or Mexican mural painting, which was extremely influential in New York at the time—modernist (vanguardist) painting was characterized by self-critique in the sense of formal expression and a mediation on the qualities of the medium of painting. This implied untying figuration from the arts, as well as an essentialist understanding of the medium of art. For Greenberg, the "purity" of art was in the political sphere, especially if it was seen as incarnation of free nation against the Soviet Union.

---

52 Institutional critique in the 1970s involved the politicization of conceptual strategies in order to reveal how institutional interests—mediated by economic and ideological interests—frame and define the production, interpretation, and visual experience of the artistic object. Drawing on theories developed by the Frankfurt School and by poststructuralism, institutional critique examined the subjection of art to ideological interests, recontextualizing aesthetic practices within their own ideological backing and linking social and ideological interests with cultural practices focused on the process of masking and neutralizing culture through "repressive tolerance." See Yves-Alain Bois, Benjamin Buchloh, Hal Foster, and Rosalind Krauss, "1971," in *Art Since 1900* (Cambridge, MA: MIT Press, 2006), 545–49.

53 See Stephan Dillemuth, Anthony Davies, and Jakob Jakobsen, "There is No Alternative: The Future is Self-Organised," in *Art and Social Change: A Critical Reader*, ed. Will Bradley and Charles Esche (London: Tate Publishing and Afterall, 2007).

Postmodernism could be understood as an effort to break with Greenberg's disciplinary reductivism. Taking up the vanguardist goals of surrealism and Dada to unify art and life, postmodernism flourished with the advent of interdisciplinarity and by fusing art with everything else. Postwar art continued the vanguardist critique of the bourgeois notions of autonomous art and expressive artists, embracing everyday objects and gestures, transforming the function of the artist while interrogating the institution of art or attacking it anarchically.[54] According to Hal Foster, art from the 1950s and 1960s represents the failure to destroy the institution of art and the institutionalization of the vanguard.[55] If Greenberg vouched for art's autonomy with the purpose of resisting illustrative meanings prone to propaganda, kitsch, and commercial forces, the interdisciplinary strategies of postmodernism took art, in Foster's words, "to become part of life under the terms of mass capitalism, while the culture industry appropriated it."[56] Due to its "post-medium" condition, as Rosalind Krauss posited it, the materials of art can range from social interaction, to scientific investigation, to montage, and so forth. With post-modernism, the politics of art's autonomy implied breaking away from Greenbergian purity, and the autonomy of art was conceived as "provisional, always diacritically defined [as something supplementary to art] politically situated, always *semi*."[57]

In that sense, Theodor W. Adorno's take on art's autonomy radically differs from Greenberg's. In his 1962 essay, "Commitment," he responds to Jean-Paul Sartre's aesthetic manifesto *What is Literature?* and elaborates a theoretical debate about autonomous engaged art and literature. According to Adorno, there are two kinds of works of art. On the one hand, there are works that "vulgarly assimilate the existence against which they protest, in forms so ephemeral, that from the first day they end up in seminaries in which they inevitably end up." These works are comfortable being fetishes or a pastime and thus fall into becoming cultural merchandise in a depoliticization that is actually deeply political. On the other hand, there is autonomous engaged art, which, as art, is necessarily detached from reality. Adorno refers to autonomous art not in the sense of "art for art's sake" in its strictly formalist aspect,

54 Hal Foster, "What's Neo about the Neo-Avant-Garde?" *October*, no. 70 (1994): 5–32.

55 Foster, "What's Neo about the Neo-Avant-Garde?"

56 Foster, "What's Neo about the Neo-Avant-Garde?"

57 Foster, "What's Neo about the Neo-Avant-Garde?"

but in the sense that it denies a direct connection with reality. The distance that autonomous art maintains from reality, however, is mediated by reality itself. This means that the work of art cannot emerge from nothingness; that is to say, its origin is a reaction against reality. Thus, Adorno, like Walter Benjamin, distinguishes between "engagement" and "tendency." In that regard, for Adorno, committed art does not have the intention of generating betterment measures, legislative acts, or practical institutions like propaganda to transmit a concrete ideology, but rather operates at the level of fundamental attitudes.

For Adorno, an autonomous and engaged artwork operates at this level, abandoning the social contract for reality, and stops speaking as if reporting fact. This is the moment in which an artwork may surprise us. According to Adorno, the *shock* of the intelligible (or ambiguous) achieves communication more than the legible and the explicit. This is how artworks are autonomous instead of heteronomous. Heteronomy means that artworks are subject to another power, to an external law. As it is autonomous, an engaged work of art is not linked to an empirical reality or to a correct or incorrect political tendency. Art's autonomy serves to avoid popularization and becoming coopted by the market, and implies freeing it from any external purpose. An engaged work of art does not transmit a message in order to convince a public. And although it opposes society, autonomous art it still part of it.

The conditions of possibility of art's autonomy, under the actual neoliberal order I have outlined, are radically different to what we understand today to be art's autonomy under modernism (during the Cold War and defined by Greenberg as *l'art pour l'art*) and postmodern interdisciplinarity, which implies the institutionalization of the vanguard and the subsumption of art to the culture industries. That is to say, the emancipatory promises of modernism (criticality, self-design, creativity) are now located at the center of our everyday lives through consumption and production processes. Under the conditions of the neoliberal order, perhaps what is at stake is the autonomy of art as a political strategy, in the sense that art does not need to justify itself or be useful; evidently, without succumbing to be design or decoration, as *art for art's sake*.

For some, the autonomy of art is only a "metaphysical residue"; however, the real problem has to do with the fact that art no longer designates a reproductive or representative realm, but a field of social production and power relationships. That is to say, art's autonomy has become a problem because it is a field of production of surplus value, not because it legitimates anything as art and anyone as artist. Beyond Warhol and Duchamp, there has been a new transformation of the work of art. After Warhol, there comes Rikit Tiravanija, by way of Fluxus, with the dematerialization in art. Thus, the artwork has dissolved and transformed in relationships, space, and context, extending into time. That is to say, the art world is part of an economy of specialization and the production of social relationships that materialize in exhibitions, conferences, symposia, vernissages, homages, VIP parties, presentations, and other mediums. The ties created are more important than the artwork itself; thus, the art world is a context, a social distribution network of creative production, producing surplus value. Daniel Montero's book about art from the 1990s, *El cubo de Rubik, arte mexicano en los años 90*,[58] which is mainly focused on institutionalization processes and the globalization mechanisms behind art from that decade—in detriment to analysis of the works and dialogues among the artists producing them, limiting himself to describing the artworks as "neo-conceptual tendencies" inherited from US art from the 1960s and 1970s—attests to this. At the same time, contemporary art is a playground for the rich, with the function of embellishing capitalism, and this is why the glamour of contemporary art is indissociable from precarity, the exploitation of forms of life and ways of making a living, the war against organized crime, the war against terrorism, shock therapies in crisis economies, and real-estate bubbles.

If the autonomy of modern art implied considering art as a distanced realm from reality, the post-medium condition of art implies that it has become a niche within reality.[59] What is thus at stake in autonomous art today is to posit it as an experience of reality fundamentally foreign and antagonistic to the prevailing reality, and not as entertainment. Beyond its instrumentalization, autonomous art would resist becoming an instrument against its own illusions, refusing to become a political force subject to interests foreign to itself, or to becoming a pleasing commodity. Unhappy to compete under the terms of the cultural and creative industries, the production of engaged autonomous art would forget the art world and the globalizing ambitions of

---

58 Daniel Montero, *El cubo de Rubik, arte mexicano en los años 90* (México D.F.: Fundación Júmex Arte Contemporáneo/RM, 2013).

59 Marina Vishmidt, "Mimesis of the Hardened and Alienated: Social Practice as a Business Model," *e-flux journal* 43 (March 2013), http://www.e-flux.com/journal/"mimesis-of-the-hardened-and-alienated"-social-practice-as-business-model.

contemporary art, and it would posit itself as a site of precarious labor. The conflict between society and culture would be reawakened instead of being soothed with pseudo-political products for its self-complacent consumption. It would be an a-democratic art form that would refuse to align itself with the neoliberal ideal of political freedom: to make visible not the collateral damage of neoliberalism, but to make visible that which does not yet exist.

Therefore, a genuinely radical approach within the field of art would mean going beyond politically correct art—art that is satisfied with the system of galleries, grants, and markets, and with serving as the government's official showcase. For example, the exhibition "A partir de mañana: todo" ("From Tomorrow On: Everything")—which touched on the theme of the subversion of the hegemonic contents of information as a launchpad for emancipation—took place at the Modern Art and Digital Cultural Center Estela de Luz, the controversial monument commemorating the bicentennial (of the Mexican Independence and Revolution in 2010). The allegedly "politicized" works in the exhibition find themselves perfectly comfortable in the exhibition space hosting them.

Dissatisfied with competing under the terms laid down by the creative and cultural industries, the production of committed autonomous art would be posited as a precarious working site, and it would reawaken the hostility between society and culture, rather than placating it with pseudo-political products for self-indulgent consumption. It would be an "undemocratic" form of art in that it would not align itself with the neoliberal ideal of political freedom. Addressing everyone, it would release itself from the circulation of content, interrupting it, communicating nothing. It would oppose the visibility of what the system declares as extant (power controls what's heard and what's seen, and therefore does not need to employ censorship). Politicized autonomous art would make visible that which does not exist from a different point of view, spreading the contagious attitude of those who have nothing to either gain or lose.

Mexico's Cultural Revolution

The advent of the cultural industries, which we could mark with the inauguration of the Georges Pompidou Center in Paris in 1977, meant making accessible to the masses the production and consumption of art, literature, film, and music with the purpose of democratizing culture. Such a project of democratization—which arrived in Mexico with neoliberalism—sets forth a dilemma for cultural policy. Do we conceive art as a field of autonomous experimentation for an informed expert elite, or do we want museums to be full of publics making art accessible—or transforming art into entertainment or spectacularizing culture—in detriment to the quality and autonomy of the work of art? Or should culture be the showcase of minority voices, a site for community gathering, a bastion of dissident public space against forms of power? The debate is ongoing if we consider culture as an expression describing a community. The response of the current regime to the global debate on the democratization of culture has been, first, to consider the Center Georges Pompidou's offer to open a Pompidou branch in Mexico (there exist branches already in Shanghai and Málaga);[60] second, a cultural center in a revitalized Chapultepec Park; third, a policy of repatriation of plundered patrimony; fourth, to prioritize the cultural expressions of originary peoples, for the Semilleros Creativos (Creative Hotbeds) program in marginalized rural and urban communities to provide art education for children and youth; and finally, to give a new role to intellectuals not as critics of power, but as direct participants in political processes. Except for the Pompidou scheme, current cultural policy is a state-led program that seems to seek to oppose itself to spectacle and elitism of the culture industries.

On December 1, 2018, the doors of "Los Pinos" were opened to the general public. "Los Pinos" has been the presidential residency since President Lázaro Cárdenas refused to take residence in the emblematic Chapultepec Castle. After López Obrador refused to live in Los Pinos as a sign of the new regime's austerity, it was announced that the space would be destined for a cultural center. The project conceives Chapultepec as "a space for the integration of a complex society in which the human right to culture will be offered."[61] Its objective is to integrate the four zones of Chapultepec Park into a single one. The leadership of the project was granted to visual artist Gabriel Orozco, who donated his labor to the State to redefine the cultural vocations of the park and create a "space of permanent cultural life." The Chapultepec complex

---

60 Sonia Sierra, "SRE evalúa abrir sede del Pompidou en México," *El Universal*, April 24, 2019, https://www.eluniversal.com.mx/cultura/sre-evalua-abrir-sede-del-pompidou-en-mexico.

61 Alejandra Frausto, "Transición en Los Pinos: Hay bienes que no estaban en inventarios ni en bodegas: Frausto," *Aristegui Noticias*, April 9 2019, https://aristeguinoticias.com/0904/entrevistas/transicion-en-los-pinos-hay-bienes-que-no-estaban-en-inventarios-ni-en-bodegas-frausto-video.

will include a site museum lodged in Lázaro Cárdenas's house; it will conceive space as a "laboratory to offer access to artistic expressions," and it will host the Carlos Chávez Orchestra, an exhibition space for recovered patrimony—which inaugurated with the display of 594 *exvotos* repatriated by the Italian government.[62]

Once the Chapultepec Cultural Project was revealed, the president publicly announced cuts to the secretary of culture's budget and the elimination of subsidy to the Morelia and Guadalajara Film Festivals and the Fénix awards. At the end of May, the president made a statement that generated a lot of unease among the cultural and academic communities: "Intellectuals and scientists got used to living full of attention." He then posited science and culture as something superfluous and declared: "The poor are first and 'academic tourism' is over."[63] A post-neoliberal role has been ascribed to culture, research, and science, in sync with the ideological goals of the "Fourth Transformation."

As we have seen, neoliberalism in culture went hand in hand with the instauration of the culture industry and with the principle that the voices of artists, writers, and filmmakers were relevant in giving shape to society. Culture was thus conceived as something *useful* for society and as a site for investment return. Attributing a decisive political role to culture, the state and the private sector invested unprecedented amounts of money to generate political, economic, and social surplus value, exploiting the diplomatic potential of art and culture, conceived as a form of human capital. Under neoliberalism, art was given the task to show, criticize, or perceive critically relevant events. Exhibitions and biennials took up "political" questions: work, poverty, exploitation, inequality, violence, globalization, war, exclusion, human rights violations, and new and insidious forms of power. Or perhaps we could say that neoliberalism implies a retrograde political economy that goes hand in hand with progressive liberal values of democracy, freedom of expression, support to arts, and culture and multiculturalism.

As explained above, under Carlos Salinas de Gortari, a system of grants and subsidy for the arts had been established with the SNCA (Sistema Nacional

---

62 Frausto, "Transición en Los Pinos."

63 Alma E. Muñoz y Alonso Urrutia, "Intelectuales y científicos, entre los inconformes por austeridad: AMLO," *La Jornada*, May 29, 2019, https://www.jornada.com.mx/ultimas/2019/05/29/intelectuales-y-cientificos-entre-los-inconformes-por-austeridad-amlo-7960.html.

de Creadores de Arte or National System of Art Creators) and FONCA (Fondo Nacional para la Cultura y las Artes or National Fund for Culture and Arts) programs. In the 2000 "democratic transition" when the PAN took over with President Vicente Fox, one of the government's priorities was "the development and democratization of culture." Taking advantage of the subsidy structures already in place, the government invested a budget—always reluctantly—to produce, disseminate, and administer culture, opening up the participation of corporate and private sponsors to collaborate and invest in the art and culture market and implement an official program. This program was not designed to guide cultural contents and symbols—as pre-neoliberal PRI régimes had done—but to satisfy the national and global demands for cultural and creative commodities. In parallel, culture was posited as a human right and as a tool for democratization. We need to bear this in mind when we contextualize the anti-intellectual climate inherent to President López Obrador's cultural policy. Seemingly, the fruits of almost three decades of cultural production, which positioned Mexico—and especially Mexico City—as a key node in the global fluxes and exchanges of culture, were attacked and began to be slowly dismantled as a sign of neoliberal-era decadence. In the current regime's National Development Plan, the debate on the meaning of the "democratization of culture" and the role the state should have in disseminating culture is dropped in favor of an ambiguous policy of cultural subsidy with the goal of disseminating, enriching, and consolidating the cultural heritage and diversity in the country.[64]

It is true that inequality in Mexico is more appalling if we consider the amount of the budget invested in cultural production, knowing that culture is produced from, by, and for privilege, and that cultural producers generally come from privileged social strata. But what was truly obscene about government and private investment in culture during the "neoliberal" era (which in truth was way below the 1 percent of the budget recommended by the UNESCO) is the government's disinvestment in public education. In parallel to the neoliberal boom in investment in culture, the public education system began to be dismantled with fatal budget cuts and austerity measures.

It has been argued that the main objective of the current regime in cultural policy is to de-subsidize the cultural structures already in place in an effort to democratize and decentralize cultural production, expanding resources

---

64 Plan Nacional de Desarrollo 2019–2024, https://lopezobrador.org.mx/wp-content/uploads/2019/05/PLAN-NACIONAL-DE-DESARROLLO-2019-2024.pdf.

to culture and education where they have not yet reached. They thus seek to offer support to folk artists in rural areas, to the creation of orchestras with children and adolescents from marginal zones; in sum, to deterritorialize cultural investment to remote communities where culture has not yet arrived. It seems that the current government's tendency is to dismantle the cultural and educational structures inherited from "neoliberal" governments and to substitute them with a centralized cultural program in sync with the regime's ideology and electoral propaganda.

Paradoxically, the cultural policies of the current regime geared toward eliminating subsidies resonate with former secretary of culture Guillermo de Tovar y de Teresa's project of slowly defunding culture, seeking to pass the bill to "the publics," implementing a "self-sufficiency model" for cultural production. Since Tovar y de Teresa, however, we never had news or instructions on how such a scheme would be implemented without further precarizing cultural production. It all points toward the reestablishment and normalization of the proto-neoliberal state relationship with cultural producers, through practices like sudden elimination of funding or releasing it in a trickling manner, of cultural bureaucrats who are hardly or not at all engaged with their function, of artists, musicians, or writers working for free to achieve visibility for their work—which is not valued by the bureaucrats. Cultural producers have been fighting for years for dignified working conditions, for salaries, against the officialist bad taste that characterized proto-neoliberal cultural production, for freedom of expression, for autonomy from the State's interests. At the same time, the goal of democratizing culture was fulfilled once mass assistance was registered in public museums, as well as the editorial boom in the past twenty years, among other examples. What is worrisome is that beyond the official delegitimizing attacks of academics and cultural producers, the current anti-intellectualist and obscurantist climate of dismissal of culture and scientific research[65] is that what can be perceived behind culture and education austerity measures is that a new script is being written for national sensibility under the aegis of the president and his collaborators' tastes and interests.

In his morning address on June 18, 2019, the president declared that what his government is supporting in terms of culture is "my conception of culture,"

65 "La titular del Conacyt ha tenido expresiones lamentables: Antonio Lazcano" *Aristegui Noticias*, August 11, 2019, https://m.aristeguinoticias.com/1108/kiosko/la-titular-del-conacyt-ha-tenido-expresiones-lamentables-antonio-lazcano.

which for him "has to do with originary peoples."[66] This declaration was made with the same tone with which President López Obrador answered journalist Jorge Ramos when he confronted the president with the number of murders in the fourth month into his administration. According to Ramos, homicide rates rose in the country, and yet the president denied it and asked him to compare his numbers with a graph that the president presented at the National Palace. The president highlighted a distinction between "my" numbers and "yours" (Ramos's).[67] Similarly, the president's cultural program seems to be centered on a kind of populist electoralism, justifying a new bet on Mexican essentialism based on "the culture of the poor" and of "the peoples." The current regime's cultural policy is thus in full continuity with the utilitarianism and instrumentalization of culture of neoliberal governments for allegedly fixing the social tissue ravaged by violence, but without freedom of expression, and is concerned with implementing an official aesthetic sensibility imposed from above de facto, eliminating the democratic apparatus of cultural—not access, but production.

We are undergoing the gradual destruction of the public sphere not only because of the post-truth situation we are living in, in which the president allows himself to delegitimize journalistic investigation, enunciating "his" truth as supreme, but also because public functionaries allow themselves to make vulgar and misogynous declarations, directly offending citizens. A study by Verificado, the Mexican fact-checking company, revealed that only 48.5 percent of declarations by the president in his daily morning addresses from December 2018 to February 2020 are true. Of 880 suspicious declarations, 24.5 percent were found to be misleading and 24 percent false.[68] To this we can add a new horizon of the cultural ideology grounded on the nineteenth-century histories by Paco Ignacio Taibo II, Alfonso Reyes's *Cartilla moral* (Moral Primer), the interests and academic ties of Dr. Beatriz Gutiérrez (the first lady and director the Coordinación de la Historia y la Memoria or the Coordination of History and Memory), and the enthronement of a new

---

66 Mañanera , June 18, 2019.

67 Jannet López Ponce, "Jorge Ramos Confronta a AMLO con Cifras de Homicidios," *Milenio*, April 12, 2019, https://www.milenio.com/politica/jorge-ramos-confronta-amlo-cifras-homicidios-libertad-expresion.

68 Deyra Guerrero, "Sólo la mitad de lo dicho por AMLO en las Mañaneras, es verdad," *Verificado*, March 3, 2020, https://verificado.com.mx/mitad-verdad-amlo-mananeras.

official cultural figure in the lineage of Diego Rivera, José Luis Cuevas, and Octavio Paz: conceptual artist Gabriel Orozco, the male artist with more visibility and intellectual and commercial credibility outside of Mexico, as director of Los Pinos Cultural Center project. There is also the suspect symbiosis between experimental performance/cabaret with the Senate of the Republic by Senator and performance artist Jesusa Rodríguez, who follows the principle of leaving aside artistic critique in favor of direct action transforming "the [cultural] mafia in power" to "the magicians in power."

In parallel to the gradual dismantling of democratic-neoliberal cultural structures, we are beginning to see the crystallization of a cultural program that promotes a simplistic national identity under the homogenizing articles "Indigenous," "marginal," or "originary" based on the centennial idea of folklore as Mexicanity, as the problematic official appropriation of the originary peoples' cultures by the government as the "essence" of Mexico. For instance, through the "National Guelaguetza" festival on December 15, 2018, which gathered cultural representatives from all states, although paradoxically, in the 2018 original Guelaguetza in Oaxaca, the communities that usually take part in the festival refused to participate because that year the government did not offer enough or dignified support. There is also the ferocious mission of the secretary of culture to repatriate plundered patrimony and to defend handicrafts and folklore art, as well as Mexican design, from further plundering and plagiarism. From the standpoint of the "originary peoples," however, the state's cultural policies on their behalf are far from legitimate: state cultural policy is appropriating once more their culture (or whatever is left of it) for its own aesthetic and ideological purposes. According to Mixe thinker Yásnaya Elena Aguilar, we must never forget that "Indigenous" is a political category derived from European colonial relationships with America's originary peoples, who were first denominated "Indians"; then, when the Republic was instituted, they became "Indigenous peoples." The problem is that this category, although it has been now changed by the more politically correct "originary peoples," and in the context of cultural programs imposed by the state favoring them, tends to homogenize, deny diversity, and erase the languages from the nations that are considered to be outside of the Mexican state. The alleged "recognition" granted to originary peoples through a cultural policy geared toward covering their "cultural needs" also obscures the erasure of the violence upon which the nation-state is still being erected and legitimized: that of the direct destruction of their life forms by megaprojects perpetuating colonial relations of oppression and continuous dispossession through extractivism. This is why, for the so-called "originary peoples" in Mexico, the current regime's cultural programs are once more instrumentalizing their culture, rendering opaque destruction and dispossession of their lands.[69] This means the intensification of the neoliberal extractivist policies in regions where the developmental project of neoliberalism has not been yet.

President Andrés Manuel López's Obrador's cultural program is also in perfect synchrony with the global backlash of identarian obsession with ethnic specificity or singularity, in tune with the authoritarian policies tied to ethnicity that have emerged following the global chaos (like Islamic fundamentalisms). The current regime's "leftist" politics is not based on anti-capitalism or the socialization of the economy, but on an essentialist identarian morality that is used to veil absolutist capitalism and extractivism, and that the state itself is operating in collaboration with corporations and transnational corporations in an open continuum of neoliberal policies. These policies and the discourses that obscure them evidence the current moment of loss of orientation that resulted in the dismissal of critique to power, in forms of aestheticized politics (the "magicians" in power), all justified by a moralizing mandate to put the poor first, which makes visible the permanent conflict that gives shape to modernity: the Christian principle of compassion and the Darwinist one of the survival of the fittest.[70] In other words, the populist morality of power putting the poor, the marginalized, and the originary peoples first, coexists without apparent contradiction with neoliberal policies. The capture of the possible communal spaces of solidarity by the State, and the effectiveness and pragmatism of cultural policy that seeks to "recognize" the culture of the "originary peoples," are the principles of power. If the "democracy for the poor" of the Fourth Transformation is an attempt to protect human life under Darwin's laws, then the further subjection of vulnerable peoples to financial and extractive capitalism implies that solidarity is superseded by competition, reaffirming and further legitimating a division

69 Yásnaya Elena Aguilar Gil, "Construir Naciones sin Estado, parece algo radical pero no lo es," *Radio UdeG Guadalajara*, October 30, 2019, http://udgtv.com/noticias/jalisco/construir-naciones-sin-estados-parece-algo-radical-no-lo-yasnaya-elena-aguilar.

70 Franco "Bifo" Berardi, "(Sensitive) Consciousness and Time: Against the Transhumanist Utopia," *e-flux jounal* 98 (February 2019), https://www.e-flux.com/journal/98/257322/sensitive-consciousness-and-time-against-the-transhumanist-utopia.

of the world, grounded on the "natural" selection of privileged and redundant populations.

The Mexican Renaissance

Everything is relative, we would need to define what we understand by culture, because if it is about supporting culture, I could tell you, there has never been this much support to culture as today, in my own notion of culture. Because culture is that which is related to the peoples and never, have originary peoples, the members of our cultures have been taken care of like now.
—AMLO, Morning Address June 18, 2019

In any case, culture and civilization, artistic creation and theoretical knowledge as well as practical application are borne out of the development of the spirit; but they are inspired by moral will or human perfection. When we lose the moral horizon, culture and civilization degenerate and destroy themselves.
—ALFONSO REYES, *Cartilla Moral*, Federal Government Edition 2019

The regime's cultural sensibility manifests in projects like Secretary of Culture Alejandra Frausto's pompous delivery of a "Presidential Declaration," a document that recognizes the center of the Tiohusco community in the municipality of Felipe Carrillo Puerto, Quintana Roo, as a Historic Monument Site.[71] The village was the cradle of the Caste War in the nineteenth century, and in the sixteenth century it became a nodal point for the Franciscan missionaries to evangelize adjacent territories. The "Presidential Declaration" is accompanied by economic support to encourage economic development in the village through what is known as "Patrimony Tourism." The secretary of culture has also put in place a program to promote "community culture" of agents formerly marginalized, like the "Pixanitos" Theater Group's production of a theatricalized version, for children, of Martin Luther King's "I Have a Dream" speech. The Yucateco group, directed by actress and theater director from Yucatán Ilse Morfin, from the municipality of Kanasin, presented their work at the Auditorio Nacional in Mexico City, accompanied by live music by

71 Secretaría de Cultura, "La memoria maya vive en Tihosuco, la nueva Zona de monumentos históricos de México," *Gobierno de México*, October 4, 2019, https://www.gob.mx/cultura/prensa/171344.

the Carlos Chávez Orchestra. The public had access to the spectacle, paying an entry fee of 1 peso to enter the auditorium.[72]

As I already mentioned, some of Secretary of Culture Alejandra Frausto's objectives are to promote culture produced by marginal agents, to promote patrimony tourism, to administer the repatriation of plundered patrimony, and to defend it from plagiarism. As far as the repatriation of plundered patrimony goes, there has been poor success, for instance, in two pre-Hispanic art auctions in France; the first comprised 120 pieces, and the second 44. The INAH (Instituto Nacional de Antropología e Historia, or National Institute of Anthropology and History) interposed a complaint to the French Ministry of Justice—but no response was received in either case.[73] In what concerns the defense of folk art to "recognize popular culture as a distinctive and as an identitarian trait of our country,"[74] Frausto explains in an article that the main objectives of the secretary of culture are: to seriously look after folk art and to support the development of handicrafts and ensure the prosperity of folk artists, by creating publics through artistic education and access to culture of the most ample sector of society possible, as well as seeking cultural agents from the most remote communities in the country, in order to aid and integrate them in an "enriching exchange between popular art and contemporary art masters."[75] In the same article, she mentions how this exchange recently materialized: in an encounter of the FONCA in Puebla and Tlaxcala in which SNCA members (photographers and stage directors) worked together with the rural communities of two municipalities, "showing the possibilities of transformation of a gaze and a reality through the lens of a camera of corporeal expression."[76] During the exchange, "photographers and directors received from the communities the plain powers of the eye and

72 Joel González, "Niños y jóvenes yucatecos presentarán obra en el Auditorio Nacional," *Sipse*, November 1, 2019, https://sipse.com/novedades-yucatan/ninos-jovenes-presentaran-obra-teatral-auditorio-nacional-348787.html.

73 Georgina Zerega, "México pierde otra batalla por 44 piezas de arte precolombino subastadas en Francia," *El País*, October 31, 2019, https://elpais.com/cultura/2019/10/31/actualidad/1572544644_868267.html.

74 Alejandra Frausto, "Normalizar el arte, diversificar la cultura," *El Universal*, June 24, 2019, https://www.eluniversal.com.mx/columna/alejandra-frausto-guerrero/cultura/normalizar-el-arte-diversificar-la-cultura.

75 Frausto, "Normalizar el arte."

76 Frausto, "Normalizar el arte."

the body as engines for life, identity, work, and art."[77] This exchange, to me, sounds very much like a state-sponsored version of intervention or site-specific art, as discussed above.

A journalist was recently given the task to visit ten *semilleros* or hotbeds across the country to gather the voices of children about art, the works they have produced, their community, and the *semillero* itself. Creative *semilleros* are part of the national Community Culture Program. Its main axis is arts education with a community approach to children and youth across the country to give them access to radio, film, creative writing, visual arts, performing arts, photography, and music. This program is conceived for the long term, and therefore it needs teachers who know the community well and know how to negotiate the varying actors to ensure that the program lasts. These agents are called "Promotores," and their goal is to create artists, to professionalize children in the arts, and to create dialogue between them and their communities, to think about the present they live in, and consider who could have agency in the transformation of the country.[78] According to the forward chronicle, due to the *semilleros*' work, art production has been decentralized.

Part of the cultural mission of the current regime also implies a ferocious defense of patrimony to "stop (Carolina) Herrera and other international brands from disseminating, on their terms, *our* national culture."[79] In 2019, the secretary of culture wrote two letters that were made public: one addressed to Carolina Herrera and the other to Louis Vouitton, accusing the designer houses of appropriating elements of popular Mexican tradition, demanding accountability for having incorporated into their designs elements from Mexican originary peoples, especially their cosmovision. Frausto demands Carolina Herrera to explain and to clarify if the communities that created the textiles—Tenango de Doria in the State of Hidalgo,[80] the Tehuantepec Isthmus, and Saltillo, Coahuila—will benefit from the sales of their collection. For its part, the designer house Louis Vuitton was accused of appropriating

---

77 Frausto, "Normalizar el arte."

78 Laura García Jiménez, "La batalla contra el monstruo verde: crónica de un viaje a través de diez Semilleros," *Revista común*, July 2, 2020, https://www.revistacomun.com/blog/la-batalla-contra-el-monstruo-verde-cronica-de-un-viaje-a-traves-de-diez-semilleros?rq=semilleros.

79 Frausto, "Normalizar el arte." My emphasis.

80 Luis Pablo Beauregard, "México acusa a Carolina Herrera de apropiación cultural por su colección más reciente," *El País*, June 13, 2019, .https://elpais.com/elpais/2019/06/12/estilo/1560295742_232912.html

designs from the Tenango de Doria community in the state of Hidalgo for its chair collection, Dolls by Raw Edges. In the letter addressed to Louis Vouitton, Frausto invited them to a dialogue table with the artisans, a proposal that the designers accepted with gusto.[81] The two appropriation controversies unleashed by Frausto are not new: there have been Isabel Marant's blouses with Mixe embroidery or Zara's clothing that has also used artisanal Mexican designs. Frausto's letter, however, must be considered in the context of Morena's legislative project to safeguard knowledges, cultures, and identities of originary and Afro-American peoples in Mexico, for which authorship laws have been explicitly written to defend Mexican peoples' creations from being used by foreign designers without their knowledge. For instance, Roche Bobois made a collection inspired by Huichol art, and for every piece sold, the Huicholes will receive an income. The principle behind Frausto's letters is an emphasis on an ethic of the recognition of authorship of the origin of the works, which is part of the government's crusade to give visibility to handicraft workers; more than author's rights, the official mission implies recognizing and disseminating the designs that "are part of indigenous cosmovisions' in specific regions in Mexico," and if someone is going to make a profit with them, the community needs to be informed, paid, and taken into account.

Paradoxically, the Mexican government is not accusing design houses of expropriating Mexican designs from their cultural meanings for massifying and selling them. Rather, they are being charged with appropriating Mexican culture without acknowledging originary peoples. In this context, Yásnaya Elena Aguilar accuses the Mexican government of having erected and legitimated itself precisely through cultural appropriation. For Yásnaya, culture is an ensemble of artistic manifestations of a given society; they are complex systems with underlying conducts, cosmovisions, knowledges, beliefs, rituals, and symbols, to mention some elements, of a given society. In the latter sense, almost every collective element seems to be a manifestation of that which we call culture.[82] The Mixe writer argues that a key element to the construction

81 Rodrigo Osegueda, "Luis Vuitton plagia los bordados artesanales de la comunidad de Tenango de Doria," *México Desconocido*, July 11, 2019, https://www.mexicodesconocido.com.mx/louis-vuitton-plagia-los-bordados-artesanales-de-la-comunidad-de-tenango-de-doria.html.

82 Yásnaya Elena Aguilar Gil, " El Estado mexicano como apropiador cultural," *Revista de la Universidad*, July 2018, https://www.revistadelauniversidad.mx/articles/0bb50a13-2ad8-40e3-9972-5f35dd35184f/el-estado-mexicano-como-apropiador-cultural.

of cultural systems is propagation or transcultural hybridization, and to limit it implies limiting freedom of expression. Aguilar Gil also notes that beyond the moral accusations of appropriation, there are unrightful forms of cultural appropriation; for instance, when it is about manifesting abuse against hegemonic cultural groups over oppressed populations or oppressed cultural groups, repeating the asymmetric colonial practices. In sum, appropriation is problematic when products are exoticized and inserted into the logic of capitalist appropriation. For Yásnaya, this is the case of the Mexican government, which has taken cultural elements from the culture it defends against international relations to create an artificial mix of what is called "Mexican culture." Although the diversity of the Indigenous peoples is underscored (and is not homogenized like in the first *Indigenista* era), this notion of culture obviates the fact that the government assigns public resources for expropriating and dispossessing the originary populations by subcontracting the exploitation of their commons. For Yásnaya, Mexican culture is the result of the unlawful cultural appropriation by the Mexican state of cultures that it has, and it keeps on disappearing.

In other words, historic nationalism and the current regime's neo-populist nationalism have recognized and valued cultural productions of the originary populations, parting from an essentialist Mexicanism originated in official culture, based on the demagogic exaltation of such peoples, which, as we have seen, consider the State as the appropriator of their cultures, and do not feel represented by it. This long-expired Mexicanismo celebrates folklore while dispossessing and promoting extractivism in originary peoples' lands. In the meantime, the president and his collaborator's idiosyncrasies in cultural themes constitute a script that sustains the cultural populist ideology of the regime. Another element constitutive of the regime's ideology is the Netflix documentary *La Patria* by Paco Ignacio Taibo II (PITII). In it, the camera follows PITTII through the scenarios that testify to fifteen years of Mexican history, which are also narrated in the three volumes of his history book of the same title. The books tell the saga of President Benito Juárez's recuperation of a "shattered country" after the liberation from Maximiliano's Empire toward building a nation. *Patria 1* encompasses the Ayutla Revolution until the Reform War (1854–1858); *Patria 2* is centered on the French Intervention (1859–1863); and *Patria 3* describes how a Republic fragmented by guerrillas managed to confront the invading French Empire until the fall of Querétaro and Maximiliano's execution. The books are nonlinearly written, and in them, Taibo scrutinizes the actions and historical role characters related to power had, such as Ignacio Zaragoza, Benito Juárez, Maximiliano and Carlota, and Porifirio Díaz. The narrative of the books is structured through microbiographies of the historical characters, told as letters addressing the "pure ones" in the second person ("Your name is Benito Juárez Maza . . . ") and the "bad guys" through indirect discourse. According to PITTII, the "pure ones" are "intelligent, sharp, and laborious as hell; they are terribly jealous of their independence and bear critical spirit; and they are honest until absolutely poor. Incorruptible, obsessed with popular education, sons of the Enlightenment, progress, knowledge, science."[83] The "bad guys" are the "Conservative crabs animated by the Church and usurers, the French military intervention and by Maximilian's Empire."[84] Taibo's documentary is a Manichean history starring the "pure ones" against the "prudish in favor of making the country go into debt and give it away to foreigners." One of the key phrases uttered by Taibo in his documentary is: "History has the capacity to return subtly, tremendously, into the present." His statement resonates with President Andrés Manuel López Obrador's well-known adscription to the legacy of Benito Juárez. PITII's history encompasses an archaeology of the concept of "Fatherland," which originated in "14 years of conflicts and passions between 'the red' and 'the pure ones.' " The parallel with the present is the legacy of neoliberalism that the president is allegedly battling against (in discourse) in which the combat between the "pure ones" and the "red ones" takes place against foreign interests in the country. In continuity with Juárez, his regime will supposedly be the end of colonialist incursions, national foreign debt, and concessions to transnational corporations. The establishment and fall of Santa Anna's dictatorship; the Ayutla Revolution to dethrone Santanismo; the debate that gave rise to the 1857 Constitution; the Reform War; the invasion of Spain, England, and France to collect inexistent debt; the flight toward the north of Juárez; and the guerrilla Republic of Chinaca, an authoritarian presidentialism based on centralization that ends up in a federalist reform, are the series of events that, according to PITII, gave way to the "Fatherland," born out of a "liberal revolution" that channeled discontent, giving birth to a nation grounded on the values promoted by "the pure ones." Should we be concerned if the president and Taibo propose to rewrite the Constitution, taking a "neo-pure" stance?

But "neo-pure" values have been already put into place by the regime, disseminated through the new edition and government distribution of Alfonso

---

83 Paco Ignacio Taibo II, *Patria* Tomo 1 (México D.F.: Fondo Económico de Cultura, 2018), 6.

84 Ignacio Taibo II, *Patria* Tomo 1, 7.

Reyes's *Cartilla Moral*. The brief primer is posited as an "ethical guide for the country." In its most recent edition, it includes a new introduction by President López Obrador, and it is being distributed through state institutions as well as by Evangelical groups throughout the country. The main purpose of the *Cartilla*, according to the president, is to encourage reflection upon the principles and values that contribute to harmonious coexistence and respect to plurality and diversity. Although none would disagree with rethinking an ethics for contemporary society and for rebuilding the social tissue, for the president, the current origins of the crisis of values are corruption and lack of jobs (as opposed to the legacy of colonialism, capitalism, modern alienation, and the current wave of primitive accumulation, which is inextricable from gender violence). In line with Evangelist religion, which promotes the individualistic values of academic self-cultivation, entrepreneurship, and the pacification of society through the values of peace, absolute respect, and nondiscrimination, the president argues that "not only of bread the man lives," because in order to be happy, both well-being of the soul and material well-being are necessary.

Alfonso Reyes wrote the *Cartilla Moral* in 1944, commissioned by then–Public Education Secretary Jaime Torres Bodet. In 1992, José Luis Martínez re-edited the text, and President Ernesto Zedillo suggested making it part of public education textbooks. In both attempts to disseminate Reyes's primer, the text did not make it to the press because it was considered to be conservative, religious, and contrary to the Mexican State's secularity. President López Obrador's edition is twenty-eight pages long and is divided into fourteen sections where moral lessons are included about respect to self, family, society, the fatherland, humanity, and nature, in a moral search of the preservation of the fundamental principles of justice, democracy, and rule of law. Part of the problem with the State dissemination of the *Cartilla* in cahoots with the Evangelical Church is that, according to ethics, the adhesion to a moral principle is individual, while right is a collective concern. It seems like the regime is not only instrumentalizing culture for its own purposes, but also for the Evangelical Church to validate its own misogynous, narrow-minded, and outdated moral regime, as is the *Cartilla Moral* itself. Further issue with the *Cartilla Moral* is that the government is promoting the participation of religion with the government in a task that, in theory, corresponds to the State. It has become evident that the current regime does not shy away from indicating religious directives and proselytizing. The "collaboration" between the state and participating churches is transforming the latter into governmental instruments with a vague and diffuse objective, establishing a dangerous precedent, without even mentioning the political ties that exist between MORENA, President López Obrador, and the Evangelical Church. We should also consider the figure of the "siervos de la nación" or "servants of the nation," which is an army of Morena militants wearing distinctive beige vests who perform specific tasks on behalf of the government. For instance, they are part of the COVID-19 vaccination campaign or are given the task to allocate government aid to vulnerable citizens. The name of this controversial figure has religious undertones, and even before the distribution of the *Cartilla Moral*, the secularity of the government had already been brought into question. In May 2019, an opera was presented at the Bellas Artes Palace as an homage to Nasón Joaquín García, leader of the Evangelical Church La Luz del Mundo (The World's Light). Even against the official prohibition to lending State spaces to organized cult events in order to preserve the government's secularity, the mise-en-scène was executed in Bellas Artes, the most emblematic building representative of culture in Mexico City.

Intellectuals and the Triumph of Democracy: From "the Mafia in Power" to the "Magicians in Power" (Or the Cabaret at the Senate)

Another questionable trait of the current regime is its aestheticization of politics, simultaneous with a politicization of aesthetics. This situation not only confuses, but also makes inseparable the political from the cultural sphere, and it is not only the result of an antidemocratic official program of cultural propaganda, but also of institutional irresponsibility, and of the propagation of demagogy and personal idiosyncrasy. If the president's definition of culture is reduced to the demagogic exaltation of Indigenous peoples, intellectuals are being assigned a new function: that of solving without contradiction the situation of being artists (without public subsidy), having to function as activists, and radical and progressive voices within the lines of power.[85] This is because now, "critiquing from within the art bubble" is frowned upon, as intellectuals now must go deep into reality on the side of power to legislate and participate democratically "from within," resolving national problems like the disappeared, femicides, corruption, violence, and the tearing of the social tissue.

---

85 Jesusa Rodríguez, keynote presentation at the 2019 Hemispheric Institute Conference on June 10, 2019, https://www.youtube.com/watch?v=TwdKg31WoJc.

Artists and intellectuals are also now giving lessons of civic values, history, and ethics. According to Senator and performance artist Jesusa Rodríguez, to put artists at work on an agenda to solve the country's problems supposes the reconversion of "the mafia in power" to "the magicians in power."[86]

This line of aesthetic-political action was inaugurated with Rodríguez's intervention in the Plenary of April 25, 2018, at the Senate of the Republic, when Rodríguez, together with Senator Ana Lilia Rivera, staged a reconstruction of Olmec Offering IV from La Venta, Tabasco, associated to maize and fertility during the presentation of a law initiative to protect maize native species.[87] Offering IV is composed of six stelae, or standing slabs, and sixteen characters that, according to Senator Rodríguez, represent a gathering of various pre-Hispanic peoples for the unknown historical event represented in the stelae. Although the original meaning of the congregation remains unknown, the characters representing the diversity of the Mexican peoples were invoked in the performance "to pray against the *chahuistle* [evil] of transgenics falling upon us and our primary divine grace [maize],"[88] nowadays threatened by transnational companies seeking to commercialize transgenic maize seeds. Rivera, the legislator, explained that the goals of her law initiative are to declare native maize as national patrimony, to promote its sustainable development, and to establish mechanisms to protect it as far as production, commercialization, consumption, and constant diversification go. The legislation also seeks to involve civil society in the preservation of native maize, including campesinos, Indigenous communities, and academics seeking to guarantee access in Mexico to maize free of GMOs. Although transgenic seeds are indeed a threat to our food sovereignty, and there have been initiatives (like Colectivas A.C.) from within civil society to struggle against the growth of transgenic products in the country through national and international legislation (which still fall short in protecting us from transnational companies like MONSANTO), one of the blind spots of the senators' show was their silence with regard to the neoliberal policies regarding agroindustry and the

---

86 Rodríguez, keynote.

87 "Jesusa Rodríguez arma ofrenda al maíz en el Senado para evitar "chahuistle transgénico," *SinEmbargo*, April 25, 2019, https://www.sinembargo.mx/25-04-2019/3571452.

88 Nación 321, "El polémico 'performance' de Jesusa Rodríguez en el Senado," April 25, 2019, https://www.nacion321.com/congreso/el-polemico-performance-de-jesusa-rodriguez-en-el-senado.

dismantling of the sustainability of the Mexican agrarian economy. These policies led to the import of transgenic maize for the past thirty years. In spite of the slogan "sin maíz no hay país" (there is no country without maize), it is a known fact that Mexico imports most of the maize it consumes. Between January and May 2018, we imported from the United States a total of 169 tons of maize and exported 429 tons of the grain during the same period; 98 percent of the maize exports come from the United States (2 percent from Brazil). The volume of imported maize augmented 3.9 percent with regard to 2017 (also taking into account that bean—another staple of Mexican nutrition—imports rocketed to 87 percent in 2018).[89] Although GMOs represent a threat to our food sovereignty, our autonomy with regard to feeding ourselves has been slowly dismantled for the past thirty years. Although the legislation to protect maize from transgenics is an important gesture, clearly more fronts need to be attacked, and a complex strategy is needed geared not only toward legally eradicating GMOs from Mexico, but also to recovering national food sovereignty, well beyond the good-intentioned government plans.

My main concern here is that Senator Jesusa Rodríguez's action imposes through political performance the mandate that artists and intellectuals be directly useful to the regime. In the case of the senate performance, the aim was to make it attractive by introducing cabaret within the senate to mobilize it and the rest of society, to get attention from the public about the deep problem of the "monsantization" of the country, an intervention that, according to Rodríguez, was successful.

Embracing her role as a leader of civic and ethical values, the performance artist/senator posted a video online in which she gives herself the challenge of climbing up the Sun Pyramid in Teotihuacán "at once and without stopping." Wearing a camera on her back, we see her climbing without stopping and stoically making it all the way to the top; once there, she declares on a faltering breath: "Our grandmothers and grandfathers taught us how to build [pyramids]. They conceived things in the long term. Our short-term project is to save the world. If they [our grandmothers and grandfathers] achieved this, we can do anything. So, Viva Mexico!"[90] The lesson on ethical and civic values continues with the senator picking up plastic bottles that are littering the top of the pyramid.

89 Susana González, "Incrementan importaciones de maíz en México," *La Jornada*, June 21, 2018, https://www.jornada.com.mx/ultimas/2018/06/21/incrementan-importaciones-de-maiz-en-mexico-4833.html.

90 Rodríguez, keynote.

The senator further imparted a history lesson at the Hemispheric Institute gathering in June 2019 in Mexico City. Blurring the boundaries between demagogy, personal opinion, and critical theory, Rodríguez offered an X-ray of the country as constituted by a series of "traumas." The senator's keynote told this story through an imagined taxi drive in which she converses with the driver. In Mexico City, the taxi ride has been the mythical encounter between the middle and lower class because, historically, cab drivers (a species about to disappear) have been one of the most politicized sectors of Mexican society. But far from being a symmetrical conversation between two informed people, Rodríguez condescendingly indoctrinates the driver by telling him the history of Mexico as a succession of collective traumas:

> Our mother earth has suffered traumas. How have we overcome them? If the Conquest of Mexico erased all of *our* culture, there is a trauma in the collective unconscious that degenerated in a co-dependency syndrome in our relationship to our mother earth. Father Hidalgo tried to cure us with a false therapy he called "Independence"; another false therapy followed called "Reforma." Things were going well until we suffered another trauma, that of Porfirio Díaz's dictatorship, which came with an irritable bowel syndrome. The therapy for that trauma was the Revolution, but then we were fucked over by 30 years of the PRI, which left us with neoliberalism, which gave Mexico Stockholm syndrome (in which the victim is complicit with her executors). The traumas of Mexican history have not been resolved and they keep on piling up. The solution to the traumas and legal corruption is AMLO. Corruption is another one of the illnesses inherited from the PAN and the PRI. If the country can heal or not, is one of the enigmas of the 4T.[91]

In the Q&A session of Senator Rodríguez's keynote, she declared that her main challenge in her role as "magician in power" is that "now the demand is absolute, wider than demands made from art or with art. In art, results are abstract. We have to deliver concrete results, like stopping the violence, to go beyond being spectators."[92] In what followed, she made a controversial and thus irresponsible declaration that the FONCA's grant system should disappear, because "art can be spared, [so] it has no social validation."[93] In that regard, and in sync with state policy of prioritizing the poor, for Rodríguez , it is necessary

91 Rodríguez, keynote.
92 Rodríguez, keynote.
93 Rodríguez, keynote.

for artists to give up not only the privilege of "living off of the State," but also to relinquish masculine, carnivorous, and class privileges. I am not sure that the figure of the vegetarian lesbian is the "ideal Mexican" of the current regime, and Rodríguez's stance represents a healthy antagonism from within government lines. And yet what is highly troubling here is the way in which Senator Rodríguez misunderstands privilege. The problem with privileged populations is that their lives are based on consumption and development at the cost of the lives and the forms of life of redundant populations, and as we have seen, among them are Indigenous populations. And yet Rodríguez claims to be speaking on their behalf, to be one of the people as well as a direct descendant of pre-Hispanic peoples (underscored by her colorful use of *huipiles*). Aligned with traditional Mexicanismo national narratives and with the current regime's neo-populism, she is appropriating originary cultures for an ambiguous purpose that is far from representing contemporary originary peoples' ordeals. Another problematic aspect of Rodríguez's declarations is the mandate of artists and intellectuals to be useful politically to the state. In that regard, she continues the neoliberal conception of art as useful.

For many, however, cultural production remains precisely one of the conditions of democracy and social wealth of a country, and market and government interests compromise these conditions. We are seeing Mexican cultural production succumb not only to dogmatism and moral tutorship, but to prejudice in an anti-intellectual climax in which intellectuals, museums, and universities are subordinated to the State project. Through official ideology, the traditional values of heteropatriarchy seep through, and social stratification based on criollismo and mestizaje is invisibilized, while religion is reintroduced into society by way of the State. The university stops being a key site for modernization and transformation of the country and intellectuals, its moral compass. The human difference that exists between mestizo and criollo and originary populations by centuries of dispossession and extermination is posited by the current state cultural hegemony as "anthropological, racial, spiritual" difference. This discourse is an illusory attempt to heal, yet again, the colonial wound with cultural production tied to a moral renovation linked to evangelist religiosity and populism. In this regard, critique is needed now more than ever, aligned with a struggle with whatever public (and private) structures to subsidize art remain.

CHAPTER FIVE

After the Neoliberal Ruin of the World in Common, Can We Share a World Beyond Representation?[1]

The Loss of the *Lebenswelt* and Modernity

Rootlessness, violence, the shattering and loss of all traditions, loneliness, ruins, a devastated environment, xenophobia, mental decay, and illness; this is our inheritance from modernity. A reflection on these forms of modern alienation traverses Hannah Arendt's work, in which she poses some of modernity's traits (humanity's increasing dependency on technology and science, the flight from the earth into the universe and into the self, authoritarianism, the trivialization and emptying out of truths, mass society, etc.) as a direct threat to the *Lebenswelt*. The *Lebenswelt* is the world of common experience and interpretation that humans share. For Arendt, the world, nature, and earth are interrelated, but they must not be confused. While the earth is the quintessence of the human condition insofar as it provides human beings with a

1 A version of this paper was delivered at the conference "Art after Culture" at e-flux on June 15, 2019, in New York City.

habitat, nature is the condition of organic life,[2] and the common world is the framework from within which understanding and judging can arise among humans. The common world therefore possesses unquestionable meaningfulness and enables common subsistence in togetherness. This is possible, Arendt argues, because men move and act in the world, and because they can talk with and make sense of each other and of themselves.[3] The "public sphere" is intrinsically related to the world in common: it is common to everyone and is distinguished from our private place within it. The common world is therefore a human artifact that results from human hands and affairs. To live together in the world, moreover, implies that "a world of things is between those who have it in common."[4] Arendt writes that this "in-between" is physical and as real as the world of things we all see. Action and speech are concerned with this "in-between" that relates and separates "men" at the same time. This is because being in the common world means to be concerned with and affected by the same things, but from different positions within that world, which constitutes the "reality" of a "web" of human relationships in which "men" disclose themselves as subjects.[5] The common world is also what we are born into and what we leave when we die, because it survives from generation to generation.

According to Arendt, modernity, which was precisely enabled by the destruction of all tradition, is characterized by the irretrievable loss of the experience of shared meaning, and talking with and making sense of each other. This loss triggered the disappearance of a space for arguing, reasoning, and argumentation: the space of politics, comprised of speech and action.[6] The loss of shared meaning began when the "sameness" of the object of the world in common began to cease to be discernible, according to Arendt, partly due to the arrival of "mass society."

For Arendt, mass society is characterized by isolation and lack of normal social relationships and, therefore, by an absence of consciousness of common interest. A couple of decades later, Félix Guattari diagnosed the ravages of modern alienation, what he described in the 1980s as a "crisis of relationality."

---

2 Hannah Arendt, *The Human Condition* (Chicago: The University of Chicago Press, 1958), 2.

3 Arendt, *The Human Condition*, 4.

4 Arendt, *The Human Condition*, 52.

5 Arendt, *The Human Condition*, 182.

6 Hannah Arendt, *Between Past and Future: Six Exercises in Political Thought* (New York: The Viking Press, 1961).

In his view, this crisis is due to the reduction of kinship networks to the bare minimum, the poisoning of domestic life by the gangrene of mass-media consumption, the ossification of family life by a standardization of behavior, and the reduction of neighbor relations to their meanest expression.[7] In this light, we could infer that what is compromised by the modern loss of the *world in common* is the relationship between subjectivity and its (social, animal, vegetable, or cosmic) exteriority. By all accounts, this gradual loss is leading to general implosion. If the establishment of neoliberalism, the economic-political program that has progressively ruled the world since the 1980s, meant that "there is no such thing as society. There are individual men and women and there are families,"[8] it means that globalization implies the disappearance of society. This can be linked to Arendt's argument that the loss of tradition in modernity also means the destruction of the world in common; the lack thereof has led to the pervasive feeling, as Franco (Bifo) Berardi has recently written, that entropy is expanding, vision blurring, and private meaning clouding, obstructing any possible path of escape.[9] We are only now realizing that the systematic undoing of the social foundations of human relationships (or the *world in common*) occurs in parallel to the degradation of nervous cells, and that the destruction of the social tissue is inseparable from environmental damage, and that climate change is, in fact, indissociable from collective psychic collapse. For instance, Hubert Sauper's feature *Darwin's Nightmare* (2004) renders this visible as it documents the misery, environmental damage, and social and self-destruction brought to a community at the shore of Lake Victoria in Tanzania by industrialized fishing. The film registers how neoliberal poverty is grounded not on a lack of development or jobs, but on a people's inability to survive, leading a sustainable life in their originary environment—either because colonization has taken away their skills to do so, or because they have been displaced. Films that show similar communities surviving their self-destruction are Ricardo Silva's *Navajazo* (2015), an "ethno-documentary" made in collaboration with its subjects (marginal, addicted, or deported people living in Tijuana), and

7 Félix Guattari, *The Three Ecologies* (London: The Athlone Press, 1989), 27.

8 Margaret Thatcher's famous statement in an interview in Women's Own in 1987; transcription available online: https://www.margaretthatcher.org/document/106689.

9 Franco "Bifo" Berardi, "Game Over," *e-flux journal* 100 (May 2019), https://www.e-flux.com/journal/100/268601/game-over.

Juan Manuel Sepúlveda's *The Ballad of Oppenheimer Park*, which is about a community of originary peoples in Vancouver in 2016 who tell, intoxicated, the story of colonization and destruction of their people and life worlds. These films can be described as a kind of apocalyptic humanism, which, according to Yuk Hui and not far from Arendt's critique of modernity, is linked to the expansion of technology by globalization.[10]

Authoritarianism in the Twenty-First Century

According to Chinese philosopher Yuk Hui, globalization is the outcome of the transformation of the world that had situated the West at its center, which led to a global axis of time constructed by technology and science that became the synchronizing metric of all civilizations. In our modern world, technology, which embodies rationality and scientific epistemology, is the true universal.[11] Modernity begins, according to Arendt, in the seventeenth century, precisely in the "Age of Reason," with the Enlightenment, which was supposed to fully realize humanity and universal values, fighting "magic thought" with science and technology. The introduction of the machine transformed both life and the world; designed to make human life easier and human labor less painful, the instrumentality of tools resulted in the increasing rule and destruction of the world. This was caused by the substitution of the world of machines by "the real world" and because machines, for Arendt, fail to offer humans a dwelling place. Part of the problem is that with machines, everything began to be put to some use or other; everything had to lend itself to achieve something else, as an end in itself.[12] We have now arrived at the point where machines have taken over and have made redundant human cognitive capacity, along with the philosophy in which technology is based. For Yuk Hui, this means the end of the Enlightenment, a void, a loss of orientation. This is because what comes after worldwide technological synchronization centered in Europe is apocalyptic humanism, embodied in the images of "ecological ruins" like Notre

10 See my text, "Self-Destruction as Insurrection or How to Lift yhe Earth Above All That Has Died," *e-flux journal* 87 (December 2017), https://www.e-flux.com/journal/87/169041/self-destruction-as-insurrection-or-how-to-lift-the-earth-above-all-that-has-died.

11 Yuk Hui, "What Begins After the Enlightenment?" *e-flux journal* 96 (January 2019), https://www.e-flux.com/journal/96/245507/what-begins-after-the-end-of-the-enlightenment.

12 Arendt, *The Human Condition*, 151–52.

Dame or the Amazon rainforest, which Paul B. Preciado proposes to honor as punk monuments, marking the loss of a world that ends (and the beginning of a new one).[13] The antidotes to self-destruction are nostalgic invocations of cultural traditions, which we have seen become violent returns to nationalism, cultural essentialisms, and ethnofuturisms.[14] The precedent to the radical totalitarian nationalisms that have sprung up across the globe in the past few years was Radical Islamism, with its aggressive return to religious essentialisms in a defense against the dissolution and homogenization of cultural specificity and identity brought about by the imposition of Western culture through globalization. One of the three worlds that are woven together in Ahmad Ghossein's *The Fourth Stage* (2015), along with magic and cinema, is the changing landscape in Southern Lebanon, where the artists' camera records contemporary manifestations of Islamic visual and material culture in private and public spaces.

In this context, the power of capitalism—of which neoliberal totalitarian corporate states (and religious institutions in general) have become instruments—works by selecting, excluding, and disseminating events and constructing visualities that structure the present that each one of us perceives, applying one possibility of reality among many possibilities according to each user. To the point that "normal" for us means living in a world in which we have the right to retreat to our own private worlds of meaning, these private worlds are tailored to the wants of each individual by the algorithms of digital interfaces constantly adapting to our individual needs. In a way, the possibility of the world in common has been replaced by the explosion of a myriad of niches for the private consumption of digitalized content disseminated in the "world" and in the Infosphere. Clearly, representation—the dispositive that enables appearance through speech and action in the world in common and the human capacity for the creation and dissemination of shared meaning and traditions—has been hijacked by capitalism, authoritarianism, democracy, the Internet, and spectacle.

For Hannah Arendt, the expansion of authoritarianism in Europe in the 1920s and 1930s was due to alienation and loneliness brought about by the degradation of the *world in common*. Clearly, further loss of the *world in common* and the crisis of relationality help us understand the resurgence of fascisms and fundamentalisms across the world in the twenty-first century.

---

13 Paul B. Preciado, "Notre Dame of Ruins," *artforum*, April 21, 2019, https://www.artforum.com/slant/paul-b-preciado-on-the-notre-dame-fire-79492.

14 Hui, "What Begins After the Enlightenment?"

Nowadays, the main ruling instruments are the mobilization of affects to achieve polarization, fear, and the mass sentiment that "something" (like our means of subsistence or the networks of safety materialized in the welfare state) has been taken away from "us," either by the 1 percent or the immigrants. With this tune, the corporate state is managing *live* mass mood swings by immersing itself within the masses, wielding the totalitarian discourse of "taking back" what has been stolen from "us" (at any cost). According to Arendt, the difference between "modern dictatorships" and premodern tyrannies is that terror is no longer used as a means to exterminate opponents, but as an instrument to rule the perfectly obedient masses. Modern terror, moreover, strikes without provocation, even if the victims are innocent from the point of view of the persecutor.[15] In the modern versions of authoritarianism, race and class thinking are instrumentalized to dominate "men," as race and class unity become the substitutes for nationalistic emancipation.[16] The resurgence of authoritarianisms across the world in the twenty-first century is also based on class and race thinking, along with the radicalization of impotence, the dissemination of toxicity in the public sphere, and the polarization of whatever is left of "society," through a phenomenon called "post-truth" or "self-truth." Only in the American continent, presidents Jair Bolsonaro, Andrés Manuel López Obrador, and Donald Trump lie systematically through their teeth to their constituents, even against numbers generated by state institutions, a global phenomenon that tends to reproduce itself. Self-truth is the perversion of public truth, which is the phenomenon that transforms truth into personal choice, and which thus destroys the possibility of truth. Realities that do not correspond to facts in reality are systematically invented. The humanist apocalypse comes together with a messianic vanguard grounded in self-truth that means the amputation of the word in its full sense. Whatever anyone says now has no value, no sense, no meaning. Brazilian writer Eliane Brum describes this situation as losing one's place within grammar. As the world in common further collapses, language extinguishes itself as mediator,[17] as in the film *Birds of Passage* (2018) by Ciro Guerra, which tells the story of

---

15 Hannah Arendt, *The Origins of Totalitarianism* (New York: Schocken Books, 1951), 143.

16 Arendt, *The Origins of Totalitarianism*, 161.

17 Eliane Brum, "Enfermo de Brasil: Cómo resistir la enfermedad en un país (des) controlado por la perversión de la autoverdad," *El País*, August 2, 2019, https://elpais.com/elpais/2019/08/03/opinion/1564785296_446106.html.

the infiltration of capitalism and corruption in a Wayuu family when illegal drug trading is introduced in Colombia in the late 1960s and 1970s. In the narrative, at the moment in which the translator or mediator among two tribes is murdered, direct passage to violence occurs, akin to the murder of language and truth by current regimes. In what follows, I will elucidate the role culture and cultural production have had in modernity as mediators, as truth, as word, as representation, as the "in-between." If, with modernity, culture becomes a kind of secularized religion as the only means to struggle for inhabiting a world in common, how do we come to terms with the current humanist apocalypse and the dispossession by authoritarianism of the world-in-common?

Culture as the Site for the Production of the World-in-Common?

In the modern political imagination, the State produced a representative form of social cohesion by disseminating a world of shared meaning, expressing the alleged "essence" of an imagined community. In this context, art and critical thought were the utmost expression of illuminist values and had the vanguardist role of announcing a visionary and emancipatory future for all. Premised on a separation between action and appearance, vanguardist art operated in a separate realm than politics and action (what we know as the "autonomy" of art), and artists adhered to the tradition of the Revolutionary take-over as the road for universal emancipation. In their rebellion, vanguardist artists made a tactical, temporary, local, contrived, problematic, and idealistic alliance with the working class and the marginalized. This alliance was based on representativity: an invisible social contract in which artists imagined themselves to be *mandated* by humanity to *address* humanity in the name of universal values, grounded on a conflict between the individual (artist) and societal structures.[18]

In the 1960s (or high modernism), artists abandoned and deconstructed representation and critiqued representativity, dismissing them as totalitarian structures, as vehicles for a bland, sexist, and racist humanism, as well as for a trite universalism. Artists replaced the invisible social contract from early modernity that had enabled them to speak on behalf of all of humanity with a new one, in which they spoke from the point of view of their own

18 See Thierry de Duve, *Aesthetics at Large, Volume 1: Art, Ethics, Politics* (Chicago: University of Chicago Press, 2019), 67–70.

gender, ethnic origin, political struggle, or sexual orientation, as colonized peoples, minorities, workers, and so forth. Paradoxically, in the 1980s and 1990s, representativity came back with a vengeance through identity politics and consciousness-raising activism (on the AIDS epidemic), although no longer as a concept subject to criticism and deconstruction, but instead as a positive, affirmative concept.[19] Equality came to mean equal access to visibility through self-representation, and a new kind of multicultural universalism flourished, celebrating difference in spite of humanism contradictions and conflicts from the real world. The return of representativity was parallel to globalization. Globalization meant the dismantling of the referential economy of political and aesthetic modernity, and the exhaustion of the social contract that had assigned artists universal representativity. Nowadays, art tends to address globalized mass society in a context in which governments and corporations have monopolized culture for the purpose of managing mass societies: along with a niche for entertainment, as we have seen, culture is an index of democracy in the sense of freedom of speech, accessibility to being cultivated, a dispositive for the dissemination of new content. Culture has become a product, merchandise that is consumed as entertainment at the service of the life process of society, embedded in the cycle of the production of the new, judged according to the standards of freshness and novelty.[20] Arendt and other thinkers lamented the beginning of art becoming "mass culture"; artists, however, either embraced this new frame for the production and consumption of art, like Andy Warhol, Jeff Koons, Damien Hirst, and others, or rejected it, creating a new niche art production in the name of politicization, counterinformation, and criticality. Under globalization, critical artists have been summoned to give up art's autonomy and to take up the task to restitute what has been broken by the system, to denounce globalization's collateral damage and the conditions of production of contemporary art, to imagine the future, to produce political imaginaries, to disseminate counterinformation, to restore social links, to gather and keep documents and traces for the "duty of memory," and so forth. For this, the genre of documentary form (under an array of experimental and self-reflexive forms) has become a privileged means of expression, as Okuwi Ewenzor's dOCUMENTA (11) demonstrated, exhibiting through an estimated 600 hours of moving images in 2002, what

19 Thierry de Duve, *Aesthetics at Large*, 75.

20 Arendt, "The Crisis in Culture: Its Social and Political Significance," in *Between Past and Future*, 201.

had become evident as the collateral damage of globalization.[21] For instance, Zarina Bhimji's *Out of Blue* (2002) was a portrait of the landscape in Uganda that the artist was forced to leave as her family was expelled by Idi Amin thirty years prior. Similar portraits of forced displacement were Sandja Ivenkovic's *Personal Cuts* (1982) and *Solid Sea* by the Milan-based collective Multiplicity, the latter of which told the story of the destiny of immigrants who drowned in 1996 in the Sicilian coast. Pavel Braila, Kultug Ataman, and Isaac Julien exhibited moving images of the Third Cinema genre, with postcolonial versions in Trin T. Minh-Ha and Group Amos. There was also Steve McQueen's *Western Deep* (2002), in which he took a camera and a microphone into a South African gold mine, and Eyal Sivan's *Itsembatsemba—Rwanda One Genocide Later* (1996). In this light, we could perhaps argue that the vanguardist role of artists has been substituted by the mandate to cultivate in spectators a feeling of political responsibility in the name of self-representation and representation of Enlightenment values.

Differentiated Representativity and Codependent Politics of Appearance

The main problem with the return of representation through differentiated representativity, speaking on behalf of the ordeal of others or in the name of the recognition of my private ordeal, is that both reproduce a moralizing realm of nonshared meaning. This form of address, moreover, has given way to what I would diagnose as a codependent politics of appearance. In psychological terms, "codependency" is the excessive reliance on a partner who requires support regarding an illness or addiction. Within differentiated representativity, the "intervener on behalf of someone else" is the relying part and the addict, the subject of the ordeal in question. This "codependent politics of appearance" is based on a melancholic restitution of meaningful singular-plural worlds, clearly devoid of the possibility of speech and action, and thus of common meaning. A codependent politics of appearance, moreover, disseminates a form of despotic empathy generated by situating oneself or others in the place of the martyr or scapegoat, seeking recognition and visibility. In other words, albeit well-intentioned, contemporary forms of

21 See Okuwi Enwezor, "Documentary/Vérité: Bio-Politics, Human Rights and the Figure of 'Truth' in Contemporary Art," *Australian and New Zealand Journal of Art* 5, no. 1 (2004): 11–42.

representation are not allowing for the in-common to occur. This is because the modern practice of "looking at the pain of others" has created a form of "reified subjectivity," as Anita Chari has diagnosed. According to Chari, this form of subjectivity is a spectacularized point of vision, uncommitted and post-political, that individuals assume with regard to the world in relationship to our own practices and habits. In this pathology, the economy exists as a domain that is apparently separate from human activity; therefore, alienated subjectivity is incapable of seeing the extent of its involvement in capitalist processes, fueling/furthering the incapacity to understand forms of domination in the context of the totality of social reality. Therefore, Chari sets forth the "culture of spectatorship" that Sontag defined in *On Photography* as something fundamentally alienating, causing blindness toward capitalist processes that we are all complicit with (incoherence) and that are the direct or indirect cause of the pain of others, and that images circulating in the sensible regime convey. As a pathology, the alienation described by Chari leaves no room for empathy, and neither does it allow one to foresee the actual power relations, as it divides the world between "the wretched of the screen" and reified spectators living in modernized enclaves, blinded to the privileged position they occupy in global economic processes—what is known in discussions about documentary and representation of underdevelopment and poverty in Latin America as "pornomiseria."[22]

Recently, I have been thinking about a possible analogy that could be made between the proliferation of documentary images, reportages, artworks, or literature about the situation of emergency in which the majority of the global population is living in, and the Baroque crucifix sculptures representing Jesus Christ's martyrdom. In late seventeenth- and eighteenth-century Southern Spain and Latin America, Christ was represented with torn flesh and wounds all over his body, hanging on the cross bleeding to death. These images had the purpose of reminding Catholics of the sacrifice that the Son of God had made dying in the name of humanity. Perhaps a Catholic unconscious is now at work, as we remain passive before the ordeal of others and are therefore unknowingly attributing to "the wretched of the screen," the

22 See Alex Horton, "Art Installations Blast Audio of Sobbing, Detained Children Across New York City," *Washington Post*, June 12, 2019, https://www.washingtonpost.com/nation/2019/06/12/art-installations-blast-audio-sobbing-detained-children-across-new-york-city.

role of redeemers sacrificing themselves in the name of the well-being of the privileged populations.

Neo-Pornomiseria and Authoritarianism: The Rule of Affect and Morality

An example of catastrophe pornography is *Carne y Arena (Virtualmente present, físicamente invisible)* (2017), the virtual reality installation by filmmaker Alejandro González Iñárritu, in collaboration with cinematographer Emmanuel Lubezki at the Tlatelolco University Cultural Center. The exhibition was shown at Cannes, LACMA in LA, and the Prada Foundation in Milan, and it had a purpose of confronting the viewer with the experience of immigrants crossing the Mexican desert to arrive at the United States, through a series of apparatuses like a 360-degree screen, a virtual reality mask, a video, and interviews with the migrants. As an ensemble, they offer reality effects from the point of view of absolute objectivity. In that regard, the technology "speaks." But beyond the elimination of mediation (that could be established by a second voice or fiction), the installation seeks to literally place the spectators in the desert in such a way that they can virtually live the experience of crossing, just like migrants. It is clear that the installation seeks to expand documentary cinematographic language: in a room with a desert landscape laid out in 360 degrees, González Iñárritu seeks to show the "out of field" and to expand the public's perspective by interpolating her through the immediacy offered by virtual reality, providing the momentary fantasy of being *vita nuda*, or non-mournable life. About this project, González Iñárritu declared:

> I never conceived it as a response or as a political project but as an artwork that would be about human crisis at the world level. . . . It has the power to transport you to the Sonora Desert so you can live in your own flesh the tragedy. [The objective is] to be seen in Washington by those who make international policies in the United States.[23]

The passion for detail in the extreme experience offered by the installation seeks to generate compassion in the viewer by subjecting her to living in her own skin the ordeals underwent by the migrants. The belief that the most vivid reality is the experience offered by technology, and that this can

---

23 From the installations' press release: https://www.gatopardo.com/portafolio/arte/carne-y-arena-tlatelolco.

be emancipatory and can bring about social change, reflects the profound alienation of capitalist society. Could we re-create rape, for instance, in virtual reality, hoping that it would work as an antidote to gender violence? The problem with González Iñárritu's installation is that the experience it provides lacks the value of revelation; its force resides in a sterile (and sensationalist) mise-en-scène that loses force in the ephemeral sensation felt by the viewer. The installation clearly responds to the current organization of ideological apparatuses; in it, the mobilization of affect (which is not the same as *con-mover*, moving or moving with), objectivity, expert knowledge, and technocracy are equated with intellectual power and are able to transmit "truths." How can it produce meaning, without eliminating contingency?

In *Tell Me How It Ends: An Essay in Forty Questions* (2017), a book that also addresses the migration crisis of Mexicans and Centro Americans to the United States, Valeria Luiselli parts from her experience as a translator of migrant children seeking refugee status in the United States to describe the migratory system and expose their ordeals. In parallel, she seeks to explain the origin of the migratory crisis and to denounce the complicity of Mexicans and the Mexican government with the United States making the crossing even more dangerous for the migrants. That is why, under Barack Obama's government, the Differed Action for Childhood Arrivals policy was created, which implies that at the moment in which children are freed form the famous "ICE Boxes," where they can spend up to two weeks in humiliating and physically dangerous conditions before they are delivered to their families, they are given twenty-one days to find a lawyer and put together a case to seek asylum. On the contrary, they are deported by a judge in presence or in absence. It must be noted that after Luiselli published her book, the situation of child immigrants has clearly gotten worse, to the point, for instance, of having children as young as three having to "defend" themselves in court without a lawyer or parent present. Luiselli explains that Obama's policy is the coldest possible response by the US government to the exodus of Central American children, and it is linked to the language with which the problem is described: a refugee undocumented child is an "illegal immigrant." The problems she herself had with the US Migration Services to obtain a green card led Luiselli to work as translator for the New York court, and this is how she translated into Spanish the forty questions of the questionnaire to access the Migration System and, into English, the children's responses. Depending on the answers Luiselli was able to extract from the children, their chances of staying in the United States decreased or increased. The key was in making the children express a narrative of extreme violence, direct persecution, and danger of death, which would allow them to build a convincing case to attract the interest of a lawyer in processing the child's asylum demand before the US Citizenship and Migration Services. The essay is divided into five parts (Border / Court / Home / Community / Coda) and is structured according to the questions of the admission's interview, but it tries to enlarge the court's narrow scope that derives from the forty answers. The narrative is punctuated by the recurrent question posed by the author's five-year-old daughter: "Tell me how it ends, mama." The impossibility of giving a concrete and hopeful answer to the child, imagining the mother living the moment of silence she takes to process her frustration, pain, and incertitude before the migrant children's situations, and then being able to articulate an answer to her daughter, achieves the transmission of her impotence and desperation and places us before the urgency of the problem. *We feel the knot forming her throat.*

In her essay, Luiselli localizes the origin of the migrant children's crisis in the poverty and violence in which they live in Central America, tied to the Mara Salvatrucha (MS-13) and Barrio 18 gangs besieging the area. The author traces the genealogy of the problem to Central American guerrilla wars in the 1980s, without omitting the role the United States played in them. She also goes back to the wave of refugees arriving in Los Angeles in that decade and the ulterior massive deportations in the 1990s, when many of the migrants were already gang members. Luiselli declares: "The whole thing is a mess, a puzzle impossible to piece together using common sense and logic."[24] At the same time, she denounces the Frontera Sur Program, Mexico's policy in collaboration with the United States to stop Central American migration and deport the undocumented people captured in the country. Luiselli describes the dangers the children suffer during the trip to reunite with their families in the United States, who are very likely to have contracted huge debts in getting coyotes to guide them to the border. Once they arrive, Luiselli tells us, the children realize they really never left Tegucigalpa, because Hempstead (a city in the state of New York) is an extension of it. This is because the gangs have become a transnational army with cells all over the United States that harass and push the newcomers, as it happened back at home, to join the gangs. According to the author, Hempstead belongs to the map of violence related

24 Valeria Luiselli, *Tell Me How It Ends: An Essay in Forty Questions* (Minneapolis: Coffee House Press, 2017), 46.

to drug trafficking, the same map to which Tegucigalpa belongs.[25] Finally, for Luiselli, the attitude of the US authorities regarding migrant children is not always negative, but in general, "it is based on misunderstandings or voluntary ignorance."[26] According to her, it is urgent to put on the table the causes of the massive exodus, while she expresses the need for the United States and Mexico to hold themselves responsible for the devastation of the social tissue in Honduras, El Salvador, and Guatemala. Toward the end of the book, we learn that the authors' students, inspired by her, have created a political student organization to contribute to ameliorating the situation by establishing a program that would enable the quick integration to their new environment of the children refugees: the TIIA or Teenage Immigrant Integration Association. Luiselli concludes: "While the story continues, the only thing to do is to tell it over and over again as it develops, bifurcates, knots around itself." *It must be told*, she writes.[27]

In an interview, Luiselli inscribed the political-literary search of her essay at the heart of Latin American debates about commitment and literary production. In the 1960s, within the context of ideological militancy, aesthetic and literary debates were assimilated to the great topics of sociopolitical debates. The questions they posed were: What can be done with communist ideology as political horizon in relationship to literary narrative? Can literature—or the author—contribute to changing the world, and in what way? The debate took place within the opposition between communism as the writers' moral guide and her own consciousness, and pushing for the need to distinguish between a vision of reality as filtered by leftist ideology and empirical or personal investigation. Luiselli declared:

> I encountered the infertile dilemma (all onanism is infertile) between the *utility* of fiction and the *duty* of the novelist before her political circumstances. The sole duty a novelist has is to write very well. And it is difficult to write very well if you want to achieve a political effect, a social reaction, or if you believe that a novel will be useful and will change or ameliorate something. Of course a novel can change many things, reader by reader, mind by mind, but writing from the belief that one must or can do that, is mere

25 Luiselli, *Tell Me How It Ends*, 83.
26 Luiselli, *Tell Me How It Ends*, 84.
27 Luiselli, *Tell Me How It Ends*, 96, 97.

arrogance and intellectual vanity. The novels written from such disoriented heights of that kind of arrogance are always unendurable.[28]

In sum, for Luiselli, a politics of writing does not reside in pretending to change the world, because it would be arrogant, because "writing from such disoriented heights" results in "unendurable" literature. The author localizes the power of writing in mobilizing the reader on the writing's quality. But at the same time, she contradicts herself when she rejects the dilemma of the utility of writing, dismissing the idea as masturbation. In that way, Luiselli takes a "non-position" based on the denunciation of the immorality of the situation through a narration of actual facts that she charges with affect and filters through her own story. In the same interview, she declares having been freed from writer's block by following a friends' advice to "transform emotional capital into political capital."[29] And that transformation is, for Luiselli, a matter related to the *form of the writing*. The essay is exquisitely elaborated, parting from the forty questions of the migration questionnaire; it is splashed with seductive phrases, exotic anecdotes (like a family trip to the south of the United States), the *charm* of her five-year-old daughter, of hipster ennui: "The day Trump won the election, when I finally gathered enough willpower to get out of bed."[30] The problem is that she never brings into question the *content* of the text itself; as Viridiana, she is surprised by the difficulties she had in getting the migrant children she helps to sympathize with her. The discourse of *Tell Me How It Ends* is a moral one of *being on the right side*. With her non-position, Luiselli evades questioning her own political tendency and the site from which she writes. The text is, in its absolute lack of reflexivity, anti-modern. She also resorts to common places (those disseminated by the mass media) to explain the genesis of the migrant crisis, establishing that "what the US government does is wrong; what civil society does is right." At any moment, we come across her text with the words "racism," "colonialism," "capitalism," "neoliberalism," or "disposession." Luiselli accuses the Mexican government of endangering the migrant's crossover through Mexico without mentioning "social cleansing," "redundant populations," or "state violence." But this is due to the fact that she is trapped in the migrant children's legal labyrinth and, as such, the labyrinth produces "nonevents" that are invisible

28 Valeria Luiselli, "Entrevista por Eduardo Rabasa," December 1, 2016, http://reportesp.mx/entrevista-con-valeria-luiselli-eduardo-rabasa

29 Luiselli, "Entrevista por Eduardo Rabasa."

30 Luiselli, *Tell Me How It Ends*, 103.

racism and state violence, tools with the goal of governing redundant populations as noncitizens, precisely placing them in legal situations like this legal labyrinth to seek asylum.

In her narrative, instead of shaking the alienated stupor of the neoliberal subject, Luiselli succumbs, along with González Iñárritu and the myriad of visual and textual artworks of catastrophe pornography, to the temptation of addressing the viewer at the affective level. She says it herself: when she pretends, by evoking her child's insistent plea, "Tell me how it ends, mama," to transform the emotional capital of her ordeal with the US Migration Services into political capital. And because language cannot get rid of its representative function, the essay flagrantly lacks a convincing analysis of the situation of the immigrant children; it presents to us the brutality of the facts of Central American violence, of Obama's policies, of Mexico's complicity as the *truth* of the situation. And what about the truth of racism? What about the truth of the racism of others? What about the actual division of the world into classes? To blow up the distance between "fact" and "truth" is a common site of the mass media; "truth" is a way of seeing and positing facts. The author claims to have "clarity," but the text says little about the history of Latino migration to the United States and about the intermittent waves of deportations; it says nothing about the refugee crisis at the global level (systemic, neoliberalism). The way she enunciates it, her truth is more offensive than illuminating, more alienated (in Anita Chari's sense) than empathic. The starting point to understand the migratory crisis would be to understand what defines contemporary politics: the opposition between neoliberal globalization and right-wing nationalism. For its part, the genesis of the immigrant crisis is the neoliberal version of colonialism, summing up centuries of destruction of the traditional forms of life and ways of making a living of many peoples who are not completely "modernized." These redundant populations have been dispossessed from their life forms and habits they have inherited, and they are suffering from rootlessness, dispossession, and intergenerational trauma. What do we do? We must part from the fact that globalization has two faces: that of the poor refugees and that of the privileged elites, without forgetting that internationalist solidarity—we must recall that the elite fought with Central American socialist guerrillas in the 1980s—has been substituted by competition of all against all. The narratives Luiselli achieves in pulling out from the broken testimony of each migrant child are competing among themselves and, at the same time, with her, for obtaining US citizenship. Citizenship is obtained by the "strongest," as the "migratory success" depends on the fact that the system clearly favors certain human types, and certain cultural identities and ways of life, based on economic success. In other words, within the frame of the global race to obtain citizenship, the identities of the Central American immigrant children are not as desirable as Luiselli's. In the case of the immigrant children, their narratives compete unevenly in the possibility they have in adjusting them to the legal immigration system of the United States. As Luiselli obviates such points, her non-position is that of an ideological (neo)liberalism that preaches recognizing the other, the defense of her human rights, inclusion, and diversity. This form of "solidarity," however, is not horizontal, but vertical, and it feeds fascism. According to Walter Benjamin, when engaged intellectuals seek to integrate to the proletarian forces, they become members of a strata situated *in between classes*, ignoring the position that as bourgeois they occupy in the production process. According to Benjamin, this "in-between" position is impossible, because engaged intellectuals run the risk of becoming ideological benefactors or patrons, falling into the trap of logocracy.[31] And it is precisely ideological patronage that Luiselli succumbs to as she covers with her privileged voice the ordeals of the immigrant children.

But perhaps the problem does not reside in Luiselli's voice, but in the iteration in her authorial voice of the "post-ideological" character of our era. As it embodies free-market common sense, post-ideology has opened up a gap between political stance and political action. It is not that the left has become obsolete in the way in which it criticizes contemporary forms of power, that it has failed in creating alternative political organizations. Rather, it is because neoliberal non-ideology thrives in the dissociation between critique, symbolic gesture, and everyday life. For instance, we can denounce hunger in Africa but drink Sudanese coffee at Starbucks; take street children as a subject for an art piece, but turn one's back to a beggar; be against slavery, but buy clothes manufactured by slaves in Southeast Asia; and so forth. The dissociation between critique, political stance, and everyday life that characterizes our era of alienated subjectivities, which leads us to believe in the possibility of the "post-ideological" allows Luiselli to remain blind about her own position at the heart of capitalist power and production relations. But her voice is also built to denounce without denouncing, to enunciate acts as truths without revealing.

31 Walter Benjamin, "The Author as Producer" *New Left Review* 1, no. 62 (July/August 1970): 83–91.

The problem resides in the fact that works like Luiselli's, along with the mass media, draw a horizon of legibility in common and thus delineate an arch of what can be said and done, what positions can be legitimately adopted, and what actions can or cannot be committed. That horizon of common legibility, however, is a matter of power relations, and it has to do with the articulation of the political borders of a discourse. In that way, social divisions become a matter of limits, creating an "inside" with concerned world citizens and an "outside" inhabited by suffering victims. This is the definition of despotic or codependent empathy.

Empathy and the World-in-Common

What do we mean when we say we feel the pain of someone else? Empathy is co(m)penetration with the pain of someone else, similar to traversing a landscape or reaching a new place whose laws are unknown to us. Empathy is choosing to pay attention by expanding ourselves to engage with something that surpasses us as individuals. For its part, despotic empathy hinders solidarity and interdependency because it is a childhood pathology that manifests itself in adults who worry too much about the problems of others, and who look after them as a means to exercise control or to satisfy egoic emotional needs. Codependent empathy, moreover, is a form of painful dependency to find approval, meaning, and self-value, but from a person who is usually involved in compulsive self-destructive behaviors, perpetuating cycles of emotional and physical pain. Currently, the other side of codependent empathy is the criminalization of solidarity, fueled by the new totalitarian sentiment that something is being taken away from "us" by "others." For instance, against Scott Warren, the activist accused of offering food, water, and shelter to Mexican immigrants stranded in the desert at the Mexican-American border; or against Capitan Pia Klempe, who is currently facing twenty years in an Italian prison for rescuing some 1,000 people from drowning in the Mediterranean, and who has been accused of "assisting illegal immigration."[32]

32 Isaac Stanley-Becker, "An Activist Faced 20 Years in Prison for Helping Migrants. But Jurors Wouldn't Convict Him," *Washington Post*, June 12, 2019, https://www.washingtonpost.com/nation/2019/06/12/scott-warren-year-sentence-hung-jury-aiding-migrants; and Harriet Brewis, "Female German Boat Captain Faces Up to 20 Years in Jail for Rescuing 'Drowning' Migrants," *Standard*, June 12, 2019, https://www.standard.co.uk/news/world/

If we think about the contemporary codependent politics of appearance in Hannah Arendt's terms, it means that the world of appearances is constituted by a moralizing Manichean perspective: that of communities formed around subjugation and worldlessness versus communities of morally concerned spectators. This single perspective is a further sign of the disappearance of the common world and of the domination of worldlessness by radical isolation that has bred disagreement and polarization across communities. Two of the consequences of being imprisoned in our own singular experience is (1) mass disablement to hear or see others, and (2) the fact that our reality is constituted only by appearance as opposed to action, speech, and relationships that make up Arendt's *world in common.* As despotic forms of empathy prevail, action and speech are reduced to sheer appearance, and thus speechless action, a demand for recognition, but lacking the disclosure of the position the speaking human occupies in the world in relationship to myself and others: not in ethnic or nationalistic terms, but in terms of the places we occupy in capitalist processes (privileged or redundant populations). If the opposite is the case, when we have gestures without speech, they are perceived as brute physical appearance without verbal accompaniment and are thus meaningless (like mass attacks). For Arendt, actions are only made relevant by the spoken word, which identifies the speaker as the actor announcing what she is doing, thereby giving meaning to her actions, but only within and in relationship to others. In other words, no other human performance requires speech to the same extent as action; in acting and speaking, humans show who they are and reveal their identities, but only when people are together with others. This "being with" is neither for nor against others, but sheer human togetherness.

Both despotic empathy and alienation destroy the in-between that contains speech and action. The world we have in common is usually seen from an infinite number of different points of view. Through speech and action, we learn not only to *understand* each other as individual persons, but to see the same world from each other's, and sometimes opposing, standpoints. Universality in this context means that while everyone sees and hears from a different position, *some* people have the capacity to multiply their own viewing position with its attending matrix and perspectives.[33] From a decolonial standpoint, however, acknowledgment of difference is not enough, because

---

german-boat-captain-faces-up-to-20-years-in-jail-for-rescuing-migrants-a4166011.html.

33 Arendt, "The Crisis in Culture," 219.

it means recognizing positions of dominance or oppression. What needs to be *in between* people is incommensurability, for instance, listening and attempting to understand the Indigenous demand for the repatriation of land, and where I am situated with regard to this demand. Incommensurability also means to acknowledge that while Europeans and descendants of Europeans in North America and in the "Global South" may not be on the receiving end of oppressive relations, colonial violence in fact impacts *everyone* insofar as privilege is hierarchical and racialized.[34] Or, following Fred Moten, to take into account Black peoples' demand to their own curriculum without the exacting standards of white society, acknowledging the desire to "take over" and adjust standards on their own terms, beyond the singular integrity of white peoples.[35] This would imply to move beyond the intersubjective validity of judgments of taste in Kantian morals, which are, for Arendt, the grounds for political consensus. For this, we would need to modify commonness on the go, bringing incommensurability into the "in-between" humans, which would imply acknowledging interdependency beyond detachment or codependent empathy.

To resist the present, I thus propose, first, to take up the urgent task to produce horizons of hope from the point of view of incommensurability by creating new relationships between creativity and critique,[36] and second, to do away with representation, recognition, and difference and substitute them with frames for relationality and reciprocity. Perhaps before we can embark on this search for relationality, we would need to flee the psychosphere (the locus where mind develops and enters into relations with other minds). Third, not to confuse the *Lebenswelt* or the "world in common" with the public sphere and relationality with relational aesthetics. For this we would need to put relationality before aesthetics (not as aesthetics). In relationality, alterity is experienced without mediation or instrumentalization and becomes a mode of listening, while reciprocity would enable a shift toward incommensurability, in the sense that it could change the focus from mediation toward the concrete effects of our actions upon others and in the world. The emphasis

34 Eve Tuck and K. Wayne Yang, "Decolonization Is Not a Metaphor," *Decolonization: Indigeneity, Education & Society* 1, no. 1 (2012): 1–40.

35 Fred Moten, *The Universal Machine* (Durham, NC: Duke University Press, 2018), 73.

36 Rosi Braidotti, "On Putting the Active Back into Activism," *New Formations: A Journal of Culture/Theory/Politics*, no. 68 (2009): 42–57.

on the *relation*, rather than on the moral demands of the subject, would enable relationships toward transformative encounters, interrelating to others as exposure, availability, and vulnerability. Relationality and reciprocity also mean acknowledging that our midterm survival depends not on the help of strangers or "foreign aid," but on "mutual aid."

This means rejecting individualism, combining self-interest with the well-being of an enlarged sense of community, which includes one's territorial or inhuman connections.[37] For this we must embrace the fact that it is our duty to look after ourselves and after each other, mainly because capitalist society is constituted as a foreign power with which it is impossible to interact. Instead of waiting for capitalism to fall apart above us, and in spite of us, we need to begin to act, taking our existence in our hands, inhabiting territories autonomously, but mostly, giving primacy to the power of togetherness, to the pleasure of togetherness. Finally, the idea that we could achieve the partialities of the common world in the context of overscaled global society with documentaries, media formations, or aesthetic and literary practices, stems from the emancipatory role modernity ascribed to art. This is clearly false, as for the world in common to appear, humans need to be formed in distinct symbolic and linguistic worlds: their different forms of knowledge and their different relations to the world and to the earth are not measurable by their uses of mass media and formal aesthetic devices.

Beyond Toxic Essentialisms: What Forms Will Our Link to the World Take?

Sa la na, a yuum, iasis/laissez faire-laissez passer (2019), by the collective Biquini Wax, is a multimedia installation that is presented as an allegorical parody of Mexico's economic liberalization. It is a three-dimensional portrait of Keiko: almost in real size, the killer whale lived in Reino Aventura, an amusement park in Mexico City from 1986 to 1996. It is realistic, but it also seems like a 3-D animation, and instead of guts, the flayed and eviscerated torso of the whale contains foam sculptures representing iconic images from the mass and visual culture of the era. Inside Keiko's guts, imaginary and real characters alluding to historical events are juxtaposed: the fall of the Berlin Wall and the first McDonald's inaugurated in Mexico in 1985; the first

37 Braidotti, "On Putting the Active Back into Activism," 54.

operating PC with Microsoft Windows behind Pike; the Soccer World Cup pet in Mexico. Behind Pike there is a goalie, in its frame appear written the acronym of the General Agreement on Tariffs and Trade (GATT), the international commerce treaty Mexico subscribed to in 1986, the same year the country was host to the Soccer World Cup. There is also Gizmo, the good Gremlin, a maguey—back then, tequila went from being something "indios" drank, to becoming a gourmet drink and an export product. There are also Koopa from *Super Mario World*, *It*, the evil clown from Steven King's novel, and allusions to Hollywood like *Rambo* and *Shark*; there is also Pikachu and a Fisher Price phone that evokes the first privatization in Mexico. Coca-Cola could not fail to be present, and Keiko pulls with its mouth two bottles tied with a rope: if Rubén Gámez's experimental film *La fórmula secreta* (1965) interrogates the coming of mass modernization halfway through the twentieth-century parting from the fact that Coca-Cola was in every Mexican's blood (including the Indigenous populations, until then excluded from modernization), with neoliberalism—which implies the intensification of late capitalism until absolutist capitalism, inseparable from extractivism and primitive accumulation—now marine life also carries Coca-Cola in its body. Along with destruction and environmental damage, Keiko's hollowed-out torso full of toxic materials also alludes to the apocalyptic imaginary of global warming and ongoing mass extinction: I'm thinking of the images circulating of marine mammals or birds aground with their guts blown up by plastic.

If Keiko is a kind of vessel containing elements of the visual culture that accompanied, characterized, adorned, and obscured the effects of the first wave of neoliberalism in Mexico (before NAFTA was signed, many Mexicans dreamed of having access to the commodities Keiko carries in its gut, which were signs of modernization, progress, and sophistication), its life story is an allegory of sorts of the dark destinies of the liberalization of the market: Keiko was the first superstar Mexican export. It showed up in the final episode of the 1989 telenovela *Quinceañera*, in the Mexican film *Keiko en peligro*, and in *Azul*, the telenovela starring Kate del Castillo in 1996. And then, in 1993, Reino Aventura's killer whale became Willy, to act in the Hollywood production *Free Willy* (of which three parts were filmed); seeing the whale being freed in the ocean through the screen, I had the faint hopes that her flaccid dorsal fin due to lack of swimming in deep waters, dehydration, and heating up in captivity, a diet of frozen fish and probable sign of chronic depression, would finally straighten. Twenty-something years after her cinematographic liberation (in truth, Keiko was liberated in 2002 and died of pneumonia in the open sea a year later), *Keiko*—or the allegory of market liberalization—appears aground with her gut full of plastic in the Palais de Tokyo in Paris.

When Keiko's body appears aground in a museum, the regime is promising to dismantle the legacy of the neoliberal regimes of generalized corruption, crony capitalism, privatization, lack of collective values, exploitation, and injury against originary peoples and rural mestizo populations that allegedly resulted in the rampant inequality that is lived in the country. Reparation of the ravages carried out by neoliberal politics is sought to be achieved through a re-statization of the economy, what President Andrés Manuel López Obrador has called "modernization from below," which includes megaprojects, Special Economic Zones, and infrastructure for transportation and resource extraction, as well as programs to mitigate "poverty." As we saw in the previous chapter, the current regime's project prioritizes "Indigenous communities," seeking to undo inequality, celebrating "community art," and laying forth a new nationalist imaginary originated in the sensible harmonization between states and corporations.

With neoliberalism, the central role the State had as administrator of the sensible until the late 1980s reconverted to give way to freedom of expression and to the antagonistic dance of civil society toward democracy. That is to say, in the context of Mexico's neoliberalization, cultural and sensible imaginary production had the role of being the windows to freedom of expression, antagonism, and sites to denounce the abuses of power. Above all, cultural producers rejected being co-opted as providers of content for a nationalist cultural imaginary promoted by the State.

Once the collateral damages of neoliberalization became palpable, a sensible imaginary tied to violence and the precarization that began to be lived in the country emerged. Following Ignacio Sánchez Prado, this led to imaginaries of fear and pain in narratives in mass media, as cultural products began to negotiate the rupture of the social contract of the welfare state that linked revolutionary nationalism to modernization. If modernization implied an allegorical relationship between individual and nation, allowing for the territorialization of marginal subjects into the State's material structures, modernization meant "Mexicaneity," and thus citizenship. Differently, with neoliberalization, sensible production began to narrate subjectivities tied to the national machines of precarization, racialized and vulnerable imaginaries of violence, uprooting, and forced displacement. Neoliberal sensible production thus registers the loss of horizon of both modernization and citizenship.[38] This imaginary was linked to the so-called discursive matrix of *narconarrativas*, inhabited by the specter of organized crime and the myth of all-powerful drug lords waging a war among themselves to achieve territorial control defying Mexican State violence. Following Oswaldo Zavala, the *narconarrativas* are the indirect result of the imaginary disseminated by official sources since the 1970s that imposed the rules of enunciation and narrative function of the "narco," creating a habitus of meaning in which state sovereignty and citizen safety is always at stake.[39]

In contrast with previous regimes, the current government established a program to orient cultural production toward an epistemic nationalism and to create a hegemonic imaginary tied to anti-corruption, conservative values, political classes' austerity, and the official appropriation of Indigenous culture. For instance, Mexico City Governor Claudia Sheimbaum is reported to perform *tequio* every Saturday in a different *delegación* (borough) in the city. *Tequio* is community work done in rural areas; or, as one of the slogans President López Obrador has borrowed from the Zapatistas, "to govern obeying." There is also the controversial dissemination of the new edition of Alfonso Reyes's conservative *Cartilla Moral* by the government and the Evangelical Church. This new populist nationalism is also anti-intellectual and adverse to criticism, as we saw in chapter 5. In parallel, a new wave of Indigenism and Mexicanism is being disseminated through official and corporate channels, which are in perfect sync; for instance, the Consejo de Comunicación's campaign #Soyincorruptible (#Iamincorruptible—the Communication Council is an association that gives voice to Mexican corporations). The campaign includes conferences in schools and universities planned for the next ten years, as well as a campaign on billboards and posters in public spaces. The campaign designs "good," incorruptible Mexicans. In the billboards, there are different citizens; for instance, a student "who does not blackmail" his teachers to pass his exams, or a woman "who does not bribe cops and pays her fine," or another "who finds work without nepotism."

---

38 Ignacio M. Sánchez Prado, "Máquinas de precarización: afectos y violencias de la cultura neoliberal," in *Precariedades, exclusiones y emergencias: Necropolítica y sociedad civil en América Latina*, ed. Mabel Moraña and José Manuel Valenzuela (México D.F.: UAM Iztpalapa y Gedisa, 2018).

39 Oswaldo Zavala, *Los cárteles no existen* (México D.F.: Malpaso, 2018).

Another instance in which the state and corporations are in sync is Coppel's campaign starring Yalitzia Aparicio. Coppel offers credit and merchandises to the working class and inhabitants of rural areas throughout the country. Yalitzia is the young Mixe woman who starred in *Roma*, Alfonso Cuarón's 2018 film for which Yalitzia was nominated for an Oscar for best actress. During the months of promotion for the successful film in festivals throughout the world, Yalitzia left her life as rural teacher behind in Tlaxiaco, her community in Oaxaca, to become a celebrity and an influencer. Recently, Yalitzia became Good Will Ambassador for Indigenous Peoples at the UNESCO. For the Coppel campaign, Yalitzia's image displays a young Indigenous Mixteca woman who achieved the neoliberal dream of success, fame, and richness, promoting the message of "better your life" through the acquisition of merchandises made available by Coppel.

The other face of the successful neoliberal subject is the "good neoliberal subject" figured by the main character of the 2019 film *La camarista*, interpreted by Gabriela Cartol. In the film, director Lila Avilés portrays the daily life of a young mestizo lower-class woman who stoically works at a luxury hotel in Mexico City. Taking up the language of cinematic duration, akin to Chantal Akerman's *Jeanne Dielman 23 Quay du Commerce, 1080 Brussels* (1975), we see "Gabriela" making daily efforts so she can be upgraded and earn more money by being assigned to clean a floor above hers; without losing hope, every day she requests a forgotten and unclaimed red dress she has obtained the right to claim. We also see her regularly calling home to inquire about her toddler son, and every night, she goes to school with a teacher who has been hired by the hotel. Silence, submission, resignation, work, effort, and desire to be better are the qualities that describe this perfect neoliberal subject, who appears grateful for her working conditions of extreme self-exploitation, representing the other face of "success" of neoliberal ideology. The reverse of this figure are the main characters from *Los Chicuarotes* (2019), Cagalera and Moloteco, inhabitants of San Gregorio Atlapulco, one of the main districts and originary populations from the Xochimilco borough in Mexico City. Urbanization ended up disappearing chinampas (small agricultural areas embedded in water bodies dating from pre-Hispanic times), knowledge of ancestral medicinal plants, and with autonomous forms of subsistence of the inhabitants, transforming them into cheap labor hands and thus precarious workers. As they lack opportunities, Cagalera and Moloteco try making a living honestly as clowns collecting money in public transportation. When they hear there is a position in the Electricians Union for sale, they kidnap the son of a neighbor to get the money and become free from their marginal and precarious life. As they get caught, their story ends badly. Aside from the fact that the film is neoliberal pornomiseria, it is a moral lesson of anti-corruption, in sync with the government's purification mission and with the Consejo de Comunicacion's campaign described above.

The current revaluing of Mexican roots is not only government policy, but also a marketing strategy that has already begun to expand in national campaigns. Last year, Grupo Lala launched its limited edition *Sabores de México* (Flavours of Mexico) product line, highlighting the flavors and ingredients from traditional Mexican crops in different states such as Tuna-Guanábana flavored yogurt (from Nayarit), Elote Miel (Honey Corn) from Yucatán, and Sueño de Ángel (Angel's dream) from Mexico City, a flavor of churro and traditional cheese. The line of products and the campaign seek to "promote the best of Mexico, its communities and culture." The Lala company, through its foundation, has three initiatives: homes for Indigenous peoples, lunches for students, and support for families in community centers, having invested 18 million pesos for the past five years, impacting almost a million people. Soon, the Lala Foundation will collaborate with Huicholes in a project called Ha Ta Tukari (Water, Health, and Food Sovereignty) in three communities in the state of Jalisco, donating 7.6 million pesos. In this case, the corporation is functioning like an NGO and an arm of the state, executing appropriation, dispossession, and reparation at the same time. Another campaign to revalorize traditional flavors and customs from Mexico was launched on the 2019 Day of the Dead by La Costeña. In Coyoacán's main plaza, a giant jaguar was erected with 10,391 La Costeña preserve cans; a race "with a cause" was organized to support La Villa San José, a "safe and dignified space" in Guasave, Sinaloa. The image of the Day of the Dead's mega-parade was also reproduced in La Costeña's campaign. The mega-parade originated in 2015, when Mexico City Governor Miguel Mancera, through the extinct (and accused of corruption) Tourist Promotion Council, paid $18 million to the producer of *Spectre 007* (James Bond's most recent film) to film the movie's first (eight-minute-long) sequence in Mexico City's Historic Downtown. The Hollywood image of the invented tradition of the Day of the Dead parade in Mexico City that appears in the film responds well to Frederic Jameson's indictment: if the nucleus of globalization was the global dissemination of American mass culture, which unleashed the extinction of local cultures, they can now only be brought back to life through their Disneyfied form. The mega-parade has been staged every year since, and for the 2019 edition, Mexico City Governor

Claudia Sheimbaum recuperated the manufactured image from Hollywood of Mexican traditions as "the most Mexican of all traditions" and "community ritual." Hundreds of "cultural community promoters" participated in the manufacturing and procession of the Day of the Dead mega-parade with "ethnic" masks they made in collaboration with populations regular to the PILARES. The PILARES are government community centers in marginal and rural areas subsidized by the government. Members of the PILARES also took part in "community dances" and elaborated "mojigangas," "catrinas," chariots, and music instruments. The goal of the PILARES is to reinforce the social tissue, share knowledges, and visibilize peripheral cultures. For the 2019 mega-parade, however, the regime exploited and exoticized vulnerable populations to deliver the Hollywood-like image of Mexican traditions while precarizing cultural worker employees of the PILARES, who had not yet been paid all year for their work.[40]

If in the current nation-sate imaginary, the state and corporations are in ideological sync when it comes to the subjectivity that prescribes "good" neoliberal subjects as those who are successful, self-exploited, and incorruptible and "bad" ones as those who are corrupt and criminal, we should not be surprised if they are also allied in other areas. For instance, the Banco de Bienestar promoted by Andrés Manuel López Obrador's government is linked to Nestlé, Bayer, and Monsanto. It competes with Bancoppel, which offers the same services as the Banco de Bienestar. It seems like, in truth, the post-neoliberal re-statization of the current regime implies close collaboration with corporations to increase acquisitive power of the poor so that they can consume within a "moderate" capitalism in full continuity with the previous neoliberal regimes.

In spite of the fact that the state agenda is oriented toward re-statizing and socializing the economy, and to confer originary peoples and "the poor" a central role in government programs, the coordinate forms of capitalist power keep on advancing, extending the extractive zones or sites where life is reduced to the capitalist reconversion of resources.[41] For instance, there

---

40 According to this note, many have gone all year without being paid. See Alida Piñón, "Artistas llevan 8 meses sin pago de Cultura CDMX," *El Universal*, November 27, 2010, https://www.eluniversal.com.mx/cultura/artistas-llevan-8-meses-sin-pago-de-cultura-cdmx.

41 Macarena Gómez-Barris, *The Extractive Zone: Social Ecologies and Decolonial Perespectives* (Durham, NC: Duke University Press, 2017), 32.

is the "Mayan Train" already discussed in chapter 1, conceived as an "integral project for territorial, infrastructure, economic growth, and sustainable tourism reordering" with the goal of achieving "social well-being of the inhabitants of the Mayan area." The negative social and environmental impact of the megaproject are well documented; we could add that Alfonso Romo Garza, current head of the presidential office, obtained in 2007 the concession to exploit water in the cenotes (a type of skin hole that contains drinking water common in the Yucatán Peninsula) from all across the peninsula, and to develop agroindustry and biotechnology in the region.[42] These megaprojects, as we know, are signs of ongoing neocolonization, dispossession, destruction, and displacement, and the "well-being" they promise is nothing but the inclusion of populations and cheap labor hands, debtors, and consumers dispossessed from their sustainable forms of life and making a living.

The current stage of neoliberalism—legitimized by the new fascisms and populisms across the world—is characterized by the intensification of extractivism, and it implies continuity with private and foreign investment in the Mexican territory, stealing the commons through megaprojects. Megaprojects imply expropriating and devastating territories, violating the autonomy of originary populations, and make forms of life vulnerable to state and corporate violence. Historically, energy and rail infrastructure have been at the center of colonial processes grounded on the rationalized cleansing of territories, famine, and environmental destruction, aside from the fact that extractivist practice is tied to colonial capitalism implanted in Latin America in the sixteenth century. Eduardo Galeano described this system as the "opening of the veins" of the territory to transform the underground materials and from nature like silver, rubber, oil, or henequen (today it is shale gas, bauxite, and water) into global merchandises. In this frame, the territories of the originary populations are considered to be *terra nullis*, their bodies racialized and exposed to dispossession and slavery. This is why, aside from fighting for self-determination, originary peoples are fighting to defend their lives, as their "usos y costumbres" (or uses and habits) that make up the interwoven structures of the reproduction of life that enable the reproduction of their lives—which are being put at risk with the arrival of megaprojects.

---

42 Janet Cacelín, Alejandro Melgoza, and Sergio Rincón, "Un cacique del agua en el paraíso maya," *Proceso*, March 2, 2010, https://www.proceso.com.mx/619955/un-cacique-del-agua-en-el-paraiso-maya-2.

As originary peoples are now denominated "communities," it seems like the current government is recognizing certain historical demands. In the San Andrés Accords (signed in 1996 as a way to pacify Chiapas after the Zapatista uprising), recognition of Indigenous communities as political entities was demanded toward endowing them with public rights within their municipalities, and with the faculty to associate freely so that they can coordinate their own actions and choices. They also demanded that authorities transfer public resources and funds assigned to them for them to administer themselves. But what is happening in reality? The current government is using these historical claims to give a new twist to state racism: communities are being recognized as collective cultural subjects, but not as political subjects with rights over their territories.[43] Although their culture and folklore is preserved and resources are channeled toward their preservation, they are under threat as the government (in continuity with previous regimes) seeks to bring development to communities through projects that only cause depredation and destruction, underscoring the status of originary peoples as non-citizens without autonomy over their territories. It is well known that concessions to extract resources of multinational companies have been put above consultation processes that have been falsified or corrupted. The spokespeople from the communities have tirelessly repeated that they are not opposed to progress, but that their self-determination must be respected so that they can do their own consultation, and from there make agreements with the government, instead of consultations being imposed on them that do not represent their voices. Territorial dispossession and violence, however, have intensified against individuals and communities resisting megaprojects. In that regard, Mexico belongs to entrepreneurs and capitalist powers, and to justify itself, the current regime has put into play the humanitarian game of recognizing the redundant population extoling folklore, instead of giving itself the much harder task of changing the global and heteropatriarchal system.

And indeed, recently a feminist current has emerged, promoted by academics like Dawn Paley, Raquel Gutiérrez, Verónica Gago, Rita Segato, and Silvia Federici, grounded on the urgent need to concatenate violence against the territory, originary peoples, and campesinos with gender violence. According with these thinkers, these kinds of violence part from the logic of capitalist absolutism of generating surplus value through a war against life,

43 Emiliano Monge, "Nuevo indigenismo institucional," *El País*, September 13, 2019, https://elpais.com/elpais/2019/09/14/opinion/1568419698_963817.html.

exercising violence against the capacity to (re)generate and (re)produce social life as a whole. That is to say, capitalism is a war against all forms of collective life. I quote Dawn Paley and Raquel Gutiérrez: "The war against drugs is entirely linked to the promotion of capitalism's interests, and particularly, of transnational capitals linked to mining, building of infrastructure, manufacturing industries, energy exploitation and finances." This thesis, as we have seen, has also been advanced by Oswaldo Zavala, Federico Mastrogiovanni, and Guadalupe Correa-Cabrera. The quote goes on:

> From this point of view, extreme violence acquires sense, as it explains territory and water dispossession of entire populations and the brutal social control exercised through State and para-State violence which weaves itself and perversely resonates with domestic violence fed by the dispositive of the couple/marriage, by nuclear family isolation and machismo which sponsors, admits and amplifies the capitalist-patriarchal system. All these forms of control, from State terror to the prison system, ranging from para-military massacres through unleashed domestic violence, result in the destruction or weakening of the very heterogeneous and varied interwoven structures of the reproduction of life that make an effort in reproducing and maintaining forms of life beyond and against capital and its ceaseless loops of accumulation.[44]

In situations of forced migration, displacement, or dispossession, due in part to agroindustrial violence and land-use modifications, parenting becomes impossible. This is why reproductive rights can be summarized as having a roof, food, and the means to assure a sustainable and dignified life, and why they are intrinsically linked to the struggle for territory defense. Linking violence against territory and originary peoples to femicide violence is the principle of the feminist strike.

In Silvia Federici's key text *Calibán y la bruja*, she explains how, in the fifteenth century, after peasants had successfully fought against feudal lords' dispossession of their lands the century prior and had achieved certain privileges, a counter-revolution was put to work that acted upon all levels of social and political life. Political authorities, according to Federici, made important efforts to co-opt young and rebellious workers through a malicious sexual

---

44 Raquel Gutiérrez Aguilar and Dawn Paley, "La *transformación sustancial* de la guerra y la violencia contra las mujeres en México," *DEP, Deportate, Esuli e Profughe, 30* (Venezia: Universidad Ca'Foscari, 2016).

politics, giving them access to free sex, which transformed class antagonism into hostility against working-class women. For instance, in France, municipal authorities ceased considering rape a crime in cases in which victims were lower-class women. A common practice in France and Italy thus became gang rape by domestic employees or upper-class youth, while the women were poor maids. Rape of poor women with State approval weakened class solidarity.[45] This situation resonates with contemporary impunity that is given by the State to perpetrators of gender violence.

In Mexico, a movement emerged since the 1990s by mothers of murdered or disappeared women, also by victims of gender violence, who have ceaselessly demanded justice and reparation from the State. The feminist strike has become a device to overcome the status of victims by women demanding justice, as, following Verónica Gago, it is a process that maps the forms of exploitations of bodies in territories from the standpoint of visibilization and insubordination, in order to show the mechanisms of precarization upon which the capitalist system is grounded. With the "strike," the feminist struggle goes beyond the realm of domestic violence to connect it with economic, work, institutional, police, racist, and colonial violence, weaving these forms of violence with financial and territorial extractivism.[46]

Bearing this in mind, I suggest we assume that all literary or artistic production is political, because it can never escape either reinscribing dominant cultural values parting from certain epistemologies, or resisting them. We can thus glimpse in a sensible register in cultural production, which I will call "autonomous," the perpetuation of a dominant or hegemonic imaginary that is invisible and traversed by matters of race and class, but also gender. This register perpetuates a racist and heteronormative imaginary according to colonial legacy and capitalist values; for instance, Gabriel Orozco's installation, *Oroxxo*, erected in February 2017 at the Kurimanzutto Gallery in Mexico City for which Orozco collaborated with FEMSA, with the purpose of opening a branch of the OXXO convenience store inside the gallery. Each one of the products had been branded with an Orozco sticker (the primary-colored circles which are his brand). The installation alludes to the inescapable status of merchandise of the work of art, while it introduces the ready-made into the

---

45 Silvia Federici, *Calibán y la bruja: Mujeres, cuerpo y acumulación originaria* (Madrid: Traficantes de Sueños, 2004), 72–73.

46 See Verónica Gago, *La potencia feminista o el deseo de cambiarlo todo* (Madrid: Traficantes de sueños, 2019).

field of financial speculation, as it empties the work of art of content, highlighting that the source of value of the work is The Artist. That is to say, the meaning of the work of art resides in its value, ascribed to the work like a supplement by the (male) artists' proper name and brand. In other words, the value of the work resides in the artist's extra-aesthetic performance, which has to do with his reputation, pedigree, his belonging (or not) to the "A-list," who collects him, and so forth. In Daniela Alatorre's video performance, *Big Dick Energy*, we see the young artists sitting inside corporate-public spaces: a Vips restaurant and an Oxxo, playing with a trophy she has given to herself in which the inscription, "Conceptual Artist," can be read. Alatorre is here underscoring the asymmetry that exists in the art world that is traversed by gender relations through a parody of a female artist charged with "big dick energy" as the condition to becoming a prized conceptual artist.

What I am trying to get at with Daniela Alatorre's video and the *Oroxxo* is articulating how an essentialist toxic heteronormative masculinity circulates in our sensible, and in spite of women's feminist fight in culture (inaugurated by Mónica Mayer in Mexico in the 1970s), this masculinist essentialism has been perpetuated by generations of men conversing between them, and who, prize after prize, exhibition after exhibition, have reproduced in the sensible register the structures of masculine privilege. This essentialism is grounded in the many technologies of subjectivity invented by modernity to establish and maintain Western masculine supremacy. For instance, let's think about the changes in the representation and language of sex and sexuality brought about by the ubiquity of pornography, and how these representations have radically transformed the ways in which we love and desire.[47] In the same way, the heteronormative sensible register reproduces the dominant imaginary of modern sexual difference through an epistemology that fixes the positions of men and women through an internal regulation. If we exist within heteronormative worlds that create stories, parting from which we create stories in literature, film, and art, in our stories we speak from our own place and position, which are already predetermined by social relations traversed by gender. This is why, instead of reinforcing the toxic imaginary of modern sexual difference (which is also racist and classist, and thus

---

47 Paul B. Preciado, *Un apartamento en Urano: Crónicas del Cruce* (Buenos Aires: Anagrama, 2013), 174.

violent), it is necessary to shatter it from the consciousness that gender analysis is a matter of social and environmental justice that concerns everyone.

For instance, the film *Museo* (Alonso Ruizpalacios, 2018) tells the story of two friends who plan a robbery at the Anthropology Museum in Mexico City, and whose adventure (or ridiculous endeavor) represents the masculine search for recognition in an attempt to capitalize privately by plundering national patrimony. For its part, *Roma* transmits nostalgia for the welfare state and for the middle urban class's identification with agrarian struggles previous to the chaos of the so-called war against drugs. The nostalgia is directly eloquent of the current machista impossibility of politicizing extractivist violence, which, as I already said, is intrinsically tied to the exploitation of feminized labor and reproductive rights. In Hari Sama's *Esto no es Berlín* (2019), art becomes a prop in the background of the vacuity of post-industrial life disguised as false existential punk radicality. The story narrates the rebellion of a young man against middle-class conventions, but without going deeper into the stories of violence and mental illness derived from capitalist alienation that also generate individual unease and domestic violence. The main character is a flaneur of counterculture and gender fluidity, and the only interesting aspect of the movie is a performance outside of the Azteca Soccer Stadium by the art collective, to which the main character belongs, during a World Soccer Cup game in which they call attention to the AIDS epidemic (such a performance never took place). *Esto no es Berlín* and *Museo* are thus an inventory of toxic masculinities that try escaping the status quo, but without being uncomfortable with the power masculinity has given to them. Rebellious antiheroes, they navigate the generational crisis previous to neoliberalization through their anger and resentment, acting out in the realm of counterculture to validate themselves defying hegemonic conventions; and in a historical moment, in which such conventions are about to lose validity at the verge of market liberalization. What interests me here is that the acting out of the characters makes them to be on the side of the "barbarian," which is one of the constitutive faces of toxic masculinity of the genius, or *poète maudit*.

Following Emily Hind's *verga* (dick) investigation, "bad boy" behavior helps creative men achieve credibility as geniuses. In this manner, creative masculinity fluctuates between the "bad boy" and the refined intellectual or civilized intellectual. The privilege of oscillating among both poles is only reserved for men and is necessary so that they can demonstrate artistic and intellectual competence.[48] The oscillation occurs in textual and extratextual performances. For instance, the protagonist of Tryno Maldonado's novel *Temporada de caza para el león negro* (2009) is Golo, the very cliché of the nineteenth-century tortured artist in a contemporary context: a young eccentric painter and genius involved in drugs, music, partying, and sex. His life is narrated by his boyfriend, who tries to get him to quit cocaine, paint, and sell his work; he fails while he observes, with a mix of sadness and adoration, his outburst of "geniality" (or self-destruction). There is also the documentary about poet Samuel Noyola by Diego Enrique Osorno, *El vaquero del medio día* (2020). Osorno is looking for the traces left by a poet who was an artist, a guerrillero, and homeless, who was very close to Octavio Paz. In his search, he interviews his lovers, girlfriends, writer colleagues, and street buddies. Noyola's life is that of a *poète maudit* who mysteriously disappeared. Although in truth, his disappearance is not so mysterious: he disappeared in a whirlwind of self-destruction, prompted by his addiction to alcohol and drugs. Osorno describes him as "the last modern poet."

It could be said that the feminine equivalent of the male, the textual and extratextual performance, is the wound, which can be subdivided into "sad" or "enraged." Leslie Jamison, for instance, writes of having unconsciously learned to repress her anger and to put on a sad face, because furious women are not beautiful, while in their suffering, they are, and even elegant. Enraged women are perceived to be messy because their pain threatens to cause collateral damage. It is as if the possibility of feminine fury endangering others would threaten a woman with taking away the social capital we have acquired by being injured. This is why society is much more comfortable with female rage when it promises to self-regulate, abstain from disaster, and remain civilized.[49]

Alcoholism and addiction in general have an important role in the construction of intellectual masculinity. It is an aggregate to the "shock value" strategy to demonstrate intellectual competence. Clearly, the link between addiction and creation is exclusively male privilege, as Leslie Jamison also notes in her chronicle to sobriety, *The Recovering: Intoxication and Its Aftermath* (2017). In it, she describes the myths of alcoholism by the famous

48 Emily Hind, *Dude Lit: Mexican Men Writing and Performing Competence (1955–2012)* (Tucson: University of Arizona Press, 2019).

49 Leslie Jamison, "I Used to Insist I Didn't Get Angry. Not Anymore. On Female Rage," *New York Times* , January 17, 2018, https://www.nytimes.com/2018/01/17/magazine/i-used-to-insist-i-didnt-get-angry-not-anymore.html.

Writers' Workshop in Iowa, haunted by the ghosts of alcoholic writers who have passed through there, including herself. In her essay, "Does Recovery Kill Great Writing?" Jamison writes: "A woman's drinking is often understood less as the necessary antidote to her own staggering wisdom and more as self-indulgence or melodrama, hysteria, an unpardonable affliction."[50] In the early days, alcohol was, for her, a ticket to enter the boy's club, and she wanted to understand her addiction as part of a history of transgressive creativity beyond the limits of comfort. When she finally understands that addiction obeys a deep desire to be absent from her own life, she realizes that alcohol can only be illumination and comfort for men; while quoting Marguerite Duras, she writes: "When a woman drinks it's as if an animal were drinking, or a child."[51] I think of the main character's timid relationship to whisky in Ave Barrera's *Restauración* (Paraíso Perdido, 2019); or in Jean Rhys or Lucia Berlin, who were not granted a license to live above the law like William Burroughs or Samuel Noyola, but who died alcoholics, poor, and alone, with very few publications and barely known as writers. I quote Emily Hind, who brilliantly dissects the Mexican context: "I cannot name a single Mexican woman writer who makes public her taste for cocaine. In fact, the gender-reversal experiment of imagining a cocaine-using Mexican woman writer proves so difficult that the effort ends up helping me see the mechanism of the bad boy role."[52]

Before I offer some antidotes to the heteronormative hegemonic sensible, I cannot avoid mentioning Julián Herbert's chronicles *Ahora imagino cosas* (Penguin Random House, 2019). The narrative voice executes by heart the textual performance of the oscillation between bad boy and civilized, as described by Hind. The chronicles narrate the writer's travels to different cities until Herbert reaches bottom, looks for sobriety, and tries to understand gender violence under the auspices of another rehabilitated addict: David Foster Wallace's essay "A Supposedly Fun Thing That I'll Never Do Again" (1997) about a cruise-ship trip, and not Foster Wallace's rehab memoir, *Infinite Jest* (1996). What interests me about Herbert's chronicles is that, aside from the textual performance of masculinity, the author explores the modern mandates of progress and development materialized in the tourism industry. Herbert

50 Leslie Jamison, "Does Recovery Kill Great Writing?" *New York Times*, March 13, 2018, https://www.nytimes.com/2018/03/13/magazine/does-recovery-kill-great-writing.html.

51 Jamison, "Does Recovery Kill Great Writing?"

52 Hind, *Dude Lit*, 93.

offers us a social, political, and personal image of Acapulco, his birth town, where he narrates his family's social ascent while seeking for the lost glamour of the city drowned in a spiral of violence. He cannot avoid describing the city in sexualized terms (which, for some creepy reason, reminded me of María José Cuevas's documentary about elderly vedettes, *Bellas de noche* [2017]): "[Acapulco] is a beauty if groped, where adolescent erotism and decrepit luxury mix, along with the hotels that cauterized the view of the ocean, the impenetrable door to the Baby'O, a prostitution house called La Huerta, and the ghost of my mother." In other chapters, he explores the expansion of tourism know-how to Mazatlán and the main cities in Baja California Sur. The writer registers the changes brought about by modernization, the impact of the tourism and commercial boom in the ways in which the social and economic tissues in these cities are configured.[53] I am not at all surprised that, in spite of evidence he himself describes, he does not question the development paradigm, as his blind spot is the existing ties between modernization, uprootedness, violence, and self-destruction. In the essay titled "Ñoquis con entraña," Herbert recounts a visit to Talca, Chile, where he was invited to give a lecture at a university. This narrative is intertwined with the case of the disappearance and murder of Talca native Aylin Álvarez Fuentes, a young woman addicted to drugs whom, upon leaving a rehabilitation center, disappears, and days later appears dead. He also discusses the #MeToo movement from the point of view of four men discussing the moral and literary problematic of a rape accusation of a young Chilean writer against another writer, and how the accusation caused a small schism in the Chilean literary community. He then tells an anecdote about Alejandro Jodorwoski: when he saves with psychomagic Enrique Lihn's suicidal girlfriend. As the story goes, she pays Jodorowski with her body and (I quote Herbert), "they fucked for hours while Linh pounded the apartment's door." Years later, Lihn and Jodoroski meet in Italy, where both hug amicably as if nothing has happened. Herbert writes cynically: "This is how psychomagic works, as it is a parallel universe where machos make up in Venice and women inexplicably disappear form the narrative after crossing the Mapocho river of sex, as if depression, as if the female body lacked narrative density."[54] As he places in the same tex-

53 Julián Herbert, *Ahora imagino cosas* (México D.F.: Literatura Random House, 2019), 23.

54 Herbert, *Ahora imagino cosas*, 94.

tual plane Aylin's femicide, the accusation of rape by the Chilean writer, and Enrique Lihn's mute girlfriend, Herbert wonders who has the moral authority to speak of these matters, because for him, on the one hand, "most of the stories of violence against women are a sort of *nouveau roman* of misogynistic and police cruelty," and on the other, he sees a rupture between how feminists who are now fifty or sixty years old understand abuse and how young women understand it today. At the end, he concludes that his opinion is inconsequential, that the lack of "narrative density of the female body" is a matter of psychomagic, and Silvia and Mónica, two characters mentioned by Herbert (his former and current partners), get lost, mute in the narrative. Herbert's conclusion is that "poetry is an uncomfortable fruit, I must accept that the perfume of cherries comes from the trash." To turn to moralism in plain bad-boy performance is typical of the archetype of the male intellectual because only a part of the body commits the crime, as Hind tells us.

From the side of incantations against heteropatriarchal epistemology are the classic novels by Josefina Vincens, *El libro vacío* (1958) and *Los años falsos* (1982), a visionary interrogation of the reproduction of gender technologies. The main characters are inheritors of traditional masculinity, confined to becoming providers, and men who must achieve recognition from those who surround them. Vincens carefully lets us observe how her characters, although they are about to break or leave the imposed role of masculinity, end up being seduced by the power heteropatriarchy offers them and thus end up reproducing it, more because they desire it and less because it is what they are mandated to do. In a first-person narrative, in both novels, Vincens gives us access to the social and cognitive structures inhabited by her characters to reproduce masculine rationality, in an attempt to understand and deconstruct heteropatriarchy. Emiliano Monge's *No contarlo todo* (Penguin Random House, 2019) reminded me of Vincens novels. It has in common with *El libro vacío* the fact that the narrative is interwoven with diary entries from one of the characters. Monge, moreover, from an insider perspective, attempts to come to terms with the inherited structures that reproduce masculinity, generation after generation. "Emiliano" (the character) is his father's (Carlos Monge Sánchez's) interlocutor, upon his request to know the story of his grandfather, Carlos Monge McKey. It turns out that the grandfather left one day at dawn, that he had bought a dead body he used to simulate his own death. As he disappears, Carlos Monge Sánchez's mother gets together with Uncle Polo, who functions as a father figure to Carlos and his siblings. In the narrative, "Emiliano" tries to come to terms with his father, a philosopher and guerrillero who spent a month in Lecumberri; he tells these and other life experiences to his son, who wants to be able to understand himself better. Emiliano Monge (the author) carefully registers the moments in which the characters express their emotions. When he recounts the episode of his father's disappearance, Carlos Monge Sánchez declares: "I swear Emiliano, I have never felt this fucked up in my entire life, so strange and lost. A mix. A mix of everything anyone can feel, but in a single and unique instant." The grandfather reappears and eventually appears in Emiliano's and Diego's (his younger brother) lives when they are children. The children become mute witnesses to Carlos Monge Sánchez's fury, who accuses their grandfather of wanting to "play family" with them. Predictably, the grandfather's presence will be intermittent in their lives, as will their father's, who leaves "Emiliano's" house when he is thirteen or fourteen years old. Emiliano "is hurt because his father chose to do what his grandfather achieved when he pretended to be dead: to leave, go away, get out from their lives. To leave everything behind and start over." That moment will be definitive for "Emiliano," who, unable to understand, will imitate his father's and grandfather's impenetrable behavior. Thus, *No contarlo todo* tells "Emiliano's" search for finding lost fragments of his own story to end the repetition, generation after generation, of the violent and painful rupture of family ties. Carlos Monge Sánchez's narration of the story of his life is interwoven with Carlos Monge McKey's diary, written in notebooks whose origin is not revealed to us, only their dates: 1939, 1943, 1958. We learn that the father—"Emiliano's" great-grandfather—also left his family, leaving a void in his son. Monge McKey wonders if the life he is living is the one he has chosen; he describes his paternity and his relationship to his wife. In the present, "Emiliano" and his father drink coffee together while the son insists that he needs his father to undo knots that are impenetrable to him, so he can understand why his father is always leaving, why he was forever absent. The explanation is luminous:

> I was those who had been before me. A pain, a void, a need to escape that I did not want to get to you. A violence that was buried in my body when I was in jail, and other violence that I carried from the beginning. Masculine, Sinaloense son of a bitch violence, from your grandparents, aunts, uncles,

grandmothers. And the feeling of being lost these can only leave behind. I did not want to pass this on to you.

The effort to unmask the mandates of masculinity from within that are inherited, but they also generate vulnerability, and masculine wounds are the beginning of an urgently needed detox that will lead us to dismantling heteropatriarchy.

I want to conclude this chapter with an experimental text by Verónica Gerber. *La compañía* (Almadía, 2019) is an experimental photo story that lays forth the ties between agrotoxicity, the physical sequels, by mining, modernism, and heteropatriarchy. Gerber appropriates Amparo Dávila's short story "El huésped" (1959), a first-person narrative of a woman whose home has been taken by a guest whom her husband has imposed her to host. The tenant behaves like a parasite and harasses the woman, her children, and Guadalupe, the domestic worker. Gerber uses fragments of Dávila's text with different names—"The Guest" becomes "The Company," "Guadalupe" is "The Machine"—and uses a second-person address, which she juxtaposes with photographs of the San Felipe Nuevo Mercurio mine in Zacatecas. With the juxtaposition, Gerber draws an analogy between extractivism in Zacatecas—at the end of the book there are fragments of interviews with San Felipe inhabitants speaking about the ravages in their mental, social, and physical health left behind by the mine—and a masculine power that is imposed in a feminized space in Dávila's short story. Some of the photographs of "La Compañía" have been intervened by figures from "La máquina estética" (*The Aesthetic Machine*, 1975) by Manuel Felguérez. "La máquina estética" is a series of forms made by a computer, programmed with algorithms with the purpose of making them. While the landscape is intervened with modern forms, the territory and the home are penetrated, leaving behind a stella of toxicity. In *La Compañía*, Gerber draws the link that is usually invisibilzed by modernity between heteropatriarchy and extractivism. To make that link visible is necessary to begin to disseminate a categorical disavowal against heteropatriarchy and its negative side effects in psyches, bodies, and territories, to begin to outline and then execute the very-much-needed epistemological rupture that will enable cognitive emancipation to understand that sex and gender are the product of an array of social and discursive technologies of life and truth-management, which are harmful.[55] Another purpose for making that link visible is to emancipate the sensible from its becoming signs to be consumed, which ends up destroying the sites we have remaining to build collective meaning. This is why we need to recuperate art, film, and literature as dissident signifiers allied to a sexual revolution that can lead to a transformation of the imaginary, of images, and of the narratives that mobilize desire and shape the sensible.

---

55 Preciado, *Un apartamento en Urano*.

CHAPTER SIX

A Country in Pain

Resignifying Violence toward Autonomous Spaces for Survival

FOR MANY, violence in contemporary Mexico is what defines the country, as violence is present in everyday life, in cities' streets, in the countryside's plantations, in the mass media, in "high" and popular culture, in urban planning, in private and public schools, in interpersonal relationships at work and at home, and thus, on everyone's mind. Since Felipe Calderón's presidency, violence has augmented exponentially and has been quantified in vague numbers. Between 2000 and 2015, official death numbers were more than 100,000 and 23,270 disappeared; as of January 2020, there is official record of 215,999 murders and 61,000 disappeared.[56]

---

56 The 2015 official numbers were quoted by José Merino, Jessica Zarkin, Eduardo Fierro, "Desaparecidos," *Nexos*, January 1, 2015, http://www.nexos.com.mx/?p=23811@nexos; and the 2020 numbers are from Fernando Camacho Severín, "La cifra official de desaparecidos se queda corta: ONG," *La Jornada*, January 8, 2020, https://www.jornada.com.mx/2020/01/08/politica/008n1pol, and "Década violenta en México: más de 200,000 homicidios y un asesinato cada 23 minutos," *Infobae*, January 1, 2020, https://www.infobae.com/america/mexico/2020/01/01/decada-violenta-en-mexico-mas-de-200000-homicidios-y-un-asesinato-cada-23-minutos.

As we saw in chapter 1, the issue of violence is usually perceived, on the one hand, as originating in the "War Against Drugs." Initiated in 2006 by Calderón, it implied militarizing vast zones of the country, especially the North. Under this lens, journalists, intellectuals, and opinionists have sought to denounce, to provide a diagnosis, to historicize, to condemn, to offer alternative definite versions to the official one. On the other hand, they have sought to give voice to victims' complaints and demands (alive or dead), attempting to show the human side of tragedies. Beyond the mediatic parade of dead bodies, victims have been invoked to be mourned collectively, enabling survivors to speak out, to claim restitution, to demand an explanation, justice, and visibility. As we have also seen, efforts to explain violence in Mexico consider it to be a problem of sovereignty: the result of the crumbling rule of law, bringing forth a "failed state," and "an-state."[57] As we have seen, this was Sergio González Rodríguez's thesis, according to whom the main problem of violence in Mexico resides in the capture and reordering of vast regions of the country by criminal groups. In his view, these groups created a shifting cartography and govern in collusion with the government, coercing citizens under a new criminalized institutional regime.[58] This form of organization has fragmented the collective and transformed the country into a battlefield, governed simultaneously by a false rule of law and the absence of the law. The consequences are dysfunctional institutions, deficient criminal justice, and lack of the self-corrective potential of the State. The collusion between the legal and the illegal forms of government has given leeway to a normative state that rules simulating legitimacy and legality.[59] To this kind of dysfunctional and differentiated governing we can add the United States' program to destabilize the country through paramilitarism and what is known as the "Plan Mérida," a binational initiative conceived to palliate violence in Mexico that paradoxically has increased it exponentially. This destabilization plan became blatant when the outcome of the ATF's (The Bureau of Alcohol, Tobacco, Firearms, and Explosives) "Fast and Furious Operation" came to light; as we saw, the operation consisted of selling assault weapons to Mexican drug cartels so they could track them and obtain information from them. Between 2010 and 2011, more than 2,500 assault weapons traceable by GPS entered Mexico illegally. Many of these weapons were found in crime scenes—and the perspective of

57 Sergio González Rodríguez, *Campo de guerra* (Barcelona: Anagrama, 2014), 15.
58 González Rodríguez, *Campo de guerra*, 15–16.
59 González Rodríguez, *Campo de guerra*, 20.

a nearly "failed," degraded, and dysfunctional state prevails. This perspective is also the official line that has justified militarization of the country to allegedly prevent organized crime from continuing to capture vast segments of Mexican public life and to "reinforce" institutions and the judicial system.

As we have seen, we could consider violence in Mexico to be the local version of the "New World Order" or the Mexican manifestation of global processes. Not only is violence in Mexico not the result of the anomalous or failed functioning of the State, but it is one of the multiple expressions of the actual world order that results in a specific form of democratic governing that characterizes the neoliberal political economy. This form of government illustrates what Aihwa Ong calls "graded sovereignty," by which she means, the differential management of populations, the creation of a diversity of zones, among them some ruled under regimes of exception. That is to say, with the neoliberal form of governing, the State can be solid and protect some regions or areas (e.g., the sweatshop industry was not affected by the violence reigning in Juárez), while it is nearly absent in others. At times, state protection has been substituted by private defense organizations such as communal police, paramilitaries, or even private armies with the aid of foreign countries. It is known that corporations like the tequila brand José Cuervo, drug cartels, or anti-immigrant groups have hired specialized agencies that offer "private armies" to administer services of surveillance, intelligence, defense, and training. It is also known that the federal government also hires private companies to train the military. For instance, in 2007. PEMEX and the CFE (Comisión Federal de Electricidad or Federal Electricity Commision) hired the services of SY Coleman, which specializes in air-space surveillance and anti-missile defense for the creation and operation of strategic surveillance and monitoring in their plants in Veracruz. Black Mamba (TPS Armoring), SandCat, and SandCat MX have also provided services to the SEDENA (National Defense Secretary), while companies like Lockheed Martin, General Dynamics-NASSCO, DynCorp, Kroll, Armor Group, MPRI, Constellis, and Raytheon have developed security-related activities in relationship to the Mérida Plan. Guadalupe Correa-Cabrera argues that Los Zetas is comparable to a transnational corporation insofar as it is a private army trained by Guatemalan ex-Kaibilies (an elite military force taught by the Israel Defense Force in the 1970s) at the border between Brownsville, Texas, and Nuevo Laredo, Tamaulipas. According to Cabrera-Correa, "hybrid wars" are taking place and drug trafficking is only one of this group's activities, as now these paramilitarized groups sell hydrocarbons and minerals and act like transnational corporations with a network of diversified businesses. Private military organizations are business and professional services intimately tied to war: military skills, combat operations, strategic planning, intelligence, risk evaluation, operational support, training, logistics, and armament systems.[60] The neoliberal mechanism of graded sovereignty, moreover, has the purpose of allowing some areas to be flexible with regard to markets—or else run the risk of losing their structural relevance in the neoliberal legal and illegal economy—and to eliminate all obstacles to the (legal and illegal) flux of merchandises, resources, money, and people. We must recall Dawn Paley's indictment that neoliberalism is inseparable from war.

Taking into account the form of governing under the logic of "graded sovereignty," we must also consider what Achille Mbembe calls *necropolitics*, the fusion between politics and war. This amalgam does not work in function of the first to limit the second, but rather results in the predatory practices of neoliberal globalization, which are inseparable from the neoliberal privatization of the public sphere. Mbembe defines sovereignty as a self-instituting and self-limitation process that implies that societies rule themselves by their own norms, deliberatively and within a space of communication. According to Mbembe, what was repudiated after September 11 (which marks the beginning of the New World Order) is the principle of self-limitation that is to say, the taboo against murder was eliminated based on the ways in which existential threats are defined and enemies are handled. In this regard, the nihilism inherent to the dynamics of violence renders inadequate the notions of "rule of law" and "sovereignty" to explain the situation.[61] That is to say, at the global level we are all facing an uncertain enemy that threatens our existence, our well-being, and our physical and economic safety, and thus, her elimination is justified beforehand.

Furthermore, necropolitics implies the instrumentalization of human existence and the destruction of bodies and populations considered expendable from the point of view of the political economy justified as "security" measures. If the Mexican State governs differentially its populations according

---

60 José Reyez, " 'Ejércitos privados,' la amenaza a la 'Cuarta Transformación,' " *Contralínea*, December 10, 2018, https://www.contralinea.com.mx/archivo-revista/2018/12/10/ejercitos-privados-la-amenaza-a-la-cuarta-transformacion.

61 Achille Mbembe, "Necropolítica, una revisión crítica," in Helena Chávez McGregor (ed.), *Éstética y violencia: necropolítica, militarización y vidas lloradas* (México D.F.: MUAC, 2012), 134.

to the political economy's needs, then the War Against Drugs is the fiction underlying a necropolitical manifestation and the result of a differentiated government of areas and populations. Characterized by the collapse of legality and illegality, and under the shadow of the legitimacy of the struggle against crime, militarization of the country has been accompanied by a series of juridical reforms to harden the State's repressive function, reducing violent phenomena and dissent to criminal cases.[62] Debatably, the purpose of this war is to destabilize the country through paramilitarism and state violence to reconfigure Mexican territory on the basis of the interests of the oligarchy and national and transnational corporations. Following Pilar Calveiro, who preceded Dawn Paley, Oswaldo Zavala, Guadalupe Correa-Cabrera, and Marcelo Mastrogiovanni in understanding violence beyond "the war against crime," it is not a war in which enemies fight against each other to death, but a form of state violence against the excluded and dissident. As everyone knows, government institutions, including the army and businessmen at the global level (through banks and corporations that launder money), even the CIA and the DEA are part of the network of organized crime.[63] This network disseminates massive forms of violence in order to control markets, dispossess citizens, disarticulate resistance, scare off or eliminate social fighters (especially territory and environmental advocates), and to negatively impact the lives of an ample sector of society. Following Calveiro, this fake war allows an extraordinary accumulation of resources while justifying a new penitentiary punitivity. Posited as a series of juridical reforms to combat corruption and to reinforce institutions, the penitentiary system (of which sectors are being privatized) condemns more and more people from the "margins" of society for longer periods and in worse conditions.[64] In this war, collective identity is being destroyed and substituted by fear, uncertainty, and vulnerability. As Subcomandante Marcos asks, "What kind of social relationships could be maintained or woven if the dominant image with which a social group could identify itself, if the sense of community is being destroyed by the shout 'every

62 Pilar Calveiro, *Violencias de Estado: La guerra antiterrorista y la guerra contra el crimen como medios de control global* (México D.F.: Siglo veintiuno, 2012), 21–29.

63 Calveiro, *Violencias de Estado*, 21–29.

64 Calveiro, *Violencias de Estado*, 21–29.

man for himself'?"[65] Terror felt daily is a form of governing through suffering, which also paralyzes and fragments communities.

The criminal network conformed by the military, National Guard, oligarchy, politics, and businessmen is confronted by citizens who identify themselves as victims of this war, proclaiming innocence. For instance, the *Movimiento por la paz con justicia y dignidad* (Movement for Peace with Justice and Dignity), led by poet Javier Sicilia, congregated to demand government reforms, restitution, and acknowledgment of the victims of crime and the war against crime. Members of the movement are mostly middle class; they marched on the streets and occupied public spaces dressed in white demanding clarity, justice, respect, and restitution of their human rights. The local situations of violence they have undergone, however, are a consequence of global processes, which, on the one hand, make their class and consumer privileges possible and, on the other, are jeopardized by violence. This contradiction, moreover, is obviated in their discourse as victims. Another problem is that victimization as a founding experience of a social movement implies taking populist positions that hinder the propagation of a collective consciousness regarding the structural origin of all violence. Some of the achievements of the *Movimiento por la paz* have been on the plane of recognition: August 30th has been named "Forced Disappearance Victims International Day," and Felipe Calderón proclaimed the "Victims' General Law" and erected a "Victims Memorial" in Campo Marte in Mexico City.

The ideological and financial underpinnings of the *Movimiento por la paz* recently came to light when Keith Raniere, leader of the NXIVM sect, was put on trial in New York for offenses against women and criminal association. It turns out that the *Caravana por la verdad, justicia y paz* (Caravan for Truth, Justice and Peace) led by Sicilia and Mormon Chihuahua leader Julián LeBarón in 2011, was financed by In Lak'ech por la Paz A.C., made public in 2007, and produced by Emiliano Salinas Occelli, son of Mexican ex-president Carlos Salinas de Gortari. Emiliano Salinas was also the director of ESP (Executive Success Program), the Mexican branch of NXIVM. They

65 Sup Marcos, "Sobre las guerras: Fragmento de la carta primera del SCI Marcos a Don Luis Villoro, inicio del intercambio epistolar sobre Ética y Política. Enero-Febrero de 2011." *Enlace Zaptista*," February 14, 2011, http://enlacezapatista.ezln.org.mx/2011/02/14/sobre-las-guerras-fragmento-de-la-carta-primera-del-sci-marcos-a-don-luis-villoro-inicio-del-intercambio-epistolar-sobre-etica-y-politica.

also financed the documentary *Encender el corazón* by South African director and NXIVM member Mark Vicente, a narrative centered on Raniere and on LeBarón's family story in Chihuahua and their struggle against violence.[66] Keith Raniere's ideas and the money from his foundation were behind the "pacific revolution" promoted by LeBarón and Sicilia. The core ideology of the movement was exposed by Emiliano Salinas in a TED talk in San Miguel de Allende in 2011. He declared that members of civil society should act as concerned citizens and transcend the role of victims of Los Zetas, the narco, the government, corruption, poverty, and so forth. He encouraged Mexican civil society to take responsibility over the country and give a three-level response to the violence: first, move beyond denial that "Mexico has cancer"; second, acknowledge the gravity of the situation and embrace the fear and take back public spaces; and third, take nonviolent action through a self-organizing society.[67] According to observers, this speech was similar to the one LeBarón delivered during the Caravana's trip across the country, and it was written by NXIVM member Antonio Cervantes. Julio Hernández López, regular columnist at *La Jornada*, noted how the influence of Keith Raniere in the movement and in the In Lak'ech NGO was intrinsically tied to elite business doctrine.[68] In 2017, when in a *New York Times* article former NXIVM member Sarah Edmonson denounced Keith Raniere for criminal acts against some of his female followers,[69] Mike Vicente delimited himself from NXIVM and declared his documentary about La Caravana por la Paz to be dead. In an interview published by León Krauze, Vicente states that the documentary was proselytism for Keith Raniere's movement, who saw himself as a messiah of Ayn Rand's brand of radical individualism.[70] Again, the

66 Polemón, "Javier Sicilia y los Le Baron fueron financiados por la secta NXIVM," https://polemon.mx/javier-sicilia-y-los-lebaron-fueron-financiados-por-la-secta-nxivm.

67 Emiliano Salinas, TED Talk in San Miguel de Allende, June 24, 2010, https://www.youtube.com/watch?v=WMahpWvAPWo.

68 Julio Hernández López, "Astillero," *La Jornada*, April 23, 2012 available online: https://www.jornada.com.mx/2012/04/23/opinion/008o1pol.

69 Barry Meir, "Inside a Secretive Group Where Women Are Branded," *New York Times*, October 17, 2017, https://www.nytimes.com/2017/10/17/nyregion/nxivm-women-branded-albany.html.

70 León Krauze, "¿Qué carajos hice? : la historia de la película de ESP en México," *Letras libres*, October 23, 2017, https://www.letraslibres.com/mexico/politica/que-carajos-hice-la-historia-la-pelicula-esp-en-mexico.

problem with this discourse is the depoliticization of violence by the individual taking of responsibility of a faceless abstract phenomenon; the urge to transcend the status of victim becomes a dubious collective empowering again, without acknowledging the structural causes of the violence and recognizing state, gender, and corporate violence in the country. The concept of "civil society," the collective site within democracy that is allegedly the framework of the operation of the movement, makes us also wonder if democratic governments can be accountable to the people who elected them, because we are paying for the price of the neoliberal policies our government implemented. Although of course democracy has become a cynical manipulation of political space, and the Caravana por la paz is thus of the antagonism that constitutes the political theater of democracy and a symptomatic expression of neoliberalism. We must note that in January 2020, Javier Sicilia approached President Andrés Manuel López Obrador in a new Caravana that arrived at Palacio Nacional from Cuernavaca, Morelos, to discuss with the president a scheme for transitional justice in the country in the face of the intensification of violence since Morena's arrival to power. The president, however, refused to receive the Caravana, personally announcing that he will not change his security strategy—the instauration of a National Guard and his "abrazos no balazos" focused on social and cultural policies.[71] One aspect I agree with in the Caravana's discourse is the need to move beyond suffering as a collective means to self-organize; indeed, social suffering is not effective as an antagonistic political organization platform: the juridical system incorporates the victims to the archive and to an inquiry (that rarely bears fruit), becoming mere numbers and thus de-corporealized, ghosts.[72] As Ulrike Meinhof stated, a collective learning process is necessary to organize individuals and to politically realize fear, indignation, and pain;[73] for instance, when these emotions turn to autonomous initiatives, such as the case in Cherán, Michoacán.[74]

---

71 Arturo Rodríguez García, "AMLO descarta un encuentro con Javier Sicilia y rechaza cambiar estrategia de seguridad," *Proceso*, November 18, 2019, https://www.proceso.com.mx/607079/amlo-descarta-un-encuentro-con-javier-sicilia-y-rechaza-cambiar-estrategia-de-seguridad.

72 Rodríguez, *Campo de Guerra*, 73.

73 Ulrike Meinhof, "Armed Anti-Imperialist Struggle," in *Hatred of Capitalism*, ed. Sylvere Lotringer (New York: Semiotext(e), 2001).

74 Thelma González Durán, "El pueblo que espantó el miedo," in *Entre las cenizas*, ed. Daniela Rea and Marcela Turati (Oaxaca: Ediciones Sur+, 2012).

The current regime combining graded sovereignty with necropolitics (the amalgam of politics and war)[75] has permeated the ways in which we apprehend and represent our fields of experience, and it has determined the ways in which battles are being fought in public spaces. In these times without faith, consolation tends to come from the outside, and this is why social mobilizations tend to make pain public. In a sense, the powerful and pleasant fantasy of transgressing the otherwise unreachable border of someone else's feelings has been put at the center of our culture. Under Felipe Calderón's presidency, the mass media and the culture industry thus multiplied violence: if public space got saturated with visions of bodies hanging from bridges accompanied by blankets with threatening inscriptions broadcast in the national news, blogs, or social media, these visions were translated into poetry, reportage, chronicle, essay, fiction films, documentaries, symposia, installations, performances, novels, and other mediums. All this violence in the sensible regime functioned clearly as a form of power, following Cristina Rivera Garza, who posited it in this manner: "Horror is the spectacle of power: State Horror."[76] Following the ethical mandates of denouncing, visibilizing human rights violations, transmitting indignation, and mourning collectively, visual and literary experiments were created to denounce and communicate the irrepresentability of trauma—from documentary to traumatic realism, to minimalism and abstraction. For instance, the "cultivated" versions of Televisa's newscasts are Teresa Margolles's pseudo-conceptual installations built from remains lifted from crime scenes, or Amat Escalante's *Heli* (2012), which is a film that established the national victimhood archetypes. "Heli" embodies the victim whose vengeance is frustrated due to his lack of ties to power, which is why he will always be fucked over, and the trauma he suffered justifies his erratic and misogynistic behavior. His preadolescent sister "Estela" is kidnapped, tortured, and raped and comes home pregnant beyond being able to have an abortion, mute, and "living dead." In *Heli*, violence is presented as a useless and self-fed cycle; Mexicans appear full of fear and degraded by forces foreign to them and without agency, learning painfully to live with violence within and around them. In her documentary *El Velador* (2012), Natalia Almada films Culiacán's cemetery—the epicenter of the drug war (which is not the same thing as the war against narco-traffic). Chris Chang speculates that this

75 Achille Mbembe, *Necropolítica* (Barcelona: Melusina, 2011).

76 Cristina Rivera Garza, *Dolerse: textos desde un país herido* (Oaxaca: Sur+ ediciones y Frontera Press, 2011), 12.

cemetery, with its capricious architectonic forms, mausoleums, tombs, and crypts, is probably the region's fastest development zone (between 2010 and 2012, it went from having 18,000 to 35,000 tombs).[77] In the film, the camera contemplates the comings and goings of the interments, as well as the masons, who are building nonstop. In the meantime, in Almada's film, we listen to the radio and see in television how the violence is quickly expanding in the region. In the moving images, Almada shows the rituals following death and the tombs as idiosyncratic individual expression of a new caste: the narcos. With an ethnographic lens, instead of showing dismembered bodies, Almada films burial rituals and printed banners with the faces of the dead, revealing a "narco-aesthetic."

With the public, private, and sensible regimes saturated with stylized, realistic, minimalist-conceptual, or raw violence—either emphasizing the human aspects, emphasizing the tragedy, or exploiting the atrocious and grotesque—the social body came to be in permanent shock (many by proxy, although there are very few families left untouched by violence in a larger or smaller degree of closeness). In this context, collective expressions of mourning were grievances that sought to catalyze pain, addressing and blaming a form of power that overwhelms us. In general, in a situation of grieving, the socially excluded, the underclass, and the poor may capitalize their complaint as an opportunity to become visible or to gain a place within society. Moreover, the identity of "victim" has a great mobilizing power: a suffering person has undergone a process of de-subjectivation, and to identify herself as a victim implies building a field in which she can regain subjectivity by drawing self-consciousness from the pain. That is to say, the victim incorporates the damage to her identity while her empowerment is tied to a feeling of virtuosity or heroism. According to Cristina Rivera Garza, "Pain is a form of the production of reality, a language that enables bodies to decipher together power relationships . . . and to produce meaning and legitimacy."[78] But although the grievance is addressed to power, instead of becoming political subjectivation, it tends to get inscribed within the frame of human rights and humanitarian crises. Thus, suffering becomes a cultural and social experience that is far from dissent or antagonism, but that rather implies proclaiming one's own exception. And although each and every grievance deserves to be listened

77 "Natalia Almada by Chris Chang," *Bomb Magazine* 116 (Summer 2011), http://bombmagazine.org/article/5110.

78 Cristina Rivera Garza, *Dolerse*, 54.

to, there are terrible eras in which compassion and empathy are not enough to account for all the complaints.[79]

Hiding Bodies, Resignifying the Violence

When living under precarious conditions in a permanent state of exception and shock became the normality under President Felipe Calderón's reign, Enrique Peña Nieto changed the narrative of the violence plaguing the country. For instance, the seventy-two bodies of Centro American immigrants buried in a mass grave in San Fernando, Tamaulipas, found in August 2010 became the anger valve under Calderón. At that moment, a total of 193 bodies had been found in 47 anonymous mass graves, and bodies continued to appear in the news, at least until 2011. The PGR (Attorney General of the Republic) recognized the complicity of San Fernando police with the massacres,[80] and this event became, for public opinion, the catalyzer to demand an "ultimatum" to violence. As I have already mentioned, mass graves evoke state violence manifested as mass disappearance from fifty years ago. In the case of the San Fernando mass graves, instead of having been politically repressed, the bodies found were signs of frustrated economic activity: redundant cheap labor hands from which even criminal gangs were unable to extract surplus value (by extorting their families for ransom money). The mass graves also evoke maximal efficiency in the privatized discarding of excess cheap labor hands. As a measure to avoid a similar scandal as the one triggered by the San Fernando mass grave findings, instead of showing violence in the mass media and through cultural expressions (e.g., by publicizing the scandalous captures of narco leaders underscoring the power of the marines and the army as Calderón had done), Peña Nieto's government minimized the blood and bodies and hid the growing numbers of the dead and disappeared. That is to say, Peña Nieto's authoritarian style was characterized, aside from the massive repression of protest and forced disappearances, by hiding as well as silencing violence and instead pushing political corruption scandals forward. Under Peña Nieto, scandals began succeeding each other, momentarily

---

79 J. M. Coetzee, *La edad de hierro*, translated by Javier Calvo (Barcelona: Mondadori, 2002), 51.

80 Paola Chouza, "México admite la participación de policía en Matanzas de inmigrantes," *El País*, December 22, 2014, https://elpais.com/internacional/2014/12/22/actualidad/1419280307_672813.html.

superseding the noise created by the preceding one (in which justice rarely prevails), as I explained through the "caja china" (or Chinese box) mechanism in Luis Estrada's film.

An event that crossed the limit of the unspeakable and that did not transcend to public opinion, as an example of the systematic invisiblization of violence under Peña Nieto, is the massive massacre in Allende, a small town in Coahuila near the border. In March 2011, the Zetas used ranches as extermination camps over a dispute of 800 kg of cocaine. It is calculated that three hundred persons, whose homes, businesses, ranches, and lands had been destroyed, plundered, or abandoned, were disappeared. It is thought that the disappeared were calcined in improvised crematorium ovens,[81] a consequence of the scandal caused by discovery of the mass body graves in San Fernando, Tamaulipas, not to leave traces of the massacres. It all began when Luis Garza Gaitán and Héctor Moreno Villanueva, prominent ranchers in the region who collaborated in smuggling cocaine with Los Zetas, denounced them and left under a witness protection program to the United States. The Zetas victims in Allende are family members, friends, and workers of both men. The case came to light some three years after the massacre had occurred, with a few notes in *Proceso* and *Vice*.[82] The Coahuila government remains silent about the case, except to announce the destruction of the homes in ruins of the disappeared owners and to declare that Geokinetics, a corporation devoted to fracking, is now operating in the area. Certainly, the disappearance of the inhabitants of the area from their ranches was very convenient to begin fracking without civil opposition. The absence of bodies is signified in their ruined properties but silenced by the rest of the community and the country, and it is an index of the new levels of terror and impunity that are being lived in Mexico.

Another recent case, also characterized by the absence of body traces but which has resonated for over three months, provoked massive mobilizations without precedent across the country and abroad. According to the official version, on the night of September 26, 2014, in Iguala, Guerrero city police patrols blocked access to buses driving students from the Rural Normal Raúl Isidro Burgos Favela in Ayotzinapa, who had kidnapped the buses to go gather funds

---

81 See the following links: www.proceso.com.mx/?p=363638 and www.proceso.com.mx/?/p=382282.

82 Diego Enrique Osorno, "El manantial masacrado," *Vice*, September 19, 2014, vice.com/es_latam/article/qbqdpq/el-manantial-masacrado.

to assist the October 2, 1968, commemorations in Mexico City. Municipal police began shooting, and after a series of events, a commando attacked the students and a soccer team traveling in another bus, resulting in twenty-six wounded. As the story is told, later on, municipal police handed forty-three of the students to members of the Guerreros Unidos cartel to make them disappear, with the Iguala mayor serving as intellectual author of the crime. This event was posited as an example of the links between organized crime and governmental entities, proof of the State's dysfunctionality: to justify the establishment of the centralization of the police force in Guerrero. It is said that the students were executed and calcined in Cocula and that their remains were thrown in the San Juan River. To date, an Argentinian forensics team was hired privately and identified one of the bodies, normalista's Alexander Mora; reports also revealed the involvement of federal forces in the crime, denying the version that the students were burned in the Cocula trash deposit and speculating that they were incinerated in the military Iguala crematorium.[83]

While many citizens are not directly linked to the victims, violent events fueled—or not—in the mass media and social networks do not cause us direct suffering, but they make us suffer insofar as they are signs of a dire state of affairs that indeed causes suffering; it is a sign of the siege on the commons, of the new authoritarianism, of the incertitude, precarity, and insecurity in which we live. The disparity of attention between the San Fernando graves, the Allende massacre—the scandal did not translate to massive protests on the streets—and the crimes against the Ayotzinapa students have more to do with how the media are controlled. With Peña Nieto, mediatic power inflated certain stories to manipulate popular emotions, creating a shift from being in permanent shock and indignation by the ceaseless parade of dismembered bodies and narco-mantas under Calderón, to being permanently scandalized by Peña Nieto's regime concatenation of shit storms linked to corruption in power and corporations; for instance, the cost of the First Lady's "White House" (Angélica Rivera) tied to Grupo Higa (an important government subcontractor), the excessive lifestyle of politicians and their families scrutinized by citizens in their social networks, or the money-laundering scandal by the HSBC Bank of Mexican cartels' assets.

---

83 "As Obama Hosts Peña Nieto, Explosive Report Ties Mexican Federal Police to Students' Disappearance," *Democracy Now*, January 6, 2015, https://www.democracynow.org/2015/1/6/as_obama_hosts_pena_nieto_explosive.

In spite of the indignation spawned by massacres or scandals, however, the law is rarely applied, as the demand for accountability hardly transcends cyberspace. The information that circulates in the mass media traverses the screen, acquiring force in reality but in a distorted form. For instance, the Iguala massacre provoked massive mobilizations across the country and abroad, as well as chaos in and around Guerrero: by January 2015 there were twenty-eight municipalities taken across the State in solidarity with the parents,[84] five armed guerrillero organizations manifested their support to the families,[85] and celebrities or intellectuals publicly pronounced themselves against the crime.[86] It was often said that the Ayotzinapa 43 were "the dead that finally counted." The slogans of "Vivos se los llevaron, vivos los queremos" ("They were taken alive, we want them back alive," created in the context of the Argentinian dictatorship in the 1970s), "Fue el Estado" ("The State did it"), and "Faltan 43" ("There are 43 missing") channeled indignation by the collusion between political and police forces with drug traffickers (that was one of the versions that explained the events), as well as racism and contempt against young campesinos, originary peoples, and students and activists. "Ayotzinapa" catalyzed collective encounters to demand accountability, to condole together, mantras counting up to forty-three were spoken in public places or events. The magnitude of indignation and of the manifestations in solidarity with the Ayotzinapa parents of the disappeared *normalistas* attest to the collective need of people to find each other on the street to feel that their indignation and frustration are shared. Here we can remit to the paradox evoked by Elias Canetti in the formation of a mass: in the affective and physical proximity of bodies, fear of others is inverted, which is to say, fear that individual limits be transgressed transcends to become an imaginary collective present or presence. When this process reverts to a mourning ritual, insofar as the ritualization of death—according to Canetti—has to do with archaic survival, equality reigns within the mass, thus creating a shared consciousness.[87] Recently, President Andrés Manuel López Obrador declared

84 Sergio Briceño, "Tomadas, 28 alcaldías por el caso Ayotzinapa," *La Jornada*, December 29, 2014, www.jornada.unam.mx/2014/12/29/politica/005n1pol.

85 José Gil Olmos, "Ante la pesadilla de Iguala, las guerrillas despiertan," *Proceso*, November 1, 2014, www.proceso.com.mx/?p=386407.

86 See the opening speech for the 2014 Teletón by Eugenio Derbez, *Aristegui Noticias*, December 6, 2014, http://aristeguinoticias.com/0612/mexico/inaugura-derbez-el-teleton-y-habla-de-la-casa-blanca-y-de-ayotzinapa.

87 Elias Canetti, *Crowds and Power* (New York: Farrar, Strauss & Giroux, 1984).

that the case of the Ayotzinapa disappeared youth is a one of "State injustice," reversing the state fetishism inherent to civil society's accusation of "the state did it" and further entrenching the discursive hegemony of the opposition.

Evidently, the social field is an affective link. In this regard, without having the purpose or intentionality, the body empathizes with other bodies because it has the capacity to put itself in the place of other people. What is experienced in public manifestations of discontent is the feeling of being part of a meaningful social field. The sensorium that is created is the fantasy of being part of something; in experiencing momentary shared intimacy, people feel empowered. The distorted image—or the political imagination—that traverses the screens to mobilize the public, however, is foreign to political identification and radically different from an image with which we could identify in the long term as a collectivity. That is to say, the image of the collectivity that is created within the mass of people in pain is ephemeral, and as Franco Berardi would say, social action is less the result of conscious and organized choices and more the result of automatic chains of cognitive elaborations and social interaction in social media.[88] It must be mentioned, however, that pain has indeed translated to action in the case of collectives of family members who search for disappeared loved ones with their own means. It is the case of the Association of Families United in Searching and Finding Disappeared People in the northern state of Coahuila documented by Dawn Paley.[89]

In spite of its momentary therapeutic powers of collective reparation, to condole is to complain and is thus pre-political noise, whose potential for actualization still needs to be realized—members of searching collectives hand in their findings to official authorities to run them in their DNA databases, after all. Therefore, it is necessary to resignify violence in order to stimulate our capacity to see beyond the mass graves or lack thereof, eliminating the temporality of what is being observed; it is about a play of figurability and legibility, of the creation or the crystallization of a discourse. In the face of the intensification of violence, the thesis of the disintegration of the State can no longer be held because it is evident that it governs selectively with economic goals in mind. Bearing this in mind, to resignify violence would be to

88 Franco "Bifo" Berardi, "The Neuroplastic Dilemma: Consciousness and Evolution," *e-flux journal* 60 (December 2014), https://www.e-flux.com/journal/60/61034/the neuroplastic dilemma consciousness and evolution.

89 Dawn Paley, *Guerra Neoliberal: Desaparición y Búsqueda en el Norte de México* (México D.F.: Tierra Adentro, 2020).

see something more than inhabiting and sharing trauma, the morbidity of someone else's suffering—to move beyond the shock. In that regard, it would also be necessary to understand that the constant presence of death in our imaginaries is indissociable from the empire of neoliberal capital and the oligarchy's desire for social cleansing and living under socioeconomic apartheid, with restricted access and privileges to basic commodities and services, and that peace might actually be impossible in a country whose policies are dispossessing and destroying the forms of making a living and the forms of life of its peoples. Beyond violence as a moral problem, from the side of power and from the side of those who denounce power, to resignify violence would mean to transcend dogma that "if you're good, you can't be a victim of evil."

In Mexico, the base structures of systemic violence have been deployed for five hundred years, which is why they have been rendered invisible; for instance, the racism inherent to the reigning caste system obstructing empathy and making ethnocentrism and classism inescapable, alluring the privileged class to isolate itself in gated and heavily surveilled communities. Another example are class, race, and culture divisions evident in the different sectors of political mobilizations: the demands and direct actions of public-school system unions (the SNTE, or Sindicato Nacional de Trabajadores de la Educación), guerrillero groups from the mountains, vigilante police in rural areas, *normalista* students, and urban students of public schools are all considered as "radical," and this is why urban civil society only partially solidarizes with popular resistance while demanding that it moderate its radicalization (e.g., condemns traffic disturbances).[90] We must also take into account the impunity that generally characterizes Mexicans' relationship to power, which implies affirming one's own superiority through violence and aggression toward others in everyday and banal situations. Due to our history of colonization, we lack a social pact for the common good, and these are some of the reasons why the justice system is inefficient and corrupt. What is needed to combat violence, besides a social pact geared toward the common good that could transcend race and class relations, would be decent salaries enabling people to prosper, to organize unions, to establish environmental controls, to have real choices with regard to transportation and other

90 Alberto J. Olvera, "La resistencia civil y la democracia en México," *El País*, February 10, 2015, http://internacional.elpais.com/internacional/2015/02/10/actualidad/1423539349_623262.html.

consumer goods, and to have equality in good quality access to goods and services, among others.

While sympathizing with victims claiming restitution is a way of transforming the act of seeing into something that transcends voyeurism and morbidity, it implies responding to an interpellation and an invitation to become others and to collectively take responsibility.[91] To mourn the lost lives, as Rivera Garza puts it, is to go beyond individual pain to sympathize in a collective act in which we display our most basic human condition: vulnerability.[92] In this regard, to recognize one's own vulnerability could serve as the ethical ground for a theory of empowerment and self-responsibility toward others: "to recognize life as lived by the other"; a public mourning ritual makes us more vulnerable and thus more human, helping us to catalyze the pain and to not respond with violence before the damage that has been done to us.[93] It is imperative, however, to tie collective suffering with the politicization of the threat to the commons by neoliberal policies and corporate harassment to the country and its citizens, transforming the claims for justice into forms of resistance to the new authoritarianism and recognizing that the destruction of life and bodies is the basis of global capitalism.

Taking this into account, resignifying violence would be to see beyond inhabiting and sharing trauma and morbidity in suffering, to transcend shock and indignation, and to understand that the constant presence of death is inextricable from a neoliberal capital's empire and the oligarchy's and middle class's unconscious desires for social cleansing and for living under socioeconomic apartheid with privileged access to basic goods and services. Evidently, peace is impossible in a country whose policy is to dispossess and destroy its peoples' means of making a living. Beyond violence as a moral problem, on the side of power, as on the side of those denouncing power, resignifying violence would imply giving the dead a symbolic status (e.g., as martyrs) to repel the epidemics of idleness, anxiety, depression, anguish, apathy, fear, and indifference that permeate the collective and to allow victims to transcend their place as a niche for semiotic consumption, conferring survivors a perspective beyond suffering, as well as a clear action and an organization program. To

91 See Susan Sontag, *Before the Pain of Others* (New York: Knopf, 2003); and Ariella Azoulay, *The Social Contract of Photography* (Cambridge, MA: MIT Press, 2009).

92 Rivera Garza, *Dolerse*, 127.

93 Rivera Garza, *Dolerse*, 127.

resignify violence is to change the discursive frame of the plea or complaint of the victim of the violation of her human rights addressed to the State and to rethink violence properly as state violence (instead of corruption and impunity) and as obeying a logic of the neoliberal political economy, which is none other than a new wave of colonial dispossession and destruction.

One example of the resignification of violence includes the situation in 2014 in Chalchihuapan, Puebla, in which José Luis Tehuatlie Tamayo, the boy who died by a rubber bullet shot by the police when he was walking with his mother by a protest, was named a "Hero Child"; a plaque was revealed condemning Puebla State Governor Rafael Moreno Valle as the responsible murderer.[94] There is also the narration of the circumstances of the deaths of thousands of people embroidered collectively throughout the country and abroad in public spaces. The "embroiders for peace" decided to put their activities to an end because they feared for themselves. Evidently, small symbolic actions such as this one are extremely threatening to a minority who has the power over the economy, political processes, and mass media. This silent, anonymous, slow, meticulous, patient, reflexive, and communal gesture is a threat because it is the active creation of a *feeling of a shared reality*, which implies an encounter with reality that is not mediated by massive communication media or social networks.

To resignify violence would also be to create forms of being in common in public spaces that could open up spaces for self-management and autonomous organizations. Instead of demanding restitution to the State, the situation demands that we turn our backs to power with the eloquence of the embroiders and with the tenacity of the Uruapan Purépecha peoples, who have self-organized to keep out violence brought on by the State and organized crime.[95] In this manner, it is also urgent to identify what values we want our society to adhere to, considering the colonial baggage, the racialization of violence, and the caste system that gives form to our society, to what level and with which means, if we decide to believe in defending the commons.

---

94 Yadira Llaven Anzures, "Proclaman como 'niño héroe' al niño asesinado en Chalchihuapan," *La Jornada de Oriente*, September 17, 2014, www.lajornadadeoriente.com.mx/2014/09/17/proclaman-como-nino-heroe-al-nino-asesinado-en-chalchihuapan.

95 Ernesto Martínez Elorriaga, "Exigen habitants purépechas la salida de la Fuerza Rural de sus comunidades," *La Jornada*, September 15, 2014, www.jornada.unam.mx/2014/09/15/politica/007n1pol.

There is no discussion happening in the world today that is more crucial than a debate about contemporary forms of resistance; the idea of justice has been crushed and overridden for a fragile moral discourse of "human rights." It has become clear that a violation of human rights is necessary to implement unjust political and economic structures in the world. These serve as collateral damage of the system and not as accidents, as the result of impunity or evil and in line with the colonial legacy of social cleansing through genocide, slavery, and colonialism. Neoliberalism controls the soil of the world.

In Mexico, the status quo that we are governed by a "Failed State" is the consequence of the paralysis of political imagination by neuro-totalitarian, faux individuation and its colonization by populist technocratic thinking. That is why, in the current conjuncture, what is needed to bring civil society together is not indignation against the government, but rather knowledge that the outcome of the model of development capitalism are civil wars and irreversibility of climate change; that the collateral damage of the economic model is presented to us in the form of hundreds of bodies circulating in refrigerated trailers, the privatization of fossil-fuel extraction (by white-collar and poor people), or in the murdering and imprisonment of dozens of Indigenous leaders against megaprojects.

It is thus our responsibility that political action be grounded on awareness that every megaproject represents environmental as well as social catastrophe originated in genocidal dispossession of the territory, in continuity with the massive dismantlement of the Mexican agricultural economy. We must be aware that the global neoliberal order is a machinery to generate forms of extreme urbanization rooted in the single goal of generating surplus value. Violence in the country must be understood through the lens of continuity of Dirty War against guerilla movements in Mexico since the 1960s in Michoacán, Guerrero, and Chihuahua, which now includes methods to maximize terror as decapitation, dismemberment, mass kidnapping, car bombs, blockages, executions, and the chemical dissolution of bodies.

In order to flee from the political imaginaries of the populist technocratic state and of the failed state, we must understand that our moralizing democracy is a mirror image of the disintegration of a shared ethical basis of our lives, and that there are no frames to produce collective meaning beyond the reproduction of private hedonism; that hedonism is making us cynical, and that the cult of winners prevails in our civilization, as those who are considered to be gods are celebrities and entrepreneurs: the caste of the "successful." And it is perhaps because we are not seeing to what extent we are profoundly immersed in the global processes of dispossession, that we are still paying taxes and are incapable of actively investing as politicized agents defending the territory. This is partly due to the fact that in our political imagination, there is no project beyond "demanding that the government function," although the existence of the redundant populations is real, as it is true that there are humans who have no need to consume or produce within the capitalist system and who are creating autonomous infrastructure. We are living in the cadaver of capitalism that is beginning to rot. Hegemonies are broken. Indigenous peoples who are deserting from the nation project-organizing autonomies, arming themselves against state violence with "Communal Policing," *exist for real.* The current opposition in Mexico is not expressed online but materializes in reality as "Consejo Nacional Indígena" (National Indigenous Council), "Consejo Regional de Pueblos Originarios en Defensa del Territorio de Puebla e Hidalgo" (Regional Council of Originary Peoples Defending the Territory of Puebla and Hidalgo), and "Prisioneros politicos indígenas por defender sus territorios" (Indigenous political prisoners for defending their territories). A transformation will come from the imminent collapse of capitalism, and this is why I want to make an urgent call for utopian speculation (fantasy) of radical political imagination that is, above all, anti-technocratic and anti-capitalist. The most valuable forms of political imagination will be those that depend on empathy and in our capacity to foresee concrete changes to the present situation substituting the direct moral relationship with the superficial qualities of the events we consume in the media or Infosphere and in the sensible regime of state- and private-sponsored industrialized cultural production.

Inhabiting Spaces of Autonomous Survival: Destituting the Legacy of Modernity

Nowadays, power manifests itself as overtly offensive and incarnates the absolute evil of intolerance through racist and misogynist discourses. In November 2017, at the United Nations Climate Summit in Bonn, California Governor Jerry Brown told Indigenous protesters demanding to stop fracking in their lands: "Let's put you in the ground." In October 2018, Melania Trump wore a Zara jacket with the phrase, "I really don't care, do you?" when she made a public visit to a migrant children's refugee center in Texas. The demise of tolerance, inclusivity, and the new identarian essentialism is operating as a public justification of social Darwinism on a global scale. Under the current naked version of absolute capitalism—stripped from the discourses of democracy, human rights, and multiculturalism that used to embellish it—it has ceased to make sense to think about the world as divided into first and third, east and west, north and south. As we have seen, with its ability to go beyond national divisions, the globalized market has long integrated first and third worlds, forcing certain areas of the third world to "develop" and creating pockets of wealth and cultural sophistication in the South, as well as areas of destitution and misery in the North. The world has been configured into territories connected in various degrees to global processes. There are modernized pockets of privilege and cultural sophistication connected to global flows of symbolic and financial capital, coexisting with enclaves inhabited by what I call "redundant populations." This sector of the population has differential or no access at all to health care, citizenship, debt, education, and jobs. By differential I mean goods, services, or lower-quality food. A portion of the redundant population lives in "zones of sacrifice," which, by many accounts, are the contemporary manifestation of coloniality. According to Naomi Klein, the zones of sacrifice are inhabited by communities surviving the toxic load of our systemic need to consume fossil fuels; they also undergo the slow violence that results from exploiting "the commons" as "natural resources."

The commons and sustainable autonomous forms of life of the redundant populations—what Raquel Gutiérrez calls *entramados de reproducción* (interwoven structures for the reproduction of life)—are the target of the current manifestation of subcontracted state and corporate violence because they pose a threat to the expansion of capitalism. Specifically, for Gutiérrez and Dawn Paley, the current "War against Drugs" in Mexico, launched in 2006, is a war against the capacities of humans to organize collective life; impunity for domestic and public forms of violence deploys a continuum of violence that maintains the overlapping heteropatriarcal and capitalist systems as war is being waged against forms of life and the interwoven structures of the reproduction of life that sustain them.[96] As I will argue, these interwoven structures of the reproduction of life are under siege because they are foreign to the process of market valorization and are thus conceived as threats to the expansion of capitalism. Technocracy and power directly consider them forms of insurgency, which is why they are being destroyed in the name of pacification and development. This form of destruction constitutes injurious forms of interdependency, as it is de facto sustaining the lives of people inhabiting privileged zones who are denying while justifying the annihilation under the logic of inclusion into the global markets; for instance, the extraction of shale gas in

96 Raquel Gutiérrez Aguilar and Dawn Paley, "La *transformación sustancial* de la guerra y la violencia contra las mujeres en México," *DEP*, no. 30 (2016).

the Canadian province of Québec in order to provide Montréal with natural gas, or the destruction of communities around the Cutzmala Dam and the Valle del Mezquital, which has served to provide a fraction of Mexico City's inhabitants with water.

Against this backdrop and in the context of the industrialization on a global scale of cultural production, art bears the mandate to give up its autonomy and be useful. This means that aesthetic quality is now measured against an artwork's criticality or the potential effectiveness it can have in the social field in constructing communities, salvaging the social tissue, or giving visibility to disenfranchised populations. "Conflict" is now a subject for curatorial and artistic intervention, and artistic practices must unleash "beautiful trouble" as a way to reconfigure ethics, propose climate solutions, and give leeway to oppositional assembly and occupation. As a niche in cultural production linked to political practice, "sensible politics," as we have seen, means that what matters in representation is how things are represented, thus delivering a form of nongovernmental politicization active at the level of encoding unstable political acts in medial forms. It also means positing art as a platform for notable acts of collective creative mobilization that could recast institutions' sense of public purpose and explore art's capacity to define a democratic field.[97] This pervasiveness in the cultural production of the ethical mandates of the visibilization of wrongs, of attempts to restitute structures of collective solidarity through "social design," implies the transformation of taste into a civic value.

This scheme of allegedly emancipatory artistic practices is currently inserted in the first variable of a false opposition that is drawn to combat absolutist capitalism, aligned with the continuation of the globalization and modernization projects, of development and democracy, and thus with promises of prosperity and emancipation. The other variable is the emergence of aggressive national identities that are behind the new fascisms, which are an attempt to contain the destabilizing effect of the dynamics of globalization by recurring to traditional forms of life. The anti-capitalist third way emerges from the formerly called *third world* that proposes as a source of resistance against globalization of old Asian, American, or African traditions. Thus, the

---

97 Johanna Burton, Shannon Jackson, and Dominic Willsdon, "Plight of the publics: An Introduction to *Public Servants*," in *Public Servants: Art and the Crisis of the Common Good* (Cambridge, MA: MIT Press, 2016), xv.

political impasse of the Left consists of being trapped in the false solutions of either resisting global capitalism, either favoring the local traditions it destroys or opposing it from the standpoint of a universalizing emancipatory project disseminated by political parties, contemporary art, and cultural practices in general through the concept of the "Global South." But even though the neoliberal politics of austerity and privatization could be halted by eventually establishing something like a universal basic income, this schema fails to consider the actual system of global interdependency sustained by the fossil fuel and financialization economy, which can no longer assure sustainable and dignified lives for most inhabitants of the planet, including nonhuman life. An apocalyptic feeling begins to spread.

Wolfgang Streeck, for instance, has described how contemporary capitalism has begun to disappear on its own because it is collapsing from its own internal contradictions. According to Streeck, what comes after capitalism is neither socialism nor another definite social order, but an interregnum, a period of social entropy and disorder. We will come to this "failed state" scenario, according to Streeck, after economic growth stagnates and inequality and redistributed conflict intensifies, which will be followed by the evaporation of the possibility of administering macroeconomics due to the ubiquity of corruption of all kinds. We will thus arrive at a moment in which capitalism as economic regime will no longer be able to sustain society.[98] To this we can add the fact that the elite is actively contributing to the collapse of the current social order, with their lack of capacity to maintain it and their lack of vision to establish a new one. That is to say, the global elites—and by this I mean the 1% and the technocrats administering their interests on behalf of which they govern us—aside from ignoring the collateral damage of the capitalist economic model and of being incapable of incrementing protocols for relating to the environment beyond extractivism, they live convinced that the world in which we are living in, although not the best possible, is the "lesser of evils" and thus believe that radical change would only make things worse. Clearly, the global plutocracy lives in a bubble (including in private refuges in the eventuality of the apocalypse),[99] in a world apart in which different rules

98 Wolfgang Streeck, *How Will Capitalism End?* (London: Verso, 2017).

99 Mark O'Connell, "Why Silicon Valley billionaires are prepping for the apocalypse in New Zealand," *The Guardian*, February 15 2018, https://www.

and laws apply because legal processes and police authorities are designed to protect them and modify the laws to please them.

The imminent collapse of the capitalist system is due to the fact that absolute capitalism means legalized corruption and the appropriation of everything to incorporate it into the field of market valorization. The former heroic figure of the worker, expressing its creative potential, was substituted by the mandate of self-cultivating human capital, the enthusiastic channeling of one's energies into work, and the tacit acceptance of precarious working conditions. Everyone now must see for themselves because collective institutions have been eroded by market forces and the community's interweaving of the sustainability of life is being directly assaulted through market valorization and corporate and state violence. And although the raw matter of industrialization—natural resources—turned out to be finite, workers now contribute to the reproduction of a capitalist society, having become *crévards*—or "greedy opportunists," as the Invisible Committee posits it—and exploiting ourselves and each other under the frame of a collaborative economy.[100] Aside from the already mentioned redundant populations living in zones of sacrifice, there are also the excluded populations from the possibility of being exploited and from consumption cycles, living in a situation of survival.

According to Streeck's apocalyptic narrative of the interregnum that follows the collapse of capitalism, the changes that will occur will always be unpredictable, and the future will be ruled by institutional disintegration and structural indetermination. But contrary to what is common belief, the collapse of capitalism will bring us a kind of generalized breakdown that will forces us to build our lives autonomously by way of making voluntary agreements among consensual individuals. This will be much harder than Streeck foresees it because we are survivors of alienation. Following Karl Marx, *Entfremdung* is the subjective condition that derives from living in a society stratified in social classes that dissociates subjects from their essence.

For Marx, salaried work also separates the workers from their essence and from production. Social alienation follows. Let's recall Margaret Thatcher's well-known slogan: "There is no such thing as society. There are individual men and women and there are families. . . . People must look after themselves

theguardian.com/news/2018/feb/15/why-silicon-valley-billionaires-are-prepping-for-the-apocalypse-in-new-zealand.

100 Comité Invisible, *Ahora* (Logroño: Pepitas de calabaza, 2018).

first. It is our duty to look after ourselves."[101] This resulted in a form of capitalist social relations with a low level of integration, without common values, and with isolation among individuals and groups of people: a notion of society constituted as a foreign power with which it is impossible to interact.

We should also consider that absolutist capitalism is attacking the interwoven structures of the reproduction of life that are working outside of markets, because the main risk of the disintegration of salaried society are neither the failed state, global warming, nor environmental collapse, but precisely the fact "that humans become able to invent unforeseen uses of their time and life and begin to take seriously the question of their meaning."[102] In that regard, in Mexico, the so-called War Against Drugs is not a conflict of armed military and paramilitary groups but a war against the working class and Indigenous women, children, and men—the redundant population, or the target of a terror strategy. The war is based on the generalized intensification of state and corporate violence against the capacities of the reproduction of life; that is to say, against the capacities of human collectivities to organize and direct collective life.[103] The War Against Drugs" thus functions through the guarantee of impunity and militarization to expand capitalism and social control and to strengthen the state. The goal of the war, I repeat, is the destruction and degradation of relations of reciprocity and mutual aid, and collaboration and trust, which have always been cultivated in precarious conditions by Indigenous peoples in Mexico, and which technocracy and the state apparatus have always considered as insurgent.

In this context, the modern idealization of the third-world peasantry as a force of resistance has been long abandoned. From Hegel to Marx to Fanon, the dispossessed, rather than passive victims of modernity, had been the agents of liberation, by way of the dialectical transformation of exploitation into a universal revolutionary struggle for freedom. And yet the neoliberal reforms rapidly transformed campesinos into a new "modern" peasant culture in which individuals dispossessed of their forms of life and ways of making a living, and thus of their dignity, have turned on their head the traditional

---

101 In an interview in *Women's Own* from 1987, quoted in *The Guardian*, April 8, 2013, https://www.theguardian.com/politics/2013/apr/08/margaret-thatcher-quotes.

102 Thatcher, "Margaret Thatcher: A Life in Quotes," 31.

103 Gutiérrez and Paley, "La *transformación sustancial*."

position that has been ascribed to them as subalterns. As "modernized consumers," but with differential or no access to credit, jobs, and merchandises, they are joining cartels and mafias seeking to restore their wounded dignity (and masculinity) to vindicate their status as handicapped consumers and dispossessed peoples. Killing for money and power, they are looking for identarian affirmation and dignity through a kamikaze logic.[104] Another side to this logic is suicide, which has come to be perceived as an effective form of a self-destructive action of the oppressed, the only means to dissipate anxiety, depression, and impotence of peoples and communities living in intolerable situations; for instance, the Attawapisakat and Wapekeka communities in Ontario, Canada, which since 2016 have suffered a crisis of mass suicides, especially of youth.[105] For Franco Berardi, suicide (e.g., of France Telecom workers, Hindu farmers, North American originary peoples, youth across the world), is functioning as a final act of self- affirmation before accepting defeat that would obliterate any sense of dignity. Expropriated from language by education, from their culture by ethnography and marketing, from songs by reality TV contests, from our flesh by mass pornography, from our city by the police, and from our friends by precarious wage labor, destruction and self-destruction are ways to regain agency.

In the current panorama of expropriation and violence, the communities that need to take care of a wound are perceived as the current "damned of the earth." Clearly, regimes of alterity no longer occupy the locus of otherness that could question hegemonic structures. On the one hand, "the Other" has lost its alterity, as modernization has created communities that have undergone what Jalal Touffic [djalal tawfiq] calls "the withdrawal of tradition past a surpassing disaster" and that are thus inhabited by damaged bodies emptied of cultural signification exposed to forms of violence that do not count as crimes. On the other hand, there is no more alterity or discursive site for opposition because now the only accepted frame for "political agency" is the demand to restitute human rights. This implies particularizing political crises by transforming them into private suffering, thereby hindering their potential to become collective political struggles.

---

104 Franco "Bifo" Berardi, *Futurability: The Age of Impotence and the Horizon of Possibility* (London: Verso Books, 2017).

105 See https://www.thestar.com/news/canada/2016/04/18/how-the-attawapiskat-suicide-crisis-unfolded.html.

From this perspective, the function of this "Global South" is to remind us of the ethical and social disaster brought about by modernity and the nineteenth-century idea that a Western and modern form of life are the "normal" and the standard to measure progress and historical change. That is to say, the spell of universal progress has been broken, along with the belief that technique would bring us limitless growth and political stability. Dogmas such as the French colonization of Haiti, but the idea that the French Revolution offered the ideological basis on which to rebel and achieve independence, now sound to us like cheap Enlightenment propaganda. Perhaps the Enlightenment can only be thought of now as the ideology of capitalism: human rights, transparency, democracy, and culture. We are living in the dead body of modernism and capitalism, and progressive European values are not helping to escape the rot. Contrary to what we believed in, the legacy of modernity resulted in being not a horizon of emancipation led by the proletariat, but a biosphere and humanity on the verge of extinction, surviving and self-destructing in a world that is already in ruins.

At the root of the normalization of the neocolonial destruction of the life forms and forms of making a living of some for the sake of the privilege of others is the modern assumption of man's domination of nature and societies, which is also bound to the project of the Enlightenment as a form of scientific and artistic mastery and political emancipation. Put differently, from a decolonial perspective, the Western "I think, therefore I am" is preceded by 150 years of "I conquer, therefore I am"; the cogito, ergo sum is therefore nothing other than an imperial being grounded on genocide, epistemicide, racism, and sexism as the foundation of knowledge and high culture of the modern/colonial world.[106] (Colonialism and modernity are inextricably bound as the first enables the latter.) The mastery of knowledge is embodied by the, rightly problematized by Donna Haraway, "knowing" Western subject that considers itself and its gaze as neutral, objective, and superior, as visionary and enlightened.[107] Let's recall Werner Herzog's Fitzcarraldo, whose mad colo-

---

106 Ramón Grosfoguel, "The Structure of Knowledge in Westernized Universities: Epsitemic Racis/Sexism and the Four Genocides/Epistemicides of the Long 16th Century," *Human Architecture: Journal of the Sociology of Self-Knowledge*, no. 1 (Fall 2013), 77.

107 Donna Haraway, "Situated Knowledges: The Science Question in Feminism and the Privilege of. Partial Perspective," *Feminist Studies* 14, no. 3. (Autumn 1988), 575–99.

nial enterprise is justified by bringing opera to the Amazonian jungle—opera being the highest embodiment of Western intellectual and aesthetic achievement at the time. Somehow, the destruction that underlies modernity is either justified or thought to be healed through culture. What I'm thinking about here is the scene in Jean-Luc Godard's *For Ever Mozart* (1996) that shows SS soldiers listening to Beethoven.

This is why, to end devastation, we must acknowledge that colonialism—masked by the technocratic belief in development and culture as forms of emancipation—is the matrix of the present fueling the wave of extraction and primitive accumulation on a global scale, constituting forms of power that link populations and territories to the logics of race, bureaucracy, and markets. But this is precisely why we have to be careful not to let decolonization become the "Orientalism" of the Anthropocene (or Capitalocene or Chthulucene). We will have failed if decolonization becomes the new constitutive other of Western civilization and culture—a mode of discourse and not a form of life; a style of thought based on the ontological and epistemological distinction between the "West" and the "Indigenous." Decolonization could easily fall into mere academic and cultural production discourse and be relegated to a metaphor, entrenching settler colonialism even more, which implies rationalizing and maintaining unjust social structures.[108] This is because decolonization does not imply reverting positions of dominance or securing identities on traditions, "usos y constumbres" (uses and habits) of the originary peoples, but repatriating the land, abolishing slavery, and abolishing the empire. It requires a change in the order of the world. Finally, in the current landscape of expropriation and violence, we will have failed if the "wretched of the earth" remain a subject of Western intervention and rescue—while, if we maintain this dichotomy, the opposite is true.

Decolonization therefore requires an unsettling restructuring beyond the logic of extractivism and dispossession and needs to be grounded on epistemological, ontological, and cosmological relationships. We urgently need to find other genealogies of thought and action geared toward autonomous and collective forms of organization guarded from capitalism. We need stories and narratives beyond crises, victims, or mere survival; stories that rely on self-determination that can bring change from within, rather than changing after being recognized from an outside. These struggles will

---

108 Eve Tuck and K. Wayne Yang, "Decolonization Is Not a Metaphor," *Decolonization: Indigeneity, Education & Society* 1, no. 1 (2012): 1–40.

be framed around a defense of the material and symbolic conditions that guarantee the reproduction of life in common; for sustaining the interwoven structures of reproduction that are not mediated by capitalism or heteropatriarchy, but grounded on agreements producing forms of obligation toward the collective.[109] The struggles to come, following Raquel Gutiérrez, will necessarily materialize in precarious small steps: change shall be permanent, yet discontinuous; change will be a rhythm present in almost all vital processes, like the diastole and systole, and will contradict the homogenous, identical, and lineal temporality of capital and the state.[110]

To begin to undermine the standpoint from which colonialism makes sense, and parting from the idea that it is impossible to go back to "zero" through decolonization or to an idealized and pastoral precolonial past, and that utopian experiments of the twentieth century to live in communities outside of capitalism failed, instead of waiting for capitalism to fall apart on and in spite of us, we need to begin to act destitute, looking for autonomous and collective forms of organization guarded from capitalism and seeking to create different relationships between forms of life and life itself. To destitute is to make colonialism make no sense. It is to produce agreements to produce forms of obligation toward the collective; it is to guarantee the material and symbolic possibility of the reproduction of life.

In their book, *Por un habitar más fuerte que lo común*[111] (For an inhabiting stronger than the common), the Consejo nocturno proposes the notion of *inhabiting* as a means to oppose or resist the current state of affairs. For them, the word that defines alienation is the "metropolis," making reference to Marcello Tarí's book that describes the experience of Italian autonomy experiments in the 1970s and 1980s, titled *A Communism Beyond the Metropolis*.[112] For the Consejo nocturno, inhabiting is precisely using our time and lives in unforeseen manners; it is the "unseen" possibility of the situation. It is a means to break through the impasse of Western thought stuck between

109 Raquel Gutiérrez Aguilar, "Común, ¿hacia dónde? Metáforas para imaginar la vida colectiva más allá de la amalgama patriarcado-capitalismo y dominio colonial," *Producir lo común: entramados comunitarios y formas de lo político* (Madrid: Traficantes de sueños, 2019), 53.

110 Raquel Gutiérrez Aguilar, *Los ritmos del Pachakuti* (Madrid: Traficantes de Sueños, 2009), 31.

111 Consejo Nocturno, *Un habitar más fuerte que la metrópoli*.

112 Marcello Tarí, *Un comunismo más fuerte que la metrópoli: la autonomía italiana en la década de 1970* (Madrid: Traficantes de sueños, 2012).

modernity and tradition, universalism and the local, fascism and communism. To inhabit means to change paradigm of the project of land repatriation and of the appropriation of the means of production because there is no more land left, and because we no longer wish to produce or consume. It means occupying the territory from outside and against power to destitute it, right before the imminent collapse of capitalism crushes us along with the apocalyptic sensation permeating the present, but above all, before capitalism completely consumes our capacity to collectively reproduce life. To destitute means especially to be opposed to "constitutive power," which expresses pragmatic reason to continue adapting the structures and resources of the country to the needs of the global market with the idea of "achieving governability with a minimum of repression enticing economic growth."[113] It also implies rejecting "constitutive power," which elaborates ideal future images of society addressing utopic reason in order to oppose technocracy with its notions of "equality," "autonomy," "community," and "the public,"[114] but without being able to do away with the unrealistic modern ideal of universal emancipation that underlies these notions. To destitute power in favor of the interwoven structures of the reproduction of life means to inhabit in common, to fight for the territory and its autonomy, to stop a deadly megaproject, a neighborhood's gentrification. In this way, destitutive power will operate to dismantle the state of affairs in the present through the creation of a constellation of autonomous worlds of resistance against market forces, instituting realities in secession against state sovereignty and in favor of the paradigm of *inhabiting* sustained by interwoven structures for the reproduction of life and for nourishing life.

Inhabiting opposes the metropolis, and the metropolis is empire, the Anthropocene, the apocalypse. The metropolis is not an easily localizable or tangible enemy. It slips through infrastructure, through human relationship networks, in betterment and restitution projects of territories and communities devastated by violence, in cyberspaces' algorithms, in shopping malls, in the waves of panic and shock we feel when we know UNAM students or tourists in Garibaldi are being attacked, that throughout the country drive

113 Carlos Elizondo Mayer-Serra, "Mal gobierno: el estado incompetente," In *¿Y Ahora qué?, México ante el 2018*, ed. Héctor Aguilar Camín et al. (México D.F.: Debate, 2017), 131.

114 Introducción to *El futuro es hoy*, edited by Humberto Beck and Rafael Lemus (Madrid: Biblioteca Nueva, 2018), 15.

containers full of dead bodies rotting without destination. Power is also embedded in our communication tools, in the food and medicine we ingest.

As colonialism, the metropolis formats life and society according to its own productivity models, transforming autonomous action into a series of conducts governed through modernity's devices: science, progress, technocracy, industrialization, design, rule of nature and societies. The metropolis is the idea that the sole destiny of humankind is production and thus the metropolis denigrates, invisibilizes and exploits reproductive labor, which is considered an uncomfortable residue of human life. The metropolis is a permanent state of exception, the creation of dependency on corporate services, the slavery of a salary and debt, and social Darwinism, all of which mean superimposing private interest above general interest.

Two of the main power instruments held by the metropolis are architecture and urban planning; through the spatialization of capital, the metropolis has become the machine for its own reproduction, subjecting all areas of everyday life to the field of valorization. Neither the situationist flaneur nor the nostalgic subject have the capacity to break with the alienation that is the metropolis. Manipulating infrastructure is no longer an option. If we consider Mexico City Governor Marcelo Ebrard's (2006–2012) ice rink at the Zócalo, to recodify public spaces is a tool that has been appropriated by the state apparatus to maintain, preserve, and perpetuate its own power. Power is sovereignty over spaces and territories and reigns over what is capable of internalizing.

We must also take into account that the metropolis as the stage for the confrontation between the proletariat and the bourgeoisie has become obsolete, as has the metropolis as polis in the sense of the site for social antagonism staging disagreement of a plurality of factions from civil society to demand proper government functioning. The metropolis works as polis in the sense of having solidified political power through police administration, as it is a machine for territorial ordaining that creates networks to enable the free flow of merchandise, commodities, and finances. The metropolis is a machine akin to ghost nets abandoned or lost in the oceans, responsible for the capture of millions of marine animals, killing them and destroying their ecosystems, killing everything as it passes through.

It follows that the metropolis is the site where life passes through the Western apparatus of dominion over nature and societies through technocracy. It is not that territory is denied, but that the metropolis is erected upon the domination and destruction of the territory to reconvert it toward the paradigm of production. This is why the metropolis implies the annihilation of life and all traces of communal life forms, be it through expropriation, privatization, salaried relationships, or the super-production of institutionalized services. The metropolis is also having become helpless in procuring our own conditions of reproduction. Because, aside from going to the bank or to the supermarket, we are incapable of building a wall, cultivating a milpa, sewing a button or repairing a fridge or a car, building an algorithm, curing an infection without antibiotics.

To drive away, to destitute the formation of the state apparatus, means to *inhabit*, because inhabiting does not coincide with any of modernity's devices. Inhabiting proposes the Consejo nocturno, which is similar to nomadism as described in Deleuze and Guattari's *Treaty on Nomadology* in the sense of distributing the self in space, holding onto spaces that are disappearing, like a forest vanishes with deforestation. Inhabiting is the purely destituent potency of organized loneliness by the metropolis, which coincides with the elaboration of affective densities and modes of conviviality, which are stronger than the needs produced by the paradigm of the government and corporations that have stolen or potency from us. To inhabit is thus to take over our own existence. To *inhabit a territory* is to make it one's own through autonomy, self-management, self-defense, community assemblies, and collective work. I want to conclude by drawing a nuance between Indigenous autonomy and workerist autonomy. Indigenous autonomy is not the self-management of the extant (of the commons); it is taking over territory through collective experimentation of forms of life beyond and against the state and the market, destituting the constellation of extractive forces and government and corporate devices. In Indigenous autonomy, exchange and use value are rejected and acquire ethical, communal, and political value differently than workerist autonomy does, which rejects work and proposes estrangement from the institution through sabotage, anti-production, ungovernability in factories. For workerist autonomy, attacking the metropolis means creating zones of mass illegality at the heart of enemy territory; for instance, through "red markets," where merchandise much cheaper than normal prices is distributed, or even through direct appropriation of merchandise, much cheaper than normal prices, or even the direct appropriation of merchandise, even home-squatting. In workerist autonomy, a battle against power is fought not to take over the state machinery, but to extend the liberated zones where a communist form of life could flourish. In the liberated zones of occupied houses, there are massive self-reductions of gas, electricity, water, and telephone services;

in this manner, workerist autonomy means the destruction of the affective and social subjection devices, absolute social cooperation, and the desire to uproot every relationship of production.

But now that the working class has disappeared as a historical figure from the political horizon, the Consejo nocturno proposes autonomy grounded on inhabiting, which implies a different use of the world; it means destituting instead of sabotaging, assuming that we first have to destitute ourselves, and then destitute the forms of power that are disseminated in the social field. To conclude, it is not about being able to choose, but to choose being able to, giving primacy to collective potency to dent our reality in ruins and begin inhabiting another world.

BIBLIOGRAPHY

Acuña, Rodolfo. "The Age of Billionaires." *Counterpunch*. December 12, 2013, www.counterpunch.org/2013/12/27/the-age-of-thebillionaires.

Adorno, Theodor W. "Commitment." *New Left Review* I/87-88 (September/ December 1974): 75–89.

Aguilar Camín, Héctor, Luis de la Calle, María Amparo Casar, Jorge G. Castañeda, José Ramón Cossío Díaz, Eduardo Guerrero, Santiago Levy, and José Woldenberg, eds. *¿Y Ahora qué? México ante el 2018*. México D.F.: Debate, 2017.

Alfie, Miriam. "Supervía Poniente: conflicto social y visión urbano-ambiental," *Estudios demográficos y urbanos* 28, no. 3 (September/December 2013). https://doi.org/10.24201/edu.v28i3.1452.

Amador Tello, Judith. "El proyecto Mundo Maya, 'salvajemente neoliberal.' " *Proceso*. July 30, 2011, https://www.proceso.com.mx/cultura/2011/7/30/ el-proyecto-mundo-maya-salvajemente-neoliberal-90161.html.

Anderson, Chris. "Mexico: The New China." *New York Times*. January 26, 2013, http://www.nytimes.com/2013/01/27/opinion/sunday/the-tijuana -connection-a-template-for-growth.html.

Aranda Luna, Javier. "No más cultura de utilieria." *La Jornada*. June 21, 2012, https://www.jornada.com.mx/2012/06/27/opinion/a05a1cul.

Arendt, Hannah. *Between Past and Future: Eight Exercises in Political Thought*. New York: Viking Press, 1968.

———. *The Human Condition*. Chicago: University of Chicago Press, 1958.

———. "Ideology and Terror: A Novel Form of Government." *Review of Politics* 15, no. 3 (July 1953): 303–27.

———. *Más allá de la filosofía. Escritos sobre cultura, arte y literature*. Edited by Fina Birulés and Ángela Lorena Fuster. Translated by Ernesto Rubio. Madrid: Trotta, 2014.

. *The Origins of Totalitarianism*. New York: Schocken Books, 1951.

Aristegui Noticias. "La titular del Conacyt ha tenido expresiones lamentables: Antonio Lazcano." August 11, 2019, https://m.aristeguinoticias.com/1108/kiosko/la-titular-del-conacyt-ha-tenido-expresiones-lamentables-antonio-lazcano.

Athanasiou, Athena, and Judith Butler. *Dispossession: The Performative in the Political*. Cambridge, UK: Polity Press, 2013.

Azoulay, Ariella. *The Social Contract of Photography*. Cambridge, MA: MIT Press, 2009.

Bailey Glasco, Sharon. *Constructing Mexico City: Colonial Conflicts over Culture, Space and Authority*. New York: Palgrave Macmillan, 2010.

Banco Mundial. "La clase media mexicana creció en la última década." November 13, 2012, http://www.bancomundial.org/es/news/feature/2012/11/13/mexico-middle-class-grows-over-past-decade.

Barillas, Sandra. "El cabildo de Cuetzalan, en session abierta, oficializa el rechazo a proyectos mineros e hidroeléctricos." *La Jornada de Oriente*, November 6, 2014, http://www.lajornadadeoriente.com.mx/2014/11/06/el-cabildo-de-cuetzalan-en-sesion-abierta-oficializa-el-rechazo-a-proyectos-mineros-e-hidroelectricos.

Baudrillard, Jean. "Disneyworld Company." *Libération*, March 4, 1996, https://www.liberation.fr/tribune/1996/03/04/disneyworld-company_166772.

———. "Towards a Critique of the Political Economy of the Sign." *SubStance* 5, no. 15 (1976): 111–16.

Bauman, Zygmut. *Globalization*. New York: Columbia University Press, 1998.

Beauregard, Luis Pablo. "México acusa a Carolina Herrera de apropiación cultural por su colección más reciente." *El País*, June 13, 2019, https://elpais.com/elpais/2019/06/12/estilo/1560295742_232912.html.

Becerra, Ricardo, and José Woldenberg, eds. *Balance temprano desde la izquierda democrática*. México D.F.: IETD and Editorial Grano de Sal, 2020.

Beck, Humberto, and Rafael Lemus, eds. *El futuro es hoy*. Madrid: Biblioteca Nueva, 2018.

Benjamin, Walter. "The Author as Producer." *New Left Review* 1, no. 62 (July/August 1970): 83–91.

Berardi, Franco "Bifo." *After the Future*. Edited by Gary Genosko and Nicholas Thoburn. London: AK Press, 2011.

———. *Breathing: Chaos and Poetry*. South Pasadena, CA: Semiotext(e), 2018.

———. "Emancipation of the Sign: Poetry and Finance During the Twentieth Century." *e-flux journal* 39 (November 2012). https://www.e-flux.com/journal/39/60284/emancipation-of-the-sign-poetry-and-finance-during-the-twentieth-century.

———. *Futurability: The Age of Impotence and the Horizon of Possibility*. London: Verso, 2017.

———. "Game Over." *e-flux journal* 100 (May 2019). https://www.e-flux.com/journal/100/268601/game-over.

———. "The Neuroplastic Dilemma: Consciousness and Evolution." *e-flux journal* 60 (December 2014). https://www.e-flux.com/journal/60/61034/the-neuroplastic-dilemma-consciousness-and-evolution.
———. "The Psychopathologies of Hyper-Expression." Translated by Arianna Bove. *transversal texts* (June 2007). https://transversal.at/transversal/1007/berardi-aka-bifo/en.
———. "(Sensitive) Consciousness and Time: Against the Transhumanist Utopia." *e-flux journal* 98 (February 2019). https://www.e-flux.com/journal/98/257322/sensitive-consciousness-and-time-against-the-transhumanist-utopia.
———. *The Soul at Work*. Los Angeles: Semiotext(e), 2009.Bishop, Claire. "Participation and Spectacle: Where Are We Now?" In *Living as Form: Socially Engaged Art from 1991–2001*, edited by Nato Thompson, 34–46. New York: Creative Time, 2012.
Borger, Julian. "Fleeing a Hell the US Helped Create: Why Central Americans Journey North." *The Guardian*, December 19, 2018, https://www.theguardian.com/us-news/2018/dec/19/central-america-migrants-us-foreign-policy.
Botz-Bornstein, Thorsten. "A Tale of Two Cities: Hong Kong and Dubai." *Transcience* 3, no. 2 (2012): 1–16. https://studylib.net/doc/8157533/a-tale-of-two-cities--hong-kong-and-dubai-celebration-of.
Bourdieu, Pierre. *Intelectuales, política y poder*. Buenos Aires: Eudeba, 1999.
Bowden, Charles, ed. *Juárez: The Laboratory of Our Future*. New York: Aperture, 1998.
Bowden, Charles. *Murder City: Ciudad Juárez and the Global Economy's New Killing Fields*. New York: Nation Books, 2010.
Braidotti, Rosi. "On Putting the Active Back into Activism." *New Formations: A Journal of Culture/Theory/Politics*, no. 68 (2009): 42–57.
Brenner, Neil, and Nik Theodore. "Cities and the Geographies of Actually Existing Neolibrealism." *Antipode* 34, no. 3 (July 2002): 349–79. https://doi.org/10.1111/1467-8330.00246.
Brenner, Neil. "Neoliberalisation." In *Spaces of Neoliberalism. Urban Restructuring in North America and Western Europe*, edited by Neil Brenner and Nik Theodore. London: Wiley-Blackwell, 2002, 18–42.
Brewis, Harriet. "Female German Boat Captain Faces Up to 20 Years in Jail for Rescuing 'Drowning' Migrants." *Standard*, June 12, 2019, https://www.standard.co.uk/news/world/german-boat-captain-faces-up-to-20-years-in-jail-for-rescuing-migrants-a4166011.html.
Briceño, Sergio. "Tomadas, 28 alcaldías por el caso Ayotzinapa." *La Jornada*, December 29, 2014, www.jornada.unam.mx/2014/12/29/politica/005n1pol.
Brooks, David. "Deliberada ambigüedad en la reforma energética." *La Jornada*, December 21, 2013, http://www.jornada.unam.mx/2013/12/21/politica/007n1pol.

Brown, Wendy. *Undoing the Demos*. New York: Zone Books, 2015.
Brum, Eliane. "Enfermo de Brasil: Cómo resistir la enfermedad en un país (des) controlado por la perversión de la autoverdad." *El País*, August 2, 2019, https://elpais.com/elpais/2019/08/03/opinion/1564785296_446106.html.
Bois, Yves-Alain, Benjamin Buchloh, Hal Foster, and Rosalind Krauss. "1971." In *Art Since 1900: Modernism, Antimodernism, Postmodernism*. Cambridge, MA: MIT Press, 2006, 545–49.
Budgen, Sebastian. "A New 'Spirit of Capitalism.'" *New Left Review*, no. 1 (2000). https://newleftreview.org/issues/ii1/articles/sebastian-budgen-a-new-spirit-of-capitalism.
Burton, Johanna, Shannon Jackson, and Dominic Willsdon. "Plight of the publics: An Introduction to *Public Servants*." In *Public Servants: Art and the Crisis of the Common Good*. Cambridge, MA: MIT Press, vii–xxv.
Butler, Judith. *Frames of War*. London: Verso, 2009.
Cacelín, Janet, Alejandro Melgoza, and Sergio Rincón. "Un cacique del agua en el paraíso maya." *Proceso*, March 2, 2010, https://www.proceso.com.mx/619955/un-cacique-del-agua-en-el-paraiso-maya-2.
Calveiro, Pilar. *Violencias de Estado: la Guerra antiterrorista y la Guerra contra el crimen como medios de control global*. México: Siglo XXI Editores, 2013.
Camacho Severín, Fernando ."La cifra official de desaparecidos se queda corta: ONG." *La Jornada*, January 8, 2020, https://www.jornada.com.mx/2020/01/08/politica/008n1pol.
Canetti, Elias. *Crowds and Power*. New York: Farrar, Strauss & Giroux, 1984.
Cano, Gabriela, and Hilda Monraza. "Un recorrido por la historia del feminismo en México." *El Universal*, March 8, 2020, https://www.eluniversal.com.mx/cultura/un-recorrido-por-la-historia-del-feminismo-en-mexico.
Carlsen, Laura. "Mexico's Oil Privatization is a Risky Business." *Foreign Policy in Focus*, May 27, 2014, http://fpif.org/mexicos-oil-privatization-risky-business.
———. "Plan Puebla-Panama Advances: New Name, Same Game." *Americas Program*, September 10, 2009, https://www.americas.org/6410.
Castañeda, Jorge G. *Mañana Forever: Mexico and the Mexicans*. New York: Knopf, 2011.
Cave, Damien. "In the Middle of Mexico, a Middle Class Rises." *New York Times*, November 18, 2013, https://www.nytimes.com/2013/11/19/world/americas/in-the-middle-of-mexico-a-middle-class-is-rising.html.
Chang, Chris. "Natalia Almada by Chris Chang." *Bomb Magazine* 116 (Summer 2011). https://bombmagazine.org/articles/natalia-almada.
Charner, Flora. "Brazil's Favela Fairy Tale: When Prince Charming Packs Heat." *Aljazeera America*, November 24, 2014, http://america.aljazeera.com/multimedia/2014/11/debutantes-ball-riodejaneirofavela.html.
Chávez McGregor, Helena, ed. *Éstética y violencia: necropolítica, militarización y vidas lloradas*. México D.F.: MUAC, 2012.

Checa Gismero, Paloma. "On *The Return of a Lake*." *Field Journal*, no. 1 (Summer 2015): 281–88. http://field-journal.com/issue-1/checa-gismero.
Chomsky, Noam. "Los pueblos indígenas están salvando al planeta de un desastre ambiental." *Ecoosfera*, March 3, 2017, http://ecoosfera.com/2017/03/noam-chomsky-activismo-ambiental-indigena-latinoamericano-video.
———. "Un movimiento genuino por el cambio social." *La Jornada*, December 7, 2014, http://www.jornada.unam.mx/2014/12/07/mundo/026a1mun.Chouza, Paola. "México admite la participación de policía en Matanzas de inmigrantes." *El País*, December 22, 2014, https://elpais.com/internacional/2014/12/22/actualidad/1419280307_672813.html.
Cid de León, Oscar. "Alista el Museo Jumex su inauguración." *Reforma*, October 26, 2013.
Clement, Megan. "Sisters in Arms: The Families Fighting Femicide in France." *Aljazeera*, December 30, 2019, https://www.aljazeera.com/features/2019/12/30/sisters-in-arms-the-families-fighting-femicide-in-france.
Coetzee, J. M. *La edad de hierro*. Translated by Javier Calvo. Barcelona: Mondadori, 2002.
Comité Invisible. *Ahora*. Logroño: Pepitas de calabaza, 2018.
Composto, Claudia, and Mina Lorena Navarro, eds. *Territorios en Disputa: Despojo capitalista, luchas en defensa de los bienes comunes naturales y alternativas emancipatorias para América Latina*. México D.F.: Bajo Tierra Ediciones, 2014.
Conaculta Cuaderno 13: Patrimonio cultural y turismo gestión cultural: Planta viva en crecimiento. Guadalajara: Encuentro Internacional de Gestores and Promotores Culturales, 2006.
Consejo Nocturno. *Un habitar más fuerte que la metrópoli*. Logroño: Pepitas de calabaza, 2018.
Corona, Sonia. "Un Estado mexicano admite que la policía use armas de fuego en las propuestas." *El País*, May 20, 2014, http://internacional.elpais.com/internacional/2014/05/20/actualidad/1400613204_366357.html.
Correa-Cabrera, Guadalupe. *Los Zetas: Criminal Corporations, Energy, and Civil War in Mexico*. San Antonio: University of Texas Press, 2017.
Cruz, Alejandro. "Pagarán vecinos de Mazaryk (Polanco) las renovaciones al área." *La Jornada*, January 24, 2014, www.jornada.unam.mx/2014/01/24/capital/033n1cap.
Danelo, David J. *Toward a U.S.-Mexico Security Strategy: The Geopolitics of Northern Mexico and the Implications for U.S. Policy*. Philadelphia: Foreign Policy Research Institute, 2011. https://www.fpri.org/docs/media/Toward_a_US_Mexico_Security_Strategy_Danelo.pdf
Dávila, Patricia. "Banco Azteca creará 'clientes cautivos' para Salinas Pliego." *Proceso*, March 19, 2019, https://www.proceso.com.mx/575944/

advierten-que-reparto-de-subsidios-en-elektra-y-banco-azteca-creara-clientes-cautivos-para-salinas-pliego.

Davis, Ben. "On Art and Investment." *art-agenda*, March 25, 2014, http://art-agenda.com/reviews/on-art-and-investment.

De Boever, Arne, and Warren Neidich, eds. *The Psychopathologies of Cognitive Capitalism: Part One*. Berlin: Archive Books, 2013.

de Duve, Thierry. *Aesthetics at Large, Volume 1: Art, Ethics, Politics*. Chicago: University of Chicago Press, 2019.

Dean, Jodi. "Communicative Capitalism: Circulation and the Foreclosure of Politics." *Cultural Politics* 1, no. 1 (2005): 51–74. https://commonconf.files.wordpress.com/2010/09/proofs-of-tech-fetish.pdf.

———. "Enjoying Neoliberalism." *Cultural Politics* 4, no. 1 (2008): 47–72. https://doi.org/10.2752/175174308X266398.

———. "Collective Desire and the Pathology of the Individual." In *The Psychopathologies of Cognitive Capitalism: Part One*, edited by Arne De Boever and Warren Neidich. Berlin: Archive Books, 2013.

Deleuze, Gilles. "Postscript on the Societies of Control." *L'Autre journal* no. 1 (May 1990).

Delillo, Don. *White Noise*. New York: Penguin Books, 1985.

Demos, T. J. "*Return of a Lake*: Contemporary Art and Political Ecology in Mexico." *Rufián Revista* 17 (January 2014). https://tjdemos.sites.ucsc.edu/wp-content/uploads/sites/374/2016/08/Demos-Alves-MUAC-copy.pdf.

———. *Return to Postcolony: Spectres of Colonialism in Contemporary Art*. Berlin: Strenberg Press, 2013.

———. "The Great Transition: The Arts and Radical System Change." *e-flux journal*, April 12, 2017, http://www.e-flux.com/architecture/accumulation/122305/the-great-transition-the-arts-and-radical-system-change.

Díaz Gómez, Floriberto. "Compartencia: Comunidad y comunalidad." ediciones patito.org, December 14, 2014, http://rusredire.lautre.net/wp-content/uploads/Comunidad.-y-ocomunalidad.pdf.

Díaz, Gloria Leticia. "Quiso, no pudo . . . y se pudrió." *Proceso*, February 19, 2004, http://www.latinamericanstudies.org/mexico/portillo-pudrio.htm.

Dillemuth, Stephan, Anthony Davies, and Jakob Jakobsen. "There is No Alternative: The Future is Self-Organised." In *Art and Social Change: A Critical Reader*, edited by Will Bradley and Charles Esche. London: Tate Publishing and Afterall, 2007, 378–83.

Dunbar-Ortiz, Roxanne. "An Open Letter to President Barack Obama: Change the Columbus Holiday to Indigenous Peoples' Day." *Beacon Broadside*, October 9, 2014, https://www.beaconbroadside.com/broadside/2014/10/change-the-columbus-holiday.html.

Easterling, Keller. *Extrastate-Craft: The Power of Infrastructure Space*. London: Verso, 2016.

Emmelhainz, Irmgard. "Self-Destruction as Insurrection or How to Lift the Earth Above All That Has Died." *e-flux journal* 87 (December 2017), https://www.e-flux.com/journal/87/169041/self-destruction-as-insurrection-or-how-to-lift-the-earth-above-all-that-has-died.

Enwezor, Okuwi. "Documentary/Vérité: Bio-Politics, Human Rights and the Figure of 'Truth' in Contemporary Art." *Australian and New Zealand Journal of Art* 5, no. 1 (2004): 11–42.

Escalante Gonzalbo, Fernando. *Historia mínima del neoliberalismo*. México D.F.: El Colegio de México, 2016.

Expósito, Marcelo. "Lecciones de historia. El arte, entre la experimentación institucional y las políticas del movimiento." Paper presented January 30, 2009, at the VIIth International Symposium of Theory of Contemporary Art (SITAC): *Sur, sur, sur, sur*. http://marceloexposito.net/pdf/exposito_sitac.pdf.

Federici, Silvia. *Calibán y la bruja: Mujeres, cuerpo y acumulación originaria*. Madrid: Traficantes de Sueños, 2010.

Fernández F., Aurelio. "Cuetzalan: defenderse y construir." *La Jornada*, April 9, 2014, http://www.jornada.unam.mx/2014/04/09/opinion/026a1pol.

Ferri, Pablo. "Interview with Yásnaya Elena Aguilar Gil: Los pueblos indígenas no somos la raíz de México, somos su negación constante." *El País*, September 9, 2019, https://elpais.com/cultura/2019/09/08/actualidad/1567970157_670834.html.

Fisher, Mark, and Nina Mönntman. "Peripheral Proposals." In *Cluster: Dialectionary*, edited by Binna Choi, Maria Lind, Emily Pethic, and Nataša Petrešin-Bachelez. Berlin: Strenberg Press, 2014, 192–97.

Fisher, Steve. "As Obama Hosts Peña Nieto, Explosive Report Ties Mexican Federal Police to Students' Disappearance." *Democracy Now*, January 6, 2015, https://www.democracynow.org/2015/1/6/as_obama_hosts_pena_nieto_explosive.

Flores, Leonor. "Política cultural ineficaz, pese a mayors recursos." *El Economista*, May 17, 2013, https://www.eleconomista.com.mx/arteseideas/Politica-cultural-ineficaz-pese-a-mayores-recursos-20110517-0177.html.

Forbes. "Se respetarán contratos de la reforma energética." March 18, 2019, https://www.forbes.com.mx/se-respetaran-contratos-de-la-reforma-energetica-asegura-amlo.

Foster, Hal. "What's Neo about the Neo-Avant-Garde?" *October* 70 (1994): 5–32. https://doi.org/10.2307/779051.

Fox, Dominic. *Cold World: The Aesthetics of Dejection and the Politics of Militant Dysphoria*. London: Zero Books, 2009.

Fraser, Nancy. *The Old is Dying and the New Cannot Be Born: From Progressive Neoliberalism to Trump and Beyond*. New York: Verso, 2019.

Frausto, Alejandra. "Normalizar el arte, diversificar la cultura." *El Universal*, June 24, 2019, https://www.eluniversal.com.mx/columna/alejandra-frausto-guerrero/cultura/normalizar-el-arte-diversificar-la-cultura.

———. "Transición en Los Pinos: Hay bienes que no estaban en inventarios ni en bodegas: Frausto." *Aristegui Noticias*, April 9, 2019, https://aristeguinoticias.com/0904/entrevistas/transicion-en-los-pinos-hay-bienes-que-no-estaban-en-inventarios-ni-en-bodegas-frausto-video.

Friedman, Thomas L. "How Mexico Got Back into the Game." *New York Times*, February 23, 2013, https://www.bajacallcenters.com/about/news/how-mexico-got-back-into-the-game.html.

Gago, Verónica. *La potencia feminista o el deseo de cambiarlo todo*. Madrid: Traficantes de sueños, 2019.

Galeano, Eduardo. "To Be Like Them." In *Juárez: the Laboratory of Our Future*, edited by Charles Bowden. New York: Aperture, 1998, 159–68.

García Canclini, Néstor. "Mexico City, 2010: Improvising Globalization." In *Other Cities, Other Worlds*, edited by Andreas Huyssen. Durham, NC: Duke University Press, 2008, 79–98.

García, Jacobo. "En el corazón de la Guerra en México." *El País*, September 9, 2019, https://elpais.com/internacional/2019/09/08/mexico/1567906718_822056.html?ssm.

García Jiménez, Laura. "La batalla contra el monstruo verde: crónica de un viaje a través de diez Semilleros." *Revista común*, July 2, 2020, https://www.revistacomun.com/blog/la-batalla-contra-el-monstruo-verde-cronica-de-un-viaje-a-traves-de-diez-semilleros.

Gasca Serrano, Leticia. "Arte en México, ¿cómo se compra?" *El Economista*, February 13, 2012, http://eleconomista.com.mx/entretenimiento/2012/02/13/arte-mexico-como-se-compra.

———. "Todos coinciden: invertir en arte es Buena opción." *El Economista*, February 13, 2012, http://eleconomista.com.mx/entretenimiento/2012/02/13/todos-coinciden-invertir-en-arte-es-buena-opcion.

Gil Olmos, José. "Ante la pesadilla de Iguala, las guerrillas despiertan." *Proceso*, November 1, 2014, https://www.proceso.com.mx/reportajes/2014/11/1/ante-la-pesadilla-de-iguala-las-guerrillas-despiertan-139211.html.

———. "El despojo interminable de los pueblos indígenas." *Proceso*, October 12, 2013, https://www.proceso.com.mx/reportajes/2013/10/12/el-despojo-interminable-los-pueblos-indigenas-124590.html.

Gil, Yásnaya Elena Aguilar. "Construir Naciones sin Estado, parece algo radical pero no lo es." *Radio UdeG Guadalajara*, October 30, 2019, http://udgtv.com/noticias/jalisco/construir-naciones-sin-estados-parece-algo-radical-no-lo-yasnaya-elena-aguilar.

———. "Ëëts, atom. Algunos apuntes sobre la identidad indígena." *Revista de la Universidadd e México*, September 2017, https://www.revistadelauniversidad.mx/articles/f20fc5ef-75e2-44d0-8d5b-a84b2a87b7e3/eets-atom-algunos-apuntes-sobre-la-identidad-indigena.

———. " El Estado mexicano como apropiador cultural." *Revista de la Universidad*, July 2018, https://www.revistadelauniversidad.mx/articles/0bb50a13

-2ad8-40e3-9972-5f35dd35184f/el-estado-mexicano-como-apropiador-cultural.
Goddard, Michel. "Media Ecology, Political Subjectivation and Free Radios." *The Fiberculture Journal*, no. 17 (2011). https://seventeen.fibreculturejournal.org/fcj-114-towards-an-archaeology-of-media-ecologies-%E2%80%98media-ecology%E2%80%99-political-subjectivation-and-free-radios.
Gómez-Barris, Macarena. *The Extractive Zone: Social Ecologies and Decolonial Perspectives*. Durham, NC: Duke University Press, 2017.
Gómez, Laura, and Alejandro Cruz. "Analizarán esquemas para concluir obra en Masaryk, ante la negativa vecinal a pagar." *La Jornada*, February 20, 2014, www.jornada.unam.mx/2014/02/20/capital/038n1cap.
Gómez, Laura, Alejandro Cruz, and Raúl Llanos. "Tesorero: impuesto por mejoras, sólo en las zonas de alta plusvalía." *La Jornada*, January 29, 2014, www.jornada.unam.mx/2014/01/29/capital/037n1cap.
González, Joel. "Niños y jóvenes yucatecos presentarán obra en el Auditorio Nacional." *Sipse*, November 1, 2019, https://sipse.com/novedades-yucatan/ninos-jovenes-presentaran-obra-teatral-auditorio-nacional-348787.html.
González, Rocío. "En Polanco desconocen que deberán pagar remodelación." *La Jornada*, January 30, 2014, www.jornada.unam.mx/2014/01/30/capital/037n1cap.
González Rodríguez, Sergio. *Campo de guerra*. Barcelona: Anagrama, 2014.
———. *The Femicide Machine*. New York: Semiotext(e), 2011.
González, Susana. "Incrementan importaciones de maíz en México." *La Jornada*, June 21, 2018, https://www.jornada.com.mx/ultimas/2018/06/21/incrementan-importaciones-de-maiz-en-mexico-4833.html.
Grillo, Ioan. *El Narco: Inside Mexico's Criminal Insurgency*. New York: Bloomsbury, 2011.
Grosfoguel, Ramón. "The Structure of Knowledge in Westernized Universities: Epistemic Racism/Sexism and the Four Genocides/Epistemicides of the Long 16th Century." *Human Architecture: Journal of the Sociology of Self-Knowledge* 11, no. 1 (2013). https://scholarworks.umb.edu/humanarchitecture/vol11/iss1/8.
Guattari, Félix. *The Three Ecologies*. London: The Athlone Press, 1989.
Gudino Terán, Uriel. "¡Sólo hazlo! Coaching, training y sujeción: sobre la producción de subjetividad neoliberal y la nueva masculinidad hegemónica en Tijuana, B.C." Master's thesis, Colegio de la Frontera Norte, August 2020.
Guerrero, Deyra. "Sólo la mitad de lo dicho por AMLO en las Mañaneras, es verdad." *Verificado*, March 3, 2020, https://verificado.com.mx/mitad-verdad-amlo-mananeras.
Guthrie, Amy. "While Negotiators Talk NAFTA, Mexicans Grapple with Automation." *The Wilson Quarterly*, Summer 2018, https://www.wilsonquarterly.com/quarterly/the-grinding-gears-of-north-america/while-negotiators-talk-nafta-mexicans-grapple-with-automation.

Gutiérrez Aguilar, Raquel, and Dawn Paley. "La *transformación sustancial* de la guerra y la violencia contra las mujeres en México." *DEP, Deportate, Esuli e Profughe, 30*. Venezia: Universidad Ca'Foscari, 2016.

Gutiérrez Aguilar, Raquel. *Los ritmos del Pachakuti*. Madrid: Traficantes de Sueños, 2009.

———. "Común, ¿hacia dónde? Metáforas para imaginar la vida colectiva más allá de la amalgama patriarcado-capitalismo y dominio colonial." In *Producir lo común: entramados comunitarios y formas de lo politico*. Madrid: Traficantes de sueños, 2019.

.———. "Los Ritmos del Pachakuti. Reflexiones breves en torno a cómo conocemos las luchas emancipativas y a su relación con la política de la autonomía." In *Hacer política para un porvenir más allá del capitalism*. México: Grietas editores, 2016.

Habermas, Jürgen. "New Social Movements." *Telos*, no. 49 (September 1981): 33–37. https://doi.org/10.3817/0981049033.

Haraway, Donna. "Situated Knowledges: The Science Question in Feminism and the Privilege of. Partial Perspective." *Feminist Studies* 14, no. 3 (Autumn 1988): 575–99.

Harvey, David. *A Brief History of Neoliberalism*. Oxford, UK: Oxford University Press, 2005.

Heath, Chip, and Dan Heath. *Switch: How to Change Things When Change Is Hard*. New York: Crown Business, 2010.

Hedges, Chris. *The Death of the Liberal Class*. New York: Type Media Center, 2010.

Herbert, Julián. *Ahora imagino cosas*. México D.F.: Literatura Random House, 2019.

Herlman, Gerald B., and Steven R. Ratner. "Saving Failed States." *Foreign Policy*, June 21, 2010, http://www.foreignpolicy.com/articles/2010/06/21/saving_failed_states.

Hernández, Gabriela. "Acusan a Moreno Valle de Infundir miedo a la oposición con la 'ley bala.' " *Proceso*, May 20, 2014, https://www.proceso.com.mx/nacional/estados/2014/5/20/acusan-moreno-valle-de-infundir-miedo-la-oposicion-con-la-ley-bala-132806.html.

———. "Comunidad indígena gana amparo contra gasoducto Tuxpan-Tula." *Proceso*, February 11, 2019, https://www.proceso.com.mx/571364/comunidad-indigena-gana-amparo-contra-gasoducto-tuxpan-tula.

Hernández López, Julio. "Astillero." *La Jornada*, April 23, 2012, https://www.jornada.com.mx/2012/04/23/opinion/008o1pol.

Hind, Emily. *Dude Lit: Mexican Men Writing and Performing Competence (1955–2012)*. Tucson: University of Arizona Press, 2019.

Holmes, Brian. "Eventwork: The Fourfold Matrix of Contemporary Social Movements." In *Living as Form: Socially Engaged Art from 1991–2001*, edited by Nato Thompson. New York: Creative Time, 2012, 72–85.

———. "Neoliberal Appetites." 16 Beaver Group, 2009, www.16beavergroup.org/drift/readings/bh_neoliberal_appetites.pdf.
Homero, Aridjis. *La leyenda de los soles.* México D.F.: Fondo de Cultura Económica, 1993.
Horning, Rob. "Social Media, Social Factory." *The New Inquiry*, July 29, 2011, https://thenewinquiry.com/social-media-social-factory.
Horton, Alex. "Art Installations Blast Audio of Sobbing, Detained Children Across New York City." *Washington Post*, June 12, 2019, https://www.washingtonpost.com/nation/2019/06/12/art-installations-blast-audio-sobbing-detained-children-across-new-york-city.
Huacuja del Toro, Malú. *Salinato Versión 2.0: reflexiones desde el periodismo cultural sobre el retorno de Carlos Salinas al poder*. México: Plaza y Valdés, 2013.
Hui, Yuk. "What Begins After the Enlightenment?" *e-flux journal* 96 (January 2019). https://www.e-flux.com/journal/96/245507/what-begins-after-the-end-of-the-enlightenment.
Huyssen, Andreas, ed. *Other Cities, Other Worlds.* Durham, NC: Duke University Press, 2008.
Illouz, Eva. *Cold Intimacies: The Making of Emotional Capitalism.* (Oxford, UK: Polity Press, 2007.
Imison, Paul. "The Ultimate Mexican Hype Machine: The Myth of the Aztec Tiger." *Counterpunch*, March 29, 2013, http://www.counterpunch.org/2013/03/29/the-myth-of-the-aztec-tiger.
Infobae. "Década violenta en México: más de 200,000 homicidios y un asesinato cada 23 minutos." January 1, 2020, https://www.infobae.com/america/mexico/2020/01/01/decada-violenta-en-mexico-mas-de-200000-homicidios-y-un-asesinato-cada-23-minutos.
Jameson, Fredric. *The Cultural Turn: Selected Writings on the Postmodern, 1983–1998.* Brooklyn: Verso, 1998.
Jamison, Leslie. "Does Recovery Kill Great Writing?" *New York Times*, March 13, 2018, https://www.nytimes.com/2018/03/13/magazine/does-recovery-kill-great-writing.html.
———. "I Used to Insist I Didn't Get Angry. Not Anymore. On Female Rage." *New York Times Magazine*, January 17, 2018, https://www.nytimes.com/2018/01/17/magazine/i-used-to-insist-i-didnt-get-angry-not-anymore.html.
Jansen, Maarten. "El oro en la Tumba 7 de Monte Albán. Contexto y significado." *Arqueología Mexicana*, no. 144 (March/April 2017): 51–57.
Johns, Michael. *The City of Mexico in the Age of Díaz.* San Antonio: University of Texas Press, 1998.
Kimmelman, Michael. "A City Rises, Along with its Hopes." *New York Times*, May 18, 2012, www.nytimes.com/2012/05/20/arts/design/fighting-crime-with-architecture-inmedellin-colombia.html.

Kittler, Friedrich, and Matthew Griffin. "The City Is a Medium." *New Literary History* 27, no. 4 (1996): 717–29.

Klein, Naomi. *No Logo*. Toronto: Random House and Picador, 1999.

———. "Rising Majority Teach-In with Naomi Klein & Angela Y. Davis." *Now This is Politics*. Live on Facebook on April 2, 2020. https://www.facebook.com/NowThisPolitics/videos/1001197546941886.

———. *The Shock Doctrine*. Toronto: Random House Canada, 2007.

———. *This Changes Everything: Capitalism vs. the Climate*. (New York: Simon & Shuster, 2014.

Korol, Claudia. "No le echen la culpa al murciélago." *Página 12*, April 3, 2020, https://www.pagina12.com.ar/256569-no-le-echen-la-culpa-al-murcielago.

Kose, M. Ayhan, Guy M. Meredith, and Christopher M. Towe. "How Has NAFTA Affected the Mexican Economy? Review and Evidence." *IMF Working Paper* WP/04/59 (April 2004). http://www.imf.org/external/pubs/ft/wp/2004/wp0459.pdf.

Kraus, Chris. *Where Art Belongs*. New York: Semiotext(e), 2011.

Krauze, Enrique. *Democracia en construcción*. New York: Penguin Random House, 2016.

———. "La carrera de Lorenzo Zambrano." *Reforma*, May 25, 2014, http://www.enriquekrauze.com.mx/joomla/index.php/biogr-retrato/99-biogra-de-la-sociedad-civil-y-la-ciudadania/874-la-carrera-de-lorenzo-zambrano.html.

Krauze, León. "¿Qué carajos hice? La historia de la película de ESP en México." *Letras libres*, October 23, 2017, https://www.letraslibres.com/mexico/politica/que-carajos-hice-la-historia-la-pelicula-esp-en-mexico.

Kuznetsov, Yevgeny and Dahlman, Carl. *Mexico's Transition to a Knowledge-Based Economy*. Washington, DC: The World Bank Institute, 2008.

La Izquierda Diario. "Anuncia AMLO resultados de consulta: termoeléctrica y Proyecto Integral Morelos." February 25, 2019, https://www.laizquierdadiario.mx/Anuncia-AMLO-resultados-de-consulta-termoelectrica-y-el-Proyecto-Integral-Morelos-van.

La Jornada. "La política cultural es un campo social privilegiado: Rafael Tovar." December 17, 2013, www.jornada.unam.mx/2013/12/17/cultura/a05n2cul.

La Jornada. "Peña Nieto lanza programa de cultura en Michoacán por la paz." January 18, 2014, www.jornada.unam.mx/2014/01/18/cultura/a02n1cul.

Lajous, Andrés. "Verse en la clase media." *Nexos*, February 27, 2014, http://andreslajous.nexos.com.mx/?p=1802.

Lamas, Marta. *Abuso ¿Denuncia legítima o victimización?* México D.F.: Fondo de Cultura Económica, 2019.

Lara González, Carlos. "Un año de gestión cultural y perspectivas para el desarrollo de la política cultural del sexenio." *Artículos*, 19–22. https://www.yumpu.com/es/document/read/32399024/un-aao-de-gestian-cultural-y-perspectivas-para-el-desarrollo-de-la-.

Latour, Bruno. *Down to Earth: Politics in the New Climatic Regime*. London: Polity Press, 2019.

Lazzarato, Maurizio. "De las sociedades disciplinarias a las sociedades de control" *Revista Euphorion*, no. 5 (July/December 2009). http://revistaeuphorion.files.wordpress.com/2012/05/euphorion_5_cerebro_y_estetica_julio-dic_2009.pdf.

———. "European Cultural Tradition and the New Forms of Production and Circulation of Knowledge." *Multitudes: une revue trimestrielle, politique, artistique et Culturelle*, January 16, 2004. http://hdl.handle.net/10760/7130.

———. "Neoliberalism in Action: Inequality, Insecurity and the Reconstitution of the Social." *Theory, Culture & Society* 26, no. 6 (2009): 109–33. https://doi.org/10.1177%2F0263276409350283.

Leal, Alejandra. "El despertar de la sociedad civil: sismo del 85 y neoliberalismo." *Horizontal*, September 24, 2015, https://horizontal.mx/el-despertar-de-la-sociedad-civil-sismo-del-85-y-neoliberalismo.

Leary, John Patrick. *Keywords: The New Language of Capitalism*. Chicago: Haymarket Books, 2018.

Leger, Marc-James. *The Neoliberal Undead*. New York: Zone Books, 2013.

Levy Dabah, Simón. "Nacionalidades creativas y capitalismo chilango." *Animal Político*, October 23, 2012, http://www.animalpolitico.com/blogueros-el-chino-taliban/2012/10/23/nacionalidades-creativas-y-neocapitalismo-chilango.

Linthicum, Kate. "La guerra del narco para controlar la multimillonaria industria del aguacate en México." *Los Angeles Times*, November 21, 2019, https://www.latimes.com/espanol/mexico/articulo/2019-11-21/mexico-cartel-violencia-aguacates.

Llaven Anzures, Yadira. "Proclaman como 'niño héroe' al niño asesinado en Chalchihuapan." *La Jornada de Oriente*, September 17, 2014, www.lajornadadeoriente.com.mx/2014/09/17/proclaman-como-nino-heroe-al-nino-asesinado-en-chalchihuapan.

Lomnitz, Claudio. *La nación desdibujada*. México D.F.: Malpaso, 2016.

López Ponce, Jannet. "Jorge Ramos Confronta a AMLO con Cifras de Homicidios." *Milenio*, April 12, 2019, https://www.milenio.com/politica/jorge-ramos-confronta-amlo-cifras-homicidios-libertad-expresion.

López Rivas, Gilberto. "Puebla: entre represión y el despojo neoliberal." *La Jornada*, April 25, 2014, http://www.jornada.unam.mx/2014/04/25/opinion/023a2pol.

Luiselli, Valeria. "Entrevista por Eduardo Rabasa." *Nación*, December 1, 2016, https://www.nacion.com/ancora/valeria-luiselli-el-unico-deber-del-novelista-es/KZHTWHBBLNHWZMHTB7DMGWIUAA/story.

———. *Tell Me How It Ends: An Essay in Forty Questions*. Minneapolis: Coffee House Press, 2017.

Magallanes, Gustavo, et al. "La rebeldía del Valle de Chalco: La lucha contra las aguas negras y el mal gobierno" *Revista Rebeldía*, no. 7. https://www.yumpu.com/es/document/view/14706827/pdf-la-rebeldia-de-valle-de-chalco-revista-rebeldia.

Marchart, Oliver. "Art, Space and the Public Sphere(s)." *transversal texts* (January 2002). https://transversal.at/transversal/0102/marchart/en.

Martínez Elorriaga, Ernesto. "Exigen habitantes purépechas la salida de la Fuerza Rural de sus comunidades." *La Jornada*, September 15, 2014, http://www.jornada.unam.mx/2014/09/15/politica/007n1pol.

Mastrogiovanni, Federico. *Ni vivos ni muertos*. México D.F.: Grijalbo, 2014.

Mbembe, Achille. "Necropolítica, una revisión crítica." In *Éstética y violencia: necropolítica, militarización y vidas lloradas*, edited by Helena Chávez McGregor. México D.F.: MUAC, 2012.

———. *Necropolitics*. Durham, NC: Duke University Press, 2019.

McLagan, Megan, and Yates McKee, eds. *Sensible Politics: The Visual Culture of Nongovernmental Activism*. New York: Zone Books, 2012.

Meinhof, Ulrike. "Armed Anti-Imperialist Struggle." In *Hatred of Capitalism*, edited by Sylvere Lotringer. New York: Semiotext(e), 2001, 63–66.

Meir, Barry. "Inside a Secretive Group where Women are Branded." *New York Times*, October 17, 2017, https://www.nytimes.com/2017/10/17/nyregion/nxivm-women-branded-albany.html.

Melchior Figueroa, Robert. "Indigenous Peoples and Cultural Losses." In *Climate Change and Society*, edited by John S. Dryzek, Richard B. Norgaard, and David Schlossberg. Oxford, UK: Oxford University Press, 2016, 232–47.

Mendoza Cota, Jorge Eduardo. "Economic Integration and Cross-Border Economic Organizations: The Case of San Diego-Tijuana." *Estudios Fronterizos* 18, no. 35 (January/April 2017): 22–46.

Merino, José, Jessica Zarkin, and Eduardo Fierro. "Desaparecidos." *Nexos*, January 1, 2015, http://www.nexos.com.mx/?p=23811@nexos.

Meyer, Lorenzo. "Por sus frutos la conoceréis (a la economía)." *Reforma*, June 6, 2013.

Milenio Jalisco. "Violencia cierra pequeños negocios, pero no afecta a maquilas en Ciudad Juárez." July 27, 2011, http://jalisco.milenio.com/cdb/doc/noticias2011/43ce1154b9b35f5df68a76643e162d88.

Monge, Emiliano. "Nuevo indigenismo institucional." *El País*, September 13, 2019, https://elpais.com/elpais/2019/09/14/opinion/1568419698_963817.html.

Monsiváis, Carlos. *Alusiones*. México D.F.: Anagrama, 2007.

Montero, Daniel. *El cubo de Rubik, arte mexicano en los años 90*. México D.F.: Fundación Júmex Arte Contemporáneo/RM, 2013.

Moraña, Mabel, and José Manuel Valenzuela, eds. *Precariedades, ociedads y emergencias: Necropolítica y sociedad civil en América Latina*. México D.F.: UAM Iztpalapa y Gedisa, 2018.

Moten, Fred. *The Universal Machine*. Durham, NC: Duke University Press, 2018.
Moten, Fred, and Harney, Stefano. *The Undercommons: Fugitive Planning & Black Study*. New York: Minor Compositions, 2013.
Moy, Valeria. "Desigualdad: La herencia regional." *Nexos*, July 1, 2018, https://www.nexos.com.mx/?p=38328.
———. "Zonas Económicas Especiales: ¿Un paso hacia el desarrollo?" *Foreign Affairs Latinoamérica*, August 29, 2016, http://revistafal.com/zonas-economicas-especiales-un-paso-hacia-el-desarrollo.
Muñoz Alma E., and Alonso Urrutia. "Intelectuales y científicos, entre los inconformes por austeridad: AMLO." *La Jornada*, May 29, 2019, https://www.jornada.com.mx/ultimas/2019/05/29/intelectuales-y-cientificos-entre-los-inconformes-por-austeridad-amlo-7960.html.
Muñoz Díaz, Patricia. "5 millones de casas abandonadas." *La Jornada*, September 4, 2013, www.jornada.unam.mx/2013/04/09/sociedad/039n1soc.
Nación 321. "El polémico 'performance' de Jesusa Rodríguez en el Senado." April 25, 2019, https://www.nacion321.com/congreso/el-polemico-performance-de-jesusa-rodriguez-en-el-senado.
"NAFTA's Impact on Mexico." *Sierra Club*, March 2014, https://vault.sierraclub.org/trade/downloads/nafta-and-mexico.pdf.
Navarrete, Federico. *Alfabeto del racismo mexicano*. México D.F.: Malpaso, 2017.
Navarro, Mina Lorena. "Luchas por lo común contra el renovado cercamiento de bienes naturales en México." *Bajo el volcán* 13, no. 21 (September 2013): 161–69.
Nigam, Adita. *Desire Named Development*. New Delhi: Penguin Group, 2011.
Nixon, Rob. *Slow Violence and the Environmentalism of the Poor*. Cambridge, MA: Harvard University Press, 2011.
Nutterwegge, Christoph. "Neoliberalism as a Variety of Social Darwinism: Ten Million More Unemployed." *Indymedia LA*, April 16, 2013, https://la.indymedia.org/js/?v=cont&url=/news/2013/04/259574.json.
O'Connell, Mark. "Why Silicon Valley billionaires are prepping for the apocalypse in New Zealand." *The Guardian*, February 15 2018, https://www.theguardian.com/news/2018/feb/15/why-silicon-valley-billionaires-are-prepping-for-the-apocalypse-in-new-zealand.
Olvera, Alberto J. "La resistencia civil y la democracia en México." *El País*, February 10, 2015, http://internacional.elpais.com/internacional/2015/02/10/actualidad/1423539349_623262.html.
Olvera, Al Dabi. "Detrás del muro del Nuevo Aeropuerto: la historia que nadie ve." *Pie de página*, June 18, 2018, https://elecciones2018mx.periodistasdeapie.org.mx/2018/06/13/detras-del-muro-del-nuevo-aeropuerto-la-historia-que-nadie-ve.
Ong, Aihwa. *Neoliberalism as Exception: Mutations in Citizenship and Sovereignty*. Durham, NC: Duke University Press, 2006.

Osegueda, Rodrigo. "Luis Vuitton plagia los bordados artesanales de la comunidad de Tenango de Doria." *Mexico Desconocido*, July 11, 2019, https://www.mexicodesconocido.com.mx/louis-vuitton-plagia-los-bordados-artesanales-de-la-comunidad-de-tenango-de-doria.html.

Osorno, Diego Enrique. "El manantial masacrado." *Vice*, September 19, 2014, vice.com/es_latam/article/qbqdpq/el-manantial-masacrado.

Paley, Dawn. *Drug War Capitalism*. Oakland, CA: AKA Press, 2014.

———. *Guerra Neoliberal: Desaparición y búsqueda en el norte de México*. México D.F.: Libertad bajo palabra, 2020.

Páramo, Arturo. "Biometrópolis, el proyecto que no prosperó." *Excélsior*, October 14, 2012, http://www.excelsior.com.mx/2012/10/14/comunidad/864232#imagen-1.

Pearce, Fred. *The Land Grabbers: The New Fight over Who Owns the Earth*. Boston: Beacon Press, 2012.

Peck, Jamie, and Adam Tickell. "Neoliberalizing Space." *Antipode* 34, no. 3 (July 2002): 390–404. https://doi.org/10.1111/1467-8330.00247.

Pérez Negrete, Margarita. "Santa Fe: A 'Global Enclave' in Mexico City." *Journal of Place Management and Development* 2, no. 1 (2009): 33–40.

Pérez Orozco, Amaia. *Subversión feminista de la economía*. Madrid: Traficantes de Sueños, 2014.

Petras, James, and Henry Veltmeyer, eds. *The New Extractivism: A Post-Neoliberal Development Model or Imperialism of the Twenty-First Century?* London: Zed Books, 2014.

Piñón, Alida. "Artistas llevan 8 meses sin pago de Cultura CDMX." *El Universal*, November 27, 2010, https://www.eluniversal.com.mx/cultura/artistas-llevan-8-meses-sin-pago-de-cultura-cdmx.

———. "El mestizaje que creó el nacionalismo es pernicioso." *El Universal*, May 10, 2019, https://www.eluniversal.com.mx/cultura/el-mestizaje-que-creo-el-nacionalismo-es-pernicioso.

"Plan Nacional de Desarrollo 2007–2011." http://pnd.calderon.presidencia.gob.mx/igualdad-de-oportunidades/cultura-arte-deporte-y-recreacion.html.

"Plan Nacional de Desarrollo 2019–2024." https://lopezobrador.org.mx/wp-content/uploads/2019/05/PLAN-NACIONAL-DE-DESARROLLO-2019-2024.pdf.

Polemón. "Javier Sicilia y los Le Baron fueron financiados por la secta NXIVM." November 20, 2019, https://polemon.mx/javier-sicilia-y-los-lebaron-fueron-financiados-por-la-secta-nxivm.

Polychroniou, C. J. "An Interview with Henri Giroux on Democracy in Crisis." *Counterpunch*, May 5, 2014, http://www.counterpunch.org/2014/05/30/an-interview-with-henry-giroux-on-democracy-in-crisis.

Power, Nina. "Conversation with Hito Steyerl at the Institute of Contemporary Art." *ICA Bulletin*, March 28, 2014, https://archive.ica.art/bulletin/video/hito-steyerl-and-nina-power.

Pradilla, Alberto. “México, el sexto país más peligroso para defensores del medio ambiente.” *Animal Político*, July 29, 2019, https://www.animalpolitico.com/2019/07/defensores-medio-ambiente-asesinatos-mexico.
Preciado, Paul B. “Notre Dame of Ruins.” *artforum*, April 21, 2019, https://www.artforum.com/slant/paul-b-preciado-on-the-notre-dame-fire-79492.
———. *Un apartamento en Urano: Crónicas del Cruce*. Buenos Aires: Anagrama, 2013.
Proceso. “La Supervía, cueste lo que cueste.” August 9, 2010, https://www.proceso.com.mx/nacional/cdmx/2010/4/7/no-habra-marcha-atras-en-supervia-poniente-ebrard-8266.html.
Public Citizen. “NAFTA at 20: One Million Lost U.S. Jobs, Higher Income Inequality, Doubled Agriculture Trade Deficit With Mexico and Canada, Displacement and Instability in Mexico, and Corporate Attacks on Environmental Laws.” Press release, January 2014, http://www.citizen.org/documents/NAFTA-at-20.pdf.
Quijano, Aníbal. “Coloniality of Power, Eurocentrism and Latin America.” *Nepantla: Views from South* 1, no. 3 (2000): 533–80.
Ramírez, Ignacio. “Arrumban Museo Xico por obra.” *Mural*, November 21, 2015, http://www.mural.com/aplicacioneslibre/articulo/default.aspx.
Ramos, Jorge. “México se convierte en nación de clase media: FCH.” *El Universal*, September 25, 2012, http://www.eluniversal.com.mx/notas/872400.html.
Rancière, Jacques. “Ten Theses on Politics.” *Theory and Event* 5, no 3 (2001): 34–48.
Raunig, Gerald. “Prácticas instituyentes: Fugarse, instituir y transformar.” *transversal texts* (January 2006). https://transversal.at/transversal/0106/raunig/es.
Rea, Daniela, and Marcela Turati, eds. “El pueblo que espantó el miedo.” In *Entre las cenizas*. Oaxaca: Ediciones Sur+, 2012.
Renzi, Alessandra. *From Collectives to Connectives: Italian Media*. Doctoral dissertation, Universidad de Toronto, 2011. https://tspace.library.utoronto.ca/. . ./Renzi_Alessandra_201106_PhD_thes.
Reyez, José. “ ‘Ejércitos privados,’ la amenaza a la ‘Cuarta Transformación.’ ” *Contralínea*, December 10, 2018, https://www.contralinea.com.mx/archivo-revista/2018/12/10/ejercitos-privados-la-amenaza-a-la-cuarta-transformacion.
Ribeiro, Silvia. “Comida que calienta.” *La Jornada*, September 8, 2012, http://www.jornada.unam.mx/2012/09/08/opinion/019a1eco.
———. “Químicamente tóxico.” *La Jornada*, February 12, 2012, http://www.rebelion.org/noticia.php?id=144530.
Rivera Garza, Cristina. *Dolerse: textos desde un país herido*. Oaxaca: Sur+ ediciones and Frontera Press, 2011.
———. *Habia mucha neblina o humo o no sé que*. México D.F.: Random House, 2017.

Rodríguez García, Arturo. "AMLO descarta un encuentro con Javier Sicilia y rechaza cambiar estrategia de seguridad." *Proceso*, November 18, 2019, https://www.proceso.com.mx/607079/amlo-descarta-un-encuentro-con-javier-sicilia-y-rechaza-cambiar-estrategia-de-seguridad.

Rodríguez, Israel, and Alejandro Cruz. "Ofrece Mancera seguir apoyando a constructores, para evitar pérdidas." *La Jornada*, May 21, 2014, www.jornada.unam.mx/2014/05/21/capital/037n1cap.

Rodríguez, Jesusa. "Keynote presentation at the 2019 Hemispheric Institute Conference." *YouTube*, June 10, 2019, https://www.youtube.com/watch?v=TwdKg31WoJc.

Rolnik, Suely. *Esferas de la insurrección: Apuntes para descolonizar el inconsciente*. Madrid: Tinta Limón, 2019.

Román, José Antonio. "Pospone Peña Nieto el envío de la reforma energética," *La Jornada*, August 7, 2013, https://www.jornada.com.mx/2013/08/07/politica/003n1pol.

Romero Sánchez, Gabriela. "Un éxito, el desarme voluntario: Mancera." *La Jornada*, December 22, 2013, http://www.jornada.unam.mx/2013/12/22/capital/036n2cap.

Romero Sotelo, and María Eugenia. *Los orígenes del neoliberalismo en México: La Escuela Austriaca*. México D.F.: FCE and UNAM, 2016.

Ross, John. "The "Dirty War" Returns to Mexico." *The Narco News Bulletin*, May 18, 2006, http://www.narconews.com/Issue41/article1831.html.

———. *El monstruo: Dread and Redemption in Mexico City*. New York: Nation Books, 2010.

———. "The Next Mexican Revolution." *Coutnerpunch*, September 21, 2010, http://www.counterpunch.org/2010/09/21/the-next-mexican-revolution.Roy, Arundhati. *My Seditious Heart (Collected Nonfiction)*. Chicago: Haymarket Books, 2019.

Rubio, Luis. *Veinte años del TLC, su dimensión política y estratégica*. México D.F.: Fondo de Cultura Económica, 2014.

Salinas, Emiliano. "TED Talk in San Miguel de Allende." *YouTube*, June 24, 2010, https://www.youtube.com/watch?v=WMahpWvAPWo.

Santoyo Orozco, Ivonne. "The Apparatus of Ownership." *Scapegoat Journal 06: NAFTA/Mexico City*, no. 6 (March 2014).

———. "From the Right to Housing to the Right to Credit: The Drama of Ownership in Mexico." In *A House is Not Just a House: Projects on Housing*, edited by Tatiana Bilbao. New York: Columbia Books on Architecture and the City, 2018, 27–39.

Sartre, Jean-Paul. *What is Literature? And Other Essays*. Edited by Steven Ungar. Cambridge, MA: Harvard University Press, 1988.

Scarry, Elaine. *Thermonuclear Monarchy: Choosing Between Democracy and Doom*. New York: W. W. Norton & Company, 2014.

Secretaría de Cultura. "La memoria maya vive en Tihosuco, la nueva Zona de monumentos históricos de México." *Gobierno de México*, October 4, 2019, https://www.gob.mx/cultura/prensa/171344.

Shaviro, Steven. "Accelerationist Aesthetics: Necessary Inefficiency in Times of Real Subsumption." *e-flux journal* 43 (June 2013). https://www.e-flux.com/journal/46/60070/accelerationist-aesthetics-necessary-inefficiency-in-times-of-real-subsumption.

———. *Post-Cinematic Affect*. London: Zero Books, 2010.

———. "Post-Cinematic Affect: On Grace Jones, *Boarding Gate* and *Southland Tales*." *Film-Philosophy* 14, no. 1 (2010).

Sholette, Gregory. *Dark Matter: Art and Politics in the Age of Enterprise Culture*. New York: Pluto, 2004.

———. "Speaking Clown to Power: Can We Resist the Historic Compromise of Neoliberal Art?" In *Imagining Resistance: Visual Culture and Activism in Canada*, edited by J. Keri Cronin and Kirsty Robertson. Waterloo, Canada: Wilfrid Laurier University Press, 2011, 27–48. http://www.gregorysholette.com/wp-content/uploads/2011/11/Speaking-Clown-to-Power.NOCROP.pdf.

Sierra, Sonia. "SRE evalúa abrir sede del Pompidou en México." *El Universal*, April 24, 2019, https://www.eluniversal.com.mx/cultura/sre-evalua-abrir-sede-del-pompidou-en-mexico.

SinEmbargo. "Chomsky, Galeano, Sicilia y más intelectuales exigen a Graco (Morelos) y Moreno (Puebla) alto al acoso de activistas." April 25, 2014, http://www.sinembargo.mx/25-04-2014/973048.

SinEmbargo. "Jesusa Rodríguez arma ofrenda al maíz en el Senado para evitar "chahuistle transgénico." April 25, 2019, https://www.sinembargo.mx/25-04-2019/3571452.

SinEmbargo. "Peñabots del PRI #EstánDeLaGreña / Que coman pastel / La uerra de nuestros tiempos." December 22, 2014, http://www.sinembargo.mx/opinion/22-12-2014/30192.

Sontag, Susan, *Before the Pain of Others*. New York: Knopf, 2003.

Sparrow, Jeff. "Soylent, Neoliberalism and the Politics of Life Hacking." *Counterpunch*, May 19, 2014, www.counterpunch.org/2014/05/19/soylent-neoliberalism-and-the-politics-of-life-hacking.

Stamenkovic, Marko. "Radical Withdrawal: Necropolitics, *Capitalismo Gore* and Other Kinds of Life." *The Johannesburg Workshop in Theory and Criticism*, no. 6 (2013): 29–36.

Stanley-Becker, Isaac. "An Activist Faced 20 Years in Prison for Helping Migrants. But Jurors Wouldn't Convict Him." *Washington Post*, June 12, 2019, https://www.washingtonpost.com/nation/2019/06/12/scott-warren-year-sentence-hung-jury-aiding-migrants/?utm_term=.7b335b1c6e54.

Steinsleger, José. "Guatemala y Honduras: ¿Bantustanes para ricos?" *La Jornada*, January 23, 2013, http://www.jornada.unam.mx/2013/01/23/opinion/025a1pol.

Steyerl, Hito. "Politics of Art: Contemporary Art and the Transition to Post-Democracy." *The Wretched of the Screen*. Berlin: e-flux journal and Sternberg Press, 2012.

———. "Too Much World: Is the Internet Dead?" *e-flux journal* 49 (November 2013). http://www.e-flux.com/journal/too-much-world-is-the-internet-dead.

Streeck, Wolfgang. *How Will Capitalism End?* London: Verso, 2017.

Sup Marcos. "Sobre las guerras: Fragmento de la carta primera del SCI Marcos a Don Luis Villoro, inicio del intercambio epistolar sobre Ética y Política. Enero-Febrero de 2011." *Enlace Zaptista*, February 14, 2011, http://enlacezapatista.ezln.org.mx/2011/02/14/sobre-las-guerras-fragmento-de-la-carta-primera-del-sci-marcos-a-don-luis-villoro-inicio-del-intercambio-epistolar-sobre-etica-y-politica.

Taibo II, Paco Ignacio. *Patria, Tomo 1*. México D.F.: Fondo Económico de Cultura, 2018.

Tarí, Marcello. *Un comunismo más fuerte que la metrópoli: la autonomía italiana en la década de 1970*. Madrid: Traficantes de sueños, 2012.

Taylor, Luke. "Canada's Gran Colombia Gold Files $700 Million lawsuit Against Colombia Over Marmato Project." *Financial Post*, April 10, 2017, http://business.financialpost.com/news/mining/canadas-gran-colombia-gold-files-700-million-lawsuit-against-colombia-over-marmato-project.

Tellez, Edward. *Pigmentocracies: Ethnicity, Race and Color in Latin America*. Chapel Hill: University of North Carolina Press, 2014.

Terranova, Tiziana. "Communication Beyond Meaning: On the Cultural Politics of Information." *Social Text* 22, no. 3 (Fall 2004): 51–73.

Tetreault, Darcy Victor. "Mexico: The Political Ecology of Mining." In *The New Extractivism: A Post-Neoliberal Development Model or Imperialism of the Twenty-First Century?*, edited by Henry Veltmeyer and James Petras. London: Zed Books, 2014, 144–71.

Thatcher, Margaret. "Margaret Thatcher: A Life in Quotes." *The Guardian*, April 8, 2013, https://www.theguardian.com/politics/2013/apr/08/margaret-thatcher-quotes.

Thompson, Nato. "The Insurgents Part I: Community-Based Practice as Military Methodology," *e-flux journal* 47 (September 2013). http://www.e-flux.com/journal/the-insurgents-part-i-community-based-practice-as-military-methodology.

Tourions, Cheyanne. "Woodland School *Kahatènhston tsi na'tetiátere ne Iotohrkó: wa tánon Iotohrha*." January 16, 2017, https://cheyanneturions.wordpress.com/2017/01/16/wood-land-school-kahatenhston-tsi-natetiatere-ne-iotohrkowa-tanon-iotohrha/.

Tuck, Eve, and K. Wayne Yang. "Decolonization Is Not a Metaphor." *Decolonization: Indigeneity, Education & Society* 1, no. 1 (2012): 1–40.

Tuhiwai Smith, Linda. *Decolonizing Methodologies*. London: Zed Books, 1999.

Turati, Marcela. "Militarización disfrazada de Cruzada contra el Hambre." *Proceso*, August 31, 2013, https://www.proceso.com.mx/reportajes/2013/8/31/militarizacion-disfrazada-de-cruzada-contra-el-hambre-122844.html.

Turrent, Isabel. "Reseña de *Mañana o pasado. El misterio de los mexicanos* de Jorge G. Castañeda." *Letras Libres*, August 11, 2011, http://www.letraslibres.com/revista/libros/el-caracter-nacional.

Uribe Sierra, Sergio Elías, and Grecia Eugenia Rodríguez Navarro. "Salaverna, el pueblo que no quiere morir: una experiencia de megaminería a cielo abierto." *REMA (Red Mexicana de Afectados por la Minería)*, July 6, 2019, http://www.remamx.org/2019/08/salaverna-el-pueblo-que-no-quiere-morir-una-experiencia-de-megamineria-a-cielo-abierto.

Valencia, Sayak. *Capitalismo Gore*. Madrid: Melusina, 2010.

Valenzuela, Alfonso. "Santa Fe (México): Megaproyectos para una ciudad dividida." *Cuadernos Geográficos* 40 (2007-1): 53–66. http://www.ugr.es/~cuadgeo/docs/articulos/040/040-003.pdf.

Vanguardia. "Refuerza Ejército presencia en municipios de Oaxaca; mientras se discute la creación de la Guardia Nacional apoyan operativos estatales." *Grieta*, February 17, 2019, https://www.grieta.org.mx/index.php/2019/02/17/refuerza-ejercito-presencia-en-municipios-de-oaxaca-mientras-se-discute-la-creacion-de-la-guardia-nacional-apoyan-operativos-estatales.

Vargas, Rosa Elvira. "Realizan mexicanos trabajos que ni los negros quieren: Fox." *La Jornada*, May 14, 2005, https://www.jornada.com.mx/2005/05/14/index.php?section=politica&article=008n1pol.

Vázquez Almanza, Paola. *Aquellos que dejamos de ser: Ficción y nación en México*. México D.F.: Siglo XXI Editores, 2020.

Vazquez, Rolando. "Precedence, Earth and the Anthropocene: Decolonizing Design." *Design Philosophy Papers* 15, no. 1 (2017): 77–91. https://doi.org/10.1080/14487136.2017.1303130.

Ventura, Abida. "Inauguran el Festival Internacional Cervantino 2014." *El Universal*, October 8, 2014, http://www.eluniversal.com.mx/cultura/2014/festival-internacional-cervantino-2014-inauguracion-1044447.html.

Vera, Rodrigo. "Despoja Salinas Pliego un paraíso a Malinalco." *El Diario de Coahuila*, October 31, 2019, https://www.eldiariodecoahuila.com.mx/nacional/2019/3/31/despoja-salinas-pliego-un-paraiso-malinalco-803656.html.

Vidokle, Anton, and Brian Kuan Wood. "Breaking the Contract." *e-flux journal* 37 (September 2012). http://www.e-flux.com/journal/breaking-the-contract.

Villamil, Jenaro. "Bienvenido a la recesión, Sr. Peña." *Proceso*, October 1, 2013, http://www.proceso.com.mx/?p=354274.

Villoro, Luis. *La alternativa. Perspectivas y posibilidades de cambio*. México D.F.: FCE, 2015.

Virilio, Paul. *The Administration of Fear*. New York: Semiotext(e), 2012.

Vishmidt, Marina. "Mimesis of the Hardened and Alienated: Social Practice as a Business Model." *e-flux journal* 43 (March 2013). http://www.e-flux.com/journal/"mimesis-of-the-hardened-and-alienated"-social-practice-as-business-model.

Vulliamy, Ed. "Ciudad Juárez Is All Our Futures." *The Guardian*, June 20, 2011, http://www.theguardian.com/commentisfree/2011/jun/20/war-capitalism-mexico-drug-cartels.

Waldrep, Michael. "Scenes from Neza: Mexico's Self-Made City." *National Geographic Online*, March 26, 2015, http://voices.nationalgeographic.com/2015/03/26/scenes-from-neza-mexico-citys-self-made-city.

Walter, Emmanuelle. *Soeurs volées: Enquête sur un fémicide au Canada*. Montréal: Lux, 2014.

Wang, Jackie. *Carceral Capitalism*. New York: Semiotext(e), 2018.

Warnholtz Locht, Margarita. "Represión en Michoacán." *Animal Político*, April 7, 2017, http://www.animalpolitico.com/blogueros-codices-geek/2017/04/07/represion-en-michoacan.

Weizman, Eyal. *Erasure: The Conflict Shoreline*. Göttingen: Steidl Verlag, 2016.

Wilson, Japhy. "La nueva fase del Plan Puebla-Panamá en Chiapas." *Boletines del CIEPAC*, May 30, 2008, http://www.ciepac.org/boletines/chiapasaldia.php?id=562.

World Bank. *Special Economic Zones: Performance, Lessons Learned, and Implications for Zone Development*. Washington, DC: FIAS, 2008. https://documents.worldbank.org/en/publication/documents-reports/documentdetail/343901468330977533/special-economic-zone-performance-lessons-learned-and-implication-for-zone-development.

Wu, Chin-tao. "Embracing the Enterprise Culture: Art Institutions since the 1980s." *New Left Review*, no. 230 (1998).

Yablonski, Linda. "Creative Juices." *artforum*.com, November 25, 2013, http://artforum.com/diary/id=44217.

Yúdice, George. *The Expediency of Culture: Uses of Culture in the Global Era*. Durham, NC: Duke University Press , 2004.

Zavala, Oswaldo. *Los cárteles no existen*. México: Malpaso, 2018.

Zerega, Georgina. "México pierde otra batalla por 44 piezas de arte precolombino subastadas en Francia." *El País*, October 31, 2019, https://elpais.com/cultura/2019/10/31/actualidad/1572544644_868267.html

Zibechi, Raúl. *Dispersar el poder*. Quito: Ediciones Abya-Yala, 2007.

Žižek, Slavoj. "Capitalism Can No Longer Afford Freedom." *ABC*, May 25, 2012, http://www.abc.net.au/religion/articles/2012/05/25/3511327.htm.

———. "Capitalism." *Financial Times*, October 8 2012, http://foreignpolicy.com/2012/10/08/capitalism.

———. "Capitalism with Asian Values." *Aljazeera*, November 13, 2011, http://www.aljazeera.com/programmes/talktojazeera/2011/10/2011102813360731764.html.

———. *The Courage of Hopelessness: A Year of Acting Dangerously*. Brooklyn: Melville House, 2017.

———. "Cynicism as a Form of Ideology." In *The Sublime Object of Ideology*. London: Verso, 1989.

———. "Fat Free Chocolate and Absolutely No Smoking: Why Our Guilt about Consumption is All-consuming." *The Guardian*, May 21, 2014, https://www.theguardian.com/artanddesign/2014/may/21/prix-pictet-photography-prize-consumption-slavoj-zizek.

———. "The World Has Never Been Better." *The Guardian*, February 17, 2013, http://www.guardian.co.uk/commentisfree/2013/feb/17/free-market-fundamentalists-think-2013-best.

Zunino, Mariela. "Integración para el despojo: Proyecto Mesoamérica, o la nueva escalada de la apropiación del territorio." *CIEPAC*, no. 584, June 8, 2010, http://www.ciepac.org/boletines/chiapasaldia.php?id=584.

INDEX

www.ingramcontent.com/pod-product-compliance
Lightning Source LLC
LaVergne TN
LVHW050148080826
844660LV00002B/116